# A MATTER OF PRINCIPLE

# A Matter of Principle

Humanitarian Arguments

for War in Iraq

EDITED BY

Thomas Cushman

**UNIVERSITY OF CALIFORNIA PRESS**  Berkeley  Los Angeles  London

University of California Press
Berkeley and Los Angeles, California

University of California Press, Ltd.
London, England

© 2005 by The Regents of the University of California

Library of Congress Cataloging-in-Publication Data

A matter of principle : humanitarian arguments for war
in Iraq / edited by Thomas Cushman.
    p.    cm.
  Includes bibliographical references and index.
  ISBN 0-520-24486-9 (cloth : alk. paper)—
  ISBN 0-520-24555-5 (pbk. : alk. paper)
  1. Iraq War, 2003—Moral and ethical aspects.
  I. Cushman, Thomas, 1959–
  DS79.76.M38 2005
  956.7044'31—dc22                2004027416

Manufactured in the United States of America

14  13  12  11  10  09  08  07  06  05
10  9  8  7  6  5  4  3  2  1

Printed on Ecobook 50 containing a minimum 50%
post-consumer waste, processed chlorine free. The
balance contains virgin pulp, including 25% Forest
Stewardship Council Certified for no old growth tree
cutting, processed either TCF or ECF. The sheet is
acid-free and meets the minimum requirements of
ANSI/NISO Z39.48-1992 (R 1997) (Permanence of
Paper). ∞

*This book is dedicated to all of those who have lost their lives in Iraq in the struggle against tyranny and for the human rights of the Iraqi people.*

# Contents

Acknowledgments / xi

Introduction: The Liberal-Humanitarian Case
for War in Iraq
THOMAS CUSHMAN / 1

PART ONE **RECONSIDERING REGIME CHANGE**

1 The Case for Regime Change
CHRISTOPHER HITCHENS / 29

2 Liberal Legacies, Europe's Totalitarian Era, and the
Iraq War: Historical Conjunctures and Comparisons
JEFFREY HERF / 39

3 "Regime Change": The Case of Iraq
JAN NARVESON / 57

4 In the Murk of It: Iraq Reconsidered
MITCHELL COHEN / 76

PART TWO **PHILOSOPHICAL ARGUMENTS**

5 National Interest and International Law
ROGER SCRUTON / 95

**6** Just War against an "Outlaw" Region
MEHDI MOZAFFARI / 106

**7** Moral Arguments: Sovereignty, Feasibility,
Agency, and Consequences
DANIEL KOFMAN / 125

PART THREE **CRITIQUES OF THE LEFT**

**8** A Friendly Drink in a Time of War
PAUL BERMAN / 147

**9** Wielding the Moral Club
IAN BURUMA / 152

**10** Peace, Human Rights, and the Moral Choices
of the Churches
MIENT JAN FABER / 160

**11** Ethical Correctness and the Decline of the Left
JONATHAN RÉE / 179

**12** Pages from a Daily Journal of Argument
NORMAN GERAS / 191

**13** Liberal Realism or Liberal Idealism:
The Iraq War and the Limits of Tolerance
RICHARD JUST / 207

PART FOUR **EUROPEAN DIMENSIONS**

**14** Iraq and the European Left
JOHN LLOYD / 223

**15** Guilt's End: How Germany Redefined the
Lessons of Its Past during the Iraq War
RICHARD HERZINGER / 233

**16** The Iraq War and the French Left
MICHEL TAUBMANN / 243

**17** Tempting Illusions, Scary Realities,
or the Emperor's New Clothes II
ANDERS JERICHOW / 259

PART FIVE   **SOLIDARITY**

18   Antitotalitarianism as a Vocation:
An Interview with Adam Michnik
THOMAS CUSHMAN AND ADAM MICHNIK  /  271

19   Sometimes, a War Saves People
JOSE RAMOS-HORTA  /  281

20   Gulf War Syndrome Mark II: The Case for Siding
with the Iraqi People
JOHANN HARI  /  285

21   "They Don't Know One Little Thing"
PAMELA BONE  /  297

22   "Why Did It Take You So Long to Get Here?"
ANN CLWYD  /  309

PART SIX   **LIBERAL STATESMANSHIP**

23   Full Statement to the House of Commons,
18 March 2003
TONY BLAIR  /  329

24   The Threat of Global Terrorism
TONY BLAIR  /  340

Contributors  /  353
Index  /  361

# Acknowledgments

I would like to thank, first and foremost, the authors of the essays in this volume for ratifying my idea for it with their participation and support. Any edited volume is only as good as the authors whose works constitute it. The authors also deserve hearty praise for meeting stringent deadlines and for their intellectual bravery in putting forth their alternative visions of the war in Iraq. They have convinced me through their writings that politics as a vocation is truly alive.

Special thanks are due to Kevin Alexander, my personal editorial assistant, who worked tirelessly and responsibly on all aspects of this project. Without his assistance, this book and other projects would never have seen the light of day. My intellectual accomplishments over the last year are a direct consequence of Kevin's diligent aid.

A special debt of gratitude is due to my friends Jonathan Imber, Jeffrey Grady, John Rodden, Nicolas de Warren, James Tucker, Greg Gomez, Guy MacLean Rogers, and Richard Wilson, who offered me personal and professional support at various times during the project. Although they may not always agree with my views, or the views put forth in this volume, they understand that true friendship is beyond politics. A note of special thanks is due, as well, to my father, Orton Cushman, who has unfailingly continued to offer his support and assistance to me over the years.

I am also especially grateful to some of my colleagues and friends at Wellesley College and elsewhere who took the time to listen to rehearsals of my arguments and ideas about the war, even if they did not share my political stance on the war. You know who you are. True liberalism and intellectual diversity are rare in the contemporary academic world but not yet extinct. Jens Kruse, professor of German at Wellesley, and Nicolas de Warren, assistant professor of philosophy at Wellesley, deserve a special note of thanks for agreeing to take on with short notice the expert translations of Richard Herzinger's and Michel Taubmann's essays that appear in this volume.

I would also like to thank my editor at the University of California Press, Reed Malcolm, for supporting the vision of this volume and for making it possible to publish a rather dissident vision of the Iraq war.

My wife, Carol Hartigan, and my daughters, Sophie and Eliza, deserve special field commendations for enduring the many times when I brought the Iraq war into the blissful space of our family life. They understand that the realities of the world do not stop at the doorstep of hearth and home, even though sometimes it is better that they should.

# Introduction
## The Liberal-Humanitarian Case for War in Iraq

THOMAS CUSHMAN

W hat exactly *was* the war in Iraq? It has alternately been seen as a move to protect the national security of the United States in light of the tragedy of September 11; a preventive war of self-defense against terrorism; a way to foster stability, security, and democracy in the Middle East; a counter to arms proliferation and support of terrorism around the world; an exercise in the expansion of the American empire and protection of American material interests in the region; a war for oil; an illegal act of aggression that has fostered hatred of the United States and helped to strengthen Islamist fundamentalists in Iraq and elsewhere; and a humanitarian intervention and an act of liberation from totalitarianism in the service of human rights and democracy. The debates about the Iraq war have been strident and polarizing at the level of personal and cultural interaction, international relations, and intellectual and political discourse.

This volume consists primarily of essays by leading world political figures, writers, scholars, and activists who supported the war on what might be broadly called liberal-humanitarian grounds; a few authors who did not support the war offer some observations about the political response to it. What unites the authors is a common recognition that, in spite of the inconsistent justifications provided by the United

States and its allies and the conflict-ridden process of social reconstruction, the war can be seen as morally justifiable: Saddam Hussein was a brutal tyrant, a gross violator of human rights, a torturer, a mass murderer, a force of global instability and terror, a threat to world peace and to what John Rawls refers to as the Law of Peoples. For more than three decades, his crimes against humanity, wars of aggression, support of international terrorism, and volatility as a destabilizing force were tolerated, aided, and abetted by world powers and the international community for the sake of political expediency, stability, and material interests. Coming to the rescue and aid of a people who had been subjected to decades of brutality and crimes against humanity is entirely consistent with the basic liberal principle of solidarity with the oppressed and the fundamental humanitarian principle of rescue. The war can be seen as morally legitimate on grounds of basic human rights as embodied in the Universal Declaration of Human Rights, which is the ethical basis for the international world order. This body of moral principles was ignored by the United Nations Security Council in the case of the Iraqi people in favor of adherence to statutory international law.

Seeing the Iraq war as justifiable on moral and ethical grounds is a distinct minority view within the liberal community. Even Human Rights Watch, which played a significant role in documenting the heinous crimes of Saddam's regime, claimed that the Iraq war was not a humanitarian war on the grounds that it was not motivated by the humanitarian concern of preventing genocide (this view leaving unanswered the question, Is prevention of genocide the only legitimate reason for humanitarian intervention?).[1] The arguments by the United States that it was removing a tyrant fell flat against the recognition that the United States had once supported Saddam Hussein in his brutal war against Iran. Moreover, the United States failed to remove the despot after its victory in the first Gulf War; instead, it fostered Iraqi resistance to Saddam but cruelly abandoned that resistance to the brutal retaliation of the Baath regime.

In this respect, though, the international community was hardly any better. The ethical foundations of the international community, as encoded in the International Declaration of Human Rights, rang hollow as the United Nations implemented sanctions against Iraq that only strengthened the brutal regime and allowed the people of Iraq to remain subject to what Kanan Makiya has referred to as the Republic of Fear, denied protection, rescue, and human rights.[2] Much of the resistance to the war was grounded in a critique of American imperial ambitions in favor of a multilateral consensus forged by the United Nations according to statutory international law rather than moral imperatives. Peace and stability, rather than justice and human rights for the Iraqi people, were the central concerns of those members of the international community who stood against the liberation of Iraq.

In being critical of both the Bush administration's handling of the war, on the one hand, and the arguments of those who were against the war, on the other, the essays in this volume constitute collectively what might be called a third view. The basic elements of this perspective are a strong liberal commitment to human rights, solidarity with the oppressed, and a firm stand against fascism, totalitarianism, and tyranny. In this regard, the authors constitute part of what Paul Berman, following the lead of the French socialist Leon Blum, refers to as a Third Force of liberal internationalism.[3] Berman articulates a vision of liberal internationalism that sees the current war on terror (and the war in Iraq in his later work, which appears in this volume), as a battle against Islamofascism that is being waged in order to protect the basic values of liberal internationalism: solidarity with the oppressed, the promotion of republican and liberal values, the emphasis on promulgating basic human rights as embodied in the UN Charter, and the promotion of democratic government. Berman calls for

> a Third Force different from the conservative and foreign policy cynics who could only think of striking up alliances with friendly tyrants; and different from the anti-imperialists of the left, the left-wing isolationists, who could not imagine any progressive role at all for the United States. A Third Force, neither "realist" or pacifist—a Third Force devoted to a politics of human rights and especially women's rights, across the Muslim world; a politics of ethnic and religious tolerance; a politics against racism and anti-Semitism, no matter how inconvenient that might seem to the Egyptian media or the House of Saud; a politics against the manias of the ultra-right in Israel, too, no matter how much that might enrage the Likud and its supporters; a politics of secular education, of pluralism, and law across the Muslim world; a politics against obscurantism and superstition; a politics to out-compete the Islamists and Baathi on their left; a politics to fight against poverty and oppression; a politics of authentic solidarity for the Muslim world, instead of the demagogy of cosmic hatreds. A politics, in a word, of liberalism, a "new birth of freedom"—the kind of thing that could be glimpsed, in its early stages, in the liberation of Kabul.[4]

Berman's vision provides us with a set of basic values of a liberal internationalism that led some to support the war, even if war itself is an imperfect means for social and political advancement. As Mient Jan

Faber notes in his essay in this volume, this kind of liberal denies him- or herself the choice of standing against the Iraqi people and the rights they are entitled to according to the international community's own fiat, the UN Declaration of Human Rights. The contributors to this volume represent the voices of a Third Force of liberal internationalism. They understand the limitations of the current system of global governance, which tolerates gross violations of human rights and which failed to prevent genocide in Bosnia and Rwanda, and the need for reform in international institutions and international law. At the same time, the authors in this volume do not attempt to apologize for the specific mistakes and deceptions of the Bush administration's prosecution of the war, and this book is not an attempt to whitewash history or to second the ideological positions of that administration. The authors share the language of freedom and liberation that the US president has adopted but ground that language in a specific body of liberal principles. (It is hard, in this sense, to see George W. Bush as the "human rights president," but the consequence of the war was, in spite of the conflicts and problems in its aftermath, a significant advance in the human rights of the Iraqi people.) For most of the authors, the liberal internationalist case for the war was not made strongly enough by the Bush administration or at least as strongly as the argument for anticipatory self-defense, which turned out to be empirically ungrounded. What is striking about these essays is the willingness of each author to voice pointed criticism of the Bush administration and its practices (as Christopher Hitchens wryly notes in his contribution, "I write as one who could not easily name a mistake that the Bush administration has failed to make").

Yet at the same time the authors also offer pointed critiques of the liberal-left opposition to the war, much of which is contradictory, reductionistic, logically flawed, or excessively emotional, and irrational. Even the most sober and reflective critics of the war occupied a stage that also displayed demonstrators toting placards of Bush with a Hitler mustache, waving Iraqi and Cuban flags, and passing out copies of the *Protocols of the Elders of Zion*. Ironically, many of the authors in the volume point out that the antiwar position was, in fact, something of a conservative one in that it aimed to preserve a regime of intolerable cruelty in order to preserve the deeply flawed system of international law that gives both tyrants and democratically elected leaders equal seats at the table of international justice. Indeed, as Daniel Kofman notes in his contribution here, it is odd that many leftists, who have built careers on challenging the unrestrained sovereignty of states and state power, would find themselves arguing in favor of the current system that supports and guarantees the power of sovereign despots and the inviolability of their states, even in extreme cases such as Pol Pot, Kim Jong Il, or Saddam Hussein. Had there been no war, Saddam Hussein would still be in power rather than preparing for his trial for crimes against humanity. He would still be tormenting, torturing, and killing his own subjects, destabilizing the Middle East, and giving succor to international terrorists who are the avowed enemies of liberal democracy.

It is from this two-sided critique that the authors offer alternative viewpoints that challenge the status quo of both the left and the right. The essays in this volume offer unique observations by those of liberal disposition who wrestled with their consciences and took a stand in support of the liberation of the Iraqi people from tyranny, all the time recognizing that in conception, execution, and consequence, there were and remain significant problems with the prosecution of the war and the process of social reconstruction. The historical value of the present volume lies in the fact that it challenges the idea that the only true liberal position on the war was to be against it.

Maintaining a consistent humanitarian and liberal defense of the war has been a position increasingly difficult to sustain in light of the postwar developments in Iraq. Indeed, some liberal thinkers who originally supported the war changed their minds and decided that their original defenses could not be maintained in light of the mismanagement of the war, the failure to find weapons of mass destruction, the increasing hostility of the global community toward the United States, and the strengthening of the resolve of Islamofascism in its war against liberal democracy. Those who saw the removal of Saddam Hussein as an act of liberation and as a first step in the democratization of the Middle East are now confronted with the messy facts on the ground in Iraq. Several of the contributors express ambivalence about the humanitarian rationale for the war and concern about the unrestrained use of American power and unilateralism, the process of social reconstruction and democratization of postwar Iraq, and the perils and dangers associated with preemptive strategies. A crucial strength of the volume, though, is that the authors consider the war and reconstruction in all of its complexity and aim, constructively and critically, to remain committed to the possibilities for the advancement of liberal democracy in Iraq and for the advancement of the principles of liberal internationalism more generally. In the spirit of liberal hope, the authors focus on positive consequences and outcomes—the restoration of sovereignty, the establishment of a new government, the hope that the Iraqi people themselves have about the future. This liberal hope, rather than the cynical pessimism and the moral indifference of realism, defines the spirit of the authors of these essays.

The need for such a volume is clear. Those who supported the war on the grounds put forth by the Bush administration enjoy the privilege of power, which affords their arguments a high degree of visibility. Those who were against the war—a group that consists of left-liberal intellectuals who are effective writers and activists—have suffered few barriers to the voicing of their views and have produced a constant stream of antiwar essays and books on the subject. In many cases, antiwar views dominate the pages of the traditional left-liberal press (as, for instance, in the *Nation*, although several liberal-minded magazines, such as *Dissent* and the *New Republic*, have been notably pluralistic in offering some of the opinions expressed in this volume). The *New York Times*, the global paper of record, has exhibited strong antiwar positions in its editorial columns. It is almost always the case that war polarizes ideological and intellectual discourse, and this is certainly the case in the Iraq war: one finds books that either support the war more or less on the grounds of the Bush administration or oppose it for a variety of reasons. No single volume, however, has collected the writings of those who defended the war on traditional principles of liberal internationalism, as a struggle against fascism and totalitarianism, or on human rights grounds. Indeed, the ideological tradition uniting many authors in this volume might be described as "antitotalitarianism," as embodied in the views of the Polish leader of the Solidarity movement, Adam Michnik, whose ideas appear in an interview in this volume. In this respect, the authors are closer to the liberal form of solidarity that motivated those activist intellectuals who supported the fight against fascism in the Spanish Civil War than they are to an organization such as the United Nations and its realpolitik practices, moral indifference, and toleration of tyrants. As such, this volume serves as an important historical document that will ensure that a different voice of liberalism, one that remains principled and idealistic rather than descending into a vortex of cynical realism, appeasement, moral indifference, tolerance of tyrants, and the denial of human rights. Such a work is more important than ever, especially for the younger generation of liberals who, as Richard Just notes in his essay, have abandoned idealism for realism, thus jeopardizing the continuation of the most important defining quality of the liberal internationalist tradition.

The volume is organized around a set of central questions, and various authors approach these questions in different ways. The intent is not to provide definitive answers but to use the Iraq war as a case to raise questions and issues about the war that have not enjoyed a prominent airing.

1. *Are the ideologies of antitotalitarianism, antifascism, and the promotion of human rights sufficient justifications for unilateral armed intervention on the part of states? Do the moral and ethical imperatives of human rights trump international law, and under what conditions? What exactly is the responsibility of international organizations such as the United Nations and the Security Council, its central political apparatus? Is the war defensible purely on human rights grounds? If so, what are the problems and paradoxes created by the use of state power and violence for the advancement of human rights?*

The Bush administration attempted to justify the war on humanitarian grounds, but this stand was more of an ad hoc rationale than one that was central to the overall argument for going to war. Indeed, as it became clear that intelligence on the existence of weapons of mass destruction was faulty and the threat posed by Saddam was not as immediate as Bush and British prime minister Tony Blair had led the world to believe, the humanitarian argument was increasingly asserted, but cynicism about the consistency of the Coalition's rationale made that argument difficult for many to accept. However, it is reasonable to assume that Saddam, given past behavior and other intelligence information, was certainly trying to acquire weapons of mass destruction, and, as Christopher Hitchens, Jeffrey Herf, and others point out in this volume, he was in material breach of specific UN resolutions, breaches that the Security Council and other member states tolerated.

When considering the human rights case for the war, or what might be called the moral argument, it is interesting to note that most world criticism of the war focused on the United States and George W. Bush. The structure and practice of the United Nations, as well as the realpolitik machinations of France, Germany, Russia, and China in standing against the war, were seldom the object of critique. So we might turn the scenario on its head and ask, Can one make a moral critique of the Security Council's failure to uphold the resolutions and ethical principles of the United Nations? Can one criticize on moral grounds the failure of liberal democratic European societies to uphold their commitments to the liberal principles of the UN Charter? The answer is an unqualified yes. There are situations in which ethical imperatives trump laws, especially if those laws are unjust (an idea that was the basis for the civil rights movement in the United States and the struggle against apartheid in South Africa, to name just two of the most prominent examples). Again, it is notable that many, if not most, left-liberal critics of the war blindly accepted the authority of UN procedures, international law, and the questionable moral righteousness of the antiwar axis. In doing so, they were clearly tolerating the intolerable injustices of Saddam Hussein and betraying their own liberal principles.

Legal scholar Brian Lepard, in a pathbreaking work on ethics and international law, notes that

> there ought to be a general principle of moral law requiring governments, international organizations, and other actors to take some reasonable measures within their abilities to prevent or curb widespread and flagrant violations of essential human rights, including genocide, crimes against humanity, and rampant and systematic war crimes or torture. The Security Council is bound by this general principle of moral law. . . . [It is] legally obligated to take some reasonable measures to prevent or stop widespread and severe violations of essential human rights to the extent of, and within the boundaries of, its lawful powers under the UN Charter. . . . It is competent and obligated to take steps to prevent and put an end to all widespread and flagrant violations of essential human rights, or more sporadic violations that threaten to become widespread or to ignite or exacerbate internal or external war, thus amounting to a "threat to peace."[5]

The Bush administration clearly tried to convince the United Nations and the Security Council of their responsibilities and obligations. These responsibilities and obligations, not only to protect the people of Iraq but also to preserve peace and stability, were not met by the Security Council, and therefore the legitimacy of the entire apparatus was deeply compromised. Thus any moral critique of the war or of the Bush administration must be accompanied by a similar critique of the failure of moral responsibility by the United Nations and the inability of international law to consistently embody and put into practice the basic ethical principles on which the international community is based. This is not to say that states ought to be given carte blanche to intervene on human rights grounds, since it is clear that just about any state could create such a pretext for aggression, as in the case for the occupation of Bohemia and Moravia made by Adolf Hitler, who argued that the act was to protect Germans from atrocities being committed by Czechs.[6] A similar argument was made in the case of Poland, where allegations of Polish atrocities against Germans were a pretext for the German invasion.[7]

### 2. Can, then, the war in Iraq be considered a humanitarian war?

As noted earlier, Human Rights Watch, one of the most esteemed nongovernmental human rights organizations in the world, declared that the war was not a humanitarian war because it was not motivated by an effort to prevent genocide.[8] This perspective, however, depends on a restrictive definition of humanitarian intervention solely as the prevention of impending genocide. This leaves open the question of whether the use of military intervention can be justified in relation to other types of gross violations of human rights. Would humanitarian intervention be justified if Saddam Hussein publicly tortured ten thousand babies per day on national television? How is it that Human Rights Watch could spend its energies over the years documenting the heinous nature of the regime but then argue against rescue?

Those who argued against the applicability of the term *humanitarian intervention* in the case of the Iraq war have a strong argument based on the lack of a coherently articulated humanitarian motivation on the part of the Bush administration. Yet there is a distinct danger in making arguments based purely on considerations of motive. One of the strongest ethical arguments for the humanitarian intervention argument lies in considering the *consequences* of the war, and in this respect the authors in this volume can see clear humanitarian results in spite of the shadowy motivations of the Bush administration. One precondition for accepting a humanitarian case for the war is the acceptance of a certain kind of consequentialist ethics that judges actions based on their outcomes rather than the intentions and motivations of the actors involved.[9] A basic principle of sociological reasoning is that social outcomes are seldom the product of the motivations or intentions of actors. In this respect, the outcomes of the war in terms of social dislocation, factionalism, and resistance were unanticipated negative consequences of the war. But in similar fashion, the victory of the Iraqi people over Saddam must be seen as a positive consequence from the standpoint of moral principles of human rights. Very few of even the most vociferous opponents of the war would deny, if pressed, that it is a "good thing" that Saddam Hussein is gone and facing justice for his crimes. If that outcome is an acknowledged positive moral consequence, then all other critiques must be made in light of it.

This point brings up the question of the legitimacy of the war in relation to its legality and/or illegality. It is a fact that many people supported the interventions in Bosnia, and later in Kosovo, even while recognizing that they were technically illegal, but later they came out stridently opposed to the war in Iraq. This stance seems inconsistent, since Saddam was a far worse tyrant than Slobodan Milošević, and ample evidence indicated that he had committed acts of genocide against the Kurdish minority in the north and the Marsh Arabs in the south. He was almost certainly a greater threat to regional and global security and peace than Milošević. Surely the commission of one or more acts of genocide is some indication of the potential to do it again, but this possibility was roundly denied in the left-liberal consciousness. Many of the authors in this volume considered intervention in Bosnia and Kosovo as morally legitimate, and their support of the Iraq war, on the same political grounds of the moral imperative of rescue and human rights, is logically consistent. It is an interesting question why those who supported the interventions in Bosnia and Kosovo, even though they were unilateral and occurred without UN sanction, turned away from supporting the war against Saddam Hussein on the same grounds. One wonders, indeed, if the war had been waged by a liberal Democratic American president rather than a Republican one (who is objectively and universally loathed by almost all liberals around the world), whether more moral support for the war among liberals would have been the consequence. Indeed, as Christopher Hitchens notes in his essay, both President Bill Clinton and Vice President Al Gore, in various speeches, called vociferously for regime change during their tenure of office, a call that was conveniently forgotten when George W. Bush was making the same argument. In any case, this volume at least raises the possibility that the war in Iraq was in keeping with other unilateral efforts to promote and protect human rights, whether or not one ultimately decides that it was not.

*3. What are the political, sociological, and ethical critiques of the anti-war movement, and how do those critiques relate to the liberal humanitarian defense of the war?*

This is an important question to ask, all the more so because there is a tendency for those who are similar ideologically not to criticize themselves or their own group but to unite in solidarity against the perceived enemy of the group (in this case, George W. Bush and his policies) and broach no dissent from within the group ("no enemies on the left," as the old adage goes). Even if one were against the war, hearing the arguments in defense of it on humanitarian grounds and the limitations of one's own arguments would be an intellectually valuable exercise in an ideal liberal free marketplace of ideas. Yet this has been extremely difficult to do in the current political climate on the left, a climate characterized by a persistent, emotional, and vehement criticism of the United States (often descending into a form of elemental anti-Americanism) and a visceral and mocking hatred and vilification of George W. Bush. The tendentious propagandist Michael Moore, who spares no effort to link emotional hatred of Bush with the purportedly objective methods of the documentary, has become the living demigod of the antiwar movement.

Several of the authors whose essays appear here have themselves suffered extreme pressure and even censure and political retaliation for violating the antiwar orthodoxies of the left. Mient Jan Faber, for instance, tells the story of how he was sacked from his position as the secretary-general of the Interfaith Peace Council in the Netherlands because he followed the ethical dictates of his conscience and could not bring himself to stand against the liberation of the Iraqi people from their despot. One author from Spain, a deeply committed liberal public intellectual who was committed to the project from its inception, found his prowar views received with such vitriolic condemnation that he could not bring himself to write another word and so recused himself from the present effort. The vilification of Christopher Hitchens's positions on the war would itself make a fascinating case study of the current tide of intellectual orthodoxy on the left in relation to the Iraq war. Thus many of the authors here have found themselves suffering the fate of the heretic: intellectual outcasts banished, scorned, and vilified among their fellow liberals for expressing their heterodox views.

In my experience, what has been so striking from a sociological point of view is the resistance to even hearing the humanitarian case for the war. Throughout the essays, we hear in detail the frustration that many of the authors faced in simply trying to articulate the humanitarian case, never mind persuading people to accept it once made. This is a

fascinating sociological problem, since the left has usually been characterized precisely by its solidarity with the victims of repression around
the globe. Yet, in the case of Iraq, this solidarity simply vanished in
favor of a critique of the United States and George W. Bush and his so-
called neoconservatives and their imperial agenda.[10] If solidarity was
expressed in any way, it was in the form of a quite legitimate concern
for the civilian victims of the war. Yet, as several authors in this volume
point out, and as survey research has shown consistently, the majority
of Iraqis welcomed the war as a means to rid themselves of Saddam and
in most cases were quite willing to make the sacrifices in civilian casualties that were necessary.[11] That is, they did not see themselves as victims but as agents of resistance to Saddam who needed the war to acti-
vate their agency and to provide them with the means to overthrow
Saddam's tyranny.

As Johann Hari notes in his essay, even more troubling is the way in
which many antiwar advocates made no effort to familiarize themselves
with actual Iraqi public opinion and in some cases even distorted that
opinion to make it concordant with their own ideological agendas.
What is striking about the antiwar movement is the way in which the
global left has turned against the United States rather than gross violators of human rights such as Saddam Hussein. Indeed, the war has been
the pretext for a global revival of anti-Americanism, much of it well
grounded, but much of it a rehearsal of a more fundamental twentieth-
century proclivity of the left to vent its rage primarily at the "empire"
rather than the various despots who have wreaked havoc on the global
stage. Indeed, such tyrants figured out very early on that they could
always gain a certain advantage by articulating critiques of the bugbear
of American empire (witness, for instance, the enthrallment of the left
wing in America with Fidel Castro, who is the personification of resistance to the United States).[12]

The central question regarding the immunity to the humanitarian
case for the war is one for the sociology of cognition: Why was the left
so unwilling to listen to or acknowledge the human rights case for the
war, even if most leftists would ultimately reject it? The response of the
left to the humanitarian argument indicates a lack of tolerance for alternative views that ought to be the hallmark of liberal intellectual life. In
this respect, the left during the war displayed a pattern of intolerance
that is not new in its history. A question that I ask of my colleagues on
the left who opposed the war is, What would you say to the Iraqi person who asked you one year later why you stood against our libera-

tion? I have not yet been able to get a meaningful answer to that question, because all of the possible answers—pertaining, for example, to resisting American empire, obeying international law, preventing the deaths of civilians, taking moral stands against war itself as a crime—would mean that the average Iraqi who desired liberation from Saddam would still be subject to his terror, enslaved to tyranny, and denied the basic human rights that liberals purportedly cherish as central to their own existences.

*4. What are the limitations of Western liberal political practices and international law in dealing with tyranny, fascism, and gross violations of human rights? How can international law be more responsive to gross violations of human rights? Is the United Nations amenable to reform, and in what ways? Or is it a bureaucratic Leviathan that will continue to be guided by considerations of realpolitik and remain ineffective against gross violations of human rights? Is the United States destined to pursue a course of unilateralism, and what are the likely effects on global governance and the advancement of liberal internationalism?*

It is clearly the case that current practices of international law and international organizations have failed rather glaringly to deal with tyrants. One has only to think of UN indifference to the plight of Bosnia, Rwanda, and Kosovo and its current ineptitude with regard to events in Congo and Sudan to see that the current structure of dealing with illiberal despots with liberal principles of law, negotiation, and accommodation is deeply flawed. The flaw consists in allowing illiberal despots the luxury of treatment according to Enlightenment ideals of toleration. If you treat an illiberal tyrant liberally, you can count on rendering him a distinct advantage.

It is seldom recognized that the war was not as unilateral as many maintain. By the time the war started in March 2003, forty-eight countries had joined the "Coalition of the Willing," and critics tended to overgeneralize about the extent of opposition to the war in the world.[13] Indeed, in Europe alone, the famous "Letter of the Eight" was a significant act of solidarity with the decision to go to war: the heads of state of England, Spain, the Netherlands, Italy, Hungary, Poland, Denmark, and the Czech Republic all supported the war in an open letter signed on January 29, 2003.[14] This act evoked great consternation on the part of French president Jacques Chirac, who opined that in the case of the former Soviet bloc countries, they were severely jeopardizing their smooth entrance into the European Union. In his now-famous words, "They missed their opportunity to shut up."[15]

Another significant act of support occurred when a group of former communist states known as the Vilnius 10—Estonia, Latvia, Lithuania, Slovakia, Slovenia, Bulgaria, Romania, Croatia, Macedonia, and Albania—signed a statement of support of the war effort. The language of this statement reflected not only an affirmation that Saddam was clearly in violation of UN resolutions but a common recognition, based on the member states' historical experiences with communist domination, of the moral importance of fighting tyranny: "Our countries understand the dangers posed by tyranny and the special responsibility of democracies to defend our shared values. The trans-Atlantic community must stand together to face the threat posed by the nexus of terrorism and dictators with weapons of mass destruction."[16]

Overall, as it turns out, *more* countries in Europe *supported* the war than were against it; one year after the war, only Spain officially rejected the original position of support. In addition, the Coalition enjoyed the support of Japan, South Korea, Singapore, the Philippines, and many other Asian states. The new postcommunist republics of Kazakhstan, Uzbekistan, Mongolia, and Azerbaijan joined the Coalition. It is also important to underscore the fact that several liberal titans, deeply respected heroes of the global left such as Vaclav Havel, Adam Michnik, and Jose Ramos-Horta, supported the war on liberal-humanitarian grounds.

Some critics of this Coalition have laid the charge that it was "bribed" or "coerced." Yet the rhetoric of those leaders who supported the war—and I would again stress that it was the *majority* of European leaders who did so—especially in the case of the former countries of the Soviet bloc, present very convincing moral arguments for allying with the United States in the war against terror, more generally, and the war in Iraq, specifically. It will be up to political scientists and historians to write the history of the Coalition of the Willing, but as it stands, that Coalition was a powerful symbolic (if not material) display of support for the war in Iraq. What has been most striking is the left's general ignorance of the reality of the Coalition, as well as its hesitance to grant it any credibility or significance whatsoever.

Obviously, then, there was far more consensus and support for the war than critics acknowledge. How is it that we are still led to believe that the effort was strictly unilateral? It is not comforting to think of war and action outside the structures of global governance as the best means to promote peace and justice. In this sense, it is wise to consider the war as functional in a sociological sense: out of this conflict, perhaps reform and improvement of international institutions and law can result. The war, in this sense, might serve as a catalyst to forge new understandings and practices that might lead to a more peaceful and just future.

*5. Do wars in the name of human rights advance the ideals of liberal democracy, or are they likely to foster outcomes that are contrary to those ideas and create more problems? Is liberal democracy possible in the Middle East, especially in light of the resentment that the war has created? Does the liberal defense of the war set up an inevitable clash of civilizations and a retrenchment and strengthening of the very forces that oppose liberal internationalism? To what extent do the cultures of the Middle East, described in this volume by Mehdi Mozaffari as a constellation of "oriental despotisms," impede the advancement of liberal democracy?*

In the wake of the victory over Saddam, we have seen the emergence of a strong Shiite resistance led by Islamists from Iraq and their supporters abroad. This response was, of course, to be expected, but it was never adequately anticipated by the Coalition forces.

Yet such resistance does not necessarily indicate a lack of desire on the part of "ordinary" Iraqis to craft a liberal democratic society. In the months immediately after the war, the organization Physicians for Human Rights carried out a rather extensive survey of two thousand households in southern Iraq. The results, as seen in figure 1, were quite striking in two regards: they reflect, first, a strong consensus in the legitimacy of a US and Coalition role in democratization and, second, a rather high degree of commitment to basic liberal values, justice, and human rights.[17]

These data are not necessarily representative of the entire Iraqi population, and much has happened in the last year that has affected the public opinion of Iraqis. But it does challenge the negative perceptions that resistance, dissatisfaction, and political strife are the only realities of the Iraqi landscape. Those who were against the war find support in their critiques by focusing on bad news; sociologically, it is important to pay attention to public opinion more generally, and the news, even now, is not as disheartening as critics might predict.

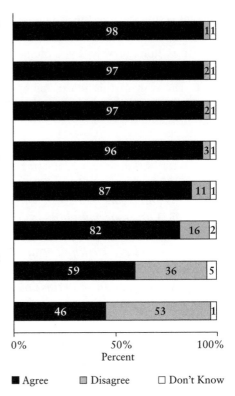

FIGURE 1. Views on Reconstruction, Government, and War Crimes

SOURCE: "Southern Iraq: Reports of Human Rights Abuses and Views on Justice, Reconstruction, and Government," a briefing paper by Physicians for Human Rights, September 18, 2003, 14, at http://www.phrusa.org/research/iraq/index.html (accessed December 29, 2004). Used by permission of Physicians for Human Rights. © 2003 by Physicians for Human Rights.

One of the most comprehensive longitudinal surveys of Iraqi public opinion is under way by Oxford Research International. The results are surprising, given the constant stream of negative news reports emanating from Iraq.[18] In answer to the question "Overall, how would you say things are going in your life these days—very good, quite good, quite bad, or very bad?" fully 71 percent of respondents answered very good or quite good, whereas only 29 percent answered quite bad or very bad. As for optimism about the future, when asked, "What is your expectation for how things overall in your life will be in a year from now? Will they be much better, somewhat better, about the same, somewhat worse, or much worse?" 81 percent of respondents answered much better or somewhat better, 11 percent about the same, and only 8 percent somewhat worse or much worse. This response is a rather stark indicator of hope for the future, which contrasts quite dramatically with news reports that focus on resistance to the occupation, terrorist acts, and disaster. Primarily, the survey shows that most Iraqis are concerned about security, jobs, living standards, and rising prices. Only 1.5 percent noted that the occupation was the biggest problem, 0.6 percent were worried about chaos, and only 0.3 percent were worried about ethnic and religious tensions.

As can be seen in figure 2, one of the most interesting findings of the survey indicates that, overall, Iraqis supported the United States–led Coalition war to depose Saddam Hussein. The percentages of people

[Ask all]
Q5 *From today's perspective and all things considered, was it absolutely right, somewhat right, somewhat wrong, or absolutely wrong that US-led coalition forces invaded Iraq in Spring 2003?*

Base = All respondents

|  | Count | % | Combined % |
|---|---|---|---|
| Absolutely right | 520 | 22.5 | 55.2 |
| Somewhat right | 759 | 32.8 | |
| Somewhat wrong | 343 | 14.8 | 44.8 |
| Absolutely wrong | 694 | 30.0 | |
| Total | 2316 | 100.0 | 100.0 |

[Ask all]
Q6 *Apart from right and wrong, do you feel the US-led coalition force invasion...*

Base = All respondents

|  | Count | % |
|---|---|---|
| Humiliated Iraq | 1093 | 49.7 |
| Liberated Iraq | 1109 | 50.3 |
| Total | 2202 | 100.0 |

FIGURE 2. Iraqi Views of the War in Iraq

SOURCE: The data from figure 2 are taken from Oxford Research International's National Survey of Iraq, June 2004, which can be found at http://www.oxfordresearch.com/publications.html (accessed December 29, 2004). Reproduced by permission of the University of Oxford and Oxford Research International (UK), Ltd.

for and against are close, but only 30 percent of the people felt the war was "absolutely wrong." In fact, one crucial finding from this study, also seen in figure 2, is that there are conflicting views of the war: 50 percent of Iraqis feel that the war liberated Iraq, whereas 50 percent believe that it humiliated Iraq. This important response indicates that positive and negative views of the war coexist: the Iraqis appear to be grateful for the deposition of Saddam's regime and reign of terror, but they also feel deeply humiliated about being an occupied country.

It is important to point out also that much of the positive reception of the war has been eroded by the failures of the postwar period, and especially the Abu Ghraib scandal, which severely damaged the ability of US forces to claim the mantle of "liberator." The evidence from the Oxford International survey indicates that the management and public relations failures of the postwar period are primarily responsible for the increasingly negative attitude toward the war and the occupation forces.

The point of these forays into public opinion is to challenge the characterization of the postwar situation in purely negative terms. Critics of the war can find it difficult to acknowledge the satisfaction of most Iraqis with the fact that Saddam's brutal regime is over, just as it was hard for them to see that before the war, widespread support for the war existed. Instead, many authors have glorified the "resistance" to the occupation without fully recognizing that this resistance is mostly composed of either former Baath Party loyalists or Islamist fundamentalists from Iraq and abroad who are using the Iraqi stage to wage jihad.

6. For many people, the war represents a severe blow to the principles of cosmopolitan universalism. The United States' unilateral action is seen as a threat to the very principles of multilateral engagement. *Does the war threaten the liberal idea of cosmopolitan universalism? What is the relationship between cosmopolitanism and the use of violent force? Can (and should) human rights be promoted "out of the barrel of a gun"? Following Kant, is it likely that the tensions and anxieties surrounding the war might lead to a renewed effort of will to strengthen the cosmopolitan world order? Or are further schisms and tensions on the horizon?*

Several authors in this volume engage the work of Immanuel Kant and John Rawls to understand the war. At first glance, it might be tempting to think that Kant or Rawls would be against the war, because it violates the laws of the federation of "perpetual peace" or the "law of peoples" as well as the Kantian injunction, clearly specified in *Perpetual Peace,* against intervention except in cases of self-defense. Yet, it is clearly the case that the United Nations, as presently structured, is not exactly what Kant (or Rawls, for that matter) had in mind as the institutional embodiment of perpetual peace or the society of peoples: for these thinkers, a global federation must consist of free and democratic *republics.* The United Nations, however, consists of a variety of types of states and makes no distinctions among them: liberal democracies, Islamic theocracies, communist totalitarian states, and failed states are all allowed seats at the table as equal partners, a situation that Kant himself would have disapproved of. The United Nations has become a site where rogue and outlaw states can form alliances and power blocs and use international law to promote and protect their own power and challenge collectively the power of liberal states that would attempt to compel them to change their ways. One has only to think of the unrelenting and sustained castigation of Israel by UN bodies and member states that use the UN structures to mount their attacks on the only democratic state in the Middle East. The UN Commission on Human Rights, headed by Libya in 2003, is an example of how the UN structures have been commandeered by illiberal states to their own political advantage. Saddam Hussein's manipulation of UN procedures and practices (as well as the United Nations' own bureaucratic inefficiency, which is infinitely amenable to manipulation by those who wish to carry it out) to maintain his hold on power is indicative of how it is that tyrants take advantage of the international community's commitment to the idea of peace at all costs to commit injustices, violence, and gross violations of human rights.

To be sure, Kant and Rawls would not argue that war is the best means for bringing rogue states to heel and turn them into liberal republics. Yet, at the same time, Kant clearly argues in *Perpetual Peace* that if war did occur (as he felt it inevitably would), it could serve as a pretext for the kinds of negotiations and reconsiderations that might reduce the frequency of future wars. In this sense, one of the more positive functions of the war might be to force reform of the United Nations. The question then remains as to whether the organization is even amenable to reform. The sociological complexities of this issue must be explored elsewhere.

In the case of John Rawls, it is not patently clear from a reading of *The Law of Peoples* whether Rawls would have supported the war in Iraq. He does note rather cryptically that war is justifiable in the case of gross violations of human rights, but he leaves open the question as to whether the decision should be made on a strictly multilateral basis with the consent of the United Nations. More important, Rawls points out that liberal peoples, should they decide to go to war and should they win, have a strict obligation to create a liberal republic in place of the vanquished outlaw state. One might imagine that Rawls would concur that the war was justifiable on consequentialist grounds: after all, one of the worst regimes in modern history was deposed. Yet, Rawls surely would have been dismayed by the postwar situation in Iraq. From a liberal-humanitarian point of view, there is no question that the postwar reconstruction of Iraq has been deeply flawed. There were clearly never enough American troops to guarantee security. Likewise, financial resources necessary for a truly invigorating liberal reconstruction have been lacking. The Abu Ghraib prison scandal severely damaged the possibility of convincing people that the American occupation was furthering the liberal principles of human rights. Indeed, it is very difficult to sustain any humanitarian case for the war in light of the fact that the occupation force engaged in the very practices that it purported to be fighting against. Nonetheless, it is important to see the bigger picture: while much of the attention of critics of the war was focused on Abu Ghraib, there has been a tendency toward moral equivocation in which the abuses of a small coterie of soldiers were seen as comparable to the magnificent and glaring atrocities of Saddam Hussein and his regime. According to the Oxford International survey of June 2004, the majority of Iraqis do not consider the Abu Ghraib scandal as official US policy; the majority feel that fewer than one hundred persons were involved in the abhorrent practices that occurred in the prison.

The narrative of the war put forth by its critics has tended to focus almost exclusively on the negative historical occurrences that would tend to support a stance of opposition. Positive outcomes are seldom the object of news reporting, and people who were against the war are cognitively disposed to consider its aftermath in purely negative terms, selecting those cases that confirm their critical agenda and ignoring positive evidence that would justify the war in terms of its intent or consequences. Here is where the liberal-humanitarian case is made stronger by conscious attention to some of the more positive aspects of social reconstruction that are often ignored by news media.

7. *What are the ongoing effects of the war on US-European relations, as well as relations among EU countries? What are the prospects for significant rapprochement between the United States and Europe? How has the war affected the liberal project of European unification, particularly with regard to new member nations from the former Soviet bloc, such as Poland, the Czech Republic, and Hungary?*

Opponents of the war, both in the United States and in Europe, express a distinct hesitance to examine the political processes and factors that led various European countries to oppose the war. In this view, American power is seen as the central object of critique, whereas European aspirations for power in Europe and in the international order more generally are not sufficiently addressed.

What was most striking about those who were critical of the United States and the Coalition is that they seldom cast a critical eye on the leading nations that opposed the war—in this case, France, Germany, and Russia. The "default" position was that these countries were acting nobly to preserve peace and multilateral institutions. What was less forthcoming, however, was an open, honest, and critical appraisal of the realpolitik considerations that led these nations to form an alliance against the war. As Kenneth Timmerman has shown in painstaking detail, France had much to lose if Saddam were to be deposed; France's alliance with Saddam's Iraq was an enduring one with strong economic benefits that Jacques Chirac was obligated to protect.[19] The situation was similar with Russia, which had long-standing political and economic ties to Iraq and stood to gain much by the preservation of Saddam's regime, especially as a check against American hegemony in the Middle East. As for Germany, Gerhard Schroeder clearly had to maintain opposition to the United States' action to ensure reelection in a political environment rife with opposition to American domination and, as Richard Herzinger notes in his essay, eager to break away from the guilt of its own fascist past. There was no way that the chancellor could have survived politically if he had joined forces with the US president and the British prime minister. The reasons for the French-German-Russian axis of opposition are complex, but the point is that in the logic of the opposition to the war, it was almost always the case that the United States was seen as acting illiberally, whereas the antiwar coalition was acting as the guardian of liberalism.

In fact, as the essays in this volume point out, it is hard to see tolerance of Saddam and his atrocities as being in any way in keeping with liberal internationalist and humanitarian ideological principles. One of the most bitter pills to swallow for those who opposed the war is that, in the end, George W. Bush might have acted more in accord with the principles of liberal internationalism than those who purported to be liberals did. If one agrees with Paul Berman that the West is at war with the forces of Islamofascism, then those who do not recognize this point or take it seriously are, objectively, part of the problem of fighting successfully against it.

George Orwell once noted in a famous epigraph, "Pacifism is objectively profascist." Extending his insights to the case of the Iraq war, it is an objective fact that those who chose to stand against the war were in one sense standing with Saddam Hussein, because if they had been successful in their efforts to stop the war, he would still be in power today. One must imagine that Saddam Hussein and his Baathist Party henchmen, in their struggle to maintain his power, were greatly appreciative of the global left's opposition to the war. Indeed, this antiwar stance appears to have been a vital component of Saddam's strategy for manipulation of the United Nations and various countries in order to get sanctions lifted so that he could begin the process of rearmament and development of weapons of mass destruction (WMDs).[20]

Overall, the essays in this volume constitute a collective effort to see the Iraq war in a different light. The authors articulate a number of liberal-humanitarian arguments and raise important issues that have not enjoyed adequate attention and that deserve to be heard amid the polarized discourse on the war. The self-critical and reflexive quality of the essays indicates the tension and ambivalence that most of the authors feel in holding the positions that they do. Taken as a whole, though, the essays are examples of intellectual commitment to the idea of what Max Weber calls "politics as a vocation":

> There are two ways of making politics one's vocation: Either one lives "for" politics or one lives "off" politics. By no means is this contrast an exclusive one. The rule is, rather, that man does both, at least in thought, and certainly he also does both in practice. He who lives "for" politics makes politics his life, in an internal sense. Either he enjoys the naked possession of the power he exerts, or he nourishes his inner balance and self-feeling by the consciousness that his life has *meaning* in the service of a "cause." . . . The serving of a cause must not be absent if action is to have inner strength. Exactly what the cause, in the service of which the politician strives for power and uses power, looks like is a matter of faith. The politician may serve national, humanitarian, social, ethical, cultural, worldly, or religious ends. The politician may be sustained by a strong belief in "progress"—

no matter in which sense—or he may coolly reject this kind of belief. He may claim to stand in the service of an "idea" or, rejecting this in principle, he may want to serve external ends of everyday life. However, some kind of faith must always exist. Otherwise, it is absolutely true that the curse of the creature's worthlessness overshadows even the externally strongest political successes. . . . It is immensely moving when a *mature* man—no matter whether old or young in years—is aware of a responsibility for the consequences of his conduct and really feels such responsibility with heart and soul. He then acts by following an ethic of responsibility and somewhere he reaches the point where he says: "Here I stand; I can do no other."[21]

What unites this volume's authors is commitment to the cause of liberal internationalism and solidarity with the weak as a political vocation. To be a dissident on this particular issue is to occupy a lonely place, but those true to their own political vocations enjoy the satisfaction and pleasure of autonomy and the inner joy of living according to an ethics of responsibility.

## ORGANIZATION OF THE VOLUME

The themes and arguments of the essays in this volume overlap considerably, yet the essays are categorized according to the general themes that are raised in each essay. The volume is organized so that the reader might comfortably begin reading at any point in the book, and the themes of each essay resonate strongly with and reinforce each other, even though they appear in groupings in various sections.

The first section is entitled "Reconsidering Regime Change." The essays in this section state the case for regime change and provide reflections on the liberal-humanitarian case for the war.

The second section, "Philosophical Arguments," presents the work of three philosophers who make philosophical interpretations of the war. These essays offer Kantian and Rawlsian analyses of the war, as well as arguments from consequentialist ethics.

The third section, "Critiques of the Left," highlights an important aspect of this volume. As noted earlier, most of the authors came to their own arguments in defense of the war based on a critical examination of the positions of their own ideological group. These essays serve as documentary evidence that there is no one politically correct left-liberal position on the war and that there is room enough in that space for articulation and toleration of dissenting arguments.

The fourth section of this volume, "European Dimensions," presents the views of four European commentators on European dimensions of the war. Most critics of the war tend to assume the hegemony of European opposition to it, but several leading intellectuals and writers in Europe supported the war on liberal-humanitarian grounds. A more in-depth examination of the European perceptions of the war would necessitate a separate volume, but the essays here present a glimpse into the more heterodox views that existed amid the dominant antiwar sentiments of much of Europe.

The penultimate section, "Solidarity," consists of essays by those who supported the war on what is perhaps the most basic liberal-humanitarian principle: solidarity with the weak. Three of the five essays in this section are by world political leaders who have struggled against despotism in their own personal lives and political practice and who have carried that struggle to the Iraqi people. With all of the openly shared doubts, ambivalences, and criticisms about the decision to go to war and its consequences, these authors—and indeed all of the authors in this volume—share one enduring disposition: that those who are in a position of strength have a responsibility to protect the weak. The very basis of liberal consciousness depends on fulfilling that responsibility. Indifference, whatever its basis, is an abdication of the duty of solidarity and the responsibility to protect.

Finally, we end the volume with two speeches by Tony Blair, the prime minister of Great Britain and a leading voice of the liberal-humanitarian argument for the war. Much of the criticism of the war focused on the administration and ideology of George W. Bush, a conservative president with a clear ideological agenda that repulses many liberals. Blair was often seen as a helpless acolyte of Bush's will. Yet these speeches show with great poignancy Blair's own liberal vision of political responsibility not only to ensure global moral responsibility to peace and security but to protect and liberate the oppressed. In this sense, Tony Blair is a model of liberal statesmanship, and his speeches serve as a reminder to all that the war can be defended on the basis of morality and principle rather than resisted on stark considerations of hegemony or empire alone.

## NOTES

1. See Kenneth Roth, "War in Iraq: Not a Humanitarian Intervention," http://hrw.org/wr2k4/3.htm (accessed November 22, 2004). Roth writes, "The result is that at a time of renewed interest in humanitarian intervention, the Iraq war and the effort to justify it even in part in humanitarian terms risk giv-

ing humanitarian intervention a bad name. If that breeds cynicism about the use of military force for humanitarian purposes, it could be devastating for people in need of future rescue." According to this strange logic, rescuing people from tyrants and totalitarian regimes endangers the future of rescuing people from tyrants and totalitarian regimes. A more detailed critique of Human Rights Watch's view of the Iraq war can be found in Thomas Cushman, "The Human Rights Case for the War in Iraq: A Consequentialist View," forthcoming in *Human Rights in an Age of Terror,* ed. Richard Ashby Wilson (Cambridge: Cambridge University Press, 2005).

2. Kanan Makiya, *Republic of Fear: The Politics of Modern Iraq* (Berkeley and Los Angeles: University of California Press, 1998).

3. In the contemporary world, the meaning of *liberal* is quite varied. In Europe and the United States, it is usually applied to progressives, social democrats, or proponents of the welfare state, yet at the same time it has been used to describe those who advocate developing free markets and easing state control on the latter (i.e., neoliberals). The term *liberal internationalism* is used in a very specific sense to describe the points of articulation among the contributors of the volume. The principles that define this position should be clear from the arguments presented here.

4. Paul Berman, *Terror and Liberalism* (New York: W. W. Norton, 2002).

5. Brian D. Lepard, *Rethinking Humanitarian Intervention* (University Park: Pennsylvania State University Press, 2002), 272–273.

6. Simon Chesterman, *Just War or Just Peace: Humanitarian Intervention and International Law* (London: Oxford University Press, 2001), 27. Chesterman argues that this is the central danger in allowing humanitarian considerations to trump international law. In his view, it is better to hold to an imperfect body of law (and seek to perfect it) than to open the door to powerful states that claim to be fighting for human rights but have rather the obverse intention. Yet, as Christopher Hitchens notes in his essay herein, there is no reason to assume that now that the United States has acted unilaterally, other powers will start unleashing wars of aggression in the name of human rights. Two years after the war, this has decidedly not been the case.

7. For a fascinating and rare glimpse of Hitler's abuse of the human rights argument, see *Polish Acts of Atrocity against the German Minority in Poland* (German Library of Information, for the German Foreign Office, Berlin–New York, 1940).

8. See Roth, "War in Iraq."

9. Samuel Scheffler defines *consequentialism* as "a moral doctrine which says the right act in any given situation is the one that will produce the best overall outcome as judged from an impersonal standpoint which gives equal weight to the interests of everyone" (Samuel Scheffler, ed., *Consequentialism and Its Critics* [London: Oxford University Press, 1988], 1). The aim of this volume is to argue not that consequentialism is the ideal ethical framework for interpreting the world but that the current disjuncture between the ethical imperatives of human rights and formal international law must be reexamined: thinking about the ethical consequences of the war allows us at least to imagine that some things can be considered morally right but against the law.

10. Danny Postel has pointed out this phenomenon of "selective solidarity" with regard to Iran: the response of the global left to the theocratic repression in Iran has been virtually nonexistent. See Danny Postel, "Iran, Solidarity, and the Left," *Radical Society: A Review of Culture and Politics* 30, no. 4 (October/December 2003): 69–76.

11. See Oxford Research International, http://www.oxfordresearch.com. The results of these surveys are discussed later in this introduction.

12. For a fascinating analysis of this phenomenon of left-wing adoration of anti-American tyrants, see Paul Hollander, *Political Pilgrims: Travels of Western Intellectuals to the Soviet Union, China, and Cuba, 1928–1978* (New York: Oxford University Press, 1981).

13. For an in-depth analysis of the numerical, geographic, and military aspects of this Coalition, see "Coalition of the Willing," http://www.geocities .com/pwhce/willing.html (accessed December 29, 2004).

14. This letter was subsequently published on January 30, 2003, in the *Wall Street Journal*. It is important to note that the acts of these heads of state were not uncontroversial in their own countries.

15. "Jacques Chirac Criticizes the Pro-American Position of Future EU Members," *Le Monde*, February 18, 2003.

16. Ambrose Evans-Pritchard, "Ten Eastern European States to Join War Effort," *The Telegraph*, June 2, 2003.

17. Physicians for Human Rights, "Southern Iraq: Reports of Human Rights Abuses and Views on Justice, Reconstruction, and Government," http://www .phrusa.org/research/iraq/index.html (accessed December 29, 2004).

18. Oxford Research International has been commissioning and carrying out successive waves of social research in Iraq. Its reports are issued at http://www.oxfordresearch.com/publications.html. The present discussion is based on results from the February 4, 2004, survey and offers a snapshot of Iraqi sentiment at that time. It is important to continue to examine the findings of ongoing research in light of continual developments, but, as of now, these are the most complete and systematic surveys available on Iraqi public opinion.

19. Kenneth Timmerman, *The French Betrayal of America* (New York: Crown Forum, 2004).

20. This book was going to press just as the Charles Duelfer's comprehensive report on WMDs in Iraq appeared. The report indicates that Saddam Hussein most likely destroyed existing stocks of WMDS in a plan to get UN sanctions lifted in order to rearm. The report makes very clear that many countries that opposed the war had rather questionable relations with Saddam's regime, a fact that was consistently and willfully ignored by anti-Bush opponents of the war. Because this volume was going to press just as the report was released, a complete discussion of its implications for some of the arguments presented in the volume is not possible. The complete Duelfer Report is available at http://www.cia.gov/cia/reports/iraq_wmd_2004/ (accessed December 29, 2004).

21. Max Weber, "Politics as a Vocation," in *From Max Weber: Essays in Sociology*, ed. H. H. Gerth and C. Wright Mills (New York: Oxford University Press, 1946), 77–128.

PART ONE

# RECONSIDERING REGIME CHANGE

# 1

# The Case for Regime Change

CHRISTOPHER HITCHENS

The case for the removal of the Saddam Hussein regime was, in most of its essential aspects, already complete by 1998, when the United States Senate unanimously adopted the Iraq Liberation Act.[1] At that period:

- Iraq's "sovereignty" had already been severely qualified by the imposition of international sanctions and by the further imposition of "no-fly zones" to prevent the repetition of genocidal attacks on the northern and southern populations of the country.

- Iraq had failed conspicuously to come into compliance with a series of important United Nations resolutions, mostly related to the identification and destruction of weapons of mass destruction (WMDs) but also to such matters as a full accounting of "missing" prisoners from the attempted erasure of the sovereignty of Kuwait. (For Iraq to destroy WMDs on its own would have been an additional grave breach of the UN resolutions, which required disclosure and registration of stocks to be handed over for destruction.)

- Iraq had become a leading sponsor and advocate of Islamist violence, abandoning its former "secular" rhetoric for tirades in favor of jihad; openly financing the suicide bombers in Israel and the occupied territories; holding conferences that called for holy war; promulgating the crudest forms of anti-Semitism; building mosques named for Saddam Hussein; and maintaining at least arm's-length contact with the Al Qaeda organization. In the meantime, the man most wanted in connection with the bombing of the World Trade Center in 1993, Abdul Rahman Yasin, was being sheltered in Baghdad.

This combination of circumstances led President Bill Clinton and Vice President Al Gore to insist, in several public speeches,[2] that another confrontation with the Saddam Hussein regime was inevitable and that the objective ought to be his removal from power.[3] A number of supporters of the previous George Bush administration, meanwhile, concluded that it had been a mistake to leave Saddam Hussein in power after his eviction from Kuwait. The year 1991 was to be viewed not just as an opportunity missed but as the regrettable commencement of a "virtual" collusion with the Baath Party, in which Iraqis suffered from sanctions while their oppressors looted the treasury, with help from the United Nations Oil for Food program, thus acquiring an immense off-the-record budget for future adventures.

Endorsement of the idea of an inescapable final round with Saddam was therefore fairly general in the political class, from centrist Democrats to neoconservatives, and had nothing surreptitious about it. In retrospect, the emphasis was perhaps too one-sidedly on Iraq as a "rogue" state and insufficiently on the danger of Iraq's becoming a "failed" state. The beggaring of the infrastructure, the immiseration of the society, with the regime's own turn to opportunist Islamism, presented the international community with the real possibility of an imploded Iraq, riven by sectarian differences and with a new lumpen underclass at the mercy of demagogy. Had such a development been allowed to run for much longer, the "failed" aspects of the state would undoubtedly have intensified its "rogue" elements—and this in a country of much greater strategic and economic importance than Afghanistan or Somalia. By international resolutions, moreover, Iraq had been adopted as a responsibility and already placed, theoretically, in our care. All that was left was to fulfill the precondition of regime change as specified in the Iraq Liberation Act. Implied in the idea of regime change, fairly self-evidently, was the embryonic concept of what we now term *preemp-*

*tion.* Presumably (and for a change), the timing of the confrontation would not be left up to Saddam Hussein to determine.

Neither major American political party quite lived up to this proclaimed responsibility. President Clinton spent the closing years of his tenure in search of an Israeli-Palestinian agreement along the lines adumbrated at Oslo (and in search also, perhaps, of a Nobel wreath). The Republican Party of George W. Bush entered the 2000 election in the guise of a quasi-isolationist force, publicly hostile to such efforts in nation building as the Clinton-Gore administration had undertaken. Iraq continued to rot and crash.

The reciprocity between the "rogue state" danger and the "failed state" danger deserves more scrutiny than it has received. Clearly, a superpower like the United States, and the world community in general, has several kinds of interest in preventing the occurrence of state failure. The first is obvious enough: it is something worse than callous to witness such developments as a spectator. The second is more specific: state failure or implosion may involve actual or attempted genocide, which nations signatory to the Genocide Convention are sworn to prevent and to punish. The third might be described as pragmatic: state failure often draws or drags neighboring countries into a "black hole." In Rwanda, where plain warnings were flatly ignored or even denied by the United Nations and by the Clinton administration, all three worst-case outcomes occurred: the state effectively ceased to function; genocide was organized and carried out by the state's former leaders and functionaries; the resulting carnage has led to a civil war in Congo that has taken millions of lives and drawn in the armed forces of neighboring states.

Had this situation been allowed to happen in Iraq, under the demented supervision of either Saddam himself or, as time wore on, his sadistic and megalomaniac sons Uday and Qusay, the preconditions for a ghastly civil war were already in place, augmented by confessional and other divisions. There can be no room for doubt that in such an eventuality, Turkey, Iran, and Saudi Arabia would have pursued opportunistic interventions, directed in each case at intensifying and exploiting the preexisting divisions rather than composing them. A major part of the international petroleum economy might have been sabotaged in the process, leading to a wide and general fall in standards of living. The result would have been Somalia or Rwanda on a far vaster scale.

In the case of Iraq, a further consideration demands attention. In the Muslim world of late, state failure has not led to widespread questioning of existing leaderships or ideologies. Instead, resentment has been projected outward, toward the supposed Crusader/Jewish/Hindu conspiracy that is at the root of all ills. Thus one can add another consideration to the aforementioned list: the general interest in denying opportunities to the forces of jihad.

All of this was to become painfully and shockingly evident in one unforgettable moment, when it was discovered that the hinterland of a failed Islamic state—Afghanistan—had been put at the disposal of a fanatical secret army, controlled in turn by a combination of crime family and crooked multinational corporations, vulgarly known as Al Qaeda. The essential facts here had also been known since at least 1998. But their lethal and toxic combustibility, in concert, had been only dimly apprehended.

I have already said that the case for regime change in Iraq was complete on its own terms, and widely understood as such, before the atrocities of September 11, 2001. We are, however, evidently compelled to review the former case through the optic of the latter. I maintain that, for the most part, the addition of the supposedly "new" emergency strengthened the case for an urgent revisiting of the longer-term one. But I would like to note in passing that what I have already described is enough to dismiss or discard all third-order distractions, such as the role of the Halliburton company, the abandoned Unocal pipeline in Afghanistan, the existence of the Carlyle Group, or the presence of a supposed Jewish cabal in Washington. Saddam Hussein was not a newly invented enemy. He was one of the oldest foes, not just of the United States but of international norms. If he was not, in the vernacular of the argument, an "imminent" threat, he was certainly a permanent and serious one. If there are to be recriminations and inquests, they should certainly begin with the question of who was right and who was wrong when the first Bush administration allowed him to resume his rule—of helicopter gunship and mass grave and meat hook—in 1991.

One may also dismiss the inexpensive suggestion that the Blair government was acting as a "poodle" or surrogate of the Bush administration. At least as early as 1999, Prime Minister Tony Blair had made a speech in Chicago saying that the welcome eviction of Slobodan Milošević did not leave the international scene devoid of psychopathic dictators, with whom coexistence was neither possible nor desirable.[4] He specifically mentioned Saddam Hussein in this context—at a time when George W. Bush was still governor of Texas—and his own timely intervention in Sierra Leone, meanwhile, undoubtedly helped to prevent another Liberia or Rwanda from occurring.

It would almost be possible to believe, when reading the memoirs of, say, Richard Clarke, that the Bush and Blair governments had never intervened in Afghanistan at all but had preferred to focus on their "obsession" with Iraq. (The fact that Clarke had been prominent among the noninterventionist faction over Rwanda has likewise escaped the notice it deserves.) The removal of the Taliban and the temporary routing of Al Qaeda was a necessary reprisal for the aggression of September 11, even if these actions were, at the time they were undertaken, violently opposed by the core leadership of today's antiwar movement. Having taken care, as it were, of the last aggression, any responsible government would have been confronted with the question, What do we do about the next one? If you doubt this point, please study the way in which the Bush administration has since been accused of overlooking the "warning signs" of an attack that had been planned since before it took office.

Leave aside, if you choose, the preexisting pledge to cease coexistence and collusion with the doomed and vicious Saddam Hussein regime. The following considerations were now added to the existing imperative:

- The Saddam Hussein regime had openly applauded the attacks on New York and Washington, adding in bragging tones that further revenge of this sort could be expected. This at a time when even regimes previously sympathetic to the Taliban and Al Qaeda, such as Pakistan and Saudi Arabia, were, if anything, disowning their previous rhetoric and commitments.

- The Saddam Hussein regime still belonged to a notorious group of nations that sought to obtain illegal weaponry by stealth. At the time, this "club" included Libya, Iran, North Korea, and a quasi-governmental and military clique revolved around the rogue scientist A. Q. Khan in Pakistan.

- The Saddam Hussein regime had offered its hospitality to Abu Musad al-Zarqawi, a venomous jihadist refugee from Afghanistan and associate of Osama bin Laden, after the eviction of

Taliban and Al Qaeda forces. This, again, at a time when other governments similarly compromised were attempting to disembarrass themselves of such links.

Over the past year or so, an apparently scrupulous yet strangely unexacting standard has been applied to undeniable facts such as the three stated here. If the Islamists praised, rewarded, and encouraged by Saddam Hussein were not clan members of the bin Laden group, it seems, then they did not really count. If Saddam Hussein refused compliance with UN resolutions on WMDs, then it was for inspectors to prove his guilt (the word *inspector,* which means "monitor," being confused with the idea of "investigator" in this context). If every other country on the illicit-weapons list proves on examination to have been even more promiscuous than had been imagined, Saddam Hussein still deserved the benefit of any doubt.

To say that this was taking the lessons of history lightly would be an understatement. A more immediate question also presented itself: Who in a position of responsibility could afford to treat such matters with equanimity? In what sense was the Baath Party entitled, in the event of doubt, to the presumption of innocence?

Later developments have vindicated the Bush and Blair administrations on these points. The David Kay inquiry, while finding no stockpiles of WMDs, established that as late as March 2003, the envoys of Saddam were meeting the envoys of Kim Jong Il in the Syrian capital, Damascus, with a view to Saddam exchanging some of his stolen money for some of North Korea's illicit missiles and for the production facilities to make more of them.[5] Shells containing illegal chemical elements have been discovered all over the Iraqi landscape, and the Jordanian authorities tell us that their ingredients have been discovered, in the hands of extremist gangs, on Jordanian territory. One report, of an Iraqi attempt to purchase "yellow cake" uranium from Niger, has been famously discredited. However, corroborative evidence suggesting that Baathist officials were trying to buy such material elsewhere in West Africa has recently come to light. Meanwhile, the Iranian mullahs have been caught flagrantly deceiving the International Atomic Energy Agency (IAEA) inspectors of their nuclear plants, while Libya has decided to surrender all of its fissile material and related product (now under lock and key in Oak Ridge, Tennessee, and, incidentally, surrendered to Blair and Bush and not Annan or Chirac or Blix). A fuller investigation of the provenance of that vast Libyan stockpile led directly to the unmasking and neutralizing of the A. Q. Khan nexus in Pakistan, which in turn stretched as far as North Korea. In terms of non-proliferation, the regime change in Iraq has had great success beyond itself. It is not unimportant, for the peace of the region and beyond, that Iraq can now be certified as disarmed. The alternative—taking Saddam's word for that condition—was never a very persuasive one.

In parallel, the unexpectedly well-organized and ruthless resistance of jihad forces, from within Iraq and also aided from outside it, must demonstrate even to the incurious that an Islamist scheme was already in preparation. This situation was actually known in advance, through the well-advertised "Fedayeen Saddam," whose very name expressed the connection. It is improbable in the highest degree that al-Zarqawi could have organized such a force, from scratch, as an indigent immigrant or refugee from Afghanistan, in a hermetically controlled country that was once as difficult to enter as it was to leave. Clearly, his group enjoyed a period of state support before the invasion. The rivalry between al-Zarqawi and bin Laden may be less than advertised (or even more). But are we supposed to be insouciant about the possibility that Saddam was setting up his own personal jihad front? Again comes the question: How much tolerance or patience could one have been expected to have demonstrated in the process of finding out?

Geopolitics also plays its part in the evolution of this argument. For many decades, the United States had been helping to run a political slum in the Middle East. The measure of the failure of this proxy system is that it once partly included Saddam Hussein himself, and during one of the worst periods of his rule at that. The relationship between this oligarchic practice, of alternating profiteering and benign neglect, and the emergence of medieval reactionary forces is neither entirely clear nor quite opaque. That some direct or oblique connection exists is seldom if ever disputed. In any case, the arrangement itself had become highly unstable and subject to abruptly diminishing returns. The project of taking a keystone state, wedged between Iran and Saudi Arabia, and of keeping the already long-made promise of helping it to throw off despotism and avoid anarchy cannot be regarded as a foolish one. The force of example might be great, but the force of any counterexample, or nonexample, would surely have been even greater. There was also the possibility, even at such a late stage, that the impact on the Israeli-Palestinian nightmare might be a positive one, in that the Palestinian rejectionists would no longer have a patron to whom they could turn, as they had after the Madrid negotiations in 1990, and the Israeli rejectionists would have one less alibi. (Before the abysmal breakdown of law and order in Iraq in April 2004, the Governing Council had gone as far as considering an invitation to the Iraqi Jews, dispossessed in the frenzy of 1947–1948, to return.[6])

This argument may seem as quixotic now as it did at the time, and it may have overestimated the number of Iraqis and Kurds who were willing to welcome a Western intervention. (Not by many, in the case of the Kurds, who had already proved the efficacy of regime change in practice.) But I have never heard a persuasive argument that it was wrong to try or that any feasible alternative was in prospect. If what was done was too little or poorly executed (and I write as one who could not easily name a mistake that the Bush administration has failed to make), then it must be borne in mind that there is a yet more severe criticism: that nothing was done at all until it was almost too late. One cannot decently forget the dozen years consumed by the locusts between 1991 and 2003.

One way to reflect on all this—because we will be back to the question of rogue states and failed states, and of the Islamic dimension of the same—is to separate what we must do for others from what we are entitled to do for ourselves. If Saddam's Iraq had been hiding weapons and harboring terrorists in the literal way that some voters were led to believe was the case, then there would have been a right to intervene that could be exerted regardless of Iraqi public opinion. As it happened, there was excellent reason to think that the inhabitants of a rogue state would see the removal of a foul tyrant as a deliverance. This unusually favorable conjunction of circumstances, which was to a great extent thrown away, is by no means certain to arise again. Many in Iran, for example, would love to see the end of theocracy. But many can also be induced to see the illegal acquisition of nuclear weapons as a question of patriotism and self-determination. What shall we do if Pakistan melts down as a society while retaining its reactors? How much do we secretly hope that Saudi Arabia is not subverted by forces even more friendly to holy war? These will be cases where realpolitik is not a perfect fit with a human rights agenda.

On the other side of the question, I believe that we have made promises and commitments to the people of Iraqi Kurdistan that involve something more than the strategic and that stretch back many decades—perhaps to as far as the time of President Woodrow Wilson. Here, a stubborn matter of principle asserts itself: We cannot betray these people again. Indeed, given the interest of the European Union in guaranteeing its liberties within Turkey as well, the time might be appropriate for an international declaration on the rights of the largest nonstate population in the region. If the Bahreini royal family can have an embassy, a state, and a seat at the UN, why should the twenty-five million Kurds not have a claim to autonomy? The alleviation of their suffering and the assertion of their self-government is one of the few unarguable benefits of regime change in Iraq. It is not a position from which any moral retreat would be allowable.

The balance of an extremely hazardous and heavily compromised intervention might be summarized, on its positive side, as follows:

- One of the worst dictators and murderers in history is in the dock, where he belongs.

- The discussion of democracy and reform, however reluctant, has been given an impetus in the region.

- The club of WMD violators has been reduced by two (Iraq and Libya), and the remaining members have been put on notice— along with the hitherto-lax UN and IAEA inspectors.

- So many are the competing demands for different kinds of Iraqi freedom that it has been dangerous as well as difficult to arbi- trate them. But how much disgrace is there in being in such a position?

- Coalition forces have acquired invaluable experience (not without some high cost in moral attrition) in how to manage the transition from rogue/failed state to survivor state. Let us hope that this experience, which will be needed again, was not acquired too late.

- The forces of jihad, who are often said to be glad of this oppor- tunity, no longer have the advantage of being the only side in the war who really know that they are fighting it. One has the impression also that they were angry and unappeasable enough already.

These points might not exhaust the list. I should say something about the returned refugees who, as in the Afghan case, may make a decisive difference simply by returning—or by exercising their right of return—to live in the country from which they had been driven. (This is another element in regime change that could have benefited from more prewar planning than it received.)

Finally, I am as ready as the next supporter of the intervention to confess to some dark nights and profound misgivings. But there was always the compensation of seeing the faces and hearing the voices of Iraqis and Kurds who had undergone the once-in-a-lifetime experience of human liberation. To have had even a small share in this historic event is a pleasure and a privilege that, to my continuing astonishment, a large proportion of the "human rights" and "antiwar" communities has decided to deny itself.

## NOTES

1. The full text of the Iraq Liberation Act is available at http://news .findlaw.com/hdocs/docs/iraq/libact103198.pdf (accessed November 22, 2004).

2. Speech by President Clinton, December 16, 1998.

3. David Sanger, "Tongue Lashings and Backlashes," *New York Times,* November 22, 1998, WK5.

4. Speech by Tony Blair, April 22, 1999, before the Chicago Economic Club. The full text is available at http://www.pbs.org/newshour/bb/international/ jan-june99/blair_doctrine4-23.html (accessed November 22, 2004).

5. David Sanger and Thom Shanker, "A Region Inflamed: Weapons: For the Iraqis, a Missile Deal That Went Sour; Files Tell of Talks with North Korea," *New York Times,* December 1, 2003, A11.

6. Dexter Filkins, "Iraqi Council Weighs Return of Jews, Rejecting It So Far," *New York Times,* February 28, 2004, A6.

# 2

# Liberal Legacies, Europe's Totalitarian Era, and the Iraq War

Historical Conjunctures and Comparisons

JEFFREY HERF

The historical irony of the war that overthrew Iraqi totalitarianism is that most liberals on both sides of the Atlantic opposed it, despite the fact that Saddam Hussein's Baath regime had ideological lineages and affinities to the fascist and Nazi regimes of Europe's midcentury.[1] The exceptions of the Blair wing of the British Labour Party, the editorial boards of the *Washington Post* and the *New Republic*, and a minority of liberal intellectuals in Europe and the United States proved the rule. Those who play a key role in defining the meaning of liberalism as a set of positions in contemporary politics, such as the editors of the *New York Times* and the *New York Review of Books*, almost all of the liberal papers in Europe, and much of the Democratic Party in Congress, opposed the war in Iraq in 2003 and did not define the issue in the context of liberalism's historical traditions of armed antifascism. To be sure, they expressed no enthusiasm for Saddam or his regime; they focused their criticism on the unilateralism of the Bush administration and on the neoconservative advisers whom they held primarily responsible for the war. Indeed, the vast majority of citizens who were not regular readers of the *Washington Post* editorial and opinion pages or of the *New Republic* were probably only dimly aware that there was a liberal case for the war.

Yet liberals and conservatives based their judgments, in part, on a set of then commonly held assertions about Saddam Hussein's weapons of mass destruction programs. The public case for a preemptive war in spring 2003 rested on the presumed imminence of the threat as well as the possibility that Iraq would give weapons of mass destruction to terrorists motivated by Islamic radicalism. As of December 2004, none of these weapons have been discovered, while the reports of the commission investigating the attacks of September 11, 2001, have found no evidence of collaboration between Saddam's Iraq and Al Qaeda in those attacks. A unanimous bipartisan report of the Senate Intelligence Committee unanimously concluded that the major justifications of the war were unfounded and unreasonable and reflected major blunders by US intelligence agencies.[2] It cannot be logically precluded that the weapons that were at the core of the immediate justifications for this *preemptive* war may yet be found; that in the months of fall and winter 2002–2003 Saddam dispersed or destroyed them; that in the chaos following the American entry into Baghdad, they were shipped out of the country, destroyed, hidden, or stolen; and that the reported hundreds of murders of Iraqi professionals since the end of the war by insurgents have silenced those who have information about the weapons. Saddam's behavior was consistent with that of a person with something to hide. Yet the American case, a case that was also supported by the intelligence agencies even of governments that opposed the war, was expressed with confidence about firmly established facts that now appear to be, at worst, simply wrong and, at best, not proven.

I shared the perfectly plausible view that Saddam was hiding a weapons program. But I supported the war not because I was sure that the threat from Saddam was an imminent one but rather because, in the face of ineradicable uncertainty about the facts, I did not believe that Saddam Hussein deserved the benefit of the doubt in any of the controversies surrounding his regime. Although I thought the preponderance of evidence did point to what Kenneth Pollack called "a threatening storm," my support for the decision to go to war rested on a judgment about the danger of leaving Saddam's regime in power.[3] Had Saddam successfully thwarted the United Nations inspection program, then, given the nature of his regime and the resources at his disposal, I believed and believe today that he would have developed an arsenal of weapons of mass destruction as the inspections regime eroded and his prestige in the Arab and Islamic world rose.

The totalitarian nature of Saddam's regime and its lineages to past examples of totalitarian dictatorship received far too little serious discussion from the Bush administration. More than any other dictatorship to emerge around the globe since the defeat of Hitler's Germany, Italian fascism, and imperial Japan, it combined the worst features of mid-twentieth-century totalitarian rule (evident also, of course, in the Soviet Union of the Stalin era, Mao's China, Pol Pot's Cambodia, and North Korea), with foreign policy aggressiveness that made it a serious threat to the Middle East and to international security. Though Saddam's "republic of fear" used the slogans of the regional and international left—pan-Arabism, anti-imperialism, socialism, and so forth—the Baath Party also drew heavily on the European legacies of French fascism and Nazism. (Oddly, the aftereffects of French fascism in Baghdad never became an issue in French debates about the war.) Like the preceding tyrannies of the extreme right, Saddam's Iraq rested on a leadership principle focused on a supreme leader held to be infallible and the use of terror against anyone who challenged his authority. As the disastrous wars with Iran and Kuwait and the devastation of the Iraqi economy under his rule demonstrated, Saddam Hussein was a more irrational and thus dangerous figure than the communist leaders of the Soviet Union and China had been during the coldest decades of the Cold War. Like that of Hitler and the Japanese leaders in 1941, Saddam's decision making was driven by an ideologically distorted view of the world that was unchecked even by collective deliberations of a politburo. The results were evident in the disastrous decision to attack Iran and then Kuwait.

Baathist ideology as manifest in Saddam's regime recalled the fascist and Nazi past in other ways as well. It rested on an ideology of subordination of individuals to the interest of the whole nation; celebrations of violence and force as higher qualities of genuine manhood; destruction of all opposition political parties and a free press as divisive forces; constant mobilization against enemies—real and imagined, foreign and domestic—through total control of the press and media; a massive secret police apparatus that enforced even the slightest dissent with terror and that left behind an estimated three hundred thousand corpses in mass graves; elimination of all debate and discussion within the government, which thus left national decisions to the whim of one increasingly ill-informed man; perception of the external world through paranoid and conspiratorial visions laced with radical anti-Semitism;

launching of two wars that led to the loss of hundreds of thousands of lives that revealed grave miscalculations; and the first use of chemical weapons in modern history by a government against its own citizens, the Kurds in northern Iraq.

As opponents of the war pointed out, Saddam's Iraq was hardly the only dictatorship with an atrocious human rights record. Indeed, President George W. Bush himself declared Iran and North Korea to be members in good standing of an "axis of evil." Yet, in contrast to North Korea and other vicious dictatorships around the world, Saddam Hussein's regime sat on top of the second largest reserves of oil in the world. In contrast to Iran, which also had considerable oil reserves, the possibility that after thirty-five years of fear and repression the Iraqis could end the Baath regime was essentially nonexistent. Oil was indeed key to the decision to invade Iraq but not because the United States was determined to control it. Oil was key because, over time, the possibility seemed excellent that United Nations sanctions would erode and then collapse, leaving Saddam with essentially unlimited financial resources from oil sales to further develop an arsenal of weapons of mass destruction. This combination of the nature of the regime and its proven record of aggression and miscalculation with money derived from oil sales meant that sooner or later Saddam could acquire weapons of mass destruction without again having to invade any other countries.

In view of all that has gone wrong since the war started, it is important to remember that the most important result of the war is that the regime of Saddam Hussein and the power of the Baath Party and its ideology in Iraq are gone. A new, fledgling Iraqi government has a chance to inaugurate the first democratic government in the Arab world. Saddam is not a successful hero to the Arab world, and he, along with other former leading officials, will be put on trial for crimes against humanity. The people of Iraq, whatever future they face, have been liberated from one of the worst dictatorships of the past half century. But our assessment must also acknowledge the following sober recollection of the justifications of the war offered by the Bush and Blair governments.[4]

First, the Bush and Blair governments' most important justification for a war—and for a war in March 2003 rather than at a later date—was that Saddam had already accumulated an arsenal of chemical and biological weapons and was still trying to build a nuclear arsenal. Those weapons have not yet been found.

Second, the Bush administration argued that there was indeed a connection among Saddam Hussein, the radical Islamists of Al Qaeda, and the attacks of September 11, 2001. Although evidence of such contacts has emerged, the commission appointed to examine the events of September 11 found no credible evidence that Saddam's Iraq cooperated in any way with Al Qaeda in the planning or execution of the September 11 attacks.

Third, both the Bush and Blair governments made the important argument that the credibility of the United Nations and of multilateral institutions and the viability of international law were at stake in the debate over whether to use force if necessary to see that Iraq implemented the terms of UN disarmament resolutions. To the enormous frustration of American and British liberals, however, these arguments fell on deaf ears among those, especially in France and Germany, who declared themselves most supportive of international institutions. While the United States was trying to save the UN from the fate of its hapless predecessor, the League of Nations and its refusal to use force against the fascist dictators of the 1930s when they violated disarmament agreements, many in the UN did not agree.

Fourth, Vice President Dick Cheney, in particular, repeatedly asserted that the armed forces of the United States and its allies would be greeted as liberators by a grateful Iraqi population and that with the destruction of Saddam's major military forces, which was expected to be over in short order, the war to defeat Iraqi Baathism would be over. This prediction by a man whose confident air is now a bad joke was absurdly optimistic. The Bush administration actually entertained the idea that Saddam's regime, his military and the Baath Party, was essentially a small criminal gang with little or no base of support. Therefore, it reasoned that after two months of war with precision, high-technology weapons that left most of Iraq's infrastructure intact and reduced Iraqi civilian casualties to a minimum, the destruction of the Iraqi army on the battlefield would mean victory in the war against Iraqi Baathism. Such reasoning entailed an astonishing misreading of the success of the US occupation in postwar Germany and postwar Japan. Had the Bush administration understood the historical connections between World War II and the postwar occupations, it would have had no reason to assume that the war in Iraq was either won or over when Saddam's statue was pulled down in Baghdad or when President Bush landed on an aircraft carrier off California and declared the "mission accomplished."

Disaster came from these unjustifiably optimistic scenarios. When, in late 2002, retiring US Army chief of staff Eric Shinseki argued for an invasion force of 200,000 troops to win the battle and secure the peace, Secretary of Defense Donald Rumsfeld dismissed the criticism and insisted on a force of only 140,000. With this reduced force, the US military and its allies failed to prevent looting and destruction of government buildings, hospitals, schools, universities, libraries, museums, and the oil and electrical infrastructure. With the collapse of the Iraqi government and dissolution of the Iraqi army, US and Coalition forces were spread too thin to prevent the collapse of law and order or even to ensure that vital documents and computer hard drives containing information about Iraq's weapons programs were secured. According to news reports, hundreds of murders and kidnappings have taken place in the past year of precisely those Iraqis professionals most able and likely to participate in building a new, democratic Iraq. In the face of such lawlessness, it is understandable that many who may have had information about Saddam's weapons programs were reluctant to come forward with information.

As of December 2004, about 1,200 of the more than 1,300 deaths and most of the 9,000-plus injuries among US soldiers had taken place after the end of "major combat operations." Faced with an insurgency that caught the Bush administration by surprise and confounded its rosy scenarios of the occupation period, an as yet not fully clarified chain of memos from the White House, Department of Justice, Pentagon, and Central Intelligence Agency (CIA) denied or cast doubt on the application of the Geneva Principles to Iraqi prisoners and included grotesque discussions of the meaning of torture. Not surprisingly, these memos from the top levels of the administration ended in the torture and humiliation of Iraqi prisoners at Abu Ghraib prison. The resulting photos and facts have disgraced the good name of the United States and constituted a blow to American credibility on an issue central to US political identity: the rule of law and defense of human rights. No one outside the most partisan supporters of the Bush administration will believe that such a shameful repudiation of principles of the rule of law was primarily the result only of the actions of a few low-ranking soldiers who engaged in these activities.

Fifth, President Bush argued that the war would make possible the establishment of a historical novelty: a liberal democracy in an Arab country in a region of authoritarian regimes from which radical Islamic fanaticism and terrorism had emerged. Such a regime could serve as a catalyst for democratization and moderation in the region as a whole. Whether this outcome happens remains to be seen. What is not in doubt is that the emergence of some kind of largely secular, democratic regime in Iraq is vital to international security and, now, to success in the international offensive against terrorism inspired by radical Islamists.

I publicly supported the war in Iraq and think that I was right to do so for the following reasons:

1.  Totalitarian movements and regimes emerged in twentieth-century Europe in a period of rapid economic and technological modernization that fostered movements of a fundamentalist nature that rejected all or parts of liberal democracy and cultural modernism yet embraced modern technology. The Baath regime in Iraq displayed a comparable mixture of technological advance combined with illiberal politics and political irrationalism that I have earlier called "reactionary modernism."[5] While the Baath regime in Baghdad was not a carbon copy of Europe's totalitarian past, it borrowed far more from it that opponents of the war were willing to acknowledge.

2.  I found the Bush administration's efforts to link Saddam to the attacks of September 11 utterly unconvincing. That many Americans had the impression that he did was a sad commentary on these misleading arguments. Rather than attempt to base a policy on reports of furtive meetings between Iraqi intelligence operatives and members of Al Qaeda, the more compelling argument for me was one about a historical conjuncture. Liberal historians are all, to some degree, heirs to Alexis de Tocqueville, Marc Bloch, and Thomas Macaulay because, like these great precursors, we believe that history is the realm of contingency and conjuncture. We liberal historians believe that great historical events—the Protestant Reformation, the American and French Revolutions, World War I, World War II and the Holocaust—have multiple and often unrelated causes whose simultaneous appearances lead to outcomes that none on their own would produce. The term *conjuncture* directs our attention to the fact of complexity, the multiplicity of causal factors, and the key importance of time and simultaneity in politics. In the past twenty years, we have been living in one of these conjunctures— namely, the coexistence of two kinds of anti-Western radicalism rooted in the Arab and Islamic world: that of secular Baathism

and the growth of terror inspired by Islamic fundamentalism.[6] Though they were not allies, the emergence of Al Qaeda took place in the same period in which Saddam was ignoring UN disarmament resolutions. The fanaticism inspired by religion and that driven by the secular totalitarian religions of modern politics have different histories and lineages, iconic leaders, and key texts. Yet the contingent fact of their simultaneous existence in geographic proximity to one another meant that both could have an impact that is beyond what they would have if they had not occurred at roughly the same time and place. In short, after September 11, no US president could exclude the possibility that Iraqi weapons would find their way into the hands of suicide bombers inspired by radical Islam. Defeating Saddam Hussein did not defeat Al Qaeda and did, no doubt, radicalize many young Muslims. But radical Islam with the Baath regime in place constituted a more dangerous potential threat than radical Islam without it. No US president should rest the security of the United States in years to come on the proposition that a Baathist regime would not hand over weapons to Islamic terrorists and thus make possible terrorist attacks on the United States or its allies. History is replete with strange alliances of previous foes who join forces to defeat a common enemy, whether they call it American imperialists or non-Muslim infidels.

3. Even if Saddam or his successors had no contacts with radical Islamists, leaving this regime in power meant taking an enormous risk. Again, the oil would remain there for the regime to use. As splits in the UN Security Council, particularly the policies of France and Russia, indicated, it was entirely conceivable that Saddam would succeed in eroding and then destroying arms control restrictions and inspections. If he had succeeded in using splits in the UN and mobilizing anti-Americanism to end the sanctions regime, all the evidence suggests that he would have continued to build a mass destruction arsenal. If and when that development happened, a Baathist regime with weapons of mass destruction would have become the dominant power in the region, potentially able to exert enormous pressures on the global economy through control over the flow of oil and its price. Moreover, an Iraq with weapons of mass destruction and a demonstrated record of aggression would have increased the

incentives for Iran and Turkey, as well as perhaps Greece, Saudi Arabia, and Egypt, to develop their own nuclear weapons, at which point efforts at nuclear nonproliferation in an area of the world filled with ideological fanaticism would have been demolished.

The fact that no weapons of mass destruction have yet been found in Iraq suggests that an intelligence failure of enormous dimensions occurred and that Saddam succeeded in a rash bluff that fooled all of the major intelligence services of the world. Perhaps. Or perhaps in the eight months from Vice President Cheney's speech of 2002 warning of a possible military campaign against Saddam until the start of the war in March 2003, Saddam destroyed, sent abroad, or effectively hid evidence of such programs. After all, by then the Iraqis had become experts at concealment and deception with twelve years of practice dealing with UN inspections. We do know that in the last weeks of the major military campaign and then in the chaotic weeks following the Americans' entry into Baghdad in April 2003, government offices were systematically looted, with files and computer disk drives with information regarding Iraqi weapons programs stolen, destroyed, and burned. The failure of the United States to secure these facilities may have meant that a great deal of evidence was destroyed or hidden. There was no reason to give Saddam Hussein the benefit of the doubt.

One of the most disappointing aspects of the debate over the Iraq war was the opposition of France, Germany, and Russia. Given the authoritarianism of the Putin government, the importance of the KGB in government, and the relative weakness today of Russia's examination of the crimes of the Stalin era and the Gulag, it hardly came a surprise that Russia opposed the war. Nor, given that the French confrontation with the legacies of Action Française and Vichy really began in earnest only in the 1970s, was it surprising that French contribution to the ideology of Iraqi Baathism played no role at all in the French debate about the war. In both Russia and France, decades of criticism of and hostility to Israel also contributed to muting criticism of Saddam's Iraq.

As a historian of Germany and of its memory of the Holocaust, I was most disappointed but not surprised that the left-of-center German government of Gerhard Schröder unequivocally opposed any war against Saddam's Iraq even if endorsed by the United Nations. Pacifism,

a certain neutralist inclination during the Cold War, echoes of Marxist anti-imperialism, and a remarkable faith in the ability of diplomacy
without force to resolve problems have long been aspects of the West
German left from which Schröder comes. In this political culture, the
memory of the era of Nazism, World War II, and the Holocaust evokes,
on the whole, not the importance of armed antifascism of the Allies but
rather the absurdity and pointlessness of war. Efforts to evoke the "lessons of Munich" and the dangers of appeasement—for example, during
the bitter debates over the euromissiles in the 1980s, repeatedly failed
to gain much traction for most of the then–West German left. Such lessons remained primarily the preserve of conservative and centrist liberal politicians in Germany and were applied in relationship to the
threat of the Soviet Union. During the 1990s, cracks in the pacifism
appeared in response to Serbian mass murder in the Balkans, but the
war there did not end until the United States intervened after Germany,
France, and Britain had tied themselves in knots and proved unable
or unwilling to use force decisively to end the slaughter. As many commentators have noted, German politicians spoke the language of shared
sovereignty, confidence-building measures, and conflict resolution that
became coin of the realm of the European Union. Rather than interpret
1989–1990 as the end point of a half century of deterrence and containment backed by armed force, the German and European left interpreted it wholly as a confirmation of the wisdom of détente.

In the name of what it called cosmopolitanism and postnational
identifications, this current of left-leaning thought in Germany and
Europe was ill equipped to respond to the possibility that a new and
different form of totalitarian rule could emerge outside Europe that
would require a possible armed response from European states.[7] The
disdain for international organizations, prevalence of religious piety in
public rhetoric, and President Bush's inability to think quickly or speak
eloquently about complex matters in public contributed to an erosion of support in Europe. However, Prime Minister Tony Blair's elo-
quence and his familiarity with the echoes of Europe's past also did
not win over much of the British press, not to mention the French and
German governments. For reasons that other commentators have frequently noted, the French and German governments reflected a widespread mood in Europe that found it hard to support the use of force in
response to a Hobbesian world in other parts of the globe. Had it been
a liberal US president who decided to invade Iraq with rhetorical justifications that resonated with French and German historical experience,

it seems to me dubious that the response would have been different. Ironically, much intellectual work needs to be done in bringing the United States' tragic perspective on international affairs to bear on European intellectual life and politics. For now it remains overly immersed in what used to be a peculiarly American optimism about the possibilities of peace and security.

The war in Iraq opened up but did not resolve the issue of similarities and differences between Europe's era of totalitarianism and the regime of Saddam Hussein. I want to conclude with two aspects of German history that bear directly on the debate over preemption and on the relationship between war and occupation. One aspect of the debate over preemption is actually not controversial among liberal opinion on both sides of the Atlantic. As wide support for the war in Afghanistan and for the international war against Al Qaeda and the radical Islamists indicates, there is broad agreement that in addition to a war of ideas, democratization, and economic development, preemptive war against terrorists willing to commit suicide has become an indispensable component of US foreign policy. Were Al Qaeda to possess weapons of mass destruction, it could not be deterred by the prospect of nuclear retaliation.

The American diplomatic historian John Lewis Gaddis has recently argued that September 11, 2001, like the Japanese attack on Pearl Harbor in 1941, brought revolutions in US foreign policy. Just as the attack on Pearl Harbor wrought the Roosevelt revolution in American foreign relations that introduced sixty years of containment and deterrence, so, too, did September 11 make preemption one necessary component of American security policy.[8] There is general agreement that someone who believes that his or her own suicide in the cause of radical Islam will lead to a marvelous future in heaven cannot be deterred by the prospect of retaliation. The case for preemption against this kind of enemy is straightforward and actually widely accepted.

Preemption applied to Iraq was another matter. The Bush and Blair governments believed that their intelligence services had gathered facts that made Saddam's threat an imminent one—that is, one that needed to be preempted in the very near future. They did not make the case for a *preventive* war, a war based on what Iraq would do some years in the future. They believed they were fighting a war of necessity, not one of choice. Yet by its very nature, every *preemptive* war must also have elements of a preventive war because it must rest on a set of political judgments and intelligence assessments, almost always about dictatorial regimes whose expertise lies in deception and terror. Leaders can never be absolutely certain that their intelligence is accurate, and they must make decisions based only on the best information available, which may not be very good. The argument for a preemptive war against Iraq rested on the best intelligence at the time; on Saddam's continued refusal to display what his government had been doing; but also on the nature of the Iraqi regime, its past policies and misjudgments, and, again, the financial resources available to the regime due to the huge reserves of oil. When all of these points were taken together, it seemed to me reasonable to assume the worst about Saddam's intentions and his present and future capabilities.

Though Saddam Hussein was not a carbon copy of Adolf Hitler, the dilemmas of preemption in the late 1930s remain relevant for the recent decision to go to war in spring 2003. Unfortunately, neither Winston Churchill's *The Gathering Storm* nor, more recently, Williamson Murray's *The Change in the European Balance of Power, 1938–1939: The Path to Ruin* appear to have made an impact on the debate over Iraq. Everyone remembers that Churchill was a critic of appeasement, but fewer recall that he labeled World War II "the unnecessary war." He meant that if the democracies and/or the democracies in alliance with the Soviet Union had made a credible threat of force in the late 1930s, Hitler might have been overthrown by a military coup in 1938 and would have been deprived of the opportunity to launch a war at the time and place of his choosing.

In his important but less well-known work, Murray argues that a preemptive war by Britain and France in 1938 or 1939 at a time and place of their own choosing would have caught Nazi Germany at a vulnerable moment well before it had the resources necessary to defeat them. He offers an abundance of evidence that Nazi Germany before the aggressions and expansion of 1940 was in a precarious economic position, lacked access to natural resources vital for armament in depth, and was thus vulnerable to a preventive war. But, he continues, Britain and France consistently made the wrong strategic choices, minimized the reality of the Nazi threat, and exaggerated German military capabilities. Murray concludes that if Britain and France had made the right strategic choices and decisions, they could have defeated Nazi Germany with a preemptive war. Had they done so, there would have been no massive invasion of the Soviet Union with the millions of lives it cost. Without the war in Europe and England's precarious position as a result, it is less likely that Japan would have attacked Pearl Harbor, thus making World War II a truly global conflagration.[9] Finally, because Nazi Germany had not yet occupied the rest of Europe along with its mineral and agricultural resources and did not have control over those areas of the continent, especially Eastern Europe, where the great majority of Europe's Jews lived, it would not have been able to implement the Holocaust, the Final Solution of the Jewish Question in all of Europe.[10]

The uncertainties and imponderables surrounding such a war would have been considerable. There would have been no blueprints of gas chambers for intelligence services to discover because they had not been drawn up by 1939. There would have been few, if any, planning documents for Operation Barbarossa. Nor would there have been an enormous paper trail of meetings and decisions by Hitler, Himmler, and Heydrich in summer and fall 1941; minutes of the Wannsee Conference of January 20, 1942; and speeches by Goebbels informing the world in 1941 that Hitler's prophecies about exterminating the Jews were "now" being realized for the victors to demonstrate the catastrophe that they had prevented. Indeed, if the British and French had attacked before January 30, 1939, Hitler would not yet have uttered his infamous "prophecy" about the extermination of the Jewish race in Europe. Conversely, in the aftermath of a successful preemptive war, there would have been legions of well-meaning anti-interventionists in France and Germany, as well as nationalists and unreconstructed Nazis in Germany, who would have insisted that Hitler had been a man of peace who was merely the latest in a long line of victims of British and French imperialism and/or of Soviet communism. In short, such a preemptive war, which could have spared Europe World War II and prevented the Holocaust, would have been extremely controversial, resting, as it would have, on a set of political judgments about what Hitler would do in the future if he had the opportunity to do so. The only things Churchill could point to were a set of political judgments, hunches, assessments, and informed opinions based on a determination to assume that Hitler meant what he said and wrote; a prescient close reading of *Mein Kampf*; his refusal to abide by the treaties of the League of Nations; and a worst-case assessment of the relationship between Hitler's ideology and German armament programs in the 1930s.

This hypothetical illustration does not impute a simple identity between the threat posed by Hitler and that by Saddam. Historical comparisons do not mean equating one thing with another, though I continue to believe that there were more similarities than the war's opponents acknowledged. Rather, I present this illustration to point out that even faced with the Nazi regime, a preemptive war, which would have saved the world many millions of lives and would have been a just and right war, would have needed to rest on political judgments and intelligence assessments that were subject to great uncertainties. The grim option of a smaller war now rather than a larger and more terrible war later was, unfortunately, not taken in 1938 or 1939. I believe that based on what we know from reading the newspapers, President Bush and Prime Minister Blair were correct to decide that a short war begun in 2003 was far preferable to the longer and more devastating war that was likely if Saddam remained in power.

Though Bush and Blair, in my view, made the right decision to go to war, Bush, Vice President Cheney, National Security Adviser Condoleeza Rice, and the architects of the war in the Pentagon, Secretary of Defense Rumsfeld and Assistant Secretary of Defense Paul Wolfowitz, all drew mistaken lessons from the success of the US occupation in postwar Germany and Japan. As Roosevelt and Churchill understood, the absolutely indispensable precondition for a peaceful, democratic Germany and Japan after the war was victory through unconditional surrender. At the end of six years of war, four million Germans had died; 600,000 of them were civilians who died in the Allied bombing campaigns that devastated every one of Germany's major cities. In the last eighteen months of the war, the figures of German battlefield deaths were overwhelming: 3,300,000 from 1944 to May 1945; 1,500,000 between January and May 1945—450,000 in January 1945 alone (or about 15,000 deaths every day).[11] In the last days of the war, Hitler and many other Nazi leaders committed suicide with no expectation that they were on the way to heaven. The German armies surrendered, and literally millions of Allied troops invaded and occupied an utterly devastated and totally defeated country. On May 8, 1945, World War II in Europe was over and fighting ceased. Warnings of massive postwar guerrilla operations turned out to be groundless. After the dropping of the atomic bombs on Hiroshima and Nagasaki, the war with Japan also ended, in August 1945.

When "major combat operations" ended in Europe and Japan in 1945, the war was over and the enemy had been defeated. Hardheaded decision makers and experienced officials in the US government, people who presumably are familiar with the history of World War II and its aftermath, seem to have become blinded by ideology and thus hopeful for a similarly clear-cut outcome in Iraq. They assumed that the Baath regime and its remnants would be definitively defeated after a war lasting fewer than two months, conducted with precision bombing that left Iraq far more intact than it would be after it was looted and burned by some of its own people in the coming month. Bush's decision to declare "mission accomplished" expressed the triumph of the power of such positive thinking over historical knowledge and common sense. In fact, as the past grim eighteen months have made clear, the period of major combat operations was only the first chapter of a much longer war against Iraqi Baathism and, in the chaos, also against terrorists inspired by radical Islam. Although Bush deserves credit for his resolute decision to launch the war, he also bears responsibility for the disaster of the occupation. Had he seen more clearly, US troops would have been provided with more heavy armor and fewer Humvees. Perhaps fewer of them would have been killed and injured. Had he sent more troops to begin with, perhaps the looting, destruction, and lawlessness of the early months would have generated more goodwill toward the occupying forces. Most important, had a larger and more armored force been in place early on, perhaps the next phase of the war, the phase to crush the remnants of the old regime, would have been more successful.

What is clearly beyond dispute is that Saddam's dictatorship is over. No longer will the vast oil reserves under the ground in Iraq be available to the Baath Party and its visions of dominating the region, threatening Israel, blackmailing the world economy through influence over oil supplies, and possibly attacking the United States either alone or in association with radical Islamists. The possibility now exists for the first time of establishing a liberal democracy in the Middle East and thus of overcoming its backwardness in relation not only to Europe and the United States but also to democracies in Asia and Latin America. No one can say with certainty whether this war will achieve its stated aims. What I do believe is that based on what I, and most of us, knew in winter and spring 2003, this war was a justified and necessary one and that the world is and will be a safer and more secure place because the Baath regime in Baghdad is gone.

Although Iraq's future remains open, one development is of particular concern to liberals, one that recalls a historical dilemma examined in my history of postwar memory in West and East Germany after 1945 and 1949. There was, I have argued, a tension between implementing rapid democratization in the West and coming to terms with the crimes of the Nazi past. De-Nazification was unpopular with crucial electoral minorities of the West German electorate. As politicians sought to win elections, the pressure to look to the present and future and forget the past intensified.[12] Since the overthrow of Saddam's regime, a parallel development has unfolded, one in which the efforts of Kanan Makiya's Iraq Memory Foundation appear to be subordinated to a policy of reaching out to former Baathists.[13] In Germany, as I indicated earlier, Nazism had been defeated on the battlefield by the end of the war, whereas in Iraq, the Baath Party has not yet been defeated and is still fighting the war against the new Iraqi government. The shortcomings of postwar German memory are well-known, but a great deal was accomplished at the Nuremberg and other postwar trials of the Nazi leaders and by historians who used surviving documentation and oral histories to detail of the crimes of the Nazi regime. It should be a particular liberal imperative to see that the history and memory of the Baath era in Iraq be brought before the people of Iraq and of the whole Arab and Islamic world in courts of law, in the recollections of the Baath regime's own oral testimonies, and in the work of historians. Recalling the truth about Saddam Hussein's Iraq will both facilitate the difficult emergence of liberal democracy in Iraq and recall the validity of the liberal case in support of the war that toppled the Baath regime.

## POSTSCRIPT, NOVEMBER 2004

If I knew in spring 2003 what I know now after publication of the Duelfer Report and other works regarding Saddam's weapons of mass destruction programs, I would not have supported the invasion of Iraq in March 2003. The United States did not go to war then with the rationale presented in this essay. It did not present its case with the uncertainties and ambiguities I mention. Rather, it did so on the basis of repeated and confident assertion that the threat from Saddam's weapons of mass destruction was so imminent that a delay of even six months or a year would have potentially catastrophic consequences. These assertions now turn out to have been false. Moreover, intelligence officials within the US government were expressing skepticism about them at the time. A political and military offensive against the terrorism of Islamic fundamentalism and confronting rogue states with weapons of mass destruction requires credibility that the current US administration no longer possesses.

Finally, a word about what the distinguished British military historian Michael Howard once called "the forgotten dimensions of strategy."[14] He referred to the importance of support for NATO from the democratic left in Europe during the Cold War. The alliance was never an alliance only of parties of the political right. Howard's comment is relevant to our current dilemmas. If the Bush administration believed that the threat from the mix of the radical Islamists and Iraq was as serious as it said it was, then, just as Churchill and Roosevelt did in 1940 and 1941, it should have governed domestically from the political center and compromised its economic and social policies at home. Instead, and in contrast to Churchill and Roosevelt, it has governed from the right and remarkably managed to divide US society and politics after it was more united on September 12, 2001, than it had been in decades. A divided and embittered domestic politics is an atrocious foundation on which to wage and win what may well be a long-term battle with terrorism inspired by Islamic fundamentalism. In seeking to have its way on every issue at home and abroad, the Bush administration has weakened, not strengthened, the capacity of the United States to prevail over the long term. The argument for a vital center and a third force in American politics and intellectual life, though, remains compelling.

## NOTES

1. On this point, see Kanan Makiya, *The Republic of Fear: The Inside Story of Saddam's Iraq* (Los Angeles and Berkeley: University of California Press, 1989; New York: Pantheon Books, 1990).

2. "Senators Assail C.I.A. Judgments on Iraq's Arms as Deeply Flawed," *New York Times*, July 10, 2004, A1 and A8–A9.

3. On the relationship between Saddam's terror and repression at home and miscalculation in foreign policy, see Kenneth Pollack, *The Threatening Storm: The Case for Invading Iraq* (New York: Random House, 2002).

4. For a series of very thoughtful liberal retrospectives on the war, see "Were We Wrong?" *New Republic*, June 28, 2004.

5. Jeffrey Herf, *Reactionary Modernism: Technology, Culture and Politics in Weimar and the Third Reich* (Cambridge, MA: Harvard University Press, 1984).

6. For an excellent liberal analysis of the rise of radical Islam and its links to European totalitarianism, see Paul Berman, *Terror and Liberalism* (New York: W. W. Norton, 2003); and Matthias Küntzel, *Djihad und Judenhass: Über die neuen antijüdischen Krieg* (Freiburg: ca ira, 2003).

7. On these points, see Jeffrey Herf, *Divided Memory: The Nazi Past in the Two Germanys* (Cambridge, MA: Harvard University Press, 1997); and Jeffrey Herf, *War by Other Means: Soviet Power, West German Resistance, and the Battle of the Euromissiles* (New York: Free Press, 1991).

8. John Lewis Gaddis, *Surprise, Security, and the American Experience* (Cambridge, MA: Harvard University Press, 2004).

9. On the links between the war in Europe and Japan's decision to attack Pearl Harbor, see Gerhard Weinberg, "Global Conflict: The Interaction between the European and Pacific Theaters in World War II," in *Hitler, Germany, and World War II* (New York: Cambridge University Press, 1995), 205–216.

10. Williamson Murray, *The Change in the European Balance of Power, 1938–1939: The Path to Ruin* (Princeton, NJ: Princeton University Press, 1984).

Germany's strategic and economic base was most narrow for the grandiose dreams of European conquest toward which her leader drove. Given the nature of those dreams it was inevitable that a European war would occur. Nevertheless, the timing as to when and in what fashion the other powers would take up that challenge was beyond Hitler's control. As he announced to his cohorts shortly after taking power, if France had any statesmen, [it] should wage a preventive war immediately. The Polish statesman, Marshal Pilsudski, apparently did think in such terms. But there was no one in France, and certainly no one in England, with the ruthlessness to "wage a war now to prevent one in the future." (361–362)

11. Rüdiger Övermanns, *Deutsche militärische Verluste im Zweiten Weltkrieg* (Munich: Oldenbourg, 2000), 238–239.

12. Herf, *Divided Memory*.

13. Lawrence F. Kaplan, "In Iraq, Silencing Memory," *Washington Post*, July 11, 2004, B7.

14. Michael Howard, "The Forgotten Dimensions of Strategy," *Foreign Affairs* (Summer 1978): 975–986.

# 3

# "Regime Change"
## The Case of Iraq

JAN NARVESON

## INTRODUCTION: WHY IRAQ?

It was widely advertised that the US invasion of Iraq was motivated by a concern about the ability of its then-dictator Saddam Hussein to use weapons of mass destruction. As is well enough known, several problems arise with that claim. One is the fact that this concern appears to have been false, at least if we construe the claim narrowly to imply that Saddam was equipped with such weapons at and immediately before the time of the invasion. It is not clear that the claim need have been quite that. It is generally agreed that he had had such weapons and was quite capable of using them against Iranians; against some of his own people, the Kurds; and no doubt against anyone whom he thought he could attack with impunity and to his own advantage.

That brings us to the second point: the possibility that he could "get away with" using such weapons is certainly false, and Saddam surely knew that. Whatever weapons he may have had at his command, he could not have used them against anyone outside the borders of Iraq without instant and devastating military response by the Americans, probably the Israelis, and likely others. It is not generally supposed that Saddam was a fool, whatever else he was. Indeed, the very fact that no such weapons have yet been found demonstrates that he was not, if anything does.

A third, difficult question is, Why does possession of weapons of mass destruction matter much? Their sheer possession is obviously not sufficient cause for war; most of America's friends have them, after all, as do the Americans themselves. It has to be the intentions of their possessor that might constitute such a cause. But intentions per se are not enough, either. There must be a realistic likelihood that they will be used aggressively. Yet, whatever is meant by "weapons of mass destruction," threats or intentions to use them in particular are quite unnecessary: the invasion of any innocent external party by perfectly familiar, ordinary weapons of war is quite enough to justify defensive response, the first Gulf War being a relevant case in point. Saddam's invasion of Kuwait mainly featured the familiar weapons of fairly modern warfare, and that fact was sufficient to justify a defensive effort.

What is special, and certainly interesting, about the second Gulf War is that its official point seems to have changed substantially: it has now become "regime change"—a category that confronts the theorist with a new (though in its way very old) question: Is it ever just for one state to invade another in order to replace the government of the latter with an improved version? It is fairly obvious, I take it, that plenty of fillings-out of the details would leave one with a thoroughly unsatisfactory case. No doubt most wars in history have been motivated by regime change: that the invaders want to boot out, or at least to dominate, the current government of the invaded state is not far from defining a war, after all, be the war good, bad, or indifferent. At the very least, then, we must take it that what is meant is that a war of this sort that could possibly be justified under the description of "regime change" is aimed at replacing an unjust government with a just government—or something along that line. Explaining more precisely the "along that line" bit then becomes a main problem, or perhaps *the* main problem.

In this essay, I shall focus on this question of when and whether regime change per se is a reasonable justification of military intervention. My general answer is a very qualified acceptance. The received view—that all states are to be regarded as immune to "outside interference" except in the sole case where they themselves are intending to engage in aggression against others—is, I shall argue, philosophically insupportable, even incoherent. That said, I then set down a list of five conditions that must be met for the category of regime change to be an acceptable reason for going to war. Finally, I consider their application to the case of Iraq. This argument is fairly straightforward; it is not unreasonable to argue—though also very far from being beyond question—that all these conditions are met in this case, in relation to the United States and its various allies in the project.

## REGIME CHANGE: JUSTICE AND INJUSTICE

What is problematic about the idea that regime change might justify invasion, at the most general level, is the uncomfortable plausibility of the thesis that all governments are unjust. Without even broaching the question of anarchism, we must acknowledge the obvious fact that whatever its intentions and however refined might be the political mechanisms for avoiding injustice, any state, inevitably, will now and then deal wrongly with somebody, and undoubtedly the "now and then" will be uncomfortably often. What else, we have to ask, is new?

Yet Saddam's Iraq presented a pretty good showcase for injustice on a rather grand scale—injustice of the kind and at the level that might provide a plausible example of a state whose operation would justify invasion if any can. Saddam's regime was famous for political murder on a fairly impressive scale. We don't know quite how impressive, but few writers question figures running to a quarter of a million or more. Such numbers put it well below the levels achieved by the most notorious of historical criminals, to be sure: Stalin, Mao, and Hitler did a lot worse, both absolutely and proportionately. But, still, the figure is impressive. The question is only whether it was enough to justify an invasion. And the problem is that, taken in and by itself, the answer seems clearly to be in the negative. At a minimum, serious questions arise about costs, in both lives and other terms; these we will address later.

But is it even a matter of "costs"? Some will claim not. They will argue that there is a serious question of principle blocking any effort of this kind. I will consider two proposals along this line.

## PACIFISM?

One view to address this matter is pacifism, according to which the only acceptable number of casualties on the other side is zero. All violence, says the pacifist, is wrong. This point is characteristically urged on the basis that human life is of supreme value or some such claim, though sometimes it is advanced more narrowly as a sort of strategy—

that nonviolence is in the end the most effective way of bringing about peace.

Without trying to be at all comprehensive, I will just point out that pacifism has enormous problems. In the first place, the familiar arguments for it are unsound. You can't get pacifism from the premise that life has supreme value, because whatever that view might mean, it is hard to see why it should justify the sacrifice of one's own life and the lives of many who are near and dear to a ruthless enemy who himself hasn't the slightest interest in peace. Moreover, most people would be hard put to accept the assessment that the life of, say, a serial rapist, has "supreme value" in any case.

In general, pacifists have a serious problem in the many cases in which resistance appears to be the only serious alternative to death. We are sometimes forced to choose—forced, one must add, by the actions of the aggressor. If the pacifist prefers death for himself in those cases, we need to ask him, seriously, how he can prefer the deaths of the good people to the deaths of the bad ones. (Note, again, that the "bad" ones are bad by the pacifist's very own criteria: for the aggressors are the war makers, the enemies of the peace that is presumably the aim of pacifism to promote and secure.) More to the point, how can the pacifist expect the rest of us to go along with this preference?

A narrower view is "war pacifism"—opposition not to all violence whatever but only to the specific violence of warfare. This perspective may well seem more attractive at first, to be sure. Yet, when the enemy is advancing on the city gates, and defense looks to be the only alternative to complete slaughter (something that, as the pacifist ought to know, has happened often enough in history), the pacifist view will appear as unpromising as in the individual case.

More abstractly, one might believe that surely the world would be a much better place if everyone were pacifist. But even if we agree with that stand, we have to point out that it would, insofar as the value of peace is what is at stake, be a similarly better place if everyone confined the use of violence to defense. Because in that case no wars would be begun in the first place, and therefore none pressed in the interest of defense, the world would be precisely as peaceable—but with the advantage that if someone fell from grace and initiated violence, then his victims would be able at least to defend themselves.

As to the idea that nonviolence is our best reaction to others' initial violence, we must agree that many wars, including the one that has inspired the essays in this collection, are hardly like that. Refraining from war with Iraq would have been easy enough, and the immediate costs of such pacificism, at least, could be expected to be few—except, of course, among those numerous Iraqis who fell afoul of their dictator's intentions, as some hundred or two hundred did every month, we are told. It is not obvious how those numerous cases could be prevented other than by violence. For Saddam's politics was the politics of the thug, of violence from the outset of his reign. Realism suggests that some people are not going to be tractable in response to purely peaceable overtures. Indeed, it certainly appears that some individuals, including notably Saddam Hussein, will cheerfully help themselves to a yard for every inch offered by well-meaning peacemakers. When we are dealing with customers as tough as that, there is no alternative to being tough ourselves.

Pacifism, then, is a mistake and, in the context of major political involvements, a potentially disastrous one. But there is no mistake at all in the view that we ought to minimize lives lost in all ventures, including military ones. Killing people is never the point of any war that can pretend to be just, and that point must be still more obvious when the object is to improve the justice of a regime. What is needed is a relevant and sensible way of estimating both the pertinent levels of justice of the invaded country's regime, before and after, and the costs in relation to the benefits of military activity—with an understanding that there are many ends to which violent means are absolutely not acceptable. Indeed, we can go further. We should accept—and I shall take it as given—that the only end for which violent means are acceptable is to counter aggression, at one level or another; in short, violence may be used only to counter or prevent initiated violence by others. We may agree, moreover, that even when violence is acceptable, the minimum of violence necessary to do the just job is the right level to employ.

## THE SANCTITY OF THE STATE?

The other principle almost universally invoked in the matter of using regime change to justify invasion is the principle of the sanctity of states: that no state may invade another except to protect itself from invasion—or, as we must immediately see the need to add, to protect itself *or its allies*, a small qualification that has been a principal cause of all the really big wars in the past few centuries. Still, the claim is clear enough. But why accept it?

I believe this question has two answers. One is that the sanctity of the state represents a pragmatic recipe for peace among nations. Wars are essentially among states, and wars, admittedly, cause great evil. We have ample reason to want to avoid them, and the best way to do so, we may well think, is to give no state cause for war against other states. That view makes sense, so far as it goes. But how far does it go? If we push a little deeper, we surely get to the other answer, which is that *for individuals* the analogous principle is indeed extremely plausible. Each individual is to be viewed as having an integrity that is not to be violated except only in the case where that individual himself is violating the integrity of other individuals who themselves are innocent. Thus, we have the classic principle of liberalism, as expounded at the level of relations among individuals by the great philosophers from Hobbes and Locke to Kant and Mill. The reasoning as applied to the present issue, then, is that the principle of the sanctity of state boundaries is simply the application of classic liberalism to the case of states.

The trouble is, though, that such reasoning doesn't follow. Classic liberalism *does* follow in the case of *voluntary* associations; the principle of freedom of association, so understood, is one of the major rights of all individuals. But states are not voluntary associations. They are defined by the powers of government to compel all to its will. And it is this very principle at the level of individuals that convicts so many states of great injustice. We would have little to gain from liberalism if, although we are protected against each other as individuals, the state is allowed to do anything it likes to us. That was Locke's point against Hobbes,[1] and I—as well as surely all readers at the turn of the twenty-first century—regard it to be solid gold. The question cannot be whether the state does indeed have the right to treat its citizens any way it likes, in total disregard of the very principle that is called in to justify the state's existence in the first place—namely, civil peace, or the protection of each individual from the violence of others. The question of government can only be, then, which sort of methods we may employ to guard ourselves against states that pay too little attention to our rights or none at all. Here, we all sympathize with Locke against Hobbes in holding that revolution—the overthrow of a regime by violence, if necessary—might be justified.

If such revolution can be justified, then certainly it becomes obvious that the sanctity of the state does not follow from the sanctity of the individual. In fact, it is unobvious to the point where it seems plainly incompatible with it, at the margin. States that make the individual subservient to their own whims and ambitions be warned: they are in the dock, and if they cannot defend their behavior toward their own citizens, then the legitimacy, in principle, of those citizens resorting to external assistance to free them from their plight becomes an option that cannot just be dismissed.

## JUSTIFIED INTERVENTION: FIVE NECESSARY CONDITIONS

I will suggest five conditions that seem to me necessary if any such intervention is to be accepted. Whether the five are also *jointly sufficient* is, of course, the interesting question. I am inclined to think that they are, but discussion of that question should be carried on more efficiently if it is cognizant of the recognized necessity of these conditions. In brief, they are as follows:

1. The new regime that is intended to replace the older, evil one must of course be at least a good deal better, whatever else.
2. The costs imposed on the invaded state must somehow be acceptable to its people.
3. The costs to the invading state must in turn be acceptable to its people.
4. The objective must be worth it to the invading state and to a just world.
5. There must be a reasonable prospect of success for the new regime.

I amplify on each point in the remainder of this essay, restating each point more precisely by way of introduction.

## CONDITION 1: A BETTER REGIME

In the previous part of this inquiry, I have said nothing, except perhaps by implication, about the desired properties of the regime that would replace the one that the invading country proposes to replace. Let's turn to that topic now. My proposal is as follows—the first of my proposed five conditions:

1. The new regime must be better in the specific respect of being liberal, the old one having been illiberal; or, more realistically, the new one must be *markedly more liberal* than the old, especially in respect of the expected safety of its citizens in relation to their government.

It will be noted that this condition does not mention democracy. It is familiar stuff to call for a *democratic* regime, as if that were a necessary and sufficient condition for satisfactory government. But—depending on how much you build into the notion of "democracy"—it is entirely possible that a government with that feature would not be satisfactory at all. In particular, if the idea is simply to give everyone the vote and have a government that is elected, our problems may just be beginning. Iraq, indeed, presents a typical problem for this purpose, for Iraq is, in effect, not one country but three: the Kurdish area, the Sunni area, and the Shiite area, the latter being more populous than the other two taken together. Both of the smaller groups, needless to say, fear domination by the other(s). Saddam Hussein, we are told, was successful in considerable part because his was the party of the Sunnis, ready to defend their interests against the more numerous Shiites. Proposing to give everyone the vote and saying no more is equivalent to fomenting civil war in such a place.

But what we outsiders want of any other state is not that it is democratic but that it is *liberal*—which may be quite another matter. A liberal regime guarantees its citizens freedoms: not only freedom from the physical violence of other privately acting individuals but freedom of religion, of association, of the press; freedom to engage in business and to choose one's occupation rather than having it imposed by others; freedom to live more or less as we please. If that can be depended on, the vote is arguably icing on the cake, or perhaps not even that. What a vote hopefully will do is enable people to protect those freedoms—and, with luck, that's what it will indeed do. But we would be foolhardy not to recognize that giving people the vote also can do just the opposite: threaten any and all freedoms, especially when majority power is exercised by ethnic or religious or political "enemies" over minorities. The very tricky problem faced by outsider states trying to improve the situation is that of achieving a stable liberal polity when that condition apparently was beyond the capability of the populace as things stood. Given the popularity of democracy in the form of an insensate demand for the vote come what may, pressures to succumb to democracy's lure are enormous. But if they aren't resisted in places like Iraq, and if devices for protecting the freedoms of minorities are not installed in the constitution in ways that can be reasonably expected to be observed, you may as well throw in the towel.[2]

Of course, I am assuming that with liberalism goes external as well as internal nonviolence. Obviously, the revamped state should be a good neighbor in the world, renouncing aggression and permitting its citizens the liberty to do business and engage in the many other modes of cooperation with people in the outside world. Nonaggression is the sine qua non for all of this activity. First things first. Nonaggression against whom, though? This is where the fundamental issue is joined. It is agreed that state A may intervene against state B in the interests of defending itself or some other threatened state, C, that asks A's aid against B's military aggression. But it seems not generally to be agreed that the fact that B's government is aggressing against *its own people* is likewise a suitable *casus belli*. The question is, Why not? That is the general question addressed in this essay, and it has been discussed in general terms in my introduction. Here we simply note that the liberalism desired for the internal government of the new regime goes hand in hand with a cooperative attitude toward the rest of the world.

## CONDITION 2: THE COSTS TO THE INVADED STATE

Now for our next two conditions, which have to do with the urgent matter of assessing the risks or costs of war. We have two cases to consider: costs to the state that would be invaded and costs to the invading state. We discuss the former first.

2. The costs to the people in the invaded country are expectedly low in relation to the gains set out in the first condition.

The point of our exercise is to improve things for the people in the invaded state. Although various kinds of improvement are possible, surely the first thing to consider is their lives, in view of the nature of war. Thus we must somehow estimate the number of lives to be lost by people in the invaded state in such an undertaking as the Iraq intervention.

We must begin with an obvious distinction. In the country ruled by any evil regime, there are the bad guys and the good guys—the ones who are imposing the very evils that we hope to rectify and the ones on whom they impose them. It is the latter whom we are especially concerned to conserve—the innocent civilians for the good of whom, we think, any government ought to be acting. Many government functionaries and agents are surely also to be considered innocent, despite their employment by the regime in question. We are not, after all, concerned to remove its postal employees—not even its incompetent ones. Others, such as the regime's bullies and torturers, will of course be among the relevantly guilty. But even when we consider its military personnel, we would surely want to count many as merely there for the job and suppose them to have been engaged, in their view, in honorable defense of their country.

In the first Gulf War, the allied invasion is thought to have inflicted a quarter of a million casualties or so—a number, we might sadly reflect, about equal to the claimed number of Hussein's own victims over the years of his regime. Probably the great majority of those soldiers were unwilling or at least had no intention of participating in the more evil activities of the regime that they were trying to defend. That point, we may agree, is sad. But worse, as we should also agree, is the prospect of killing Iraqi civilians. Ideally, no such lives would be taken. Realistically, despite the remarkably sophisticated weaponry employed by the United States and its allies, we know that some people will be killed, and were killed, and in the case of the present postwar circumstances, will continue to be, even though fairly few of those losses are due to US arms. (Detractors put the estimate at about eleven thousand; supporters much lower.)[3] These casualties rightly bother us. Again, the question arises, How many? Though easy enough to ask, it is not easy to answer. Yet answer it we must somehow, if we are to have a reasonable answer to the main question.

For this purpose, I propose that the reasonable way to look at this question is from the point of view of the typical citizen of the invaded country—in this case, Iraq. Would, or could, such a citizen applaud an intervention such as this invasion, all things considered? The short answer is of course, and many Iraqi citizens in this case did. The people of Normandy prior to D-day, if asked, would overwhelmingly have approved the invasion had they known of it, and they overwhelmingly did approve of it once launched, despite the fact that many thousands, not just some few, were killed by misguided bombs and shells, or by aroused Germans, or by mistaken aim or inaccurate precision in the weaponry of advancing soldiers. That was the risk, and they were for the most part prepared to take it. Similarly, it is possible that typical Iraqi civilians would reckon the likelihood that they and their loved ones might be accidental targets or caught in the crossfire, and so on, and weigh this possibility against the disadvantages of continued life under a rather terrible tyrant.

The situation is enormously complicated by the fact that the risks of war do not fall equally on all, as well as by the fact that the benefits of life as it was are likewise decidedly unequally distributed among the

Iraqi people. For present purposes, however, it is perhaps enough if we suppose, first, that some of those who benefited from the evil regime did so because they themselves were collaborators; while among the others, it has to be asked whether they are, even though not witting agents of the previous regime, in effect profiting from the misfortunes of their far more numerous fellows who could expect to be targets of the regime. It is probably the case that scarcely a family in Iraq would not be able to cite a cousin or brother or other close one who was either murdered or imprisoned or tortured by Saddam's henchmen. To be free of so terrible a regime is surely worth appreciable risk. It is not, however, worth an unlimited risk. The probability of the typical Iraqi's being a victim of the invasion must, then, be very low for such a thing to be just. The plausible rule of thumb, I think, would be to insist that this figure be *lower than* the probability of death or great loss imposed on innocents by Saddam's regime. Was this scenario in fact the case? We do not know a great deal about the level of civilian casualties in the second Gulf War, but we have reason to think that they have been fairly low. Not zero, certainly, but low.

We must also remember that if the invasion is successful in its object of changing the government very much for the better, then the expected benefits to the population project indefinitely into the future. It is not enough merely to compare civilian casualties during the invasion with expected civilian victims of tyranny in a similar period. The main point of revolution—and, more generally, the point of imposed regime change—is to make the indefinite future very much better for all. A modest level of civilian casualties during a short period is balanced against a far, far lower number of victims of the state for the indefinite future—if all goes well. (Condition 5 addresses the latter caveat.)

## CONDITION 3: THE COSTS TO THE INVADING STATE

This brings us to the other column in the ledger: "ours," the question of how many lives among the invaders, especially among their armies—in the present case, the US and other Coalition soldiers—we can contemplate the loss of before the idea of invasion should be abandoned. Civilians in Coalition countries were not directly at risk from the violence of war. To be sure, there is the vexed question of terrorist activities in the United States and elsewhere, but that question, it seems, is or at least was almost entirely independent of the Iraq invasion, and so for the present case it can be left to one side. (It certainly might not be so for other cases—notably Afghanistan; nor can we be sure it won't become a question at some time in the future.) We might, indeed, suggest that we can come very close to agreeing with the pacifists on one narrow front: that invasion of some other country for the sake of regime change would expectedly cost *no* lives among civilians in the invaders' country. However, the case with soldiers is very different. Different again is the case of financial costs, because of the taxes needed to pay for the invasion, met by citizens of the invading state.

Let's begin, then, with the matter of expected military casualties. We would, of course, prefer that no lives be lost on either side, but this is war and that preference is essentially idle. But the new case of the United States in Iraq brings up aspects of this question that are unusually interesting. First is the fact that all of the US military personnel are *volunteers*. That point is very important. No one was compelled to take the risks of battle. Those willing to take those risks make their own "calculation"; they reckon that a risk of some magnitude is worth taking in relation to the personal gains they see themselves to be making by engaging in the military profession. It would be absurd to go into the army on the condition that one never be exposed to risk, and every soldier is well aware of this fact. What the soldier can hope and expect, however, is that his life will not be wasted: that responsible and well-trained command is in place that will take care that exposure to the risks of battle is as small as it can reasonably be made given the objectives, and also that the objectives themselves are just and worthwhile.

The second point regarding the United States in Iraq is the former's huge military superiority, not only in arms but also in the quality of sheer military technique and training; this distinction has kept casualties down to remarkably low levels, even when the enemy has turned out to be mostly terrorists rather than regular soldiers. (In relation to the latter, only a tiny number were casualties of standard combat: 122 American and 33 British.)[4] In the first Iraq war, which is probably a better comparison, the number of such "standard casualties" was remarkably close to nil (148 American, 47 British, 2 French, and 14 Egyptian).[5] Furthermore, the US Army, at least in recent times, is noteworthy for its extreme concern with casualties, and it is still more notable for this concern in its contemporary version. These points taken together make a major difference. US military action is undertaken on terms about as favorable to the involved soldier as they can easily be imagined to be. The better those terms are, the less problematic is the factor of our-side casualties. Of course, this consideration does not eliminate the tragedy of someone's spouse, son or daughter, or friend being killed in conflict. But it does put such an outcome in perspective.

The latter point is so important that the question of economic cost—though no doubt one will be accused of being crass to say so—to the US taxpayer can easily be considered as more serious. Spending a hundred billion dollars of people's involuntarily provided money really does need justifying in a major way, and it is fair to ask whether, in the present case, such spending is worth it. In fact, however, there is an index on this matter that we can hardly ignore. Taxes are involuntary, of course, which is why justifying them is no easy matter. But I think we can to some degree finesse this question, as it were, by asking the following: How many Americans would be willing, if they *did* have their choice, to pay how much for accomplishing the purpose for which the Iraq invasion was undertaken?

If that invasion were aimed at preventing threats to the American people—as the US administration has tended to represent the situation—then we may be sure that the figure in question would be very high indeed, as it was, for example, during World War II, which after Pearl Harbor was hugely popular on the domestic front. We may be fairly certain that the overwhelming bulk of the American people regarded the very high costs of that war as worthwhile. It is very much less obvious, of course, that they would support the Iraq venture at the levels of cost that have in fact been entailed. But at least we have a conceptual tool for addressing the matter. We ask, as I put it earlier, simply whether what is at stake in the Iraq venture, in whatever terms can be correctly represented, is worth the $X price tag to the particular people who pay it. If enough Americans are willing to pay enough so that those costs would be covered, then we may conjecture that in this respect, the war was justified.

Contemporary libertarians complain, rightly, about any and all taxes on the ground that they are involuntary. Some among them imagine the possibility of privately organized armies doing the sort of thing we are discussing here. But in the real-world circumstances of today and the past few centuries, military action on this kind of scale by privateers is essentially not possible. Perhaps it should be—the point is, in my view, at least debatable—but it is not.

Moreover, another, crude but nevertheless fairly effective mechanism is available for instantiating this very idea of justifying war costs when the war is not strictly necessary for defense: elections. If a war is too costly, politicians who supported it will pay with their jobs, up to and including the president. The reelection of George W. Bush indicates that Americans, on the whole, did not think that the situation in Iraq was grave enough to warrant the removal of the president from office. I by no means wish to propose that a war is all right if and only if the administration that initiates it is elected or reelected on the basis of its military actions. Still, democracy offers something of a check, given that our other conditions are met. This check is indeed considerable enough to have inspired Kant to the conjecture that if all the nations of the world were republics, we would have Perpetual Peace.[6] It seems to me that his conjecture was at least plausible.

## CONDITION 4: THE OBJECTIVE FOR THE INVADING STATE AND A JUST WORLD

If we should attack Iraq because of its rotten government, then why not *every country on Earth* with a rotten government? This question comes naturally to mind when we propose replacement of a government by one that we hope to be far better. And the point is well taken. We certainly should not just go around saving people from their regimes whenever and wherever opportunity presents itself. Of course, a part of the answer is quite simply that even the wealthy United States can't afford to do so and must perforce choose. But choose how? On the basis of what? There needs to be some real interest on the part of the invading state or states—sheer altruism is not enough. Here is my very vague suggestion, though I hope it puts things in the right perspective: There must be a suitable national interest on the part of the invading country, "suitability" being constrained (but not determined) by the principles of liberalism, with its commitments to human rights.

What has been argued for thus far is only that states may be justified in invading other states for reasons of "regime change." But when, if ever, should they actually do so? It will be objected, and properly so, that not even the contemporary United States can spring to the aid of every oppressed country around the world. (One could also object that the United States is in ample need of internal liberalization, for that matter, but we must leave any such discussions aside for our present purposes.) The reply to the objection is that what is in question at that level is only the *legitimacy* or *propriety* of such assistance. It is not, in the view taken here, the *duty* of each country that can do so to lend such military assistance as it can. International politics is power politics, and each state is presumably attempting to do the best it can for itself. The fact that in some states people are under the thumb of a despot, their very lives in constant peril from his whims, is perhaps a necessary but by no means sufficient condition for undertaking armed assistance by some other state that can render such aid. But what would make the case sufficient as well?

The general answer remains what it has always been: the national interest. To be sure, with the onset of liberalism, the range of legitimate options among national interests that can figure in justifications of war is tightly constrained. An interest in empire for the invading state's own sake, for example, is absolutely not acceptable. An interest in *exploitation* of other states for its own presumed economic or other good is likewise not acceptable. By contrast, however, an interest in enabling its own citizens as well as those in the invaded country to engage in commerce and other mutually beneficial activities is indeed in the national interest. It is, arguably, also in everybody's interest everywhere, if obviously more so in some areas than in others. Interaction with the citizens of other states in the world redounding to the benefit of those concerned is a highly worthy goal. It does not, by itself, constitute a justification for war, but that is not what is being maintained here. What is being maintained is that *when* the *other* conditions are met, then *this* one may decide in favor of a particular undertaking and against some other.

It may be worth mentioning a somewhat parallel case. The warm-hearted citizen may read in the papers of various peoples in distant lands suffering from this or that affliction or misfortune. She might realistically decide that she can do a bit of good, but only a bit, with her very limited budget, and the question is, Which among the eligible recipients should she decide to benefit? She can answer in any number of ways that are morally acceptable: help the people she herself was descended from, help people altogether different from herself, help the ones who like music—or just flip a coin. She cannot be accused of any moral shortcoming when she provides a benefit that, after all, she has no fundamental duty to provide to anyone but provides anyway, out of sheer good-heartedness, to some few. Better some than none.

The precise nature of the US (and British, and some other countries') interests in a freer Iraq is a matter for debate. No doubt some people think that the interest consists in access to Iraq's oil wealth in particular, for example. But those who make that claim fail to understand the logic of modern economics. Oil is in huge international demand. Those with resources to exploit do so by marketing them on the international market. If they don't want to sell them directly to nation B, well, so what? Why should B care? For the controllers of the oil resources in question must sell to *someone*, or else they will derive no benefit from the resource (beyond local use, which is tiny in relation to potential sales at the Iraq level). Suppose, then, that they sell to C. If so, then that scenario in turn will free up C's suppliers to sell to B. And buying oil is cheaper than going to war for it—to put the matter very mildly. The same, generally speaking, goes for virtually any economic good one can think of. The old idea of imperialism—conquering for profit—is simply beyond the pale of economic rationality, an absurdity that needs to be junked. It is high time for discussants of public affairs, along with any politicians who may be tempted to engage in such rhetoric, to jettison the idea. Imperialism of old is *dead*—at least among the major nations today.

On the other hand, the United States, and more generally most or all of the world's "advanced" states, has an interest in liberalization in the entire Middle East, as do we all. If there is prospect of a genuinely liberal (or, more guardedly, more nearly liberal) Iraq, then to have such a large and strategically located state joining the ranks of reasonably peaceable, forward-looking states in the modern world instead of ones harboring self-aggrandizing or fanatical dictators can only be a great good, both for the Middle East in particular and for the world more generally. This point arguably provides a reasonable justification for having an immensely powerful and wealthy state such as the United States doing the job. It could easily not do so for the much less powerful and poorer states of the world. Various other countries, notably Great Britain, have joined with the Americans in this undertaking, each no doubt for reasons of its own. But again, fair enough. That is what we should expect and even welcome.

## CONDITION 5: THE NEW REGIME'S PROSPECT OF SUCCESS

This brings us to the last condition for a just intervention of this type: will the new regime succeed? This condition is perhaps the most important of all, at least from many citizens' points of view. My working condition formulation goes as follows:

5. There is a reasonable expectation that the whole thing will actually *work*. That proposed military action will effect change to an improved regime is a realistic possibility in the case in question:

the improved regime really is likely to be substantially helped toward realization, without entailing still further serious costs over and above those cited in conditions 2 and 3.

Interventions that don't work run up significant human costs for nothing or less than nothing. Our slogan here may well be "Remember Vietnam!" In the cold light of reason, the sacrifices for the sake of liberating that unhappy nation went, as we must soberly conclude, for naught. We want it to be the case that the many people who make sacrifices, including the supreme sacrifice of life itself, do not make them in vain. An undertaking known in advance to be futile is immoral, especially when the cost is reckoned in lives and not only in dollars.

To assess this important aspect of the case is no easy matter. It requires knowledge of the people and their politics that we may very well not have. It is too much, for example, to point to the liberal democratic government as the final solution to all problems and assume that the solution is so salient as to be embraced by any reasonable people anywhere.

Is this condition met in the case of Iraq? One important point is that the Iraqi people were by no means backward and devoid of political experience. Another is that its internal factions had ample history of bitter conflict and machination. Thoughtful Iraqis today, with their ample experience of the evils of dictatorship as well as their memories of past difficulties, are arguably in a position to see the merits of liberal government. As of this writing (begun in the winter of 2004, concluded after the new provisional government has begun to function), it seems reasonable to say that we don't know for sure how the prospects stand for success, but we have ground for hope—a reasonable expectation that the whole thing will actually work, in the sense that the transition to an improved regime is really possible in Iraq's case, without entailing still further serious costs beyond those cited in conditions 2 and 3. To be sure, the small-scale though spectacular violence of suicide bombers, self-styled jihadists with rifle grenades, roadside bombs and mines, and various other raids continues almost daily, and such value has multiplied the Coalition casualty list many times. Still, things are in sufficient control that it is fairly certain that elections will be held before very long. The Americans insisted that they would turn over the reigns of government to Iraqis by a certain time, and they did. (Few others, one might add, can make that statement.) They have striven to enable the local leaders to lead effectively, and continue to do so, along with military and other personnel from many other nations. What happens after that is not easy to predict. Iraq is sorely divided—and if it weren't, we may well conjecture that the American hope of a prompt withdrawal would have been long since realized. Everything depends on whether Iraq's divisions will be somehow sufficiently reconciled and made consistent with peace and order—and thus prosperity, in the longer run. Who can say for sure? All we can say at the moment is that there is considerable ground for hope. If the stakes are very high, as most of us think, then that ground for hope may, arguably, be enough.

*Are* the stakes that high in this case? One suggestion has been that they are because what is at stake is international terrorism and the sort of regimes that would be empowered if terrorists were to succeed. At the other end of the spectrum is the familiar idea from critics that the war is really on behalf of private interests hoping to amass fortunes in the oil business. Somewhere in between is simply the interest in having decent regimes in which people will be able to live their lives more safely, more richly, and more interestingly, and with whom we and others can have peaceable and mutually beneficial relations, commercial and otherwise. The former goal is an absurdity, but the latter goal is, I think, credible and worthy. However, it is not one for the achievement of which huge sacrifices in either the recipient population or our own would be justified. At present, it appears that it may be achievable—at modest cost to the Iraqis, at quite modest cost in lives to the Coalition, and at very considerable financial cost to the Americans. Many of the pieces are in place, others are being gradually put into place—even if it is taking longer than was at first hoped—and we may be forgiven for thinking that the end of overt intervention by the United States and its allies is, if not quite in sight, then not so very far over the horizon.

## CONCLUSION

Was, and is, it all worth it? I shall settle for a rather modest answer: It is credible to say that it is, in retrospect. Was it justified in prospect? Again, perhaps so. In the end, so far as the United States' role in the war is concerned, the people will somehow speak. US politicians may be reelected or defeated on the strength of the outcome of this war. Election results will provide some index, but they are unlikely to settle the matter fully. I have argued here only for the more modest conclusion that we should not reject out of hand the possibility of an affirmative answer. External military intervention is a serious matter and not to be undertaken frivolously. Without question, the regime that the US and British soldiers have eliminated was up toward the top of the scale in tyranny, and I have argued that rigid opposition to intervention for reasons other than narrow self-defense is conceptually incoherent. Human liberation is a worthy undertaking, though fraught with peril when pursued via military means against a sizable modern state. The claim here is only that such liberation is in principle capable of being justified and, more modestly, that it may have been worth it in this case.

## NOTES

1. John Locke, *Second Treatise of Civil Government* (New York: Prometheus Books, 1986) xviii, xix.

2. Russell Hardin, "Democracy at the Margin," in *Understanding Democracy*, ed. Albert Breton, Gianluigi Galeotti, Pierre Salmon, and Ronald Wintrobe (Cambridge: Cambridge University Press, 1997), 249–266.

3. According to www.Iraqbodycount.net, as of January 19, 2005, the number of civilians killed is between 15,365 and 17,582.

4. John Keegan, *The Iraq War* (Toronto: Key Porter Books, 2004), 204.

5. Ibid., 82.

6. Immanuel Kant. *Perpetual Peace* (Boston: Pearson Education POD, 1998).

# 4

# In the Murk of It
## Iraq Reconsidered

MITCHELL COHEN

Homage begets friends; truth, enemies.
> Terence

Let's begin with this assumption: Forceful arguments were made in good faith by foes and proponents of the Iraq war, even if bad faith also characterized many political players as well as intellectuals in the United States, France, Germany, Iraq, and elsewhere. The consequences of the war are what matter most now. They are still unclear. Collateral damage in a war is often visible quickly; collateral benefits may take years to emerge. One undeniable good is self-evident: Saddam Hussein's murderous rule is over. Nonetheless, reconsideration leads me to a paradoxical, unsatisfying, and unsatisfactory conclusion about the Iraq war: Most of the arguments against it were significantly wrong, but the arguments for it were palpably not all right.

Prewar claims are appropriately subject to postwar scrutiny. No decision in a democracy demands public justification more than going to war, than opting to risk and sacrifice citizens (your own as well as your foe's). Postwar developments as well as an array of investigations raised very serious questions for proponents of the war, especially those who worried about Iraqi weapons of mass destruction. No investigation—by the government or the press—and no intelligent foe of the war challenged how proponents depicted Saddam's malevolence. True, some loud voices from the far left think otherwise. But they side congenitally with any anti-Western leader no matter what he does to his own population.

Saddam's regime assassinated an estimated three hundred thousand Iraqis for political reasons. The war that he launched against Iran incurred nearly a million casualties, and his regime executed massive numbers of Iranian prisoners of war. More Muslims died due to the Iraq-Iran war than in all of the Arab-Israeli wars and intifadas. Five thousand Iraqi Kurdish villagers were exterminated by chemical weapons at Halabja, and Saddam's murderous ethnic cleansing—Arabization—campaigns against Iraqi Kurds also displaced about a million people (approximately one hundred thousand from the Kirkuk area alone between 1983 and 2003) and destroyed four thousand villages. Saddam's forces expelled an estimated quarter million of southern Iraq's Marsh Arabs and killed thousands of them, too.[1]

It is difficult to call Saddam's Iraq "a sovereign nation," except within a narrow and strictly Westphalian definition that precludes any democratic content. The people of Iraq were not sovereign in the state of Iraq. Saddam's dictatorship governed by means of its monopoly of terrorizing force; it rested on a mix of nationalist fascism and tribalism. For decades the Iraqi state warred against Iraqis; foreign military intervention, for all its many flaws, ended that war in 2003.

## II

Had Saddam not been ousted, I believe that an unjust peace would have prevailed, and war would very probably have come at a later date because of the weapons issue. Unjust peace is not always avoidable; sometimes a brutal reality secures it. For instance, the West could not act against the Soviet Union after the invasion of Hungary in 1956 because the consequences would have been world catastrophe. Nonetheless, the failure to do so brought grave injustice to Hungarians. Had Saddam's army remained in Kuwait in 1991, where it committed massive war crimes, that scenario, too, would have constituted an unjust peace.

Circumstances different from the Cold War enabled an American-led, UN-endorsed international coalition to oust Saddam's invaders in 1991 without world-catastrophic consequences. However, the Gulf War ended with an American call to Kurds and Shiites to rebel against Saddam followed by a US failure to aid them. Saddam's forces then exterminated some 30,000 Kurds and 30,000 to 60,000 Shiites. (In contrast, 2,278 Iraqi civilians died in the Gulf War itself, according to Iraqi authorities.)[2] A half million Kurds became refugees because of Saddam's onslaught. Commentators who were perplexed in 2003 by a lack of Iraqi welcome to the US Army might consider whether many Iraqis recalled the events of 1991 and the danger then of pouring into uncertain Iraqi streets.

The first Bush administration (hereafter, Bush I) made a political decision: Saddam's invasion of Kuwait could "not stand" (in the president's words). Washington mobilized global support and determined that Kuwait would be liberated, but not Iraq. American reluctance to break Saddam's power fully (Britain opposed this restraint) and the decision not to proceed to Baghdad were based on realistic calculations and also international legal ones. Washington feared the costs, in both lives and political fallout, of extending military action. It did not want the onerous responsibilities of managing a post-Saddam Iraq. Along with—probably prodded by—the Saudis, Washington worried that Saddam's collapse would also break Sunni dominance of Iraq. The United States calculated that after Desert Storm dissipated, a weakened but still Sunni-Arab-dominated Iraq would remain the most plausible obstacle to the regional ambitions of Shiite Iran's fundamentalist rulers. Finally, the UN authorized force to expel Iraq from Kuwait, not to end the occupation of Iraq by Saddam's dictatorship.[3]

Even if these reckonings made sense, Iraqi Kurds and Iraqi Shiites were sacrificed to them. A considerable moral-political debt on account of vast suffering was thereby incurred. It was mainly an American debt to Iraqis. Inaction by the UN and other Coalition members earned them a share of the responsibility, too. That debt could be paid, so far as I can see, only by replacing Saddam's dictatorship with a government that maintained at least minimal respect for human rights. The debt could not be paid by "containment" because containment sought solely to restrict Saddam's menace to within Iraq's borders. The establishment of no-fly zones and protecting semiautonomy for the Kurds in northern Iraq were minimal reparation. UN sanctions may or may not have impaired Saddam's pursuit of weapons and boxed him in. Their declared target, however, was not his regime, itself the real smoking gun, and Iraqis were still targets in his merciless box. And just as Saddam's budget priorities after the Iran-Iraq war were military restoration rather than civilian reconstruction, so his preoccupation during thirteen years of sanctions, which theoretically permitted the sale of oil for medicine and food for civilians, was to exploit difficult circumstances on behalf of his military and domestic power bases rather than to alleviate civilian suffering. One suspects that had Iraqis—60 percent of whom are Shiite and 20 percent of whom are Kurds—been able to deliberate democratically in the spring of 2003 on whether they should remain under Saddam's rule, on the grounds that the UN Security Council would not endorse outside military intervention, or be freed from Saddam's rule by outside intervention, they would very likely have opted for intervention. One might imagine them responding to UN secretary-general Kofi Annan's assertion of the war's illegality by borrowing from Anatole France's famous remark about law under capitalism—that in its "majesty," the law allows equally millionaires and beggars to sleep under a bridge—and by saying that international legality, in its majesty, protected equally citizens living in the European Union and in Saddam's Iraq.[4]

## III

Plainly, the second Bush administration (hereafter Bush II) did not go to war in Iraq in 2003 because of the moral failure of Bush I in 1991. In fact, Bush I included many of the key decision makers of Bush II (e.g., Dick Cheney, Donald Rumsfeld, Paul Wolfowitz, and Colin Powell). How, then, could a liberal or someone on the left (like me) support a war led by American conservatives? The answer is not difficult although it is unpleasant. It is sometimes possible, even necessary, to sanction an action by a political foe. It depends on the circumstances and the stakes, both practical and moral. Politics on occasion compels an uncomfortable "concurring opinion," to borrow the term used when Supreme Court justices align on a decision without sharing all of each other's thinking or general perspective. An old-fashioned way of saying this is, Strange bedfellows are not novel features of politics. Roosevelt and Churchill allied with Stalin against Hitler, and their concurring opinion did not make them supporters of the Soviet dictator or advocates of a postwar communist East Germany. Vietnam invaded Cambodia in 1979 in violation of international law and in its own interests, but the moral imperative to concur with this illegal regime change—the ouster of the Khmer Rouge without permission of the United Nations—was overwhelming because it ended genocide. And so, someone on the left who dissented sharply from the general agenda, including in foreign policy, of a conservative US president might still have good reasons to support his use of force to rid Iraq of a fascist regime in 2003. After all, many critics of the Iraq war presented cogent arguments that should not be confused with the concurring antiwar views of right-wingers such as Patrick J. Buchanan in the United States, Jean-Marie le Pen in France, and Jorg Haidar in Austria or, for that matter, of those of Leninist groups that helped to organize many antiwar demonstrations, in some cases in alliance with Muslim fundamentalists.[5]

Historical examples do not by themselves justify strange political bedfellows. Justification depends on circumstances, independent judgment, and an appropriate bearing toward those bedfellows, those circumstances, and, indeed, one's own judgments. In the case of Iraq, appropriate bearing had in my view to be informed by a priority: relief to Iraqi suffering. Now, an honest observer would have to admit that any outside effort to define Iraqi needs was a murky matter, both morally and politically. Saddam's police state stifled all voices within Iraq, and it was somewhat presumptuous of foreign powers (and intellectuals), whether in Washington or Paris or, indeed, on the East River, to be their ventriloquists. Only Iraqi exiles could speak with significant legitimacy. Some of them were exemplary advocates for their country, while others were seedy, perhaps criminal, opportunists. None could speak with complete surety about internal developments in Iraq.

What can be said with surety is that many decision makers together with many public voices that were raised against or for their decisions had priorities other than the fate of Iraqis. Governments usually have inescapably particularist concerns in specific national interests to consider. As "realist" theorists of international affairs argue, it would be naive and simplistic to expect otherwise. Moreover, if the government is democratic, then it would be undemocratic to expect otherwise, at least to a very considerable extent, since democratic governments must be responsible to their constituents. But if you accept, as I do, Max Weber's proposition that politics unavoidably entails some element of coercion, that it is never entirely "clean," then it is an ongoing imperative to pose publicly regulative, "idealist" questions to governments and political officials. In the case of the Iraq war, the first regulative question ought to be where Iraqis, in whose country a war was to be fought, fit into their principal arguments.

Two leading European foes of the war, one on the left and one on the right, would have some difficulty responding frankly to this question, as would many Arab leaders. In September 2002, German chancellor Gerhard Schröder, a Social Democrat, exploited ruthlessly the prospect of war in Iraq to aid his own reelection campaign. In other words, he staked out his position on a war with his own (domestic) political concerns chiefly in mind. French president Jacques Chirac, leader of his country's conservative bloc, did likewise, although in his case—in his concurring opinion with his Social Democratic counterpart—foreign policy ambitions seem foremost in his calculations. Chirac explained on French television in March 2003 that he opposed the war because he favored a "multipolar world." His chief concern was evidently not securing the fate of Iraqis but furthering a neo-Gaullist vision in which a French-led Europe would have a new world role counterbalancing American power (and thereby compensating for the contemporary weaknesses of the French state). It is notable that he did not say "multilateralism," which implies a common effort by like-minded—say, liberal democratic—political forces. Paris often echoed the ancien régimes of the Arab world, whose leaders insisted that Iraq was a distraction from the Israel-Palestine conflict, the "real key" to all their region's difficulties. But here, again, Iraqi suffering vanishes from the picture, as if the political murder of three hundred thousand Iraqis by the Baath government were little more than a minor dimension of "the question of Palestine."[6]

My regulative question does not aim to exhaust all the issues at stake in Iraq—the dangers posed by Saddam's regime to his region and beyond cannot be discounted simplistically now that there appears to have been no weapons of mass destruction—but it needs to be posed repeatedly in public debate in order to clarify, as much as they can be, the murkier dimensions of the war's political morality. After the war ended and weapons of mass destruction were not found, Hans Blix, who directed the UN's prewar arms search, declared that the American-British military action "was like surgery intended to remove something malignant finding that the malignancy was not there."[7] This may be so in the case of the weapons. However, a more probing diagnosis tells us that the real malignancy was what Blix himself acknowledges was "one of the bloodiest regimes the world has seen."[8] But for that regime, there would have been no weapons issue at all.

## IV

My regulative question ought also to be posed to intellectuals and public voices such as filmmakers and media celebrities who play loud, often disproportionate roles in current political debates. It is the sort of question that reveals political sensibilities. Compare, for instance, the political sensibility of Adam Michnik, the Polish intellectual who played a prominent role in ending decades of communist dictatorship in Warsaw and went to prison for his efforts, to that of Michael Moore, whose documentary about September 11 and the Iraq war, *Fahrenheit 9/11*, was one of the most widely discussed films of 2004. When Michnik explained to an interviewer why he supported the war, he did not embrace George Bush's worldview but said that he sought to see events "through the eyes" of political prisoners in Saddam's dungeons. "I think you can be an enemy of Saddam Hussein even if Donald Rumsfeld is also an enemy of Saddam Hussein," Michnik added.[9] By contrast, Moore's film presents Baghdad on the eve of war as if it were a contented Middle American town of the 1950s. Saddam's dungeons don't exist; nor do the thousands upon thousands of mass graves that the Baath regime dug and filled amply. Folks just go about their lives in Michael Moore's Baghdad, and their kids play merrily—that is, until bombs fall and they all become America's victims. Michnik saw the conflict through the eyes of a cosmopolitan human rights champion (rooted, of course, in his own country's experience), whereas Moore's prism is that of the ethnocentric part of the American left. Its reality was so dictated by anger at a very disagreeable US presidency that it could not see the reality of Baghdad's dictatorship.

Moore's film, like Michnik's comments, was made before the revelation of torture by Americans of Iraqi prisoners in Abu Ghraib. Before the war, this prison was long the site of abuse—perhaps the most infamous site of the most appalling abuse—of political prisoners by Saddam's regime. If an Adam Michnik condemns hideous American behavior at Abu Ghraib, he carries moral authority; Moore's condemnation can carry none because Saddam's prisoners are air-brushed out of this filmmaker's version of Saddam's Baghdad. Indeed, Moore's picture of Baghdad is a little like a picture of Stalin's Moscow without Lubyanka prison.

## V

Neither Michnik nor Moore were decision makers. Washington justified its resort to arms on three major grounds: liberal democracy versus totalitarianism, the danger posed by Iraq's pursuit of weapons of mass destruction, and alleged links between Saddam and Osama bin Laden.

The last of these had no factual basis. The same may be said, however, of the contention made by some critics of the war that such links were impossible because Saddam was secular and bin Laden a religious fundamentalist. After all, if Roosevelt, Churchill, and Stalin could have concurring opinions against Hitler, and if Patrick J. Buchanan and Michael Moore could concur in their opposition to the Iraq war and to neoconservatives, then it is not unreasonable to imagine Saddam and bin Laden, who had concurring anti-Western opinions, might act together on them. Syria's secular regime, whose ruling Baathist ideology was not significantly distinguishable from Saddam's ruling Baathist ideology, has had an antagonistic relation with Al Qaeda, yet it has supported Hamas and Palestinian Islamic Jihad. In the 1980s and 1990s, Baathist Damascus was often allied with Tehran's fundamentalist regime against Baathist Baghdad. Saddam began a partial remake of his regime's image in the early 1990s to enhance its Islamic credentials. He encouraged Iraqi Baath rapprochement with Sunni Islamists (particularly the Muslim Brotherhood and Wahhabists). In short, although no empirical evidence sustained Bush's claim that Saddam and bin Laden collaborated, no student of the Middle East could have been surprised had it been otherwise.

The second Bush rationale also remains unsubstantiated. The failure to find weapons of mass destruction led to charges of mendacity against Bush and British prime minister Tony Blair. It also led to harsh criticism of intelligence services for providing unreliable information to decision makers. The CIA and other intelligence services have been accused of "groupthink" in their estimation of Saddam's weapons capacities, which may well be so. However, critics of the war who insist that the weapons issue was simply a ploy and nothing else may be guilty of their own groupthink. If it is true that Saddam no longer had those weapons—postwar developments indicate that this was the case—or a substantial capacity to reconstitute them, then one principal argument for the war is undermined. But it is undermined only in retrospect. If the weapons were not there, that does not prove that the issue was a hoax. Indeed, if Bush and Blair, politicians known for exceptional savvy in public relations, manufactured a threat of this enormity or knew all along that it was fraudulent, why would they have

- gone through all of the war's damaging diplomatic prelude;
- been willing to face domestic criticism;

- · dispatched huge armies around the globe;
- · made war plans that included a hunt for the weapons, budgeted "several hundred million dollars" to destroy the weapons once found, and urged the UN inspectors to act "aggressively" and to expand their searches rapidly;[10]
- · and then fought a war,

without preparing a final, obvious step—planting the evidence?

A key feature of Saddam's rule was his consistency in violating or discarding major agreements, especially when he made them in pressured circumstances and regardless of the partner. When he declared his weapons to be gone and that he was acting in accord with international obligations, there was no reason to take his word. Indeed, a levelheaded person would have thought otherwise based on his past political behavior. Here, again, his political behavior differed significantly from that of his ideological kin—though frequent antagonist—in neighboring Syria. Hafiz al-Assad, the murderous *Raïs* (boss) of Baathist Damascus from 1970 to his death in 2000, tended to keep important agreements, particularly with those he considered his worst enemies. For instance, Assad reached an accord with Israel through American mediation in the aftermath of the 1973 war. In it he agreed that there would be no terrorism across the Golan Heights. There has been none since. Yitzhak Rabin, who was Israeli prime minister then, recounted in 1983 that these were the most difficult negotiations in which he had ever participated but that Assad followed through on commitments. In Rabin's view, this was Assad's way of saying that however much the Israelis disliked him and his regime's ideology, they could deal with him.[11] In contrast, any historian of modern Iraq can list the many victims of agreements with Saddam Hussein. They include the Kurds, Iran, the Iraqi communists, Kuwait, and, in a somewhat different way—it was only deceived and not slaughtered or invaded—the United Nations.

We know that Saddam pursued weapons of mass destruction in the late 1970s. Israel bombed his reactor in 1981 before it could became an imminent threat. (It was only a predictable threat in 1981, but had Jerusalem waited until enriched plutonium or uranium was in the reactor, the Israeli air force would have been unable to destroy it without producing radioactive calamity throughout Iraq).[12] Saddam deployed weapons of mass destruction during the Iran-Iraq war of the 1980s; at different times, he invested huge sums in biological, chemical, and nuclear arsenals. His rule was ruthless and reckless, and outside monitoring of his lethal ambitions, while in fact accomplishing a good deal, was always inconclusive and often unreliable. For instance, in spring 1990, the International Atomic Energy Agency under Blix inspected Iraq and declared that Baghdad was fulfilling its responsibilities under the Nuclear Non-proliferation Treaty. After the Gulf War, it was revealed that Baghdad had somehow hidden from inspectors a formidable nuclear program. The regime had invested somewhere between ten and fifteen billion dollars in it, and some twenty thousand people worked in its thirty-odd sites. A principal goal was enriching uranium, and each important level of this effort had a duplicate (for safekeeping, as it were).[13] "The revelation that Iraq had secretly enriched uranium without being detected shook the world," Blix later recounted, and he observed, in something of an understatement, that "weaknesses" in the "verification regime" for the Non-proliferation Treaty had thereby come to light.[14] Then, for a dozen years after the Gulf War, Saddam continued to do his best to thwart inspections.

In 1998, the year in which the United Nations Special Commission (UNSCOM) was forced out of the country, one American inspector, Scott Ritter, declared that "Iraq still has prescribed weapons capability." Baghdad had "disassembled weapons into various components" in order to hide them throughout the country. Absent effective monitoring, he insisted, Saddam's government could rapidly "reconstitute chemical biological weapons, long range ballistic missiles to deliver these weapons, and certain aspects of their nuclearization program."[15] In an October 2002 interview, David Kelly, the British microbiologist who visited Iraq thirty-seven times as an inspector for the United Nations (and who later committed suicide during the argumentative aftermath of the war), was asked whether there was an "immediate threat" from Iraq's unconventional weapons. He answered, "Yes, there is. Even if they're not actually filled and deployed today, the capability exists to get them filled and deployed in a matter of days and weeks. So yes there is a threat."[16]

By a 15–0 vote, Security Council Resolution 1441 declared in late 2002 that Saddam was in "material breach" of scores of previous disarmament resolutions. Saddam then handed over thousands of pages of outdated, misleading information. On March 18, 2003, French president Jacques Chirac spoke on French television of "the necessary disarmament of Iraq," and his ambassador to the United States, Jean-David Levitt, said that French policy toward Iraq would change "if Saddam were to use chemical and biological weapons."[17] France opposed the US-led war, but these statements indicate that its government, with its long, complex, and unsavory ties to Iraq, believed that Saddam had dangerous weapons. After the war, Paris advocated a UN-coordinated weapons inspections effort of Iraq.[18]

When David Kay, the American expert who headed the postwar search for weapons under the auspices of the Iraq Survey Group, concluded that there were no weapons—"we were almost all wrong"—he noted that France and Germany, like the United States and Britain, had believed that Iraq had chemical and biological weapons and was also possibly developing nuclear arms. Before the war, he reported, "the best intelligence that I had seen was that Iraq indeed had weapons of mass destruction."[19] In short, intelligence agencies of all Western powers, including French intelligence, according to Blix, believed that Saddam had them. In fact, Berlin was the most apprehensive about nuclear weapons; it was German intelligence that said that Baghdad could have nuclear arms within three to six years.[20] Finally, Kay reported that the Iraq Survey Group, although discovering no biological or chemical arms, also found that officers in Saddam's Special Republican Guard were convinced that those arms were to be found in units other than their own.[21]

I do not rehearse these points in order to maintain against all the postwar testimony of massive intelligence and political failure or manipulations that Saddam had the weapons. Still, if Saddam was not an imminent threat, he was certainly a predictable one in the long run. I present these points to urge against simplistic approaches to the weapons issue. Some critics of the war contend that inspections would have resolved the problem without recourse to military action. But this view also assumes that he posed real danger. If not, then Saddam was surely playing a cat-and-mouse game that would have been endless because nonexistent weapons cannot be found. If he had them, then he was likewise playing cat-and-mouse, probably expecting the cat would tire first. He readmitted inspectors only because 150,000 US and British troops stood at Iraq's border, not because of yet another UN resolution.[22] He undoubtedly calculated (with good reason) that political and economic pressures would render the military threat unsustainable over a protracted period of time. He could evict inspectors the moment it dissipated. He probably gambled that French, Russian, and German opposition would thwart Bush and Blair, but if not, at least time would be gained to prepare an underground. Given these circumstances, a cynic might say that Jacques Chirac's neo-Gaullist foreign policy reinforced Bush's unilateralism. Chirac refused French participation in the military buildup that pressured Saddam into readmitting inspectors, all while he insisted inspections ought to resolve the problem.

There is, however, another reason to shun facile judgments about Saddam's weapons (or, rather, the absence of them). Today's astonishingly "sophisticated" nuclear black market takes materials designed in one country, moves them to another for manufacture, and then ships and reships them through different lands and channels until they reach distributors and purchasers.[23] Little of this market was known until very recently when Libya renounced its nuclear ambitions and revealed many details. If we place the inability of Western intelligence to read Iraq accurately in the context of the apparently similar inability to detect the spread of weapons of mass destruction and their technologies elsewhere, from Pakistan to North Korea to Iran to Libya, then the Iraq failure becomes just one aspect of a very dangerous, more general pattern of failure. In one case, the menace may have been vastly overestimated; in the others, it was vastly underestimated. The frightening implications should not be lost amid postwar posturing.[24] Shouting "liar" at Bush and Blair may be satisfying to some, but it is not serious politics in these circumstances.

## VI

The Bush administration's first rationale—let's call it the idealist rationale—was that war against Saddam Hussein would result in the replacement of a totalitarian regime with liberal democracy. In principle, this makes Iraqi needs a priority, although it is difficult to imagine how anyone who knew Iraq's history and political cultures could imagine its quick, painless, and inexpensive transformation into a liberal democracy. It is baffling that the same Washington decision makers who characterized Saddam's hold on power as brutally tenacious, which it was, did not envisage brutally tenacious resistance to US intervention by those Iraqis who were vested in his rule. Perhaps this also helps to explain why commitment to Iraqi democracy by Bush II often seems to have weakened as rapidly as difficulties multiplied in Iraq.

It is evident that Bush II prosecuted the war more with the president's domestic political fortunes than Iraqi needs in mind; in this, his political behavior is comparable to that of Chirac and Schröder. But Bush II also sought to conduct a war without the costs of war, privatizing many dimensions of the effort and cutting taxes at home. This approach makes for an unstable, untenable political recipe. In the peculiar version of patriotism that accompanied the Bush II policies, young American soldiers were expected to risk their lives for the public good while the wealthiest segments of their society could not be asked to pay a fair proportion of taxes for the public good. Then, in March 2004, the president who had ordered these soldiers to Iraq turned the search for weapons of mass destruction into a public joke by sending to journalists a picture of himself searching for arms under his White House office furniture.[25] Combine these factors, and it becomes evident why Bush II increasingly lost credibility in its conduct of the war by the summer of 2004.

Consider its military calculations. These were based partly on a doctrine that emerged in the 1990s. It projected military success, particularly in "third world" theaters, by means of new technology and battlefield mobility rather than by the type of large troop concentrations that become prey for guerrilla strikes. The calculation was right until Saddam's statue fell. That is, it was militarily right at first but politically wrong. Only massive numbers of troops could have secured Iraq once its ancien régime was gone. They needed to be complemented immediately by an overwhelming humanitarian aid program to persuade Iraqis that a decent future was at hand and by rapid efforts to internationalize the governance of Iraq until Iraqi self-government became plausible. American disarray after initial military success was due significantly to disregard of local conditions, needs, and political cultures and then to attempts at corrective moves, like the "transfer of sovereignty," that seemed keyed less to Iraq than to Bush's electoral season.[26] There is an unhappy similarity here between the political choices made by the first and the second Bush administrations in their Middle East wars: in both cases Iraqi needs became lower priorities in the endgame. The first Bush administration left Iraqi wounds to fester. The second Bush administration festered in them, extending the endgame, as it were.

Disregard of local Iraqi realities and conditions was due partly to the ideological predispositions of Bush II. This administration, or at least the idealists within it, tended to impose Cold War categories, especially the idea of totalitarianism, onto Middle Eastern realities. According to the old domino theory, communist victory in one land would lead to the fall of one capitalist (or pro-Western) state after another. Bush II's Middle Eastern version proposed that Saddam's end would lead to the fall of the authoritarian regimes that long dominated Arab lands, one after the other.

Middle Eastern realities disappeared into a theory of totalitarianism. This is not to suggest that the theory had no use. The one party in Iraq's one-party state had fascist intellectual progenitors, and its leader had Stalinist fantasies. But Iraq, like every country, has particular, local realities (e.g., its tribal, ethnic, and religious structures and political cultures) that were apparently lost on those American decision makers who imagined they were involved in no more than an extension—or reinvention—of Cold War battles between totalitarianism and liberalism. Theories of totalitarianism usually link totalitarian regimes to the atomization of society. But for all of Saddam's totalitarian aspirations and the cruel, terrifying realities that they created, Iraq wasn't simply atomized by them. Tribal, ethnic, and religious structures weaved a more complex fabric of power under the Baath dictatorship than the word *totalitarianism* allows. That is one reason why Baathist Iraq was unlikely to unravel into Jeffersonian democracy. Imagining how Iraqi particulars might translate successfully into Iraqi democracy, or at least into a minimally decent regime, is a much harder—indeed, daunting—task than applying mechanically the theory of totalitarianism. Here imagination seems to have failed. Bush II might have been more successful had its theory been a function of Iraq rather than the reverse.

Part of the antiwar left made a comparable mental error by using imperialism as its all-explanatory idea. It is true that modern Iraq—indeed, the entire region—cannot be explained apart from the miserable history of imperialist intrusions there. But Middle Eastern politics is not simply a function of imperialism or struggles against it. The region's cultures and political cultures have distinct and diverse characteristics. And Saddam Hussein's thirty-year reign should be given its own responsibility for the vast misery it produced. The luxury of an all-explanatory dogma is that it makes complex matters—and political choices—simple. Part of the left, particularly what is now called the "postcolonial" left, "understands" the brutality of Iraqi Baathism and Saddam's rule only in light of imperialism's sins. Those sins were, of course, real and copious, but this is a little like "understanding" Nazism on the grounds that the Treaty of Versailles was unfair to Germany (which it was).

## VII

Here, then, are the elements that constituted a coherent case for the use of force against Saddam's regime, regardless of one's views of Bush II:

- the fascistic nature and dangerous ambitions of Saddam's state;
- the vast suffering it caused over more than three decades;
- its repeated acts of aggression against neighbors;
- its past use and pursuit of weapons of mass destruction and the improbability that this issue would be resolved completely by monitoring;
- its repeated violation of UN resolutions as well as of its major foreign and domestic agreements;
- the great moral debt incurred by the victors at the end of the Gulf War;
- the prospect that Iraq's wounded population might have a reasonable government and a better life.

Many of these elements link with one another, and we now know that some of them do not persuade as they did (some of us) before the war. Although it is a mistake (and politically naive) to assume, as some foes of the war did, that anyone you disagree with must be incompetent, it is now evident that Bush II mishandled a great deal in Iraq and made many bad, even obtuse, political decisions that may combine to produce potentially grave long-term consequences. One argument against the war was that it would not be carried out properly by this administration. In retrospect, this argument carries considerable force. But had there been no war, Saddam would still be in power. Does that counterbalance postwar turmoil and the nonappearance of weapons of mass destruction? These are times that try one's theories, not to mention one's analyses. They demand of intellectuals as well as policymakers a keen sense of moral burden in murky circumstances, a sense of unsettling contingencies and complexities, a willingness to argue against oneself rather than reiterating stubbornly idées fixes.

## NOTES

"In the Murk of It: Iraq Reconsidered" is © 2005 by Mitchell Cohen.

1. For some of the estimates, see *The Economist*, December 20, 2003, 59.

2. *International Herald Tribune*, June 11, 2003, 3. Saddam's regime had its own reasons to minimize the number of civilian casualties since it also reflects on the consequences of its own Kuwait policy.

3. In 1991, I supported the war and also thought it should not continue beyond Kuwait's border, although I did not anticipate Washington's call to and then refusal to support rebellion by the Kurds and Shiites.

4. I repeat here a point I made in "Comment on Suzanne Nossel on Liberal Internationalism," *Dissent* (Fall 2004). In my arguments in this essay, I also draw arguments and some details from several pieces that I wrote before and during the war: "Symposium: War and Iraq," *Dissent* (Winter 2003); "Writers, Artists and Civic Leaders on the War," *openDemocracy* (online), February 6, 2003; and "Mitchell Cohen Replies," *Dissent* (Fall 2003), Letters to the Editor section.

5. On the British case, see *The Economist*, November 29, 2003, 55. Considerable argument also took place among American antiwar activists about the role of Leninist organizations in their activities.

6. This is not to belittle the suffering of Palestinians and Israelis. It is to insist, however, that the history, dynamics, and causes of Iraq's problems and those of Israel-Palestine are distinct.

7. Hans Blix, *Disarming Iraq* (New York: Pantheon Books, 2004), 259.

8. Ibid., 255.

9. See Thomas Cushman, "Anti-totalitarianism as a Vocation: An Interview with Adam Michnik," *Dissent* (Spring 2004): 28–29.

10. In September 2002, the National Defense University, which is run by the Pentagon, had secret meetings attended by Defense planners, former UNSCOM inspectors, and military officials to map out a hunt for weapons covering hundreds of sites. *International Herald Tribune*, July 21, 2003, 4. Blix, *Disarming Iraq*, cites the budgeting (256). He also reports the US desire for an aggressive search (13).

11. Rabin told me this in an interview on July 21, 1983, in the Knesset, Jerusalem.

12. Iran tried to bomb the reactor ten months earlier, during the early phase of the Iran-Iraq war.

13. See Chen Zak's summary in "Iran's Nuclear Policy and the IAEA," Washington Institute for Near East Policy Research, Paper #3, 2002.

14. Blix, *Disarming Iraq*, 24, 16.

15. Scott Ritter interviewed by Elizabeth Farnsworth on the *NewsHour with Jim Lehrer*, August 31, 1998, as transcribed on *Online NewsHour*, http://www.pbs.org/newshour/bb/middle_east/july-dec98/ritter_8-31.html (accessed January 19, 2005). Ritter had just quit UNSCOM when he made these statements and later seems to have reversed this position, claiming that Iraq had disposed of its weapons.

16. See the *International Herald Tribune*, January 22, 2004, 1, 3.

17. *New York Times*, March 19, 2003, A12. He later retracted this statement.

18. *New York Times*, April 25, 2003, A15. Blix reports, however, that Chirac told him that he didn't believe that Iraq had the weapons. See Blix, *Disarming Iraq*, 128.

19. *International Herald Tribune*, January 29, 2004, 1, 4.

20. On French intelligence, see Blix, *Disarming Iraq*, 127. On German intelligence, see *The Economist*, February 7, 2004, and Reuters, February 24, 2002.

21. *New York Times*, February 12, 2004, A16.

22. Iraq's foreign minister, Naji Sabri, declared in his official letter to UN secretary-general Kofi Annan accepting the return of inspectors that "the measures and procedures" in Resolution 1441 were "contrary to international law" and the UN Charter. *New York Times*, November 14, 2002, A14.

23. According to Mohammed el-Baradei, director of the International Atomic Energy Agency. See the reports in the *International Herald Tribune*, January 24–25, 2004, and *Haaretz*, July 8, 2004.

24. A historical dimension to these intelligence failures is worth noting. The CIA failed to anticipate (or adequately verify) Soviet missiles in Cuba, the Soviet invasion of Afghanistan in 1979, Iraq's invasion of Iran in 1979, the collapse of Soviet communism, or Iraq's invasion of Kuwait in 1990.

25. The picture was sent by Bush to the annual Radio and Television Correspondents Dinner in Washington.

26. For the resulting mistakes on the ground, see Peter Galbraith, "How to Get Out of Iraq," *New York Review of Books*, May 13, 2004.

# PART TWO

# PHILOSOPHICAL ARGUMENTS

# 5

# National Interest and International Law

ROGER SCRUTON

Two rival views of international relations now compete for influence among our political elites, the national and the transnational, and the war in Iraq has sharpened the conflict between them. Neither view clearly justifies the war or clearly condemns it. But it seems to me that the national approach is a better guarantee of peace and stability than the transnational alternative, and cases like the Iraq war provide some evidence for this conclusion.

According to the national view, the business of politics is to maintain law, order, peace, freedom, and security within the borders of a sovereign state. Dealings with other states are premised on the assumption that they, too, are sovereign and that they, too, have the business of maintaining law and security within their borders. However, there is no assumption that other states perform these tasks well or justly, or that their subject peoples enjoy the benefits of citizenship under an impartial rule of law. The rulers of Inland may be outraged by the way in which the rulers of Outland govern their people. But Inland has a mandate to exert force against Outland only if and insofar as this action is necessary for Inland's own security. The way to maintain peace, on the national view, is to uphold national sovereignty in every area where it might be threatened and to maintain a balance of power among neighbors. Threatening behavior from one state must be met with a counterthreat sufficient to deter aggression. And wherever possible, the balance of power must be supplemented by pacts of nonaggression and treaties recognizing common interests—provided only that such treaties do not weaken or compromise national sovereignty. When such treaties break down or are manifestly disregarded, the alternative is first deterrence and then, if deterrence is ineffective, force—including preemptive force, if that is what the situation requires.

The wisdom of that approach ought to have been fully established by World War II, in which the failure to adopt a deterrent strategy against Hitler or to use preemptive strikes at the time when these would have prevented German rearmament led first to Munich and the seizure of Czechoslovakia, then to the Soviet-Nazi invasion of Poland, and finally to all-out war. Britain and France renounced the deterrent strategy that would have prevented this outcome. Why? Because their ruling elites had fallen prey to the transnational view of conflict. The national view had been assumed until the French Revolution and reaffirmed at the Congress of Vienna. It had remained in place as the guiding light of foreign policy right up to World War I, during which period the peace of Europe had been seriously interrupted only by the Franco-Prussian War. But World War I, with its senseless slaughter and incomprehensible goals, discredited, in the minds of many people, the national approach to conflict. The League of Nations was founded with the express purpose of replacing the national view with the transnational alternative. And the European Union was conceived by its conspiratorial founders as the means to liquidate the European nation-states.[1]

According to the transnational view, belligerence between sovereign states cannot be prevented by the threat of force but only by a rule of law. Disputes between states should be resolved in the same way as disputes between citizens—namely, by recourse to law and the imposition of a judgment. This scenario will require transnational government, with lawmaking and law-enforcing institutions. The authority habitually cited in defense of this approach is Kant, who, in *Perpetual Peace*, argues for a League of Nations as the way to secure permanent peace in the civilized world.[2] Under the League, sovereign nations would submit to a common jurisdiction, to be enforced by sanctions. This is the idea embodied first in the League of Nations, which consciously honored Kant in its name, and then in the United Nations.

What Kant had in mind, however, was very far from transnational government as it is now conceived. He was adamant that there can be no guarantee of peace unless the powers acceding to the treaty are republics. Republican government, as defined by Kant, both here and elsewhere in his political writings, means representative government under a rule of law,[3] and his league of nations is one that binds self-governing and sovereign nations, whose peoples enjoy the rights and duties of citizenship. For Kant, the kind of international law that is needed for peace "presupposes the separate existence of many independent states . . . [united under] a federal union to prevent hostilities breaking out." This state of affairs is to be preferred to "an amalgmation of the separate nations under a single power."[4] He then gives the principal objection to transnational government—namely, that "laws progressively lose their impact as the government increases its range, and a soulless despotism, after crushing the germs of goodness, will finally lapse into anarchy."[5]

It seems then that Kant can be taken only as partly endorsing transnational government as we now know it. His league of nations could be a reality, he thought, only if the states united by it were republics—in other words, genuinely sovereign, genuinely representative of their people, and genuinely governed by law. These qualities are manifestly not the case of a great many members of the UN today and certainly not the case of those, like Saddam's Iraq or Kim's North Korea, that have posed the greatest threat to their immediate neighbors. Such states are not really sovereign bodies but rather conscript armies in the hands of thugs. Power is exercised by those thugs, not by representative government, still less by law, and by the machinery of one-party dictatorship, supplemented by mafia clientism and family ties.

Advocates of Kantian internationalism are therefore caught in a dilemma. If law is to be effective in the resolution of conflicts, all parties must be law-abiding members of the community of nations. What are we to do, then, with the rogue state? Are we entitled to depose its rulers, so as to change subjects to citizens, rulers to representatives, and force to law? If not, are we to regard ourselves as *really* bound by laws and treaties by which the rogue state merely *pretends* to be bound? In which case what guarantee do those laws and treaties offer of a "perpetual peace"?

Kant's caveats notwithstanding, advocates of the international idea have persistently maintained that all disputes between states ought to be submitted to international law and that belligerence can never be justified until all legal channels have been thoroughly explored and exhausted. This position has been maintained even when one party to the dispute is an entirely despotic or totalitarian power, which rules by force but not by law. For, it is maintained, such a power can be compelled to abide by its obligations under international law by sanctions, and sanctions fall short of belligerence, because they respect the sovereignty and independence of the state against which they are enforced.

Now there is no doubt that sanctions hurt the people of the states to which they are applied. Shortages of vital supplies, collapse of export- and import-dependent businesses, the general undermining of social relations by the black market—all serve to spread poverty and distrust among the people, leading to hardship and even (so it was claimed of Saddam's Iraq) starvation. But, for that very reason, sanctions enhance the power of the ruling elite. The Kim family and its clients have benefited enormously from the starvation that they have inflicted on the North Korean people, and the cooperation of the international community in ensuring that the North Koreans live without hope has been only one more gift to the ruling tyranny. The privations endured by the North Koreans mean that they have neither the strength nor the mutual trust to challenge their oppressors. The same was true of Saddam's Iraq. Moreover, Saddam's circle of Baathist thugs enriched itself through smuggling and the black market, just as the party elite in Soviet Russia enriched itself through the deprivations of the Soviet people. Sanctions make a substantial contribution to power based on privation, and they have never hurt a single despot in the whole history of their use.

Furthermore, the inherent corruption of transnational bureaucracies ensures that the UN has become a channel for escaping law rather than a means to impose it. The recent report to the Iraqi Governing Council on the effect of sanctions is a case in point. Saddam, it seems, was able to use the massive flow of money under the ancillary Oil for Food program to enrich not only himself and his cronies but also his foreign supporters, without in any way improving the lot of the poor Iraqis who were the intended beneficiaries of the deal. Indeed, it proved easier for the Iraqi elite to fatten themselves through oil sales constrained by sanctions than through peacetime sales on the open market.[6]

Those are not the only negative effects of sanctions, however. By helping to maintain the fiction of a "legal" route to the goal of compliance, sanctions postpone the force that might be required to reach it. Of course, international law recognizes the legitimate use of force—in particular, to counter aggression or repel invasion. But it always sets strict limits to its use, seeing force as a last resort whose purpose is to rectify force used by others. Hence, the United States obtained the endorsement of the UN for the first Gulf War on the understanding that the intention was to expel the invader from Kuwait. But any further action, such as the invasion of Iraq and the deposing of Saddam Hussein, remained illegal. The United States respected the law, so creating the conditions in which Saddam could reassert his grip over the Iraqi people and punish those, such as the residents of Basra, who had been briefly misled into thinking that the tyrant's time was up. Once again, international law acted to postpone the resolution of a conflict and, by preventing the march on Baghdad, ensured that the march would occur only in circumstances far less likely to gain the consent of the Iraqi people.

Kant's *Perpetual Peace* proposes an international jurisdiction with one purpose only: to secure peace between neighboring jurisdictions. The League of Nations broke down because the background presupposition was not fulfilled—namely, that its members should be republics, or states bound together by citizenship and the rule of law. (The rise of totalitarian government in Russia and Germany meant the abolition of citizenship in those countries; and, of course, it was those countries that were the aggressors in World War II.) The defenders of transnational government have cheerfully ignored Kant's presupposition. Worse, they have also ignored Kant's restriction of international jurisdiction to the goal of peace. Our national jurisdictions are now bombarded by laws from outside, even though many of these laws originate in despotic or criminal governments, and even though hardly any are concerned with the maintenance of peace. We, the citizens, are powerless in the matter, and they, the legislators, are entirely unanswerable to us, who must obey them. This state is exactly what Kant dreaded, as the sure path first to despotism and then to anarchy.

It is important here to recognize that laws imposed by a transnational body, under the cover of a treaty, are not subject to repeal by any electorate and do not need the endorsement of an electorate in order to come into effect. The growth of the transnational view of conflict resolution has therefore led to a serious tying of the hands—not of the lawless states, whose hands may need tying but can never be tied by law, but of the law-abiding democracies. We, who regard ourselves as bound by our treaties, are also bound to lose their benefits.

One example deserves mention, since it is a major contribution to the loss of security in Europe. The Geneva Convention on Refugees and Asylum was ratified in 1951, when there were no refugees uncatered for in Europe and very few applicants for asylum. This pronouncement has bound the legislatures of the nation states ever since, despite radically changed circumstances. The convention enables dictators to export their opponents without earning the bad name that comes from killing them. The entire cost of the convention is therefore borne by the law-abiding states, many of whose legal and fiscal systems are now under intolerable strain as a result of the influx of refugees. Delicate matters over which our legislators and judiciary have expended decades of careful reflection (e.g., planning law), with the all-important aim of sustaining national loyalty by reconciling *us* with *our neighbors*, are thrown into disarray by a measure that we can only pretend to influence.

An uneasy silence, induced by self-censorship and intimidation, has so far prevailed concerning this matter, the most important issue facing modern Europe. But people are beginning to wake up to the effect of unwanted immigration not merely on national loyalty but on the idea of citizenship, which has until now been taken for granted. Many of those claiming asylum bring with them the Islamist frenzies of the countries from which they have escaped. Many of them claim the benefits of citizenship, even sue for them as "human rights," while acknowledging no duty to the state in return. British citizens are now engaged in a jihad against the British people,[7] for whom the accusation of treason is as incomprehensible as the suggestion that there is treason on the moon. The idea that the citizen owes loyalty to a country, a territory, a jurisdiction, and all those who reside within it—the root assumption of democratic politics, and one that depends on national sovereignty as its moral foundation—has no place in the minds and hearts of many who now call themselves citizens of European states.

As a result, our cities now contain uncounted numbers of Islamists who are plotting atrocities of the kind we have recently witnessed and that threaten to become a regular feature of European life. There is no way in which we can defend ourselves without being in defiance of a treaty signed long ago by people who never envisaged that it could have any such result. At the same time, the treaty cannot be undone without rejecting the ethos of transnational legalism, and no politician has the courage to take that path. Put our asylum laws to the national vote, and the citizens of the European states would reject them by a crushing majority. But because these laws issue from a transnational jurisdiction, the citizens who are compelled to obey them are also powerless to alter them. To think that this is a contribution to peace is, under the circumstances, laughable. For these laws are being used by Al Qaeda as a vital part of its preparations for war.

Nor should we ignore the impact of the asylum laws on conflicts like that in Iraq. The United States now finds itself in the position of handing over power to a country whose indigenous elite has been so depleted by emigration that it is doubtful whether the expertise remains that would permit effective modern government, still less the kind of secular rule of law that is engendered only by a stable, prosperous, and liberal-minded middle class. The instability of the Middle East is not unconnected to the fact that the class on which stability depends has been siphoned away by Europe, leaving the half-crazed mullahs to run the show.

Even if those criticisms of the transnational approach are accepted, it does not follow that the national approach is any better at securing peace. Indeed, the war in Iraq seems easier to justify on transnational than on national principles. President George W. Bush has even found himself obliged to invoke the transnational perspective when endeavoring to make the war acceptable to his liberal critics, arguing that the goal is not to secure American interests but to allow the Iraqis the right to choose their own government. In other words, the goal of belligerence was to change a rogue state into a republic. It was to allow Iraq at last to join the community of nations as a law-abiding member. Machiavelli wrote in *The Prince* that "the Prince must first use law, which is natural to man, but must be prepared to use violence, which is bestial, in order that the rule of law be maintained." In a similar way, someone who really believes that states must order their affairs by an international rule of law must also believe that the force necessary to maintain that law is justified.

We can have no confidence that transnational jurisdiction, when applied unilaterally, so as to govern only the actions of law-abiding states, does anything but weaken our defenses and confer legitimacy on the powers that principally threaten us. (Consider the effect of disarmament treaties during the Cold War and of nonproliferation treaties since.) But the transnational perspective is seldom taken to its logical conclusion by those who adopt it. Transnationalists tend to endorse legal constraints on law-abiding states, regardless of their effect on the rogues. Transnationalists tend also to be cosmopolitans, who identify themselves as "world citizens," and consciously repudiate the old national loyalties that bind them to a particular nation, a particular country, and a particular jurisdiction. Cosmopolitanism was expounded in antiquity by the Stoics, endorsed by Marcus Aurelius, entertained by various medieval thinkers (notably by Dante in his defense of "world empire"), and is attributed to Kant by those who see *Perpetual Peace* as a call to replace national jurisdictions with a worldwide rule of law. Kant does indeed uphold what he calls "cosmopolitan right," as a legal duty incumbent on national jurisdictions. But the federation that he believes to be necessary for the avoidance of war is a federation of nation-states, whose people are tied by their political loyalties to sovereign and territorial jurisdictions. As now understood, cosmopolitanism involves a deliberate renunciation of the national loyalties that underpin the territorial rule of law.

Cosmopolitanism appeals to executives of multinational businesses, to bureaucrats employed by the UN and the European Union, and to the nerds and whiz kids who play the global economy from their base in cyberspace, escaping any obligation that is merely local in its claim. Cosmopolitanism is popular, too, among leftist intellectuals. Many of those who might once have repudiated national loyalty on behalf of the communist international are now rejecting the simple patriotism of their fellow citizens in the name of cosmopolitan liberalism. As with the previous left-wing enthusiasms, however, this ideology owes its appeal less to any positive conception of the transnational future than to a reaction against the national present. If the evidence of history is anything to go by, the cosmopolitan yearnings of our liberal elites may offer comfort and support to tyrannies like the Soviet empire, which disguise international aggression as cosmopolitan benevolence. But they do nothing to secure the peace of the world or to provide any viable alternative to our national forms of government. Besides, as I argue elsewhere, the known benefits of constitutional government in our tradition—the separation of powers, the rights of minorities, the tolerance of opposition, not to speak of democracy itself—are predicated on territorial jurisdiction of the kind that only a national loyalty can sustain.[8] This does not mean that national loyalty can be easily revived or that cosmopolitan intellectuals can be somehow compelled to embrace it. But maybe our elites would be more reluctant to turn their scorn on the national homeland idea if they were aware of the real cost of losing a specific, localized, law-governed homeland of their own.[9]

Moreover, it could be that the national perspective is more favorable to national security and also to world order than the woolly cosmopolitanism that construes all people everywhere on the model of the armchair liberal. The national perspective encourages realistic assumptions about the sympathies, budgets, energies, and intellects of human beings. It is a direct expression of the limited sympathies and egocentric interests of ordinary people. It is therefore inherently peaceable. For it renounces the attempt to change the constitution or ruling elite of any other state, preferring mutually beneficial agreements among friends, together with implacable deterrence of enemies, in order to safeguard the privileges and the comforts of home.

Finally, the national approach is intrinsically self-correcting. The people of democracies will accept war in the national interest; but only the high-minded minority among them will accept war in the interest of democracy, human rights, or the League of Nations. Of course, that high-minded minority may enjoy priestlike powers of persuasion, sufficient to persuade the majority to join them in a call for war. Nevertheless, electorates quickly respond to realities and begin to call for a change of policy when the war is manifestly not in their interest.

An electorate will in general endorse a declaration of war, however, only if it is persuaded that a real and present threat exists or that war can be undertaken (as in Bosnia) at little real cost to the nation. In World War II, it took Pearl Harbor and the near-simultaneous declaration of war by Germany to persuade President Franklin Roosevelt to do what the national interest by then manifestly required, and it was almost too late. Likewise, President Bill Clinton was aware of the threat posed by Al Qaeda but did nothing other than exercise the presidential prerogative in a way that might alienate the people. Besides, liberals tend to believe that the United States should always open negotiations before using force, even against an enemy that believes in force first, dictatorship thereafter. It took September 11 to persuade the American electorate that the threats to the United States are real.

As that instance showed, democratic electorates are not pacifist. And most patriotic citizens recognize that it is better for the United States to be prepared to confront threats as they arise rather than wait until threats have been translated into action. It is too late now to deter Al Qaeda, and it is undeniable that threats made by lunatics who have no sovereign territory to lose and who use suicide as a weapon are extremely difficult to deter. But these lunatics depend in the last analysis on the states that harbor them, and it is surely a legitimate *casus belli* against another state that it gives protection to your enemy.

When it comes to furnishing a justification for the war in Iraq, however, the national view is at a disadvantage compared with the transnational alternative. If it is really true that Saddam had no weapons of mass destruction, it might well be argued that he presented no danger that could justify the use of force. He may have been a danger to his neighbors, but he was no danger to the United States. This is the kind of argument that is beginning to carry weight with the American and British electorates, most of whom couldn't care whether Iraq itself is ruled by a despot, an elected government, or a family of chimpanzees.

However, to argue in that retrospective way is to misrepresent the kind of reasoning that must precede any decision to go to war. Suppose we are confronted with a state that is manifestly despotic, which is neither a republic nor a law-abiding member of the United Nations, in which people are denied elementary rights, and in which crimes are regularly committed by the ruling power. It has invaded neighboring states without cause, has committed genocide against its own minorities, and seems determined to advance its own interests, whatever the costs to others. The state nevertheless claims a voice in the UN, endeavoring to influence policy and international law in order to perpetuate and enhance its power and to tie the hands of its principal enemies.

Suppose that this state makes threatening noises against the United States and its allies, and suppose that intelligence that we have no reason to doubt gives grounds for fearing its ultimate purpose. Suppose that the United States goes to war intending not to possess the territory or resources of the despotic state but to remove a perceived threat and create the conditions in which local people can decide for themselves on their form of government.

Would it be right for the United States to go to war against my hypothetical despotism? I can envisage circumstances in which the answer, even from the national perspective, would definitely be yes. There is no question of having to prove the existence of weapons of mass destruction or anything else beyond the known facts about the despotism's past behavior. Of course, the intelligence that prompted the war may have been incomplete or erroneous. But we should remember that actions are justified by their motives, not by their unforeseeable effects—else who should 'scape whipping?

## NOTES

1. On this point, see the evidence presented by Christopher Booker and Richard North in *The Great Conspiracy* (London: Continuum, 2003).

2. Immanuel Kant, *Perpetual Peace*, in *Kant: Political Writings*, 2nd ed., ed. Hans Reiss, trans. H. B. Nisbet (Cambridge: Cambridge University Press, 1991).

3. See Kant, *Perpetual Peace*, 99f., where Kant gives one of several definitions, none of which exactly coincides with any other but all of which point in the same direction.

4. Ibid., 113.

5. Ibid.

6. Report by Claude Hankes-Drielsma to the U.S. Congress, April 21, 2004.

7. The case of *al-muhajiroun* is now sufficiently notorious—see John Marks and Caroline Cox, *The "West," Islam and Islamism* (London: Civitas, 2003); and my *The West and the Rest* (Wilmington, DE: ISI Books, 2002). It is only one case of many, however, all of which illustrate what happens to citizenship when it is detached from the national idea. It is bought and sold like a forged passport, to become a tax on other people's loyalty.

8. See my *The Need for Nations* (London: Civitas, 2003).

9. This statement is not to imply that all left intellectuals are antipatriots or unable to see the dangers and the self-deceptions of the cosmopolitan idea. The tradition of left patriotism counts many distinguished names among its proponents, notably George Orwell (perhaps the founding father) and, in the American context, James Schaar (*Legitimacy in the Modern State* [New Brunswick, NJ: Transaction Books, 1981) and Maurizio Viroli (*For Love of Country: An Essay on Patriotism and Nationalism* [Oxford: Clarendon, 1995]).

# 6

# Just War against an "Outlaw" Region

MEHDI MOZAFFARI

Outlaw states are aggressive and dangerous; all peoples are safer and more secure if such states change, or are forced to change, their ways. Otherwise, they deeply affect the international climate of power and violence.

John Rawls, *The Law of Peoples*

The Kantian-inspired democratic peace theory is based on a simple and powerful idea that democracy in itself is a peace-generating leitmotiv. The universality of this theoretical assumption continues to be the subject of lively debates among scholars. Some argue that liberals should exercise restraint when contemplating war or the use of force *regardless* of the regime type of the adversary,[1] others admit that liberal democratic societies have often engaged in war against nondemocratic states, but since 1800, firmly established liberal societies have not fought one another.[2] My purpose in this essay is not to add further to an already fairly crowded domain.[3] Rather, the inquiry here consists of outlining and assessing the liberal grounds for intervention and war against a nonliberal country/regime/region.

According to John Rawls, there are five different categories of peoples: (1) reasonable liberal peoples, (2) decent peoples, (3) outlaw states, (4) societies burdened by unfavorable conditions, and (5) benevolent absolutisms. In this essay, the focus is on reasonable liberal peoples' policies toward outlaw states and the specification of the conditions and justifications for launching war against them. My aim is to apply perspectives from John Rawls's classic work, *The Law of Peoples*, to the understanding of the war against the regime of Saddam Hussein and broadly to the whole idea of democratization of the greater Middle East. What is novel in the approach is that Rawls's perspectives are applied to the larger problem of what might be called "outlaw regions." In this case, the goal of liberal states is self-defense not simply against a lone outlaw state such as Iraq but against the entire region of the Middle East, which is characterized by what Karl Marx referred to as "oriental despotisms" representing a regional threat to world peace and stability.

## ON DEMOCRATIC WAR AGAINST AN OUTLAW STATE

Democratic peace theory authorizes liberal and well-ordered peoples to go to war against outlaw states, or, as Rawls puts it, "what measures liberal peoples or decent peoples—may justifiably take to defend themselves against them."[4] Liberal and well-ordered peoples' principles are based on liberty, equality, love of peace, and toleration. The principles of outlaw states are in diametrical opposition to the principles of liberal and decent peoples. It should be noted that Rawls, who built his theoretical edifice on the idea of "peoples," significantly (and intentionally) avoids applying the appellation of "people" to describe an outlaw state. Instead, he uses the term *state*, which in his understanding is not a moral actor, whereas liberal *people*s are firmly attached to political and moral conceptions of right and justice.

Departing from a general principle, Rawls emphasizes that "no state has a right to war in the pursuit of its *rational*, as opposed to its *reasonable*, interest."[5] Only in self-defense do the well-ordered peoples have the right to go to war (*jus ad bellum*). More specifically, Rawls requires that "when a liberal society engages in war in self-defence, it does so to protect and preserve the basic freedom of its citizens and its constitutionally democratic political institutions. Indeed, a liberal society cannot justly require natural resources, much less to win power and empire."[6] Consequently, a war that has the purpose of promoting territorial, financial, or economic interests or an increase in power cannot be supported by liberal-democratic theory. Liberal and well-ordered peoples are also restricted to be respecting rules in conduct of war (*jus in bello*).[7]

After a brief presentation of Rawls's thesis on war against an outlaw state, we move to an elaboration of the main characteristics of Middle East societies as well as the Muslim world and consider how these characteristics have motivated the military interventions of the United States.

## ON DEMOCRATIC WAR AGAINST AN OUTLAW REGION

While Kant's view on international society is based on *states*, Rawls, in his ideal theory, prefers *peoples* as units for inquiry. However, there exist some situations in which neither "state" nor "peoples" constitute the appropriate designation. For instance, if the general behavior of a region or perhaps a large community of peoples closely corresponds to what characterizes the behavior of an outlaw state, should we still talk about "state" or "peoples"? Or is it more accurate to talk about outlaw regions (e.g., the Middle East)? Labeling the Middle East an outlaw region appears problematic and certainly provocative. My motivation in discussing outlaw states, as was Rawls's, is purely academic.

As a point of departure, considering the Middle East (with some exceptions) as an outlaw region provides a more accurate theoretical construction than those of states or peoples. The following are my main arguments:

· The Middle East is effectively an outlaw region.
· The US-led Coalition's war against Saddam's regime in Iraq can be considered a liberal, humanitarian, and entirely *reasonable* war that was intended to foster a process of democratization and to incorporate states in the Middle East increasingly into the Society of Peoples.

## THE MIDDLE EAST: A STATIC AND DANGEROUS REGION

Stagnation and backwardness, especially when supported by dictatorial power, is a calamity in and of itself, but it cannot be a justification to launch a military intervention, unless the regional situation represents a concrete and immediate danger to liberal-democratic peoples. Is this the case of the Middle East?

The Middle East is the world's most static region. Since the Islamic revolution in Iran in 1979 and until the fall of Saddam's regime in 2003, nothing has substantially changed in this region. Meanwhile, the entire world has gone through tremendous transformations. The Cold War has ended, the Soviet empire disintegrated, apartheid is finished, and all of Europe has become democratic. In Latin America, democracy is replacing military dictatorships; communist China is becoming capitalist; and so on forth. In the Middle East, however, non-democratic and brutal regimes continue their domination. Israel and

Lebanon are the only democratic countries in the region, though the former is an occupying power and the latter is a confessional democracy. Many had hoped that the Oslo and Washington arrangements of 1993 would bring a real change in the region. The opposite has happened. The world was expecting that the end of the Gulf War in 1991 would lead to a "new world order." Nothing in this direction happened. In Saudi Arabia and in the sheikhdoms of the Persian Gulf, tribalism and discrimination of all kinds (religious, political, gender, and ethnic) continue. In Iran, when Mohammed Khatami was elected president in 1997, a large majority of Iranians had hoped that this event would change the Iranian situation and that the reform movement would prevail. The result was catastrophic. Under the first presidency of Khatami, assassination of intellectuals and members of the opposition was continued by agents of the Ministry of Intelligence. In 2001, Iranians gave him a second chance. He spoiled it dramatically. In Syria, Bashar al-Asad succeeded his autocratic father, and the Baath old guard is continuing its absolute control over the destiny of the country. In Jordan, the young Abdullah II became king after the elimination of his uncle, Prince Hassan, by the late king Hussein. In Egypt, since 1981, President Hosni Mubarak reigns over the land of the pharaohs. In Israel and in Palestine, the vicious circle of occupation, resistance, violence, and terrorism is becoming a part of the daily life without any real solution in sight. In this situation, the continuation of a false sense of "stability" that is perpetuating stagnation is threatening the world's security.

There are two sorts of stability: mechanic and dynamic. The former refers to dictatorial stability and the latter to democratic stability. Rawls talks of "stability as a balance of forces" and "stability for right reasons."[8] *Dictatorial stability* applies to a situation where order is established by force, terror, and systematic intimidation and where there is no substantial free adherence of the population to the regime. Because of the lack of free support of the population and the lack of genuinely democratic control over political decisions, such stability leads to an arbitrary foreign policy. Great issues such as war and peace, cooperation and conflict, are decided by either a single person or a limited nonelected group. Dictatorial stability seems robust on the surface but is, at its core, actually quite fragile. There is no political flexibility or interaction with any rival forces. Under conditions of dictatorial stability, accountability is an alien practice, and responsibility remains hidden and unquestionable.

*Democratic stability* refers to a situation where order is established on the basis of the population's free participation in the political process. Decisions on foreign policy are made after a careful deliberation between the responsible and elected authorities. Under conditions of democratic stability, political flexibility is high, and the entire construction constantly interacts with the rival forces. Democratic stability appears fragile on the surface, but in reality it is a robust construction that is able to react prudently and adequately to both internal and external shocks. Democratic stability is a responsible order where transparency is required.

Middle Eastern stability prior to September 11, 2001, was and still is a mechanical and a dictatorial stability. Until 9/11, the situation was *grosso modo* bearable for the United States and other Western countries. To them, this stability was profitable, too. As President George W. Bush said, "For decades, free nations tolerated oppression in the Middle East for the sake of stability. In practice, this approach brought little stability, and much oppression. So I have changed this policy."[9] The radical change in US policy is due to the tragic events of 9/11. These events were, in reality, the last straw that broke Americans' backs. September 11 came after a series of events during two decades in which American and Western citizens, embassies, and installations had been targets for terrorist activities: in Tehran, Beirut, Paris, Nairobi, Dar es-Salaam, Luxor, Cairo, and many other places worldwide (Argentina, Indonesia, the Philippines, etc.).

September 11, 2001, represents for the Middle East what November 9, 1989, represented for the Eastern European countries. On one important point, though, these two major events are different. The stability that governed in the Eastern European region was of the dictatorial type imposed by the USSR. As part of a dependent region, the Eastern European countries did not independently represent a threat to the Western European countries or to the United States. The real threat came from the USSR. At that time, NATO had a single rival and interlocutor: Moscow. In the Middle East, however, the situation is completely different. In this region, there is no superpower equivalent to that of the USSR, which, by itself, can make comprehensive decisions about regional or global security. Furthermore, there is no single clear interlocutor but several hostile ones. The entire region is fragmented among small and large states; all are nondemocratic and without any cohesive political constructions. Existing regional associations such as the Arab League or the Gulf Cooperation Council (GCC) are far from being unified institutions. The lack of centralized institutions or a powerful state in this region makes impossible any compromise, any deal, or any political opening that could ensure a durable pattern of stability. The protracted political stagnation, on the one side, and the great danger that this situation contains for the world's peace and stability, on the other, are two factors that make political change in the Middle East urgent.

One should probably ask why, precisely, the Middle Eastern and the Muslim world at large are threatening the security of the world, while, in terms of casualties, other parts of the world, Africa in particular, dramatically exceed the number of casualties brought about by the Middle East. More than one million people were massacred in Rwanda and Burundi in the 1990s. Each year, millions of people die of hunger, AIDS, and other diseases in Africa. Despite the cruelty of the facts, the rude reality is that the African tragedy is primarily limited in scope to Africa itself and has limited contagious effect over other parts of the world. The world political, social, and economic situation is not significantly affected by the African tragedy. This is not the case for the Middle East. An explosion in Jerusalem, or a quick Israeli military expedition in Syria, or Saddam Hussein's reluctance to cooperate with international inspection agencies has an immediate impact in Tokyo, New York, and elsewhere. The impact on oil prices in the world market is even more dramatic. Furthermore, experience has shown that great events in the Middle East can directly affect the results of American presidential elections. The case of President Jimmy Carter's defeat and Ronald Reagan's victory in 1980 was largely a consequence of the hostage crisis in the US embassy in Tehran. The pro-Arab policy of President George H. W. Bush is often mentioned as being a major cause of his defeat in 1992. The considerable impact of the crisis in the Middle East on the presidential election of November 2004 seems obvious.

Based on these facts, it is legitimate to consider the Middle East as a "particular" region with a special potential to affect the world's peace and security.

Moreover, during the last three decades, the Middle East has been and still is the world's greatest producer and exporter of oil, terrorism, and emigration. It is a well-established fact that not only are the world's largest oil reserves found in the Muslim world but that also the large majority of worldwide terrorist actions are undertaken by people calling themselves Muslims. Furthermore, the majority of world emigrants are Muslims. These three elements together constitute what might be called the *Islamic triad*. In this situation, allowing a group of autocrats to repress their own population, to violate the basic human rights, and to produce global terrorism is not tolerable. In justification of their acts, some Middle Eastern autocrats evoke Islamic, tribal, and national values and particularities (*Islamocracy*). It is highly objectionable that all these values and particularities are always interpreted in favor of repression and arbitration, and never in the direction of freedom, justice, and political plurality. Stoning, cutting hands, feet, and ears off, and committing other acts of torture and terrorism do not belong to the culture of humanity in the twenty-first century. Other autocrats of the region use the threat of Islamists as a pretext for their repressive policies. This is a false argument. Precisely, it is the very nature of these regimes that is producing Islamism.

The general backwardness of the Arab societies is confirmed by the United Nations Development Programme (UNDP). Consider only a few examples of the UNDP reports: The overall gross domestic product (GDP) of the entire region at the end of the twentieth century (US$604 billion) was little more than that of Spain (US$559 billion). After the oil boom of the 1970s, most of the economies of the Middle East and North Africa either stagnated or declined. One in five Arabs still lives on less than $2 a day. The Arab countries have the lowest level of dire poverty in the world (measured at less than $1 a day). The entire Arab world translates about three hundred books annually, one-fifth of the number translated in Greece alone.[10]

Middle Eastern particularity is enhanced by its complexity. The complexity essentially emanates from the fact that in the Middle East, instead of one or two elements blocking or hindering progress, a number of closely interrelated elements coexist. In such a situation, it is hard to identify the "cause" and distinguish it from the "effect." Is imperialism and constant external interference in this region the cause of backwardness, or is the latter the cause of the former? Is Islam an obstacle to political modernization, or is its political activation in the form of Islamism caused by other factors? We must consider a number of factors in order to better understand the Middle Eastern situation. The most important, from my point of view, are (1) the Asiatic mode of production (or nonproduction) and persistence of the rentier economy, (2) Oriental despotism, (3) religious obscurantism, and (4) strong external interference.

Historically, these four elements are self-reinforcing and constitute a closed vicious circle. Therefore, the Middle East has not been witnessing any qualitative change consisting of a transition from an undemocratic stage to a more democratic and progressive one. My focus in the rest of this essay is on the first two elements—the Asiatic mode of production and Oriental despotism—not because these are any more important than religious obscurantism or external influence. Rather, these latter two have been discussed extensively elsewhere, and I wish to make an original theoretical contribution here.

## THE ASIATIC MODE OF PRODUCTION THESIS AND THE RENTIER ECONOMY

The Asiatic mode of production (AMP) is a social condition specified by Marx in his historical typology of "modes of production." In Marx's schema, the Asian, ancient, feudal, and modern bourgeois modes of production may be designated as successive and progressive epochs of socioeconomic order. In Marx's view, "the mode of production of material life conditions the social, political and intellectual life-process in general."[11] In *The German Ideology*, he specifies the mode of production as follows: "the way in which men produce their means of subsistence depends first of all on the nature of the actual means they find in existence and have to reproduce." He adds that the mode of production is a definite form through which humans express their mode of life.[12] This statement is reminiscent of the famous statement of Ibn Khaldun (1332–1406), a native of North Africa and the author of *Prolegomena/ The Muqaddimah*. Departing from a general principle, Ibn Khaldun states that "differences of condition among people are the result of the different ways in which they make their living. Social organization enables them to co-operate toward that end to start with the simple necessities of life, before they get to conveniences and luxuries."[13]

The AMP represents the longest and the most stubborn mode of production. This distinction is due "to the fundamental principle on which it is based, that is, that the individual does not become independent of the community; that the circle of production is self-sustaining, unity of agriculture and craft manufacture, etc."[14] In the contemporary Middle East, the AMP is essentially expressed through the rentier economy. A *rentier economy* is defined as an economy in which the rent situation predominates. Second, a rentier economy is an economy that relies on substantial external rent. Third, in a rentier state, only a few are engaged in the generation of this rent (wealth), the majority being only involved in its distribution or utilization. Fourth, as a corollary of the role of the few, in a rentier state, the government is the principal recipient of the external rent in the economy.[15]

In his well-documented study "Does Oil Hinder Democracy?" Michael L. Ross demonstrates that more than half of the government's revenues in Saudi Arabia, Bahrain, the United Arab Emirates, Oman, Kuwait, Qatar, and Libya have, at times, come from the sale of oil. The governments of Jordan, Syria, and Egypt variously earn large locational rents from payments for pipeline crossings, transit fees, and passage through the Suez Canal. Workers' remittances have been an important source of foreign exchange in Egypt, Yemen, Syria, Lebanon, Tunisia, Algeria, and Morocco, although these rents go (at least initially) to private actors, not the state. The foreign aid that flows to Israel, Egypt, and Jordan may also be considered a type of economic rent.[16]

Ross has explored the alleged link between oil exports and authoritarian rule following three causal mechanisms: the rentier effect, the repression effect, and the modernization effect. Referring to Beblawi and Luciani, Ross states that the rentier effect "is through what might be called a 'taxation effect.' It suggests that when governments derive sufficient revenues from the sale of oil, they are likely to tax their populations less heavily or not at all, and the public in turn will be less likely to demand accountability from—and representation in—their government."[17]

The repression effect is the second causal mechanism that transforms a rentier state into a "rentier absolutist state." The reason for this transformation originates from the power of repression. There is no doubt that "citizens in resource-rich states may want democracy as much as citizens elsewhere, but resource wealth may allow their governments to spend more on internal security and so block the population's democratic aspirations."[18]

The final and third explanation is derived from modernization theory. In this connection, the question is about whether the linkage between development and democracy is due to wealth per se. The answer is no. If democracy automatically resulted from wealth alone, then Kuwait and Libya would be model democracies, which is not the case. Ross believes that rentier repression and modernization effects are largely complementary. The rentier effect focuses on the government's use of fiscal measures to keep the public politically demobilized, the repression effect stresses the government's use of force to keep the public demobilized, and the modernization effect looks at social forces that may keep the public demobilized. All three explanations, or any combination of them, may be simultaneously valid.[19]

Ross's four findings confirm four conclusions. First, oil does hurt democracy, particularly in poor states. We assume that by "rich states" Ross means "productive states" or at least states where wealth is predominantly based on no-rentier production. Second, the harmful influence of oil is not restricted to the Middle East. Oil wealth has probably made democratization harder in states such as Indonesia, Malaysia, Mexico, and Nigeria. Third, nonfuel mineral wealth also impedes democratization. Finally, there is support for at least three causal mechanisms that link oil and authoritarianism.[20]

Related to the rentier economy, the taxation system or the lack of such system constitutes a major obstacle to a democratization process. It is a confirmed fact that taxation has played a major role in the fall of despotism in Europe and the rise of democratic regimes. This was the case in the French and English revolutions as well as in Sweden, Denmark, and other European countries, often behind the slogan "no taxation without representation." In the Middle East, where the rentier economy is dominant and a personal taxation system is either nonexistent or quite weak and disarticulated, the slogan would be "no representation without taxation." Consequently, when citizens pay little or no tax and where the state is financially independent from citizens' contributions, for those kings, ayatollahs, generals, and sheikhs with financial resources, "representation" could be, in the best case, nothing else than procedural and cosmetic or, in the worst case, nonexistent.

## THE THESIS OF ORIENTAL DESPOTISM

Oriental despotism is perhaps the oldest thesis on the situation in the Middle East. Aristotle said that "barbarians are more servile by nature than Greeks, and Asians are more servile than Europeans; hence they endure despotic rule without protest. Such monarchies are like tyrannies, but they are secure because they are hereditary and legal."[21] Niccolò Machiavelli in *The Prince* puts this crucial question forward: Why did the kingdom of Darius, conquered by Alexander, not rebel against the successors of Alexander at his death? Machiavelli's answer is clear:

> I answer that the principalities of which one has record are found to be governed in two different ways: either by a prince, with a body of servants, who assist him to govern the kingdom as ministers by his favour and permission; or by a prince and barons, who hold that dignity by antiquity of blood and not by the grace of the prince. Such barons have states and their

own subjects, who recognize them as lords and hold them in natural affection. Those states that are governed by a prince and his servants hold their prince in more consideration, because in all the country there is no one who is recognized as superior to him, and if they yield obedience to another they do it as to a minister and official, and they do not bear him any particular affection.[22]

Charles de Montesquieu also thought that the lack of stable private property or hereditary nobility is derived from Oriental despotism. Moreover, Oriental despotism did not rest merely on an abject fear but also on an evasive equality among its subjects—for all were alike in their common subjection to the lethal caprices of the despot. For Montesquieu, "men are all equal in a republican state; they are also equal in a despotic state; in the first, because they are everything; in the second, because they are nothing."[23]

Marx establishes a close relation between the Asiatic mode of production and the Oriental despotism. He states that "the despot here appears as the father of all the numerous lesser communities, thus realising the common unity of all. . . . Oriental despotism therefore appears to lead to a legal absence of property."[24]

The most famous theorist of Oriental despotism, however, remains Karl Wittfogel. Wittfogel "took Marxism as a starting point, not as a sacred text, and applied it to non-Western societies."[25] Wittfogel's thesis is on the relation between Oriental despotism and what he calls "the hydraulic problematic." Wittfogel emphasizes the importance of water in the rise of Oriental despotism. Because hydraulic agriculture needs a division of labor, a kind of bureaucratic system becomes a necessity. This situation will lead to the rise of a powerful leader who has double qualities: he is a great "engineer" and a "priest" at the same time. Therefore, in Wittfogel's view, the origin of Oriental despotism lies in the historically particular hydraulic condition in Oriental societies.

Based on various works on the subject, Perry Anderson crystallizes Oriental despotism's main characteristics as follows: "state property of land; lack of juridical restraints; religious substitution for law; absence of hereditary nobility; servile social equality; isolated village communities; agrarian predominance over industry; public hydraulic works; torrid climate environment; and historical immutability."[26] Anderson concludes that "the political history of the Orient was thus essentially cyclical: it contained no dynamic or cumulative development. The result was the secular inertia and immutability of Asia, once it had attained its own peculiar level of civilization."[27]

Finally, Oriental despotism is not a uniform construction; it takes various forms and different shapes. Throughout their history and to the present day, Middle Eastern societies have been characterized by the following forms of Oriental despotism: monarchical (Jordan and Morocco), tribal (Saudi Arabia, Kuwait, and other emirates); religious (Iran and Afghanistan under the Taliban); and military (Algeria, Egypt, Libya, Pakistan, Tunisia, Syria, and Yemen).

The persistence of Oriental despotism and the hidden instability that characterizes it comprise reason enough to argue that the Middle East represents a dangerous region that is threatening the world's security. It is implausible to expect that any radical change in the direction of democracy and peace within the Middle East should occur as a result of internal forces. Therefore, an external benign intervention with the right intention is necessary and justified. Now, the question is as follows: Are the motivations and intentions of the United States liberal or material?

## ARE US MOTIVATIONS LIBERAL OR MATERIAL?

A liberal war is a war of self-defense. When a liberal-democratic state is a victim of aggression or is seriously threatened, it has a right to launch war against an outlaw state in accordance with the international legal system. The same principle must be valid in relations between an outlaw region and a liberal-democratic community (e.g., the West).

It seems obvious that the United States had no territorial ambition in Iraq. The colonial period is over, and colonialism has, in any case, never represented the main trend in US policy. The most fundamental criticism against the war on Iraq consists of the United States' alleged intention to acquire or at least to control Iraqi oil, in particular, and the Middle Eastern oil, more generally. This view is a widespread belief among large numbers of people, especially within the Middle East itself.

This belief is baseless. Let me mention briefly only a few facts among many others. First, the United States is already in control of the main resources of oil (Saudi Arabia, Kuwait, the Emirates, the Caspian Sea, etc.).

Second, other big oil producers such as Iran and Iraq (under Saddam Hussein) have repeatedly sought cooperation with US oil companies. In the mid-1990s, Exxon, a giant American oil company, nearly concluded a very lucrative contract with the Iranian national oil company. However, the contract was never finalized—not because of Iranian reluctance but because of a decision by President Bill Clinton that, in fact, ordered Exxon to back off. According to two presidential executive orders (12957 and 13059), investing more than $40 million in Iranian oil industries was declared punishable. These orders still remain in force. Similarly, under Saddam's regime, high-ranking Iraqi officials (e.g., Tariq Aziz, the then–acting prime minister) invited US citizens to take part in Iraqi oil concessions. Again, it was the US administration that declined the Iraqi invitation.

Third, in the present world, it is not the United States or other industrial countries that decide on the price and the level of production. Decisions on these matters are made by the Organization of Petroleum Exporting Countries (OPEC) and non-OPEC individual countries.

Fourth, oil today constitutes the principal financial resource for the Middle Eastern oil-producing states. The urgent and constant need for oil is independent from the political identity of persons who will be in charge in this region. The shah or ayatollahs, Saddam or non-Saddam, King Fahad and even bin Laden—all of them are heavily dependent on oil for their income. Therefore, there is no need to put military pressure or to "colonize"' these countries to assure the production and circulation of oil.

Finally, the financial cost of the Iraq war is the best evidence against the alleged lucrative intention of "war for oil." Until the summer of 2004, the United States spent more than $100 billion on war and reconstruction in Iraq. Since Iraq's oil revenue in recent years has been only approximately $12 billion per year, how many years does it take to cover the United States' expenses during only a single year of the war?

Consequently, it is fair to conclude that the oil issue was not the real motivation behind the US-led military intervention in Iraq. It is equally fair to claim that even if oil has played a role in the war, it has not been the primary or the major motivation of Americans. The United States has, of course, an interest in the Middle East, but this interest is not of an immediate material nature.

Without the oil argument, it appears that the war in Iraq is a *strategic* war against the deep roots of terrorism, while the war in Afghanistan can be seen mostly as an *operational* war, a kind of "theater of operations." At first glance, the motivations of war against Afghanistan look different from the motivations of war against Iraq. The internal logic, however, is the same. It is true that bin Laden used and abused the territory of Afghanistan for the preparation of his devastating terrorist activities, but the Taliban's rudimentary regime, despite its brutal and primitive policy, did not as such represent a danger to world security. The real roots of both terrorism and Islamism were to be found elsewhere. They were and still are in the Middle East. Consequently, to eradicate the roots of global terrorism and its ideological basis required a radical change of the Middle East as a whole. Ironically, Saddam's Iraq was not a primary source of terrorism or Islamism. How, then, to explain or justify a war against Saddam's regime? It is not an easy question insofar as it raises a large number of questions related to subjects such as international security, international law, ethics and morality, and humanitarian intervention. But, if we admit to the dangerous and unbearable character of the current Middle East, we have at the same time to accept the obligation and the necessity to promote change in this region.

In this connection, the choice of Iraq is motivated mainly by two factors: the highly suspicious character and activities of Saddam's regime and the element of feasibility. There can be raised no doubt about the *aggressiveness* of the regime of Saddam Hussein (the war against Iran, 1980–1988, and the occupation of Kuwait, 1990–1991). Neither is there any doubt about the possession and utilization of weapons of mass destruction by the Iraqi regime (against Iranians and even against the Iraqi population). Furthermore, there was no doubt on the noncompliance of Saddam's regime with the United Nations resolutions. However, a major question remains: Did Saddam's regime represent an imminent threat to the world security *after 9/11*? This question is disputable and subject to different interpretations. Based on the knowledge that we have acquired after the occupation of Iraq, the war does not appear to be justified on the liberal grounds of self-defense. But, if we put the Iraqi question in a larger picture (the greater Middle East), admit that the whole area is a danger to its own population and the world, and consider that a total and radical change in this area is a necessity for general peace, then the war against Saddam's regime can be justified. The element of feasibility must be considered. At the particular moment in 2003, a war against Saudi Arabia (where the majority of terrorists came from) or against the Islamist regime of the ayatollah in Iran was not feasible. The war against Iraq was.

Having made the case for war, there can be hesitation in calling to account the absolute wrongdoing of the US and UK armies in various aspects of the conduct of the war. On conduct in war, Rawls identifies six imperative principles that liberal societies must obey:

- The aim of a just war waged by a just well-ordered people is a just and lasting peace among peoples, and especially with the people's present enemy;
- Well-ordered peoples do not wage war against each other, but only against non-well-ordered states whose expansionist aims threaten the security and free institutions of well-ordered regimes and bring about the war;
- In the conduct of war, three groups must carefully be distinguished: the outlaw states' leaders and officials, its soldiers, and its civilian population;
- Well-ordered peoples must respect, so far as possible, the human rights of the members of the other side, both civilians and soldiers;
- The well-ordered peoples are by their actions and proclamations, when feasible, to foreshadow during a war both the kind of peace they aim for and the kind of relations they seek; and
- Finally, practical means-end reasoning must always have a restricted role in judging the appropriateness of an action or policy.[28]

In this perspective, torture of prisoners of war under the custody of US and UK armies is not only a clear violation of the Geneva Convention but also a completely immoral contradiction of any liberal and civilized behavior. In this connection, a new and fundamental question arises: Is reprehensible conduct of groups of individuals that have been strongly condemned by the US president, among others, all it takes to disqualify *in principle* (not politically) the real causation of the war? The answer should be, Wrong conduct in war cannot in and of itself alter the right intention and the just cause of the war.

Finally, the aim of democratization of the entire Middle East is evoked as a major justification of the war. As I have explained earlier, I consider the entire Middle Eastern region to be a threat to the security of the world, due to its nondemocratic character as well as its protracted political and social stagnation. On this basis, the democratization of this vast region, stretching from Mauritania to Pakistan, represents an imperative necessity for peace in the world. Now, the question is whether all various countries in this region are what Rawls would refer to as "outlaw states."

Rawls presents a very clear categorization of types of states. Accordingly, the greater Middle East can roughly be seen as consisting of two different types of "peoples/states." The first one is what Rawls calls a "decent state"—he offers us the imaginary example of "Kazanistan." Kazanistan is not aggressive against other peoples; "it honors and respects human rights; and its basic structure contains a decent consultation hierarchy."[29] By "consultation hierarchy," he means "a common good idea of justice."[30] According to this definition, there is no such state in the greater Middle East that corresponds perfectly to Rawls's criteria. The imperfect examples would in different degree be Lebanon, Jordan, Morocco, Tunisia, Oman, Egypt, and Pakistan. All other states (including Iraq under Saddam and Afghanistan under the Taliban) have characteristics that would make them, in Rawls's formation, outlaw states. It is true that frontiers between these two categories and within each of them are blurring (e.g., Libya's recent attempts to shed its outlaw state image).

The United States' strategy toward Kazanistan-type states and more generally toward the whole region represents a policy of the *democratization of the greater Middle East*. Democratization is a painful and violent process. It can originate internally or be stimulated by external intervention. There are five different types of democratization: revolution (the French Revolution of 1789); war (Germany and Japan after World War II); coup d'état (Portugal in 1976); soft transition (Spain after Generalissimo Franco and Eastern European countries after the disintegration of the USSR in 1989–1991); and cloning (Australia, Canada, and New Zealand). The problem in the Middle East is that it has not experienced liberation or democratization in spite of revolutions, coup d'états, or any other force. Paradoxically, the two "tentatively democratic" societies, one in Egypt under the Wafd Party and the other in Iran under Mohammad Mosaddeq in the 1950s, were interrupted. The former was interrupted by a combination of UK interests and corruption of the monarchical system that led to the "revolution" of the Free Officers in July 1952. The latter was interrupted by the CIA's coup against Mosaddeq's democratically elected government in August 1953. Similarly, neither the coup against King Faisal in 1958 and the instauration of the republic in Iraq, nor the Baath coup in Syria by Hafiz al-Asad in 1970, nor even the fall of the regime of the Imams in Yemen in 1962 brought democracy to these countries. The Islamic revolution in Iran in 1979 and the fall of the shah did not produce democracy, either. Even worse, a modernizing dictatorship was in fact replaced by a totalitarian religious regime.

These examples are far from being exhaustive. Despotism in its various forms (tribal, military, religious, and kingship) is the general and invariable trend of the Middle East. Faced with this hopeless and dangerous situation, a liberal external intervention seems to be right and just.

It is in this perspective that President George W. Bush's initiative to the democratization of the greater Middle East must be situated. Already before the war against Iraq, he stated that "the United States will use this moment of opportunity to extend the benefits of freedom across the globe. We will actively work to bring the hope of democracy, development, free markets, and free trade to every corner of the world."[31] In this important text, expanding democracy, prosperity, liberty, and respect for human dignity is accentuated in different formulations that all point in the same direction: changing the world not only to a safer but also to a better place. The National Security Strategy stipulates that "the United States of America is fighting a war against terrorists of global reach. The enemy is not a single political regime or person or religion or ideology."[32]

Furthermore, in one of his speeches, President Bush emphasizes that "we support . . . democracy in the Middle East, because it is a founding principle, and because it is in our interest."[33] He has repeated the same argument in almost every speech he has given since the Iraq war.

In an American paper to the G8 Conference (June 2004), three major approaches have been suggested to combat dictatorship and the lack of human and economic development in the Middle East: promoting democracy and good governance, building a knowledge society, and expanding economic opportunities. A detailed program follows for each of these issues. This program resembles the Marshall Plan offered and implemented in Western Europe after World War II. American projects of democratization of the greater Middle East have been received by scholars such as Amitai Etzioni as an "American fantasy,"[34] by others as a "liberal crusade" or even as a demonstration of "America's revolutionary power."[35] Perhaps the right expression is "a Grotian moment": we feel that something quite different is ongoing, but we do not know what will come out of this ongoing process. This is what Hugo Grotius felt in anticipation of the Westphalia Treaties of 1648, which dramatically shaped the future of international relations and human history.

I started this essay with a quotation of John Rawls. Let me finish it with a quotation of Karl Marx: "England [the United States] has to fulfil a double mission in India [Iraq]: one destructive, the other regenerating the annihilation of old Asiatic society, and laying the material foundations of Western society in Asia [the greater Middle East]."[36]

# NOTES

1. John MacMillan, "Liberalism and the Democratic Peace," *Review of International Studies* 30, no. 2 (April 2004): 179–200.

2. John Rawls, *The Law of Peoples* (Cambridge, MA: Harvard University Press, 1999), 51.

3. Both theses have been challenged; see, for example, Bruce Bueno de Mesquita, James D. Morrow, Randolph M. Siverson, and Alastair Smith, "An Institutional Explanation of the Democratic Peace," *American Political Science Review* 93, no. 4 (December 1999): 791–807.

4. Rawls, *The Law of Peoples*, 5.

5. Ibid., 91.

6. Ibid.

7. Ibid., 94–96.

8. Ibid., 44–45.

9. George W. Bush, "Speech for Peace in the Middle East," University of Southern California, May 10, 2004.

10. Information from United Nations Development Programme, *Arab Human Development Report*, 2002–2003 (New York: Author, 2003).

11. Karl Marx, "A Contribution to the Critique of Political Economy," in *Selected Works of Karl Marx and Frederick Engels* (Moscow: Progress, 1973), 1:503.

12. Karl Marx, *Pre-capitalist Economic Formations*, trans. Jack Cohen (London: Lawrence & Wishart, 1964), 121.

13. Ibn Khaldun, *The Muqaddimah*, trans. Franz Rosenthal (Princeton, NJ: Princeton University Press, 1989), 91.

14. Marx, *Pre-capitalist Economic Formations*, 83.

15. Hossein Mehdavi, "The Pattern and Problems of Economic Development in Rentier States: The Case of Iran," in *Studies in the Economic History of the Middle East*, ed. M. Cook (London: Oxford University Press, 1970), 428; Hazem Beblawi and Giacomo Luciani, *The Rentier State* (London: Croom Helm, 1987), 51–52.

16. Michael Ross, "Does Oil Hinder Democracy?" *World Politics* (April 2001), 329.

17. Ibid., 332.

18. Ibid., 335.

19. Ibid., 337.

20. Ibid., 356–358.

21. Aristotle, *Politics* (Malta: Cambridge University Press, 1994), III:ix, 3.

22. Niccolò Machiavelli, *The Prince/Ruler*, trans. Peter Rodd (London: Bodley Head, 1954), chap. 4.

23. Charles de Montesquieu, *De l'Esprit des Lois* (Paris: Gaimer, 1956), I:81.

24. Marx, *Pre-capitalistic Economic Formations*, 69–70.

25. George Taylor, "Karl Wittfogel," in *International Encyclopedia of Social Sciences* (London: Collier, 1979), 812.

26. Perry Anderson, *Lineages of the Absolutist State* (London: Atlantic Highlands Humanity Press, 1975), 472.

27. Ibid., 483.

28. Rawls, *The Law of Peoples*, 94–97.

29. Ibid., 5.

30. Ibid., 71.

31. George W. Bush, *National Security Strategy* (Washington, D.C.: White House, 2002), preamble.

32. Ibid., 5.

33. George W. Bush, "Remarks by the President at the United States Air Force Academy," June 2, 2004.

34. Amitai Etzioni, *International Herald Tribune*, April 5, 2004.

35. Thomas L. Freidman, *International Herald Tribune*, April 3, 2003.

36. Karl Marx, "The Future Results of British Rule in India," *New-York Daily Tribune*, August 8, 1853.

# 7

# Moral Arguments
## Sovereignty, Feasibility, Agency, and Consequences

DANIEL KOFMAN

as it "the wrong war in the wrong place at the wrong time"? Between that view and its diametric opposite are other possibilities—for instance that it was the right war in the right place at the wrong time, or even the wrong war (because conducted inappropriately) in the right place at the right time. Those of us—including myself—who opposed this war because of apprehensions in the vicinity of the latter positions nevertheless often found ourselves more in agreement with the arguments of the architects than the detractors of this war. The antiwar movement seemed preponderantly to rely on outmoded concepts of sovereignty, or an incoherent jumble of agent-relative and consequentialist considerations, or some vague combination of both errors: a biased selection of undesirable consequences of going to war mixed in with an assertion of agent-relative duties not to violate another's sovereignty. If one rejected these arguments but still hesitated to support the war for fear that the stated goals, worthy in themselves, might be too difficult to achieve, then one's practical stance would be affected. One might have doubted whether victory in the form of establishing a stable democracy in Iraq without undue loss of life was achievable, but hate the forces trying to defeat it (the motley alliance of Baathist and Islamist fascists known so reverently in the antiwar movement as "the Iraqi resistance") while hoping against hope that contrary to one's doubts the goals could be achieved.

In what follows, I shall examine these two main areas of normative controversy giving rise to confusion in the antiwar movement: rights and duties concerning sovereignty, and agent-restrictive or consequentialist considerations.

I begin with the argument from sovereignty. There are variations, but the general thrust is that since Saddam's Iraq was a sovereign state, it had the right not to be invaded regardless of its internal practices. At the time of invasion, Iraq was not violating international law in any way that could justify invasion, itself among the most egregious illegal acts. In other words, the savagery of the Baathist regime, however objectionable (as antiwar spokesmen hastened to add), could not provide a reason to violate international war by invading and overthrowing a sovereign UN-member state. The myriad variations on this argument need not be examined in detail at this point. More significant, I believe, is that the entire family of such arguments relies on a mindset that is still deeply entrenched but dependent on no more than contingent historical circumstances having little current normative force. It is often difficult to argue against an entrenched mind-set with its constellation of seemingly obvious intuitions. To try somewhat to undermine those intuitions, then, I would like to borrow a quaint philosopher's device: the construction of an imaginary world similar to ours but differing in the relevant contingent alternative, in this case the emergence of a different—and I would suggest more just—international system.

Let us imagine, then, in a very distant galaxy, a planet remarkably like our own. So similar is it, in fact, that it has a geography, flora, fauna, and evolutionary history nearly identical to that of Earth. *Homo sapiens* emerged at the same time in their evolutionary history as ours, the same ancient civilizations bearing the same names rose up and fell, the same roles and characters—pharaohs, soothsayers, kings, conquerors, prophets, philosophers, peasants, slave owners and slaves—crossed swords, preached, taught, and toiled. Sometime in their late medieval period, however, subtle differences from our history emerged. Their science and Enlightenment made inroads farther and faster, such that what we consider our scientific revolution blossomed for the Twin-Earthians already in their late Renaissance: their Galileo, Boyle, Newton, Descartes, and Leibniz lived over a century earlier, as did their Hobbes, Locke, Paine, Rousseau, and Voltaire. In fact, their historians don't distinguish between the Renaissance and the Enlightenment, the two having so overlapped. Even while the Reformation and Counter-Reformation raged across their Europe, modern secularizing and liberalizing tendencies were consolidating their forces, culminating in a French Revolution 150 years earlier than our own.

The comparative histories of Twin Earth and Earth is a fascinating field, but we shall restrict ourselves here to a single phenomenon: the emergence of international state systems. On both planets, something referred to as "sovereign states" began to emerge in the late Renaissance as outgrowths of absolute monarchies and free cities. Their Jean Bodin, as ours, wrote sixteenth-century apologies for the new absolutism, which our Saddam Hussein, manacled and dragged before an Iraqi judge in June 2004, unwittingly paraphrased in retorting to his accusers, "If Saddam made the laws, how can he violate them?" In Bodin's words, "It is the distinguishing mark of the sovereign that he cannot in any way be subject to the commands of another, for it is he who makes law for the subject, abrogates laws already made, and amends obsolete law."[1]

This view was soon transformed by the conception, first urged in both worlds by John Locke and others and eventually entrenching itself in the liberal societies of both planets, that "the people" are sovereign and that those who govern hold merely "fiduciary power," power held in trust that the people can withdraw when that trust is broken. Government officials were no longer automatically above the law, and whatever special entitlements they might still enjoy required justification in terms of their ultimate service to the people. More interesting for present purposes, however, is how the two planets developed their distinct concepts of state sovereignty and their attitudes to those nations on each planet that remained outside the ambit of these liberalizing trends.

On our planet, the conception developing out of the absolutist monarchies and free cities was reinforced by the great compromise that terminated the unprecedented bloodletting of the religious wars of the Counter-Reformation. Although our international system is sometimes named after the Peace of Westphalia (1648) that ended the Thirty Years War, that treaty did little more than consolidate a system already well entrenched in Europe. A more important turning point was the principle adopted earlier in the Peace of Augsburg (1555) that allowed the rulers of each little princedom of the Holy Roman Empire to establish the religion for that state (*cuius regio, eius religio*)[2] free of external interference. Bodin's earlier-cited notion of unlimited sovereignty, intended to lend support to the monarchy in its *internal* struggle against competing feudal powers, became oddly fused in our planet's development with the Augsburgian-Westphalian conceptions of *external* sovereignty: that each government was free from external interference to adopt the religion and more generally the style of governance of its choice. While the internal notion of absolutism gradually gave way to liberalizing trends within most European states and beyond, the external absolutism of nonintervention became the norm of what our neorealists love to call the "anarchic" international system. There were, of course, historical challenges to this, notably the Napoleonic ideal of exporting Enlightenment at the point of a bayonet.[3] But until the genocides of the twentieth century spawned the development of human rights law and the notion of peremptory duties of intervention to prevent genocide, and except for these duties, the absolutist nature of our sovereign state system has held remarkable sway.

Consider now how things developed on Twin Earth. Hardly had their religious wars begun when both sides of those conflicts found themselves under greater pressure from liberal secular forces. Before any norms between states were established, liberals seized power in the major states of Europe and demanded of others to liberalize or else. Instead of treaties ending religious wars by ratifying noninterference between different illiberal regimes, as on our planet, new wars erupted between liberal and nonliberal states, culminating in the much-heralded Treaty of Marianne of 1648. A central provision of this treaty determined that only liberal democratic states meeting specified "natural rights" standards enjoyed rights of nonintervention; these states, in turn, bore peremptory duties to intervene in states falling significantly short of these standards, if necessary by overthrowing their regimes.

It may be worth mentioning that on both planets a sort of political identity called "the left" developed in the advanced liberal states and lasted well into the twenty-first century, albeit (especially on our planet) in increasingly frivolous and self-indulgent form. While it continued to derive a lingering prestige from its historical association with earlier serious thinkers and movements who had sought deeper forms of social justice than that offered by liberal capitalism, especially in the heyday of industrialization, the identity became too often associated with fashionable (and frequently affluent) youths whose most consistent conviction seemed to be that they were better than everyone else, especially their parents and political leaders. There were, however, some differences across the galaxies. On both planets, twenty-first century activists, wearing woolen hats imitating white pop stars imitating black gangsta rappers imitating or sometimes emulating the gangsters themselves, denounced "the Bush-Blair alliance," but not for the same reasons. On Earth the activists chanted "Hey hey! Hey ho! We won't fight for Texaco," rhythmically more hip-hop than the old march beat of an earlier generation's "Hey hey, LBJ, how many kids did you kill today?" Suppose in discussion you managed to corner one into admitting that overthrowing Saddam could actually have certain long-term benefits, not least for ordinary Iraqis; suppose you reminded him that had his government followed the advice of Tony Benn, Noam Chomsky, Edward Said, and their other gurus, then Milošević, the Taliban, and arguably Stalin's and Brezhnev's progeny in Eastern Europe would still be in power. Suppose, finally, that your interlocutor happened to be a cut above the average "It's for the Iraqi people to do it themselves" ilk. You were still bound to have flung in your face something akin to "First Afghanistan, now Iraq. So who's next? Syria? North Korea? Iran? Where will it all end?" If these illegal interventions are permitted to continue, the implication seems to be, pretty soon, horror of horrors, no murderously repressive regimes might remain.

On Twin Earth, by contrast, the leaders of the West are regularly denounced for leaving repressive regimes alone. Chanting "Saddam is not the only scum," left-wing activists demand to know why their governments refuse to confront the Burmese (Myanmar) regime and why China gets away not only with propping up Myanmar and North Korea in defiance of US-backed UN sanctions but with failure to introduce its own democratic reform. Their political "right," like ours, ogle the fastest-growing, potentially massive market of the Far East and explain that economic growth will inevitably bring political reform in its wake. Unlike our "left," however, theirs denounce this reasoning, pointing out that similar excuses were made to oppose sanctions against apartheid South Africa and that capitalism has often done very well, thank you, under fascism (or communism, toward which their left has been less sentimental than ours).

Most interestingly, while their left call Bush and Blair hypocritical for not supporting more regime change around the globe, as long required by Twin-Earthian international law, their chief villains are the European governments, especially the French and German, denounced as reactionary outlaws and "rogue powers" not only for having opposed regime change in Iraq but for being consistently much softer than the United States and Britain on Myanmar, China, North Korea, Iran,

Syria, the Congo—in fact, virtually wherever vicious regimes dwell. Of course, on our planet, too, the left is bothered by what they take to be hypocritical selectivity, but their counterparts on Twin Earth don't make the outlandish inference of our activists that no intervention is better than hypocritical selectivity. Since regime change of repressive states is the norm on Twin Earth and regarded as the foundation of the liberal order, "progressiveness" in international affairs is measured by compliance with this norm, "reactionariness" by noncompliance; support for *some* coercive liberalization of vicious regimes is considered more progressive than not supporting any.[4]

Even without this imaginary comparative history, one might find aspects of the opposition to the war in Iraq somewhat peculiar. It is nearly comical to observe both philosophical and political anarchists getting themselves all in a tizzy about the possible violation of some international law. (The former include prestigious liberal philosophers who deny that we have any *pro tanto* obligation to obey domestic law; the latter think progressives should smash the state and its bourgeois laws at least as soon as it smashes capitalism.) If anything, one would have thought, the domestic law of democratic societies—deriving from elected representatives, constrained by liberal principle and constitutions, and reviewed by independent judiciary—has considerably more to recommend it by way of obligating individual citizens than any treaty between various states neither necessarily representative nor liberal. (That is true even if one follows H. L. A. Hart in rejecting skepticism about whether "international law," with no legislator and tenuous enforcement, is even law at all.)[5] It is particularly amusing to contemplate anarchists fastidiously fretting over the lack of a further Security Council resolution—that is, the absence of an endorsement by the likes of Russia, China, Syria, France, Pakistan, Cameroon, Guinea, Angola, and Germany, among others, for deposing the Baathist dictatorship. (Noam Chomsky, author of an enthusiastic preface to a book on anarchism,[6] deems the invasion of Iraq and the new preemptive doctrine of the United States as nothing less than the tearing apart of the foundations of the international system of the last four hundred years. Perhaps, but why this should be regarded as the worst of calamities, however, or even just worse than the continuing rule of the likes of Saddam and the Taliban—or Milošević, the bombing of whose country by NATO, though justified at the time by an older doctrine, led indirectly to his ouster and was equally opposed by Chomsky, Edward Said, Tony Benn, and others—is nowhere sufficiently explained.)

What the comparison with Twin Earth reminds us of, however, is that our own international system, dubiously defensible from a moral standpoint, has a very contingent history. Its protection of vicious and unrepresentative governments from external intervention is an accident, not obviously a morally happy one, of our early modern history: a deal among premodern religious regimes to impose religions univocally in individual princedoms, with dissenters enjoying nothing but *ius emigrandi* (the right to emigrate).[7] If the compromise had some justification at the time to stop the worst religious massacres (though not all—however, these would soon be regarded as "internal affairs"), it is certainly more difficult to defend this aspect of its legal legacy nearly half a millennium later, when other, nonsectarian principles have become widely accepted.

The Twin Earth comparison suggests how equally contingent is the current conglomeration of politically correct views. To be sure, it has always been rather questionable why the particular cluster of beliefs endorsed by the left and liberal left (or, for that matter, by the right) at any one time had to hang together, despite some valiant past attempts to demonstrate such links.[8] What logical relations, that is, hold among the current "left's" views on Afghanistan, abortion, the Cold War, distributive justice, Bosnia, Al Qaeda, animal rights, Jerusalem, global warming, Kosovo, and Iraq? Far more accident and fashion have glued this cluster than its partisans (as well as some opponents) seem prepared to admit. But, in particular, the accidents that have given rise to our state system have equally shaped the international aspects of this cluster. If anything, one might have thought that the demand to change vicious regimes by force is much closer to the higher-level principles thought to animate the left: universalism and social progress, not to mention a historical fondness for (as left consequentialists coyly used to put it) breaking eggs with the aspiration of making an omelette.

We'll return to the issue of consequentialism later. First, however, it will be useful to distinguish between a few general types of opposition to any war. One possible stance of opposition, which we might dub the *position of feasibility skepticism* and which happened to be my own, was based on a lack of confidence that the war aims could succeed. By contrast, the chief arguments of opponents of the war in a sense (to be qualified later) questioned the morality of the war aims themselves (independently of whether these could be achieved). This *position of principled opposition* can be illustrated with the example of Vietnam. Suppose that one opposed the war for the following reasons. First, one recognized that, as Eisenhower had acknowledged in the late fifties, at least 80 percent of the Vietnamese would have voted for the Vietminh (and later the Vietcong) had free elections been held. Second, even if, unlike other opponents of the war, one did not delude oneself about the nature of the Communists, one was equally unblinkered about the US-backed dictators in the south. Thus, one opposed the war because it was wrong to impose a government against the clear wishes of the majority, all the more so if that government was at least as bad as the one being deposed. In such a case, one would have reason to disapprove of any American military success; on the contrary, one would have reason to approve of its setbacks and even to wish, in principle, for its ultimate defeat. (To be sure, an American's emotive attachment to her nation might produce psychic dissonance in practice, but on the assumption that patriotic loyalty ought to have been overridden by just war principles, if one really held the war to be morally wrong, one ought to have given or withheld approval, however reluctantly or conflictedly at the level of emotions, to ensuing military events in consonance with those principles.)

Alternatively, one could have taken the *position of feasibility skepticism* toward this war, regarding it as otherwise justified by global strategic considerations in the struggle against communism but as unlikely to be winnable. But here we can usefully distinguish between two possible skeptical positions.

*Total feasibility skepticism* is based on *certainty* that the war is ultimately unwinnable. In such a case, a surprising American military success in some limited offensive would be lamented as merely sucking the US further into a swamp; one might even hope for a quick American defeat as the best way of saving lives (on either side) in the long run. We can note in passing that unlike in the case of the position of principled opposition, it would be consistent with this view to temper the hope for an American defeat by a deeper regret, arising not merely from loyalty and feelings of attachment but from disappointment that the *morally* more desirable outcome of enhancing liberty by resisting communism was not available.

*Diffident feasibility skepticism*, on the other hand, is based not on certainty that the war is *un*winnable but only on lack of confidence that it is *winnable*. Noteworthy about such a stance is that one's reasons for approving or disapproving of military victories and defeats would differ from those of a total feasibility skeptic; one might have reason to welcome victories of a US military offensive with the hope that one's diffidence will be proved ultimately unjustified. (Certainty and doubt admit of degrees; at some point one might not know whether to welcome the American victories or not. All of this, to reiterate, is based on the assumption that feasibility aside the war aims are on balance justified.)

Two complications need to be brought in at this point. In the opening paragraph, I qualified the war aim of bringing about a stable democracy in Iraq with the proviso that there not occur "undue loss of life." We can postpone the agonizing question of how one goes about deciding how much is "undue," except to note quickly that opponents of the war cannot escape the same question (except through bad faith and self-righteous posturing) for their preferred choice (all things considered, to be sure) of leaving Saddam and sons in power. The more immediately relevant point is that if such a proviso is built into a war aim (as it surely must be if the war is ever justified), then that, too, becomes part of what one can be more or less skeptical about the possibility of achieving. Consequently, a diffident feasibility skeptic should be gratified not merely by surprising military victories per se but by those that promise the possibility of achieving the war aim as qualified by the proviso and that do not already violate it themselves. This might seem to blur the boundary between principled opposition and feasibility skepticism. A diffident feasibility skeptic who accepted the moral proviso would not, I take it, have been heartened by the prospect of a "victory" in Vietnam achieved through even more carpet bombing and even greater use of napalm and lethal defoliants or worse. And that is a principled opposition in some sense.

Conversely, principled opponents of the war in Iraq do not usually deny that bringing about a stable democracy in Iraq is good in itself. One might then say that they merely oppose the means that have been adopted to bring it about. And that is acceptance of the aims in some sense. So the two positions cannot be distinguished on the basis that one (the skeptic) accepts the aims but not the means, whereas the other (the principled opponent) rejects the aims themselves. Rather, while they both might accept some aims in some abstracted form, the principled opponent rejects the concept of going to war to achieve these aims as wrong in itself—that is, not merely because some will die but because it is a violation of sovereignty, a breach of international law, or an arrogation of power to coerce others to accept one's preferred sort of regime. The diffident feasibility skeptic, let us stipulate, does not reject war on any of these grounds and does not reject war per se as a justified means of achieving the war aims. But such a skeptic need not then be committed to the opposite extreme of accepting any military means whatsoever of achieving the ends; we can allow that part of her skepticism might be with regard to the ability to achieve the ends within the conditions of a reasonable moral proviso about the loss of life.

The second complication is that the feasibility of winning a war is often affected by the degree of support that the war effort receives. So if everyone sits on the fence, diffidence becomes a self-realizing pessimism.[9] It has been a time-honored complaint by supporters of war, from World War I German nationalists to Vietnam War hawks, that they were defeated (not to say "stabbed in the back") not by their external enemy but by the home front. More generally, it is a familiar phenomenon of human affairs that prophesies can be self-fulfilling or self-defeating.[10] So a diffident feasibility skeptic needs to take this into account by attempting to assess whether her own skepticism, and that of others like her, is an important factor in the overall probability of success. The influence can be various. The most obvious way it can be a factor is if it translates into political support for a candidate who is not committed to the war or withdrawal of support for one who is. For instance, a Spaniard who opposed the war not from principled opposition but from one of feasibility skepticism, and who consequently voted against the Aznar government, might himself have become a factor in realizing the pessimistic outcome.[11]

At any rate, I shall contend that diffident feasibility skepticism has been the only justified stance of opposition to the war in Iraq. It is a position that distinguishes its adopters from most of the antiwar movement in the two countries that launched the war: the United States and Great Britain. Diffident feasibility skepticism implies that, while there may have been sufficient doubt about the possibility of success to withhold initial support, there were otherwise sufficient reasons to go to war. Moreover, had subsequent events shown that the pessimism was unwarranted and that the primary objective of the war was sufficiently successful— to replace the Baathist dictatorship by a stable and decent regime in Iraq, without undue loss of life—then the war would have been justified. That scenario further implies that had sufficient progress occurred along the way, as might have been the case had it been prosecuted differently, such progress could have provided a reason to set aside one's doubts and throw one's support behind the war.

The most contentious aspect of diffident feasibility skepticism is its assumption that, except for the question of feasibility, the war would have been justified. Before defending this view, however, it might be useful to clear away some fallacies that clutter the workplace. My unsurprising contention will be that it is the humanitarian component of the war aim—to bring a stable democracy to Iraq in place of a savagely repressive regime—that would have justified the war were the aim feasible. But many critics of the war object that humanitarian concerns have little or no role in the motivations of the war's planners, and therefore humanitarian concerns could not have justified the war. In fact, I think the premise is an unwarranted exaggeration, but I have no wish to defend that claim here. The point, rather, is that the argument commits the *intentional fallacy*: it assumes that person A may support or justify an action of person B only if A agrees with B's intentions in performing the action. The assumption is surely false. We are not trying here to evaluate whether Bush or Blair are nice guys; that is a topic for their biographers. The question is, rather, the independent one of whether people of conscience should have supported the war. Outcomes can have sufficient moral value—in this case, putting an end to a barbaric regime—to justify supporting actions that bring about those outcomes even if performed by the agent for the wrong reasons. (Just because Lincoln's primary motivation may have been the preservation of the union, not the abolition of slavery, that does not negate the fact that what actually justified the Union's waging civil war was that the outcome of its victory would be the abolition of slavery.)

In other words, if in situation S one ought to support an act X if done (by another agent) from some motive M because of the moral value of consequence C arising from X, then in the same situation S, one ought to support act X if done from any other motive, so long as C is still a predictable consequence of X and the alternative motives do not have such intrinsic negative value or lead to other consequences (besides C) of sufficient negative moral significance to outweigh the good of C. It is unlikely that the ridding of such a brutal regime as the one in Iraq, with its systematic practices of torture and repression, could be worthy of achieving only if the agent had the right intention: the consequences are too valuable in themselves for that to be the case. (The Vietnamese invasion of Cambodia to depose Pol Pot, or the Tanzanian intervention in Uganda to depose Idi Amin, falls under the same rule).

It is also irrelevant that the West allegedly once "supported" Saddam, a favorite claim in the antiwar movement. If the claim is meant as evidence of the Coalition's bad intentions, it is just a variant of the intentional fallacy that has just been rejected. It is difficult to see what other normative significance it can bear. Even if the Allies were soft on fascism in the thirties, that doesn't mean they shouldn't have fought it in the forties. On the contrary, if it was a moral error to have been soft on fascism in the thirties or to have sold arms to Saddam in the eighties, then, if anything, the agents of those errors have even stronger duties than would otherwise be the case to reverse the effects of the errors as soon as possible.

One may note in passing that it is too often with an irresponsible smugness that some activists mock Western leaders for having supported Islamic forces against the Soviets in Afghanistan (albeit not "the Taliban," as is sometimes alleged; no such organization or movement then existed) or Saddam's Iraq in its war against Iran. In the real world, those in positions of power—as opposed to those without influence who thereby have the luxury of frivolously adopting self-righteous postures while never having to pay the consequences of them—sometimes have to make compromises, supporting what seem at the time like lesser evils against greater threats: Soviet imperialism or Khomeinyist fundamentalism. State departments are clumsy bureaucracies that are painfully slow to shift policies and alliances when changing circumstances demand it, but that fault is not quite equivalent to the Machiavellian cynicism (which no doubt sometimes exists) attributed so regularly and with such relish to them.

The humanitarian case can now be put briefly for the war, after which we can turn to issues of consequences and agent duties. The case for the war is simple. The Saddam regime was one of the most morally objectionable among current states, highly arbitrary and repressive, systematically practicing the torture and killing of political opponents of any sort, genocidal toward ethnic groups deemed enemies (Kurds, Shiites, Marsh Arabs), and with a record of attack without provocation against at least four neighboring states. On the assumption that the goal of establishing a decent and stable regime could have been achieved, the cost of some ten thousand lives during the war and aftermath to bring this about would likely have been a net gain in human life alone, leaving aside the immeasurable gain in liberty and stability and its benefits in the long term. The current civil war is being waged by Americans and liberty-seeking Iraqis against Baathist fascists and both Sunni and Shiite Islamofascists; that is a war as worth fighting as any antifascist struggle. The justification of the war, then, would have been that it saves lives overall, ends tyranny, promises in the long term to bring invaluable liberty to the Iraqis (with concomitant benefits such as the opportunity already enjoyed by the majority Shiites to practice their traditions), and contributes to the stability, liberalization, and democratization of one of the most politically retrograde, violent, and dangerous regions (despite its formidable natural resources).

Some objections to this account focus on alleged evil consequences that it has omitted. A common objection is that the invasion of Iraq has harmed the war on terror and even provided a boon to Al Qaeda. This objection is sometimes leveled at one of the stated justifications of the war: that it was intended to advance the war on terror. Of course, even if the justificatory claim were false, it would commit the intentional fallacy to take that claim by itself as a reason to oppose the war. Nevertheless, the claim that the war harms the campaign against terror can stand on its own as a consideration against the war. In rebuttal, however, weigh a number of considerations.

First, the alleged harm to the war on terror still has to be weighed against the overall benefits of the war cited previously. These might well include (and some experts on terror alleging the harm done do not disagree) long-term advantages against short-term losses in the campaign against Al Qaeda and other Islamist terrorists. In other words, there is no contradiction between the objector's claims that the chaos in Iraq has provided a new haven, rallying cause, and boon to recruitment for Islamist terrorists as well as having siphoned away resources from Afghanistan, and the claims of the US administration that coercively initiating a process of liberalization in Arab society by ridding the world of one of its worst offenders of human rights (with documented aspirations to acquire weapons of mass destruction and a record of having used them) is the best *long-term* strategy for reversing the cultural support for terrorist groups and the logistical potential for them to acquire weapons of mass destruction in the future.

Second, and of more immediate practical significance, even strategists alleging harm done do not deny that once the war was launched and the environment allegedly favorable to terrorists created, it might be necessary in order to reduce the short-term damage and move toward reaping the potential long-term advantages to defeat the terrorists as soon and as extensively as possible, while to cut and run might exacerbate the harm to the point of disaster.

Another set of objections contends that the war should be opposed because it violated international law and was launched on the false pretext of disarming the unarmed. The latter need not rely on the intentional fallacy; rather, the claim is that it is a moral harm in itself for a government to lie to its people, particularly in order to muster support for an illegal violent act. And that is surely correct. Democracy, transparency, and honesty are valued because they enable people to live autonomous lives with mutual respect as moral equals; deception by government officials impairs and diminishes this autonomy. The problem with these objections, however, lies in how they assess these harms relative to those ensuing from continuing rule by Saddam. Some appear to think that they don't need to weigh these other harms at all. One possible reason someone might think that is if that person believes in an ethical doctrine that has sometimes gone under the name of "deontology." According to this doctrine, certain duties are incumbent on agents irrespective of overall consequences of discharging or not discharging them (call them agent-relative duties). But what justifies holding people to such duties? If one does not think that they derive from divine revelation, and if one doesn't believe, as Kant seems to have, that a pure procedural test can generate them, then the rational view is that the duties are justified by the moral worth of preventing the harms that failure to discharge them would allow. I may not punch an innocent person in the face, quite simply, because it harms him. But if preventing this harm is what justifies holding one to a duty in the first place, then in a given circumstance where complying with the duty will actually cause more of the same or worse harm then the amount of harm that will be prevented, what rational basis is there for nevertheless complying with the duty?[12]

The objection of writers sometimes called deontologists is that the evaluation of actions in relation to resultant overall states of affairs, themselves evaluated in terms of some net aggregate good, ignores the ethical need to respect the interests of each individual independently of any overall state of affairs. It is wrong, say these writers, to sacrifice some individual(s) merely for the sake of increasing the aggregate social good. This point is common to influential writers of the 1970s as different as Robert Nozick on the one hand and John Rawls and Ronald Dworkin on the other.[13] The metaphors of side-constraints and trumps were meant to convey both the potential opposition between social goals and the interests protected by rights, and the absolute priority of the latter over the former when they do conflict. But both points were left by writers of the seventies in what has charitably been described as a state of "incompleteness."[14] The target of seventies deontology, including Rawls's well-known attack on theories that fail to take individuals seriously, was utilitarianism. It is easy to see a potential dichotomy between social goals and individual rights when the only valid social goals are those of maximizing aggregate happiness, satisfaction, or welfare (depending on the version of utilitarianism). The situation is more complicated when so-called hybrid versions of consequentialism include distributive, egalitarian, or other "moral goals."

As mentioned earlier, the notions of trumps and side constraints imply that social goals or benefits cannot override rights-based duties. But, as many have observed, it is difficult to make this view plausible. Many rights protect individuals from relatively minor harms, such as, to borrow Judith Jarvis Thomson's example, the right not to be kicked in the shins.[15] It is implausible that this right should never be violated even if doing so would prevent violations of much more severe rights— say, the torture and murder of hundreds of innocents. A more persuasive conception holds that rights establish thresholds, such that trade-offs in a downward direction—that is, for no matter what quantity of benefits or to prevent no matter how much harm of a qualitatively lower sort—are impermissible, while upward trade-offs (e.g., shin kicking to prevent death or maiming) would be permissible or even obligatory. (Horizontal trade-offs might be allowed depending on the degree and sort of relative gain.)

While this conception seems intuitively plausible for a limited range of personal rights that can be lexically ranked with relative ease—in the shin-kicking example, rights of bodily integrity—the gamut of moral and legal rights embedded in the complex of practices and institutions of a society or in international relations is less obviously amenable to this sort of treatment. Could one really rank harms and benefits, many of which might be incommensurable, in such a way as always to know which trade-offs were permissible?

In fact, however, one need not be committed to such a view to hold a nonabsolute conception of rights and duties that is still useful and retains an appropriate sense of stringency or urgency. As long as rights protect against some specified sorts of trade-offs—no matter how high the aggregated benefit of the sort in question—then the concept will have the stringency or urgency distinctive of it. To borrow an example from Joseph Raz, one should never take a human life no matter how much ice cream one might thereby produce.[16] The question under discussion, however, is whether the offenses committed by the Coalition leaders resemble the ice cream or the shin-kicking example. Is it really defensible to hold that one may never violate a law or deceive[17] the public no matter how much harm will be prevented? Considering the sort of harms we are talking about—on the one hand, violating law and deceiving the public; on the other hand, gross and systematic violations of human rights on a massive scale—it seems, on the contrary, that this is much like the shin-kicking case: a permissible and possibly even obligatory upward trade-off.

To reiterate, it is one thing to reject trade-offs of individual welfare for the sake of aggregate maximization, and quite another thing to go on to hold that there are things we must never do, rules we must never violate, regardless of any consequences whatsoever. An exponent of the latter extreme view, Elizabeth Anscombe, advocated Western unilateral nuclear disarmament because nuclear arms by their very design target innocent civilians. All talk of deterrence was for her immorally "consequentialist" (an expression she coined as a term of opprobrium). It was simply impermissible to target, far less to actually harm, an innocent person, even to prevent many more innocent from being harmed. As a devout Catholic, Anscombe regarded this as an obvious rhetorical point: "Come now. If you had to choose between boiling one baby and letting some frightful disaster befall a thousand people—or a million people, if a thousand is not enough—what would you do?"[18]

But Anscombe's rhetoric cannot hide her underdescription of this "frightful disaster" and having rendered its victims "people," implying adults. A more acute test of her extreme conception of agent-relative duties would be to ask her in turn whether she would condemn the boiling of one baby to prevent one million babies from being boiled the same way. Or even only a thousand? How about fifty, if a thousand is "too much"? Perhaps she would, but it would not be obvious that hers was the morally superior position.

To be sure, when one takes a broad view of things, one sometimes worries about long-term effects of breaking a well-established rule. Will it undermine future compliance in cases where it would be better to comply? Is it the beginning of a slippery slope that will lead to other rules being violated for no good moral reason? These worries, it will not go unnoticed, are themselves consequentialist and beg examination with respect to the entire gamut of relevant possible effects.

The objection now is that quite beyond attaching value to compliance with the rule itself, the violation of international law is not only evil in itself but evil because of its potential demonstration effect: encouraging other states to wage war illegally on the flimsiest of excuses. Let's consider whether these concerns have been appropriate for evaluating the war in Iraq.

If the Coalition could succeed in its goal of establishing a relatively decent and stable regime in Iraq in the next ten years, what effect will the illegality of the war have had on subsequent practice? It does not, to my mind at least, seem plausible that because the war was illegal (as we assume for argument's sake) that otherwise law-abiding states will become unruly and aggressive. Perhaps the architects of this war have been overly optimistic about the *positive* demonstration effects of over-throwing the Iraqi regime. Perhaps not every vicious regime will immediately fall into line or introduce liberal reform, whether the much-touted Libyan case exemplifies this or not.[19] But the opposite contention that the illegality of the war will produce a spate of aggressive wars masked as humanitarian intervention seems quite unconvincing. A stated aim of the war is to spread democracy and liberalism in a region and culture among those most egregiously lacking them. The aim might or might not succeed, but principled opponents worry that even if it did succeed, the illegality of the war would have destabilizing consequences. But as Michael Doyle has famously argued, "Even though liberal states have become involved in numerous wars with non-liberal states, constitutionally secure liberal states have yet to engage in war with one another."[20] The spread of constitutionally secure liberal states in hitherto tyrannical—*and war-torn*—regions, is a prescription for diminishing the prospect of war, not increasing it. Nor does the demonstration effect have to extrapolate beyond what is in fact being demonstrated: the coercive liberalization of a hitherto tyrannical unpopular regime. One can be as vigilant about enforcing *this* constraint on just wars as the objector would like to be regarding his favored legal practice. In other words, international law on Twin Earth, with its robust endorsement of humanitarian interventions, need not be enforced less scrupulously than our current norms.

A more weighty consequentialist consideration, however, is the sheer toll in human lives required to achieve the stated aims. Yet it is not obvious how one should assess this factor. Agent-relativists of an older school might be inclined to deny responsibility for the deaths and suffering caused by the Saddam regime. Saddam is responsible for those deaths, they might say, while we are responsible for those that we cause through our actions. Perhaps, one might reply, but then we are not responsible for the majority of killings in Iraq since the fall of the regime, because those are probably committed by Baathist loyalists and Islamic terrorists. In other words, one may not apply selectively doctrines of double effect (distinguishing between "intended" and "unintended" consequences), distinctions between omissions and commissions, or my agency versus another's. If these doctrines are applied universally rather than selectively they will hardly have the implication that the objectors to the war would like.

For instance, on the first of these distinctions, the Coalition is not even responsible for the deaths of innocent bystanders, the collateral damage of its bombing, since these deaths were "unintended." I agree that this claim is dubious, but then we have to take some degree of responsibility for the crimes Saddam and Sons would commit had we left them in power. There seems little alternative, then, to weighing up the entire range of harms and benefits both from acting against the regime and from leaving it in power. Once again, it appears that the assessment will turn largely on feasibility. If the aims could have been achieved with less suffering, death, repression, and whatever else bears negative moral value than what would have been experienced under Saddam throughout the years that he would have remained in power, then it will have been a morally good thing that the war took place. If the aims can be achieved only at a very high cost, which now seems undeniable, then one will have the harder task of comparing incommensurables such as death and liberty, a judgment that ultimately only the Iraqis will be entitled to make. If the aims simply cannot be satisfactorily achieved in the foreseeable future, which appears increasingly likely, then the war will have been a moral disaster. The blameworthiness of its architects will still depend in such a case on how diffident they ought to have been given available information at the outset, and especially how this information should have led them to conduct the war differently.

For diffident feasibility skeptics, however, their objection to the decision to have gone to war may continue for some time to be tempered by the hope against hope of some success for the Coalition and democratic Iraqis. To be sure, there are moral traps. As I. F. Stone once remarked, everyone thinks that the world can be made better by just a little more killing. Neither Kennedy nor Johnson set out to kill three million Vietnamese; World War I generals never intended to kill eleven million. The more that died, the more one wished their deaths not go in vain; a bit more might do the trick. Yet the alternative of a Zarqawi-run terror regime is too unpalatable to cut and run, and Shiites, Kurds, and democratic Sunnis will soon need to choose whether they will let this happen or not. That the choice was forced on them, however, will get no moral support if feasibility skepticism is vindicated.

# NOTES

1. Jean Bodin, *Six Books of the Commonwealth*, trans. M. J. Tooley (Oxford: Blackwell, 1955), 197. It should be borne in mind that Bodin's aim was to abolish the motley privileges and powers of the nobility and to bring about an efficient state bureaucracy before which citizens had equal status. In the late feudal context, Bodin could thus be regarded as a modernizer.

2. The translation of this Latin phrase is "He who rules a territory determines its religion." Joseph Strayer, *On the Mediaeval Origins of the Modern State* (Princeton, NJ: Princeton University Press, 1970); Eugene F. Rice and Anthony Grafton, *The Foundations of Early Modern Europe, 1460–1559*, 2nd ed. (New York: W. W. Norton, 1994), 196.

3. It should be borne in mind that Bonaparte's armies were popularly regarded across Europe as liberators, an image preserved in operas from *Fidelio* to *Tosca*; recall also Hegel's remark at the sight of the French emperor in Jena that "there goes the spirit of history."

4. Our activists love to mock assertions of progress in Afghanistan by claiming that Hamid Karzai's government hardly controls territory beyond Kabul, as if, even if true, this situation were not enormously better than his controlling no territory and the Taliban allied with Al Qaeda controlling all territory.

5. H. L. A. Hart, *The Concept of Law*, 2nd ed. (Oxford: Clarendon; New York: Oxford University Press, 1994), chap. 10.

6. Noam Chomsky, "Preface," in Daniel Guérin, *Anarchism: From Theory to Practice*, trans. Mary Klopper (New York: Monthly Review Press, 1970).

7. Rice and Grafton, *The Foundations of Early Modern Europe*, 196. In fact, Iraqis lacked even this right under Saddam and frequently paid dearly for attempts to exercise it.

8. For example, Jürgen Habermas, *Legitimation Crisis*, trans. Thomas McCarthy (Cambridge: Polity, 1988).

9. I owe this point to Tom Cushman.

10. Alan Ryan, *The Philosophy of Social Science*, Oxford Readings in Philosophy series (Oxford: Oxford University Press, 1970). An old example in politics was the Second International debate over activism and quietism of the party and the "spontaneity" of the masses.

11. A certain New York–based writer went around conferences and public debates in the spring of 1995 announcing that "lift and strike"—the policy then advocated by many of lifting the arms embargo on the Bosnian government and implementing punitive air strikes against the Bosnian Serb army—was "not going to happen," that "no one in Washington is considering it," and that consequently the Bosnian government should capitulate as soon as possible to put an end to the war. Fortunately, his assessment and predictions were wrong, but that outcome opens the question of the extent of his *moral* culpability in proselytizing such pessimism when the possibility of achieving a more satisfactory moral outcome was wide open.

12. This is a point made by Samuel Scheffler in *The Rejection of Consequentialism*, rev. ed. (Oxford: Oxford University Press, 1994).

13. Robert Nozick, *Anarchy, State, and Utopia* (New York: Basic Books, 1974); Ronald Dworkin, *Taking Rights Seriously* (Cambridge, MA: Harvard University Press, 1978).

14. "Accounts of agent-centred restrictions in the literature are often incomplete, leaving open, for example, the question of when exactly the restrictions may be overridden to produce a good outcome or avoid a bad one." The text then refers in a footnote to Nozick's discussion of side-constraints in *Anarchy, State, and Utopia*. See Scheffler, *The Rejection of Consequentialism*.

15. Judith Jarvis Thomson, *The Realm of Rights* (Cambridge, MA: Harvard University Press, 1990).

16. Joseph Raz, *The Morality of Freedom* (Oxford: Oxford University Press, 1984).

17. For all the attention that has been given to the claims about weapons of mass destruction, it is still not obvious that the US and British administrations *lied* in claiming that they believed there were such weapons. They may have lied or exaggerated about minor details, and they certainly used the issue as a pretext to justify a war they wished to launch for independent reasons. But anyone who heard Tony Blair's address to the British parliament the day Baghdad fell will have difficultly doubting that Blair actually believed that *some* weapons existed somewhere in the country. With all attention focused on scenes of rejoicing, tearing down statues, and beating effigies of Saddam with shoes, Blair went out of his way to remind the audience that the official justification is still the weapons of mass destruction, which he asserted confidently we will now find. This was hardly the behavior of a leader who knew there were none to be found.

18. Elizabeth Anscombe, quoted in *Ethics, Religion and Politics: Collected Philosophical Papers*, vol. 3 (Minneapolis: University of Minnesota Press, 1981), 34; quoted in James Rachel, *The Elements of Moral Philosophy*, 4th ed. (New York: McGraw-Hill, 2003), 119.

19. Doubts about this point have been expressed by some, including Ibrahim Faradi of the UN. On this view, the Libyan leader had been making similar offers to the West for more than a decade in an effort to get sanctions lifted, but the US would not take yes for an answer, even after the Lockerbie issue was resolved to Britain's satisfaction. When things went sour in Iraq and it was necessary to find some positive development from the war, the US administration then decided to open negotiations with Kadaffi and accept his offer of disarmament.

20. Michael Doyle, "Kant, Liberal Legacies, and Foreign Affairs," *Philosophy and Public Affairs* 12 (1983): 213. As Rawls, who dubs this Doyle's law, points out, the law has held between "well-established and well-ordered liberal democracies that are significant if not major powers." There are a number of cases of major powers such as the US subverting and indeed overturning the governments of smaller and less established or secure democracies (in Chile, Guatemala, and Iran). The kitchen variety of Doyle's law was suggested by Thomas Friedman: that countries having a McDonald's don't wage war against each other. Alas, this claim has already been disproved by the NATO bombing of Serbia. Nor, I reckon, will Indians and Pakistanis, Taiwanese and Chinese, and several African states lose their security concerns at the revelation of golden arches or other indications of foreign investment in their neighbor's land.

# PART THREE

# CRITIQUES OF THE LEFT

# 8

# A Friendly Drink in a Time of War

PAUL BERMAN

A friend leaned across a bar and said, "You call the war in Iraq an antifascist war. You even call it a left-wing war—a war of liberation. That language of yours! And yet, on the left, not too many people agree with you."

"Not true!" I said. "Apart from X, Y, and Z, whose left-wing names you know very well, what do you think of Adam Michnik in Poland? And doesn't Václav Havel count for something in your eyes? These are among the heroes of our time. Anyway, who is fighting in Iraq right now? The Coalition is led by a Texas right-winger, which is a pity; but, in the second rank, by the prime minister of Britain, who is a socialist, sort of; and, in the third rank, by the president of Poland—a Communist! An ex-Communist, anyway. One Texas right-winger and two Europeans who are more or less on the left. Anyway, these categories, right and left, are disintegrating by the minute. And who do you regard as the leader of the worldwide left? Jacques Chirac? A conservative, I hate to tell you."

My friend persisted. "Still, most people don't seem to agree with you. You do have to see that. And why do you suppose that is?"

That was an aggressive question. And I answered in kind.

"Why don't people on the left see it my way? Except for the ones who do? I'll give you six reasons. People on the left have been unable to see the antifascist nature of the war because . . ."—and my hand hovered over the bar, ready to thump six times, demonstrating the powerful force of my argument.

"The left doesn't see because . . ." thump! ". . . George W. Bush is an unusually repulsive politician, except to his own followers, and people are blinded by the revulsion they feel. And, in their blindness, they cannot identify the main contours of reality right now. They peer at Iraq and see the smirking face of George W. Bush. They even feel a kind of Schadenfreude or satisfaction at his errors and failures. This is a modern, television-age example of what used to be called 'false consciousness.'"

Thump! "The left doesn't see because a lot of otherwise intelligent people have decided, a priori, that all the big problems around the world stem from America. Even the problems that don't. This is an attitude that, sixty years ago, would have prevented those same people from making sense of the fascists of Europe, too."

Thump! "Another reason: A lot of people suppose that any sort of anticolonial movement must be admirable or, at least, acceptable. Or they think that, at minimum, we shouldn't do more than tut-tut—even in the case of a movement that, like the Baath Party, was founded under a Nazi influence. In 1943, no less!"

Thump! "The left doesn't see because a lot of people, in their good-hearted effort to respect cultural differences, have concluded that Arabs must for inscrutable reasons of their own like to live under grotesque dictatorships and are not really capable of anything else, or won't be ready to do so for another five hundred years, and Arab liberals should be regarded as somehow inauthentic. Which is to say, a lot of people, swept along by their own high-minded principles of cultural tolerance, have ended up clinging to attitudes that can only be regarded as racist against Arabs.

"The old-fashioned left used to be universalist—used to think that everyone, all over the world, would some day want to live according to the same fundamental values and ought to be helped to do so. They thought this was especially true for people in reasonably modern societies with universities, industries, and a sophisticated bureaucracy—societies like the one in Iraq. But no more! Today, people say, out of a spirit of egalitarian tolerance: Social democracy for Swedes! Tyranny for Arabs! And this is supposed to be a left-wing attitude? By the way, you don't hear much from the left about the non-Arabs in countries like Iraq, do you? The left, the real left, used to be the champion of minority populations—of people like the Kurds. No more! The left, my friend, has abandoned the values of the left—except for a few of us, of course."

Thump! "Another reason: A lot of people honestly believe that Israel's problems with the Palestinians represent something more than a miserable dispute over borders and recognition—that Israel's problems represent something huger, a uniquely diabolical aspect of Zionism, which explains the rage and humiliation felt by Muslims from Morocco to Indonesia. Which is to say, a lot of people have succumbed to anti-Semitic fantasies about the cosmic quality of Jewish crime and cannot get their minds to think about anything else.

"I mean, look at the discussions that go on even among people who call themselves the democratic left, the good left—a relentless harping on the sins of Israel, an obsessive harping, with very little said about the fascist-influenced movements that have caused hundreds of thousands and even millions of deaths in other parts of the Muslim world. The distortions are wild, if you stop to think about them. Look at some of our big, influential liberal magazines—one article after another about Israeli crimes and stupidities, and even a few statements in favor of abolishing Israel, and hardly anything about the sufferings of the Arabs in the rest of the world. And even less is said about the Arab liberals—our own comrades, who have been pretty much abandoned. What do you make of that, my friend? There's a name for that, a systematic distortion—what we Marxists, when we were Marxists, used to call ideology."

Thump! "The left doesn't see because a lot of people are, in any case, willfully blind to anti-Semitism in other cultures. They cannot get themselves to recognize the degree to which Nazi-like doctrines about the supernatural quality of Jewish evil have influenced mass political movements across large swaths of the world. It is 1943 right now in huge portions of the world—and people don't see it. And so, people simply cannot detect the fascist nature of all kinds of mass movements and political parties. In the Muslim world, especially."

Six thumps. I was done. My friend looked incredulous. His incredulity drove me to continue.

"And yet," I insisted, "if good-hearted people like you would only open your left-wing eyes, you would see clearly enough that the Baath Party is very nearly a classic fascist movement, and so is the radical Islamist movement, in a somewhat different fashion—two strands of a single impulse, which happens to be Europe's fascist and totalitarian legacy to the modern Muslim world. If only people like you would wake up, you would see that war against the radical Islamist and Baathist movements, in Afghanistan exactly as in Iraq, is war against fascism."

I grew still more heated.

"What a tragedy that you don't see this! It's a tragedy for the Afghanis and the Iraqis, who need more help than they are receiving. A tragedy for the genuine liberals all over the Muslim world! A tragedy for the American soldiers, the British, the Poles, and every one else who has gone to Iraq lately, the nongovernmental organization volunteers and the occupying forces from abroad, who have to struggle on bitterly against the worst kind of nihilists and have been getting damn little support or even moral solidarity from people who describe themselves as antifascists in the world's richest and fattest neighborhoods.

"What a tragedy for the left—the worldwide left, this left of ours that, in failing to play much of a role in the antifascism of our own era, is right now committing a gigantic historic error. Not for the first time, my friend! And yet, if the left all over the world took up this particular struggle as its own, the whole nature of events in Iraq and throughout the region could be influenced in a very useful way, and Bush's many blunders could be rectified, and the struggle could be advanced."

My friend's eyes widened, maybe in astonishment, maybe in pity.

He said, "And so, the United Nations and international law mean nothing to you, not a thing? You think it's all right for America to go do whatever it wants and ignore the rest of the world?"

I answered, "The United Nations and international law are fine by me, and more than fine. I am their supporter. Or, rather, would like to support them. It would be better to fight an antifascist war with more than a begrudging UN approval. It would be better to fight with the approving sanction of international law—better in a million ways. Better politically, therefore militarily. Better for the precedents that would be set. Better for the purpose of expressing the liberal principles at stake. If I had my druthers, that is how we would have gone about fighting the war. But my druthers don't count for much. We have had to choose between supporting the war or opposing it—supporting the war in the name of antifascism, or opposing it in the name of some kind of concept of international law. Antifascism without international law, or international law without antifascism. A miserable choice—but one does have to choose, unfortunately."

My friend said, "I'm for the UN and international law, and I think you've become a traitor to the left. A neocon!"

I said, "I'm for overthrowing tyrants, and since when did overthrowing fascism become treason to the left?"

"But isn't George Bush himself a fascist, more or less? I mean—admit it!"

My own eyes widened. "You haven't the foggiest idea what fascism is," I said. "I always figured that a keen awareness of extreme oppression was the deepest trait of a left-wing heart. Mass graves, three hundred thousand missing Iraqis, a population crushed by thirty-five years of Baathist boots stomping on their faces—that is what fascism means! And you think that a few corrupt insider contracts with Bush's cronies at Halliburton and a bit of retrograde Bible thumping and Bush's ridiculous tax cuts and his bonanzas for the superrich are indistinguishable from that? Indistinguishable from fascism? From a politics of slaughter? Leftism is supposed to be a reality principle. Leftism is supposed to embody an ability to take in the big picture. The traitor to the left is you, my friend. . . ."

But this made not the slightest sense to him, and there was nothing left to do but to hit each other over the head with our respective drinks.

## NOTE

"A Friendly Drink in a Time of War" is reprinted from *Dissent* (Winter 2004): 56–58.

# 9

# Wielding the Moral Club

IAN BURUMA

ere is Gore Vidal, often hailed as the most important literary essay-
ist in America, a liberal maverick, whose languid but always
spirited voice of opposition to most US administrations since
Kennedy's Camelot never fails to find the keen ears of the European
liberal-left. He was asked on Australian radio about what Vidal calls
the "Bush-Cheney junta" and how the Iraqis could have been freed
from Saddam Hussein's murderous regime without US armed force. His
answer: "Don't you think that's their problem? That's not your problem and that's not my problem. There are many bad regimes on Earth;
we can list several hundred. At the moment I would put the Bush regime
as one of them."

He was asked on the same show what he thought might happen in
North Korea. Answer: "I don't think much of anything is going to happen; they'll go on starving to death as apparently they are, or at least so
the media tells us." And what about those media, specifically Fox TV?
This is when the elegant drawl of the habitual old wit suddenly gathered heat: "Oh, it's disgusting, deeply disgusting. I've never heard people like that on television in my life, and I've been on television for fifty
years, since the very beginning of television in the United States. And
I have never seen it as low, as false, one lie after the other in these

squeaky voices that you get from these fast-talking men and women—it was pretty sick."

The Bush-Cheney junta as bad as Saddam's dictatorship. Starvation in North Korea, who cares? It's probably American propaganda anyway. But Fox News, now that's truly disgusting. I am no fan of Fox News, but there is an odd lack of proportion here that could be interpreted in various ways: the callous frivolity of a decadent old man; the provincial outlook of a writer whose horizons end at the shores of the United States, or perhaps even at the famous Washington, D.C., Beltway. Or is there a little more to it? Two more examples, from different writers this time.

Tariq Ali, in the *Guardian*, about the brutal "recolonisation" of Iraq by the United States and "its bloodshot British adjutant." It is to be hoped, he writes, "that the invaders of Iraq will eventually be harried out of the country by a growing national reaction to the occupation regime they install, and that their collaborators may meet the fate of former Iraqi prime minister Nuri Said before them."

Nuri Said, lest people forget, was a pro-Western leader, under whose rule Iraq was relatively calm and prosperous. He was murdered in a military coup in 1958. His death marked the beginning of a cycle of coups and countercoups that led to the Baathist regime five years later. The Baathists had modeled themselves on German National Socialism. One does not have to have the fertile mind of a Tariq Ali to imagine what would happen if his wish for an uprising (by Shiite extremists or former Baathists, most likely) came true: massacres, more massacres, and another dictatorship.

And, finally, Arundathi Roy, Indian novelist and favorite "postcolonial" agitprop voice in the European liberal press. In an article denouncing the United States for unleashing a "racist war" on Iraq, bringing "starvation" and "mass murder," she can muster just one paragraph about Saddam Hussein himself. "At the end of it all," she sighs, "it remains to be said that dictators like Saddam Hussein, and all the other despots in the Middle East, in the central Asian republics, in Africa and Latin America, many of them installed, supported and financed by the US government, are a menace to their own people. Other than strengthening the hand of civil society (instead of weakening it as has been done in the case of Iraq), there is no easy, pristine way of dealing with them."

Strengthening civil society. Well, that would indeed be a fine thing. Perhaps more could have been done to strengthen civil society in

Hitler's Germany, Stalin's Soviet Union, Mao's China, or perhaps in Kim Jong Il's North Korea, too. What is astonishing here is not the naiveté but the off-handed way well-heeled commentators in London, California, or New Delhi talk about the suffering of the very people they pretend to stand up for. Vidal dismisses it as "not my problem." Tariq Ali calls for more violence. And Arundathi Roy prattles about civil society.

There are, to be sure, perfectly valid reasons to be critical of US foreign policy, especially the neoconservative revolutionary mission. I was not persuaded that going to war in Iraq was right, because the official arguments were fuzzy, shifty, and changed from day to day. Once democratic governments cannot trust their people to respond to honest persuasion but resort instead to half-truths and propaganda, democracy suffers. But this does not answer the question of what to do, as citizens of the richest and most powerful nations on earth, about dictators who commit mass murder or happily starve millions to death. Why are our left-liberal intellectuals so hopeless at answering this vital question?

In the case of Gore Vidal, there has always been an old-fashioned isolationist screaming to be let out of the great man's bulky frame. But Tariq Ali, and many of his readers, would surely consider themselves to be internationalists. They profess to care about oppressed peoples in faraway countries. That is why they set themselves morally above the right. So why do they appear to be so much keener to denounce the United States than to find ways to liberate Iraqis and others from their murderous Führers? And how can anybody, knowing the brutal costs of political violence, especially in poor countries split by religious and ethnic divisions, be so insouciant as to call for more aggression?

Perhaps it is a kind of provincialism after all. In a short essay about becoming Anglicized, Arthur Koestler, a witness of communist purges and Nazi persecution, described a basic difference between the English and Europeans like him, who saw England as "a kind of Davos for internally bruised veterans of the totalitarian age." To the ordinary Englishman, such things as gas chambers and Siberian slave camps were inconceivable, literally beyond his imagination. These were things that were so far removed from English normality that they "just 'do not happen' to ordinary people unless they are deliberately looking for trouble."

Saddam's Iraq, where people were gassed, or fed to shredding machines, or tortured just for fun by the dictator's son, or Serbia under Milošević, where "ethnic cleansing" was official policy, were indeed a long way from Hampstead or Holland Park. And yet I can't believe that, for example, Harold Pinter's foaming rages about the United States and his denunciation of the NATO war over Kosovo as "a criminal act," while ignoring that without that war, hundreds of thousands of Kosovans were slated to disappear, is just parochial ignorance. Pinter is aware of human suffering far from Holland Park. He has done his bit for Kurdish victims of Turkish brutality and for Central Europeans under the Soviet lash.

So even if Tony Benn's cheery waffle about the achievements of real existing socialism can be dismissed as good old English eccentricity, the same cannot be true of the deliberate obtuseness of Tariq Ali, Pinter, Vidal, or Noam Chomsky. The main issue, for them, is the power of the United States. This clouds all other concerns. Pinter, a great artist if not a subtle political thinker, is perhaps a special case. His subject is power or, rather, the abuse of power. When applied to human relationships, Pinter's artistic intelligence produces brilliant insights. But when it comes to international politics, he becomes unhinged. US power—always abusive in his view—fills him with such fury that he cannot be rational on the subject. It also, incidentally, affects his artistry. Just read his crude poems on the Iraq war.

Anti-Americanism, by which I don't mean criticism of US policies but a visceral loathing, has a rich history, more often associated with the right than with the left. To prewar cultural conservatives (Evelyn Waugh, say), America was vulgar, money-grubbing, rootless, brash, tasteless—in short, a threat to high European civilization. Martin Heidegger had much to say about "Americanism," as a soulless, greedy, inauthentic force that was fatally undermining the European spirit. To political conservatives, especially of the more radical right-wing kind, the combination of capitalism, democracy, and a lack of ethnic homogeneity was anathema to everything they stood for: racial purity, military discipline, and obedience to authority.

It is sometimes forgotten in Britain how closely anti-Americanism resembles old-fashioned European Anglophobia. Modern capitalism, after all, was a British invention.

In the eighteenth and nineteenth centuries, reactionaries as well as radical romantics in continental Europe denounced England as a society driven by nothing but the lust for profits. London was seen as a soulless city of bankers and stockbrokers exploiting the poor in their pursuit of ever more wealth. British imperialism, unlike the French Mission Civilisatrice or the German spread of Kultur, was seen as a commercial enterprise dedicated to the expansion of economic and financial power. And worst of all, in the eyes of some, was Britain's relatively mixed population. As the British-born racist Houston Stewart Chamberlain observed to his patron, Kaiser Wilhelm II, British citizenship could be bought by any "Basuto nigger" with enough cash. Not wholly accurate, perhaps, but a telling image nonetheless.

The left's distaste for Anglo-Saxon capitalism goes back at least as far as Karl Marx. But the leap from right-wing Anglophobia and anti-Americanism to the left-wing variety really came only after World War II. Soviet propaganda no doubt had much to do with it, and especially the legacy of antifascism that the Russians exploited. Anglo-American capitalism was linked to fascism in Soviet propaganda and seen as the great enemy of all the downtrodden peoples of the world. To be on the left was to be in favor of third world liberation movements. Not every supporter of Mao, Castro, or Ho Chi Minh was pro-Soviet, but he or she certainly was anti–United States—even though the United States actually did much to end the European empires.

When liberation finally came to many colonized countries, celebration quickly turned to massive bloodletting. Dictatorships, some supported by Moscow, some by Washington, were established. Millions in China, Africa, and Southeast Asia were murdered, starved, or purged by their own "liberators." America's dictators (Suharto, Pinochet) were denounced by the left, while Soviet clients received special pleading.

But by the late 1980s, there were not many Western leftists around anymore who still admired the Soviet Union or held much brief for violent third world revolutions. Memories of Pol Pot, Vietnamese boat people, and the Cultural Revolution were a quiet source of embarrassment (one hopes). Even the promises of socialism itself had begun to fade in the aftermath of 1989. What got stuck, however, was anti-Americanism.

Anti-Americanism may indeed have grown fiercer than it was during the Cold War. It is a common phenomenon that when the angels fail to deliver, the demons become more fearsome. The socialist debacle, then, contributed to the resentment of American triumphs. But something else happened at the same time. In a curious way, left and right began to change places. The expansion of global capitalism, which is not without negative consequences, to be sure, turned leftists into champions of cultural and political nationalism. When Marxism was still a potent ideology, the left sought universal solutions for the ills of the world. Now globalization has become another word for what Heidegger meant by Americanism: an assault on native culture and identity. So the old left has turned conservative.

This defense of cultural authenticity comes in the guise of anti-imperialism, which is, of course, the same, these days, as anti-Americanism. Israel plays a significant part in this, as the perceived cat's-paw of US imperialism in the Middle East and the colonial enemy of Palestinian nationalism. Israel and the United States have a way of triggering the reflexes of European colonial guilt that overrides almost anything else.

Israeli policies, just as US policies, are often wrong, and sometimes even wicked, but even if they were always right, Israel would still be hated as the Western invader on Arab territory. On this, the contemporary anti-Zionists of the left sound just like the crusty old Arabists of the old Foreign Office school, who never had any truck with socialism. The fact that Jews can now safely be compared to Nazis, as they frequently are, is an added sop to European guilt about another horrible blot on our collective conscience.

The moral paralysis of the left, when it comes to non-Western tyrants, may also have a more sinister explanation. The Israeli philosopher Avishai Margalit calls it moral racism. When Indians kill Muslims, or Africans kill Africans, or Arabs kill Arabs, Western pundits pretend not to notice, or find historical explanations, or blame the scars of colonialism. But if white men, whether they are Americans, Europeans, South Africans, or Israelis, harm people of color, hell is raised. If one compares Western reporting of events in Palestine or Iraq with far more disturbing news in Liberia or Central Africa, there is a disproportion that suggests that non-Western people cannot be held to the same moral standards as us. One could claim this is only right, since we can only take responsibility for our own kind. But this would be a rather racist view of world affairs.

Again, there appears to have been a reversal of roles between left and right. The conservative right (I'm not talking of fascists), traditionally, was not internationalist and certainly not revolutionary. Business, stability, national interests, and political realism ("our bastards" and so on), were the order of the day. Democracy, to conservative realists, was fine for us but not for strange people with exotic names. It was the left that wanted to change the world, no matter where. Left-wing internationalism did not wish to recognize cultural or national barriers. To them, liberation was a universal project. Yet now that the "Bush-Cheney junta" talks about a democratic revolution, regardless of culture, color, or creed, Gore Vidal claims it is not our business, and others cry "racism."

There is, of course, a strong rhetorical element in all this. The US deputy defense secretary, Paul Wolfowitz, could well be a genuine believer in democratic revolutions, but his more conservative colleagues in the Bush administration may not have their hearts set on such radical goals. It is nonetheless interesting to see whom the neoconservatives in Washington managed to convert to their cause, at least as far as the war on Saddam Hussein was concerned. One of the noisiest journalistic cheerleaders for Bush's war was Christopher Hitchens. Since he has a Trotskyist past in common with some of the older American neoconservatives, there is a certain consistency in his promotion of revolutionary projects. Then, again, sending in the US Army is a strange way to promote democratic revolutions.

More significant, by far, is the backing that Bush received from Václav Havel, Adam Michnik, and especially Jose Ramos-Horta, the Nobel Peace Prize winner from East Timor. These are men, who, unlike most commentators in London or New York, know what it is like to live under the cosh. They paid the dues of voicing dissent when it was a matter of life and death. Havel and Michnik were subjects of Soviet imperialism. But the case of Ramos-Horta is more interesting, since he opposed a US-backed government, General Suharto's Indonesian regime. East Timor was a cherished cause for Chomsky and others on the left.

In an article published just before the Iraq war started, Ramos-Horta recalled the suffering of his people. He wrote, "There is hardly a family in my country that has not lost a loved one. Many families were wiped out during the decades of occupation by Indonesia and the war of resistance against it. Western nations contributed to this tragedy. Some bear a direct responsibility because they helped Indonesia by providing military aid." Thus far, none of our left-wing critics would disagree. The split comes in the conclusion. Ramos-Horta remembers how the Western powers "redeemed themselves" by freeing East Timor from its oppressors with armed force. Why, then, should the Iraqis not be liberated, too?

Ramos-Horta respects the motives of people who demonstrated against the war, although he wonders why, in all these demonstrations, he never saw "one single banner or hear one speech calling for the end of human rights abuses in Iraq, the removal of the dictator and freedom for the Iraqis and the Kurdish people." He knows that differences of opinion and public debate over issues like war and peace are vital. We enjoy the right to demonstrate and express opinions today— something we didn't have during a twenty-five-year reign of terror— because East Timor is now an independent democracy. Fortunately for all of us, the age of globalisation has meant that citizens have a greater say in almost every major issue. But if the anti-war movement dissuades the US and its allies from going to war with Iraq, it will have contributed to the peace of the dead.

One might disagree with these words. But they have a moral authority mostly lacking in the polemics of those [who were] anti–US intervention on principle. He has, however, stated a case that must be answered. Unless, of course, one really believes that the problems of faraway peoples are for them to solve alone, and that we have no business intervening on their behalf against tyrants, and that any attempt to do so has to be, by definition, racist, or colonialist, or venal.

This belief may indeed be more pragmatic, even realistic. But those who hold it should at least have the honesty to call themselves conservatives, of the Henry Kissinger school, and stop pretending they speak for the liberal-left.

## NOTE

"Wielding the Moral Club" is reprinted from *Financial Times*, September 13, 2003.

# 10

# Peace, Human Rights, and the
# Moral Choices of the Churches

MIENT JAN FABER

In 2002–2003, Christian churches were at the forefront of the campaigns against a US-led military intervention in Iraq. The unified position of the churches was quite remarkable. All over the world, Catholics and Protestants joined forces to counter the American "threat." To lend rational support to the resistance, the Christian *just war* tradition was revived. Criteria qualifying the war as just or unjust were used in numerous statements, letters, and articles, with a predictable outcome: that the war against Iraq was unjust. This was a predictable conclusion because Christian doctrine today favors pacifism and is based on the assumption that wars are unacceptable, except in clear cases of self-defense. It follows that the long-lasting massive violations of human rights by the regime of Saddam Hussein were not considered a *casus belli*, since humanitarian intervention of a military nature is also perceived as an act of war (and obviously not a case of self-defense). Either the churches neglected the massive human rights violations in the prewar period in Iraq, or the latter were simply subordinated to the issue of peace.

In my previous job as secretary-general of the Interchurch Peace Council (IKV) in the Netherlands, I was deeply involved in the debate over Iraq. Visiting northern Iraq (Iraqi Kurdistan) on a regular basis and talking to many ordinary people about their tragic experience under a brutal dictatorship, I became convinced that despite the valid criticisms of a military intervention, one could not ignore the other side of reality—namely, the fate of the Iraqi people. For most of them, the probability of a military intervention meant the emergence of a unique moment in history to be liberated from a repressive regime. I denied myself the right to oppose them. They faced circumstances where, for them, human rights had become a higher priority than peace. I myself was stuck somewhere in the middle. However, for the churches, peace was the alpha and omega. My persistent pleas for consideration of the human rights abuses in Iraq were met with sharp criticism and were misconstrued as a plea for war. In public, church leaders asked for my removal. In the middle of the war, on April 1, 2003, the board of the Interchurch Peace Council made the decision to discontinue the function of secretary-general. Soon after this decision, I left the institute.

## JUST WAR TRADITION

The just war theory or tradition is a form of moral reasoning that traces its origins to Aristotle and more explicitly to St. Augustine in fifth-century North Africa.[1] For more than fifteen centuries, the just war way of thinking has allowed men and women to avoid the trap of moral indifference and to think through the tangle of problems involved in the decision to go to war and in the conduct of war itself. The theory insists that no aspect of the human condition, including politics, falls outside the scope of moral reasoning and judgment.[2] The just war tradition is an attempt to relate the morally legitimate use of proportionate and discriminate military force to morally worthy political ends. As a tradition of statecraft, the just war tradition recognizes that there are circumstances in which the most urgent obligation in the face of evil is to stop it. Thus, at times waging war is morally necessary in order to defend the innocent and to promote the minimum conditions of international order. In a way, the just war tradition shares Clausewitz's view that war is an extension of politics. Indeed, if it is not, it is simply wickedness.[3]

Despite its reluctance to the use of force, George Weigel argues that the just war tradition, as a theory of statecraft, should not be reduced to a checklist of means tests based on the presumption against violence.[4] The just war tradition begins by defining the moral responsibilities of governments, continues with the definition of morally appropriate political ends, and then takes up the questions of means. In other words, considerations about the decision to go to war (*jus ad bellum*) precede considerations about the conduct during war (*jus in bello*). But in the case of Iraq, an overwhelming majority of statements, letters, and commentaries of churches and church representatives made use of the just war tradition in its reverse order. Its main emphasis was put on questions of war conduct, particularly questions of proportionality and discrimination between combatants and noncombatants. The *jus ad bellum* questions—just cause, right intention, competent authority, reasonable chance of success, proportionality of ends, and last resort— were almost completely neglected, with the exception of the question of whether the war was going to be waged by a competent authority, in this case the UN Security Council. The latter is, of course, a relevant question because international law restricts war engagement mainly to self-defense against an armed attack.[5] The churches, however, mostly used the competent authority principle to support their presumption against violence. Actually, I have not come across a single church statement in support of a military intervention in Iraq, even if mandated by the UN Security Council.

## THE KOSOVO WAR

Before analyzing in detail the debate during the Iraq prewar crisis, let us focus for a moment on the Kosovo war. This conflict was important because it became a harbinger for a new approach inside many church bodies: to combine and strengthen a pacifist (nonviolence) position with the criteria of the just war tradition. On March 24, 1999, NATO air forces attacked the Federal Republic of Yugoslavia (FRY) in order to force President Slobodan Milošević to sign a document that guaranteed self-rule for Kosovo. The next day, the National Council of Churches in the United States distributed a statement claiming that "peace in Kosovo . . . will be realized as the residents are given the opportunity to engage in the resolution of the issues which have become barriers to peace and justice."[6] Moreover, "no true resolution of the issues can be achieved by the application of force." This is a manifestly pacifist position.

The same day, a similar position could be found in a pastoral letter to the council's member churches in FRY, in which the secretary-general of the World Council of Churches (WCC), Konrad Raiser, expressed his profound emotion and solidarity with the Serb churches following the NATO-led bombing of Yugoslavia. According to him, "war can only bring further destruction and human suffering."[7] In the letter, no reference whatsoever was made to the position of the overwhelming majority of the Kosovar Albanians, who considered the NATO campaign the only way to freedom. The Kosovar Albanians received no attention, either, when, on March 29, four international church bodies with headquarters in Geneva appealed to the UN: "Each day of bombing makes the solution more distant, and increases the risk of regionalization of the conflict. It also enhances the danger of a renewed divide within Europe."[8] Here, the church bodies made use, implicitly, of the proportionality principle of the just war tradition to underline their rejection of the NATO campaign. The bombing campaign lasted seventy-eight days, but no signs of regionalization became visible, and, apart from some frictions with Russia at the very end of the war, a new divide within Europe did not emerge.

At the time, not everybody in the churches was convinced that pacifism was the right answer to the Kosovo crisis. It is interesting to note the mixed feelings of the Roman Catholic bishops in the Netherlands toward the bombing campaign. Well aware of the fact that a minority of the Albanians were Roman Catholics, the bishops expressed some sympathy with NATO's intervention. However, in the same breath they also pressed Western countries to make use of every opportunity to stop the air campaign.[9] In the United Kingdom, the most outspoken senior religious leader of the Church of England, Richard Harries, the bishop of Oxford and an expert on the theory of just war, was asking "those responsible for taking such decisions [on war] to consider in their calculations the tradition of moral thinking associated with the idea of the 'just war.'" Harries rightly underlined that any application of the just war criteria will produce "a variety of conclusions and that ultimately this is a decision that political leaders have to make and stand by." Harries's personal view was that air strikes against military targets in Yugoslavia are "understandable but regrettable."[10]

In reaction to the discussion in the United Kingdom, Jamie Shea, the well-known spokesperson of NATO, addressed the issue of just war in a speech at the Reform Club in London on July 15, 1999.[11] He started by saying that in the present day, wars based purely on wars of national interests are being replaced by wars of conscience. Wars of conscience are waged because countries feel "a duty to uphold certain human rights and social values against states which abuse those values vis-à-vis their own citizens." Shea calls these wars "humanitarian interventions." Nowadays, public opinion expects that the military campaigns themselves should also be conducted in a more civilized way and legit-imized by a UN Security Council resolution or some other grounding in international law. In Shea's words: "Democracies expect the maximum political results from the minimum use of force." As a result, Shea con-cludes that the principles of just war dear to Aristotle, Augustine, and Thomas Aquinas are making a major comeback.

Shea distinguishes, however, only four principles in the just war tra-dition: two *jus ad bellum* principles (last resort and chance of success) and two *jus in bello* (proportionality and discrimination) principles. He counters the last resort principle by arguing the intervention came much too late. Had NATO sent some gunboats to respond immediately to the Serb artillery shelling of Dubrovnik in 1991, the misery and destruction of the subsequent breakup of Yugoslavia could have been avoided. "There would perhaps not have been several hundred thou-sand deaths, no two and a half million refugees and untold dislocation to the social and economic life of an entire region."

Next, Shea converts the reasonable chance of success principle to the principle "the end justifies the means." Of course, by doing so, it is no longer a principle *ad bellum* but has become a rather senseless principle in retrospect. The principle is respected, Shea says, because "Kosovo is now free" [*sic*]. Faced with the *jus in bello* principle of proportionality, Shea does respond to the following crucial question: "Hasn't NATO bombing only provoked Milošević into expelling hundreds of thou-sands of Kosovar Albanians? Instead of stopping a humanitarian disas-ter, haven't you caused one instead?" He is quite honest and direct in his answer: "All military interventions are based on the premises that you have to exacerbate a crisis in order to solve it." Using a metaphor, Shea says, "The ulcer cannot be removed from the stomach unless the patient is operated upon."

Finally, let us examine the principle of discrimination. Shea asserts that collateral damage was kept to a strict minimum. In Operation Allied Force, NATO dropped more than twenty-three thousand bombs, with only thirty misdirected—but not on purpose, Shea claims. One of those accidents occurred when an aircraft attacked a railway bridge. The video footage shows that at the moment the pilot released his bomb, no train was on the bridge, but a split second after the bomb had been launched, the passenger train appeared, with the tragic results that everybody knows. There is little reason for doubt in this case, but the question about discrimination between combatants and noncombat-ants still must be answered. Indeed, the number of combatants killed during the Kosovo war was relatively low—there were no NATO casualties and according to Belgrade about a thousand on its side. Thus, the impression was left that the "only" people who were dying in this conflict were (more than eleven thousand) civilians. So, discrimination occurred but in reverse.

The four criteria of the just war tradition not addressed by Shea must have been rather obvious to him. Indeed, he seems to think that the NATO campaign served a just cause and with the right intention, because it has been defined as a humanitarian intervention. In a way, he falls in the trap of (or, if you wish, is saved by) his own definition. That the NATO air campaign was originally launched as an enforcement operation does not bother him anymore. At the end of the day, the public at large perceived the campaign as a humanitarian intervention and as such was justified. (Note: Despite the fact that human rights violations in Iraq were much more serious, even monstrous, than those in Kosovo, all attempts to redefine the Iraq war as a humanitarian intervention have failed. In my view, this result is partly because of the massive opposition against the war and partly because of the troublesome postwar situation.)

Personally, I was also in favor of a humanitarian intervention in Kosovo. In the summer of 1998, I witnessed with my own eyes how tens of thousands of Kosovar Albanians were forcefully removed from their homes, fleeing into the mountains. Asked what they wanted the international community to do, many of them responded, "Please, send NATO to protect us." Since then, I have advocated a ground operation, including close air support, with the explicit aim of protecting those people—in other words, a "real" humanitarian intervention. In March 1999, when NATO launched its air strikes, I knew that this action was not a humanitarian intervention. But in face of Milošević's reaction of massive ethnic cleansing, I found it rather immoral to focus my criticism on NATO.

To say, as Jamie Shea does, that all military interventions are based on the premise that you have to exacerbate a crisis in order to solve it is a kind of heresy for church leaders. For them, the use of violence should be restricted to policing. The fire has to be extinguished immediately and not be fanned first. At a seminar in New York on November 13, 2003, the secretary-general of the WCC, Konrad Raiser, told the audience about WCC's reservations regarding the notion of humanitarian intervention.[12] Recognizing the dilemma inherent in the UN Charter—that is, the tension between the prohibition of intervention into the internal affairs of sovereign states[13] and the affirmation of the universal validity of human rights and fundamental freedoms for all as essential for international peace[14]—Raiser suggested a solution for this dilemma by rephrasing some formulations. We should speak less about the "outside right to intervene" and more about the "responsibility of a state to protect its citizens." In other words, we should stress human protection instead of humanitarian intervention. This approach also broadens the concept of "national security" to the wider principle of "human security," Raiser argued. The objective of the international community should be "to restore the capacity and willingness of the authorities of the given state to provide for human security relying on their own forces." According to Raiser, humanitarian intervention should only be considered in situations where the international community is confronted with a failed state, but human rights cannot be enforced by military means.[15]

Certainly, the proof of the pudding is in the eating. Therefore, it is a pity that Raiser did not apply his conception to the case of Saddam Hussein and his authority as the leader of the state of Iraq. In doing so, Raiser would have had to acknowledge that for a brutal dictator such as Saddam, "the responsibility to protect" only applied to members and supporters of his own regime. At first glance, it might look like an interesting approach to replace the notion of intervention by the notion of protection, since the latter avoids war and refers directly to citizens. But on further inspection, Raiser's reasoning is quite misleading. In the name of peace, the primary actors have been changed, with the international community being replaced by a repressive state.

## THE IRAQ WAR AND THE AMERICAN DEBATE

In his column in the *Daily Southtown* on September 25, 2002, the Catholic priest and sociologist Andrew M. Greeley observed that just war theory is under attack within the Christian communities.[16] "There is no such thing as a just war, it is argued, because modern weapons are so horrific. All wars, therefore, are unjust, and the only alternative for Christians is passive resistance to those who attack them." Insofar as this position would deny humans the right of self-defense, it seems to lack common sense, Greeley stresses. "If it were followed in the early 1940s, either Hitler or Stalin would have ruled the world and most of us would be either dead or unborn." For him the weakness of the pacifist argument is that if all wars are evil, then one cannot make a particular case against a specific war. Indeed, one cannot even argue that a US invasion of Iraq seems unnecessary because, by definition, all wars, even necessary wars, cannot be justified. Greeley therefore wants a rehabilitation of the just war tradition. He needs the principles of just war in order to answer the question, What might justify a preemptive strike against an enemy whom one suspects of preparing an attack against oneself? According to him, there had been no proof, yet, of the seriousness or the imminence of an Iraqi attack. Still, "the United States might stumble into a war that is evil and unjust and in which thousands and perhaps tens of thousands of people will die horrible deaths."

Whereas Greeley distanced himself from the pacifists, his colleague George Lopez, the director of policy studies at the Catholic B. Kroc Institute at Notre Dame University, criticized the dominant American culture in which going to war is very much accepted as a means of politics.[17] Lopez, too, wants to save the just war tradition, but, contrary to Weigel, he is of the opinion that the just war theory is based on the presumption against the use of force. Lopez observes that US elites are doing the opposite. They understand the just war tradition as permitting the use of force once certain conditions are met. In doing so, he argues, they misuse the just war principles developed to serve as "uncompromising pillars whereby an exception might be granted in only this specific case." Lopez asserts that in practice, most just war thinkers present a pro forma checklist that must be addressed by decision makers who seek to have the use of force considered moral and legal by the populace. At the top of the checklist sits the selection of a norm-laden nom de guerre—Operation Just Cause, Operation Enduring Freedom, and the like—that suggests an adherence to *jus ad bellum* concerns. But the bulk of the checklist focuses on the *jus in bello* concerns of proportionate response: sensitivity to civilian casualties and ensuring no wider gains for the United States as a result of war. Lopez reminds his readers that this approach was fully manifest in the debates of the US Congress from November 1990 through January 1991 regarding the first Gulf War against Iraq. He could have added that Jamie Shea's defense of the Kosovo war fits this model as well.

Lopez also points out three unresolved dilemmas, one regarding *jus ad bellum* concerns and two *jus in bello* controversies. These dilemmas comprise the legacy of the three US wars over the last twelve years. The Gulf War, Kosovo, and Afghanistan were all fought under *jus ad bellum* criteria as wars designed to defend and reestablish important international norms. According to Lopez, those widely accepted international norms are to turn back aggression, to prevent genocide, and to halt international terrorism. Yet only in the first case, that of the Gulf War, did the United States seek authorization through the UN Security Council. But in each case the action taken to support an international norm was sufficiently strong to prevent large-scale dissension with US action, Lopez says. In other words, circumstantial evidence made up for the lack of a mandate of the UN Security Council. However, given the long-standing commitment to deal with Iraq through the Security Council, Lopez is afraid that the absence of Security Council authority will raise serious questions about the notion of "competent authority" within the just war tradition. If US military action engenders widespread condemnation in the international community, these doubts could be further complicated. Which is exactly what happened.

In retrospect, and if the aim was to prevent genocide, Lopez seems to agree with the Kosovo intervention. This is remarkable, first, because he must have been aware of the fact that this intervention was not launched for that purpose and, second, because in view of his strong rejection of the Iraq war, he should have drawn some parallels between Kosovo and Iraq. There was also a long-standing tradition to deal with Kosovo through the UN Security Council, and, given the horrifying record of Saddam, there was no reason to exclude the risk that under heavy internal and external pressure, the dictator would once again resort to genocide. It is true, however, that the Bush administration didn't give that risk a central place in its argument for military intervention. But neither did the Clinton administration, in the case of Kosovo. In the end, large-scale consent was created only by circumstantial evidence. That did happen in the case of Kosovo, but not in the case of Iraq.[18]

The two *jus in bello* concerns put forward by Lopez are interrelated. Faced with the near certainty that with the use of precision-guided munitions (PGMs) one could hit any target without concern for inadvertent civilian death, Lopez claims that US war planners will dramatically expand the list of targets considered as "military." He refers to the air–land battle strategy that was adopted in the Gulf War that resulted in huge destruction of the civil infrastructure: "After the war, in 1992 more than one hundred thousand civilians died from the lack of clean water, the impotency of electrical supply sources to meet the needs of basic hospital systems, and the inability of citizens to rely on basic waste sewage disposal." What Lopez does not take into account here, however, is the main difference between the Gulf War of George H. W. Bush and the military intervention that was considered by the administration of George W. Bush. In fact, the latter Bush wanted regime change, which implied occupation and the obligation to restore the infrastructure as soon as possible.

The contributions to the debate by Greeley and Lopez, two academics, had quite an impact on the positions that were adopted by numerous churches and church bodies in the United States and elsewhere during the fall of 2002 and the following winter. They also had an impact on the debate outside the United States, but in a far less important way. In general, the American contributions to the debate were more political. In Europe (and Canada as well), a dominant Christian-pacifist tendency combined with a dose of anti-Americanism and international legalism was often enough to lead to a strong stand against a unilateral military intervention. Most church bodies in the United States were rather conscious of the necessity to take into consideration the events of 9/11 and the Afghanistan war when formulating their position on Iraq. In a letter[19] to President Bush on September 13, 2002, on behalf of the Conference of Catholic Bishops in the United States, Wilton D. Gregory, the bishop of Belleville, reminded the president of a letter[20] from his predecessor, Bishop Joseph Fiorenza, written a year earlier, in support of a possible military response to the perpetrators and their allies of the terrorist attack on the United States on 9/11. However, he noted that this strategy has to be considered under the condition that any military response must be in accordance with "the norms of the just war tradition." In his own letter to Bush, Gregory put his finger on the *casus belli* for a military attack on Iraq. He emphasized that the catechism of the Catholic Church limits just cause to cases in which the damage inflicted by the aggressor on the nation is "lasting, grave and certain"[21]—in other words, only in cases of self-defense. Having made that hard restriction, Gregory writes that even if this condition is fulfilled, the legitimate authority for using force must be supported by some international body, "preferably by the UN Security Council." Because the bishop also feared that the use of massive military force to remove the current regime in Iraq could have incalculable consequences for the civilian population, he urged the president to pursue alternatives to war.

Two months later, on November 13, 2002, in a statement on Iraq, the US Conference of Catholic Bishops underlined the concerns of its chairperson.[22] As an alternative to war, the bishops expressed their

support for an "effective enforcement of the military embargo and
maintenance of political sanctions." Although the American bishops
made it clear that war should be avoided, contrary to the Vatican in
Rome and many other Christian bodies, they were not ready to free
Saddam Hussein from his international isolation.[23]

Perhaps the most radical opposition to a military intervention from
an official church body in the United States came from the general secretary of the National Council of Churches, Bob Edgar. After visiting
Iraq and meeting with Tariq Aziz, the Iraqi vice prime minister, he
declared that "pre-emptive war is immoral and illegal. It is theologi-
cally illegitimate and profoundly violates our Christian beliefs and religious principles. As disciples of Jesus Christ, the Prince of Peace, we
know this war is completely antithetical to his teachings. Jesus Christ
taught peace, justice, hope, and reconciliation and rejected revenge,
war, death, and violence."[24] Christian pacifism is also the ideological
basis of the Canadian Council of Churches in a letter to Prime Minister
Jean Chrétien.[25] The council strongly criticizes those who say "we are
not in the business of negotiating with Saddam Hussein." And they
continue: "Negotiations cannot open minds and possibilities if the universe is divided beforehand into two camps, the good and the evil, with
'our' side being only good. . . . We urge the Government of Canada to
stay in dialogue with all relevant parties, and to insist on treating all as
fellow human beings with human dignity and human rights." The
prime minister is also informed that Christian colleagues in the Middle
East have asked the council to teach its own society about "how crushing the international sanctions have been for the health, livelihoods and
hope of most Iraqi men, women and (especially) children." The Canadian Council is ready to do so, although it stipulates that "the suffering
of Iraqis lies *also* at the feet of President Saddam Hussein and his government." It even continues by saying that there is "no doubt that
many residents of Iraq long and pray for a regime change." But not by
force because, in their (mistaken) view, that is against the wish of the
same Iraqi people. Indeed, the council writes, "All the more striking,
then, is the strength with which voices from that country and region
urge us not to bring about a new regime by means of a violent invasion
from outside."

Who were these voices? Of course, they came from the Middle East
Council of Churches and the Iraqi churches whose leadership was
totally dependent on the regime of Saddam Hussein. The Chaldean
prelate, Bishop Shlemon Warduni of Baghdad, was speaking with his

master's voice when he declared to an Italian news agency that the Chaldean patriarchate is against all war and aggression.[26] Asked about human rights in Iraq, he pointed to the West (United States/United Kingdom) and the UN: "Whom do we have to defend? Are not our children the first victims of violence? Are not our elderly and sick, left without care and assistance, perhaps the same as yours?" By identifying themselves so closely with the leadership of the Christian churches in Iraq, Western churches were running the risk that most Iraqi people would consider them fellow travelers of the Iraqi regime. Which did, indeed, turn out to be the case. But the Western churches were not the only ones. Millions of antiwar activists marching through the streets of capitals all over the world in February 2003 were met with the same criticism from ordinary Iraqis (see, for instance, the essays in this volume by Ann Clwyd and Pamela Bone).

As we will see, the national Councils of Churches in the United States and Canada were closely in line with the dominant European way of reasoning and, unlike most of their Catholic colleagues in North America, were quite ready to meet with, and in some ways legitimize by doing so, the regime of Saddam Hussein. Let us now turn to Europe to examine the debate there.

## THE IRAQ WAR AND THE EUROPEAN DEBATE

The debate in Europe kicked off in June 2002 with a document released by the British chapter of the Catholic peace movement Pax Christi.[27] Pax Christi UK considered an attack on Iraq "both immoral and illegal." It stated that eradicating the dangers posed by malevolent dictators and terrorists can be achieved only "by tackling the root causes" of such phenomena. This could be done through "the transformation of structures of injustice and politics of exclusion." For Pax Christi, the people of Iraq should not have been made to suffer further because they were living under a dictator who in his early years in power enjoyed the collusion and support of Western nations. The people of Iraq have already paid a terrible price through a combination of UN sanctions and US/UK bombing, "including the premature deaths of hundreds of thousands of children." Initiating a military preemptive action was illegal, in the eyes of the Catholic peace movement, "except in the case of self-defense when an armed attack has actually occurred against a sovereign state. . . . However dangerous Iraq's mass destruction weapons programme might be, there is no justification for war by another state unless and until the Iraqi government itself launches an attack [on that state]." Although Pax Christi welcomed a return of UN weapons inspectors to Iraq, it also added that "the demands made on Iraq should be matched by the actions of the existing eight nuclear weapons states." In other words, those states should open up and give up their nuclear weapons programs as well. In passing, the declaration noted that its reasoning was based on the traditional just war requirements of lawful authority, just cause, right intention, and last resort.

The Pax Christi declaration is a good example of making an argument based on the concept of the lesser evil. For Pax Christi, the greater evil had to be located in the Western nations that once colluded with the lesser evil Saddam. Moreover, they were the main architects of the structures of injustice and the politics of exclusion in the world (including the injustice to and exclusion of Iraq). Since some of these Western nations (i.e., the United States and the United Kingdom) prepared for war against Iraq, Pax Christi argued that the peace movement should start to rally against war, in support of the suffering people in Iraq. The question of whether these "suffering people" agreed with this argument was never put forward, let alone answered.

At the end of August 2002, the Central Committee of the WCC joined the public debate on Iraq.[28] It expressed support for a call from the Middle East Council of Churches "for a sustained and determined diplomatic and political effort that engages the Iraqi government directly, and a sustained campaign to re-empower the Iraqi people and restore their dignity." It welcomed the Christian Declaration launched by Pax Christi UK and shared the view that the root causes of the conflict should be addressed. But foremost, it reaffirmed the words of the WCC First General Assembly (1948): "War as a method of settling disputes is incompatible with the teaching and the example of our Lord Jesus Christ." In short, what the statement wanted to convey was that good Christians should be pacifists, that the regime of Saddam Hussein should be freed from its isolation, and that the Iraqi people should be reempowered by putting an end to the sanctions.

In the months preceding the war, many church bodies issued numerous declarations in which various doomsday scenarios prevailed. A typical example is the declaration of church leaders gathered in Berlin on February 5, 2002, at the invitation of the WCC and hosted by the EKD (Evangelical Church in Germany).[29] The church leaders from Europe, North America, and the Middle East predicted a war with enormous consequences: large-scale displacement of people, civil war and major unrest in the whole region, intense hatred, extremist ideologies, global instability, and insecurity. "The plight of Iraqi children and the unnecessary deaths of hundreds of thousands of Iraqis over the past twelve years of sanctions regime weighs heavily on our hearts." Of course, the church leaders were against a military intervention in Iraq. "As people of faith, our love of neighbor compels us to oppose war." But Saddam Hussein was also criticized: "Iraq must cooperate fully with UN inspectors, and guarantee . . . human rights for all its citizens. The people in Iraq must be given hope that there are alternatives to both dictatorship and war."

But what kind of pressure did the church leaders put on Saddam Hussein in order to force him to guarantee human rights to his citizens? What kind of pressure *could* they put on him? In the West, the churches were not involved in the few and small rallies organized against Saddam Hussein, while the huge antiwar demonstrations, actively supported by many church bodies, were broadcast in Iraq over and over again, as a symbol of the massive support for the peaceful policies of the Iraqi leader. Visiting northern Iraq in February 2003, I was approached by many people who were deeply shocked after seeing the TV images, expressing their anger over the naiveté of the marching peace activists. "They really have no clue whatsoever about the dictatorship that we have had to endure for so many decades," I was told.

When all was said and done, for the WCC the antiwar campaign was a Christian "jihad" based on a kind of *status confessiones*. When war broke out on March 20, 2003, an ecumenical service of prayer was held at the WCC headquarters in Geneva. In his address,[30] WCC secretary-general Konrad Raiser rebuked President Bush's attempts to invoke divine legitimation for his war against Iraq. For Raiser, the president "must be confronted by God's concrete commandment: 'Let me hear what God the Lord will speak, for he will speak peace to his people, to his faithful, to those who turn to him in their hearts.'" The Christian response to the military posturing of George W. Bush should be "an act of defiance: denouncing this misuse of religious language in order to justify an act of war that violates the legal order developed to protect world peace." Raiser emphasized that although "many now feel helpless, full of anger and fear," the fact that all churches are acting together in "common, prophetic discernment" was an encouraging development. "We should celebrate that, for the first time, the churches together have placed the commandment of God above their respective political loyalties."

Raiser's address left no room for the slightest reference to the tyranny of Saddam Hussein. In the face of Bush's war, Saddam's tyranny had disappeared. The gathered community prayed[31] for "the women in Iraq, who will be subjected to a lot of pain and suffering. . . . Mothers will lose their sons, wives their husbands, daughters their fathers. Families will be torn apart, and many women will have to shoulder heavy burdens alone." They also prayed for "the Iraqi children . . . that they may have an opportunity to enjoy the same rights as our children—the right to be a child." I agree, but my question to the WCC is, With Saddam Hussein still in power?

The churches expressed compassion, of course, for the suffering Iraqi people under the dictatorship of Saddam Hussein. But given the churches' own pacifist conviction—that war was an act against God—church bodies, especially in Europe, wanted to believe that the Iraqi people in a way shared their view that human rights violations are bad, but war is worst of all. In a fall 2002 letter to the Dutch government, the Dutch Council of Churches expressed its deep concerns over the plight of the Iraqi people: "The regime of Saddam Hussein is oppressive and guilty of serious violations of human rights."[32] But the council was also convinced that numerous ordinary people would be victimized in a war. Moreover, it strongly doubted that a military intervention could contribute to democracy in Iraq. Before reaching the conclusion that it was against a military intervention, the council remarked that it had paid great attention "to the views of the Iraqi people in all its variety." Implicitly, this remark suggested that a majority of the Iraqi people are also against war as a means to end oppression and restore human rights. At the time, most people in Iraq would have felt manipulated by this suggestion. But for the Dutch Council, this point seemed to have been of little relevance.

## CONCLUSION

When human rights and peace come to a tête-à-tête, the churches and the majority of the peace movements will give priority to peace. Such was already the case during the Cold War. In the 1980s, only a small part of the broad Western peace movement and very few church leaders openly allied themselves with dissident groups such as Charter 77 and Solidarity in Eastern Europe. Indeed, the movements and the churches were forerunners in the antinuclear campaigns but kept silent on human rights abuses in Eastern Europe. My own organization, the

Interchurch Peace Council (IKV), was among the main initiators of the rallies against nuclear weapons. But it was also heavily criticized by most other church bodies because of its numerous public and secret contacts with a range of dissident groups in Eastern Europe. The other groups perceived our solidarity with the dissidents as destabilizing the peace between East and West. This way of thinking falls into the same pattern that we have seen during the wars in Kosovo and Iraq. The IKV has never been a propagator of war in the Clausewitzian tradition, but it was conscious of the fact that the end of the Cold War had brought a fundamental change to our world order. New and greater opportunities were created not only to raise issues of human rights but also to solve them. Since the end of the Cold War, the IKV has campaigned for a reorientation of political and military means with a focus on human security, human rights, and humanitarian intervention. Unfortunately, we did not receive much support from other church bodies.

For me, the most important question is this: How do we avoid the risk of advocating peace at the expense of human rights, and vice versa? As long as we do not live in a perfect world, the dilemma will remain. But in order to apply military means as a measure of last resort only, I propose that an "escalation ladder" for attacking human rights violations should be developed and officially introduced through the UN. In essence, this ladder should be based on the principle that all human rights violations can and should be matched with adequate and adjusted (military and nonmilitary) means. Thus, facing numerous human rights violations, varying in scale, intensity, and horror, the international community can make use of a scheme of different instruments that it will apply, particularly on the request of the Security Council. Such instruments include warnings, missions, monitors, ultimatums, political and economic sanctions, and so forth, up to humanitarian interventions in case of (impending) massive violations of human rights and genocides. To be sure, in 2003 Iraq didn't face an impending genocide, although the rights of many Iraqis were seriously violated. Iraq was a totalitarian state, plain and simple. In my view, nonmilitary measures should have been used to address these violations. But I could not forget and I was often reminded by my Iraqi friends that Saddam Hussein had already planned and executed two genocides, one against the Kurdish population in the late 1980s and another against the Marsh Arabs in the 1990s. In the 1980s, the Iraqi armed forces and security services systematically destroyed four thousand Kurdish villages and several small cities, attacked two hundred Kurdish villages and towns with chemical weapons in 1987 and 1988, and organized the deportation and execution of up to 182,000 Kurdish civilians. In the 1990s, the Saddam regime drained the marshes of southern Iraq, displacing half a million people, half of whom fled to Iran, and killing some forty thousand. In addition to destroying the five-thousand-year-old Marsh Arab civilization, draining the marshes did vast ecological damage to one of the most important wetland systems on the planet. Even so, the one and only measure related to human rights violations that has ever been taken against Saddam was a warning, issued as Resolution 688 of the UN Security Council, April 1991. Is it any wonder, then, that most Iraqis considered the military intervention of March 2003 as a late but justified instrument to restore their human rights?

## NOTES

1. James Turner Johnson, *The Just War Tradition and the Restraint of War: A Moral and Historical Inquiry* (Princeton, NJ: Princeton University Press, 1981); Roland Bainton, *Christian Attitudes toward War and Peace: A Historical Survey and Critical Re-evaluation* (New York: Abingdon, 1960).

2. Robert D. Kaplan, *Warrior Politics: Why Leadership Demands a Pagan Ethos* (New York: Random House, 2002), holds a different view. He suggests that only a pagan ethos can provide us with the kind of leadership capable of safely traversing the global disorder of the twenty-first century.

3. George Weigel, "Moral Clarity in a Time of War," the Second Annual William E. Simon Lecture, October 24, 2002, http://www.eppc.org/publications/pubID.1554/pub_detail.asp (accessed January 20, 2005).

4. Ibid.

5. Charter of the United Nations, article 51.

6. National Council of Churches, "CWSW Unit Committee Calls on NATO to Cease Bombing in Kosovo," http://www.ncccusa.org/news/99news37.html (accessed January 20, 2005).

7. World Council of Churches, "Pastoral Letter to WCC Member Churches in the Federal Republic of Yugoslavia, http://www.wcc-coe.org/wcc/news/press/99/03pu.html (accessed January 4, 2005).

8. Joint letter of the World Council of Churches (WCC), the Conference of European Churches (CEC), the Lutheran World Federation (LWF), and the World Alliance of Reformed Churches (WARC), "International Church Bodies Call for a Halt to the NATO Intervention and a Return to the Negotiating Table," March 29, 1999, http://www.wcc-coe.org/wcc/news/press/99/09pre.html (accessed January 4, 2005).

9. "Bisschoppen vragen gelovigen om stilte voor Kosovo, eedere dag," March 31, 1999, http://www.katholieknederland.nl/archief/rkkerk/media/persberichten/index_persberichten_archief_1999_3720.html (accessed January 4, 2005).

10. "Kosova: A Statement by the Rt Rev Richard Harries," March 29, 1999, http://www.cofe.anglican.org/news/kosova-a_statement_by_the_rt_rev_richard _harries,.html (accessed January 20, 2005).

11. Jamie Shea, "The Kosovo Crisis and the Media: Reflections of a NATO Spokesman," address to the Summer Forum on Kosovo organized by the Atlantic Council of the United Kingdom and the Trades Union Committee for European and Transatlantic Understanding, Reform Club, London, July 15, 1999.

12. "The Responsibility to Protect," unpublished presentation, November 13, 2003, sponsored by the World Council of Churches in New York City.

13. UN Charter, article 2.7.

14. UN Charter, articles 1.3 and 55c.

15. At this crucial point, Raiser distances himself from the authoritative report "The Responsibility to Protect" of the International Commission on Intervention and State Security, initiated by the Canadian government. Indeed, one of the basic principles of the responsibility to protect reads, "Where a population is suffering serious harm, as a result of internal war, insurgency, *repression* or state failure, and the state in question is *unwilling* or unable to halt or avert it, the principle of non-intervention yields to the international responsibility to protect."

16. Rev. Andrew Greeley, "Proposed War Amounts to Using Evil to Fight Evil," September 25, 2002, http://www.stpeters.sk.ca/prairie_messenger/Greeley _09_25_02.html (accessed January 20, 2005).

17. George A. Lopez, "The Fading Relevance of the Just War Tradition," September 27, 2002, http://www.passievoorvrede.nl/upload/waronterrorism/Lopez %20pxusa%20on%20%20Just%20War%20Tradition%2027-9.doc (accessed January 20, 2005).

18. After the liberation of Kuwait in 1991, the then–Turkish president, Turgut Özal, advised the United States to march on to Baghdad. If the US Army would have removed Saddam Hussein from power, circumstantial evidence would probably have created broad legitimacy for this (UN-) unauthorized military intervention. At the time, both the Shiite and the Kurdish populations were ready to revolt against the regime; moreover, Saddam Hussein still possessed weapons of mass destruction.

19. Bishop Wilton D. Gregory, "Letter to President Bush on Iraq," September 13, 2002, http://www.nccbusco.org/sdwp/international/bush902.htm (accessed January 4, 2005).

20. United States Conference of Catholic Bishops, letter to President Bush, September 19, 2001, http://www.usccb.org/comm/archives/2001/01-166a.htm (accessed January 4, 2005).

21. Catechism of the Catholic Church, article 2309, http://www.vatican .va/archive/ENG0015/_P81.HTM (accessed January 4, 2005).

22. United States Conference of Catholic Bishops, "Statement on Iraq," November 13, 2002, http://www.usccb.org/bishops/iraq.htm (accessed January 4, 2005).

23. The personal envoy of the pope, Cardinal Roger Etchergaray, visited Saddam Hussein in Baghdad on February 14, 2003. At the same time, the pope

received the vice prime minister of Iraq, Tariq Aziz, in Rome. Together, the Vatican and Baghdad made a last effort to prevent a war.

24. Bob Edgar, "Sowing the Seeds of Peace," press statement, January 3, 2003, New York, http://www.ncccusa.org/news/02news104a.html (accessed January 20, 2005).

25. Canadian Council of Churches, "No to War against Iraq," September 25, 2002, http://www.zenit.org/english/visualizza.phtm?sid=25818 (accessed January 4, 2005).

26. Statement published in the Italian newspaper *Awenire*, September 24, 2002.

27. Pax Christi, "The Morality and Legality of War against Iraq: A Christian Declaration," June 2002 (presented to Tony Blair on August 6, 2002), http://www.paxchristi.org.uk/documents1.htm#declaration (accessed January 20, 2005). The declaration is also endorsed by a number of religious leaders in the UK.

28. Central Committee of the World Council of Churches, meeting in Geneva, August 26 to September 3, 2002, "Statement on the Threats of Military Action against Iraq," http://www.ctbi.org.uk/intaff/iraq/wcco1.htm (accessed January 20, 2005).

29. "Church Leaders United against War in Iraq," February 5, 2003, http://www.ncccusa.org/news/03news6.html (accessed January 20, 2005).

30. Konrad Raiser, "Reflection in a Service of Prayer for Peace," Geneva, March 2003, http://www.wcc-coe.org/wcc/what/international/raiser.html (accessed January 4, 2005).

31. "Prayer for Peace," Ecumenical Centre, Geneva, http://www.wcc-coe.org/wcc/what/international/iraqpeaceservice.html (accessed January 4, 2005).

32. Dutch Council of Churches, letter dated October 19, 2002.

# 11

# Ethical Correctness and the Decline of the Left

JONATHAN RÉE

The venture was certainly risky; regime changes always are. The hundreds of murders, rapes, and miscellaneous cruelties may not have been part of the plan, but they were clearly unavoidable once it began to be implemented. The subsequent loss of thousands more lives must have been predictable, too, along with the looting and wanton damage to historic treasures. It did not help that planning and intelligence came not from within the country but from exiles and émigrés—many of them political neurotics who had got a little out of touch with the country that they wanted to lead and from which they could not expect much of a popular welcome when they returned. In addition, there was every likelihood that the enterprise would lead to protracted civil war and bring terrible instability to international relations for years or even decades to come.

But the Russian Revolution happened less than a century ago, and it is still too soon to draw up a final balance sheet. On one hand, many would agree that the Soviet system eventually became a disaster; on the other hand, it would be hard to deny that the czarist regime deserved to be overthrown, that it could not have lasted much longer anyway, and that its passing was bound to be attended by appalling violence. Still, that leaves plenty of room for controversy about Lenin and the particular kind of revolution he led. The case against him has always been easy to make, and it seems to get easier as time goes by. But even now it is hard to be sure what the real alternatives were in 1917, let alone whether any of them would have been more successful or, in the long run, more desirable.

The question is complicated by the fact that the Russian Revolution rapidly became a political symbol as well as a historic event. For most of the twentieth century, it was the ruling political obsession of all who liked to regard themselves as clear-minded friends of peace and progress. We may not have known what to call ourselves—socialists, communists perhaps, radicals (mainly in the Untied States), or leftists (in Britain)—but we formed a more or less close-knit family, no more than ordinarily dysfunctional. Like any family, we were defined as much by our quarrels as by mutual loves and loyalties, and the dispute that gave us our identity more than any other was the one about the Russian Revolution. The question was not so much whether it was justified in the first place as whether it had been betrayed at some point and, if so, when and by whom. By Lenin himself? Stalin? Even perhaps Krushchev? Gorbachev? Or by social democracy abroad, or the reactionary, belligerent nationalisms of the European working class?

The question of revolution—revolution in Russia, followed by China, Vietnam, Algeria, Cuba, and elsewhere—has always provided the left (as I will call it from now on) with its shibboleth, the test by which it has sought to differentiate itself from other strains of politics and most particularly from mainstream progressive liberalism. We leftists have always said that we revere liberal values as much as anyone reasonably could. We have declared our horror at violence, militarism, and all forms of authoritarianism and dictatorship, and in principle we have approved of everyone's right to political dissent, freedom of expression, and due legal process. But we have also insisted that liberalism is not enough and that harping on about rights can be a distraction from more pressing social issues. Rights in a narrow sense, we have pointed out, have no meaning outside the specific systems of law by which they are implemented, while in a broader but fuzzier sense ("human rights" or "natural rights"), they probably express no more than a sublime utopianism that is utterly disconnected from real social processes.

We leftists have always maintained that the injustices we want to correct are so enormous, so pervasive, and so deeply rooted in the existing social order that there is little chance of correcting them by insisting on rights in either the broad or the narrow sense. In a world where one old duke owns half of London while dozens of beggars sleep rough on the streets, a campaign for universal rights will leave fundamental injustices intact. If one community threatens to massacre another, it may be irresponsible to pay punctilious regard to the rights of all those involved. A group that faces violent attack may be justified in forgetting about rights and answer back in kind. And in a society where some groups of children are denied the educational opportunities that are open to others, a system of equal competition for jobs will only serve to perpetuate social inequalities from one generation to the next. (In such a world, as Karl Marx put it in one of the classic explanations of the difference between liberal and leftist politics, an "equal right" will turn out to be in reality "a right of inequality.")[1] In a world where tyranny rules, abrogating violence may be equivalent to acquiescing in slavery. If liberals always got their way, promoting the ideology of human rights and fussing over nice points of morality and legality, then radical social change would be off the agenda forever. Indeed, a society in which the abstract liberal dream came true might be one in which no real human being would want to live.[2]

The leftists of the twentieth century cannot all have been right about the Russian Revolution; indeed, perhaps none of them were. But in insisting that, in a world of vast inequalities, liberal values are not enough, they were standing up for a venerable intellectual tradition that reaches beyond Lenin or Marx—a tradition that goes back to classical Greece, always insisting on the dignity of politics as a practical discipline distinct from ethics or morality and perhaps even superior to it. (The idea that political obligation could conflict with individual virtue, and especially with loyalty to family and friends, was a fundamental theme of Greek tragedy, most notably the *Antigone* of Sophocles, and the answering philosophical doctrine that politics reigns supreme goes back to Plato and Aristotle.)[3] The peculiarity of politics in this classical sense is that it is concerned with the long-term welfare of a community as a whole, and not just with the happiness or virtue of particular individuals. And if moral judgment can often proceed by an unmediated appeal to fine sentiment or high principle, political judgment never can: it will always involve something more like scientific knowledge, though no doubt falling sadly short in terms of certainty and completeness. Political judgment requires much more than a moral understanding of the difference between right and wrong. It involves a calculation of the various forces at play in the community where you are proposing to intervene and an evaluation of each of the possibilities it opens up. It is largely our commitment to this conception of political rationality—to what Leninists used to call "analysis of the situation"—that differentiates us leftists from the liberal mainstream.

No doubt the Leninist wing of the left got many things badly wrong, in theory as well as in practice. The Leninists were far too willing to follow the classic philosophical line about politics—too eager to treat politics as the card that trumps all others or as the only field of practice that deserves serious attention. They should surely have done more to guard against what might be called the fetishism of politics, and if they had been better students of Karl Marx, they would have remembered that one of the many projects he sketched out, as an enthusiastic young leftist in Paris in 1844, was nothing less than a "critique of politics" as a whole.[4] But if they were guilty of fetishizing politics, they at least avoided the mistake of reducing it to morality.

The tradition of political leftism as distinct from ethical liberalism came close to collapse toward the end of the twentieth century. Of course, it has always been easy to despise politics in general, but that contempt has usually been balanced by a recognition that politics could have a dignity of its own and that it could denote a set of obligations rather larger than those of ethics or morality, though no less binding or arduous. Now, however, both conservatives and progressives began to slip into an automatic assumption that the defining characteristics of politics were venality, dishonesty, and a self-seeking nature. To act from political motives no longer meant giving priority to collective as distinct from individual welfare, or to others as opposed to oneself; instead, it implied nothing but scrambling for personal or factional advantage in some kind of intragovernmental brawl. Indeed, all the classical political skills—the ability to negotiate the shoals of social conflict, to build alliances in some areas and to break them in others—came to be dismissed as mere dishonesty. The old and noble arts of rhetoric—which have always been central to politics—came to be equated with cant or hypocrisy. By the beginning of the twenty-first century, the idea of politics as an honorable field of selfless endeavor had been given a distinctly bad name.

Then came terrorism and a new crisis over Iraq. For died-in-the-wool leftists like me, the steady accumulation of terrorist initiatives that culminated in the attack on the World Trade Center has been deeply troubling. It had at least as much impact on our inherited assumptions as the collapse of the Soviet Union or the rise of neoliberalism. I for one

had up to that time always used the word *terror* with precaution-
ary quotation marks. I was quite taken with the commonplace idea
that one person's terrorist is another person's freedom fighter; indeed,
because it is only those who are oppressed by the state or excluded
from it who need to resort to terrorism, there seemed to be a fair presumption that the causes espoused by terrorists would be good ones,
deserving the support of all progressive opinion, liberal and leftist alike.
Surely no one would resort to terrorism unless he had been subject to
monstrous injustice?

I was rather proud of the defiance shown by my father on this point.
As a British soldier, he had run a resistance network in occupied France
in World War II, sabotaging factories and railways and causing a good
deal of damage and destruction, though few if any deaths. I was
impressed, many years later, when he reacted to alarmist press stories
that sought to delegitimize various resistance movements—in Ireland or
Palestine, for example—by labeling them "terrorist." "I was a terrorist,
too," he would say, "and I got a medal for it from George VI."

With a little bit of help from the outrageous but brilliant novels of
Michel Houellebecq,[5] I have managed to put my romanticism about
terror behind me. I still think that states are often oppressive and
unjust, but after rereading Hobbes and reflecting on the phenomenon
of so-called failed states, I think that unconditional resistance to state
power as such is even more dangerous, indeed reactionary. Under the
conditions of modern life, people are nearly always better off living
under some functioning state than under no state at all. I have begun to
think that terrorism, apart from being unpleasant in itself and often
counterproductive, could as likely as not be harnessed to objectionable
and unjust causes. This point is particularly true of Islamicist terrorism,
insofar as it aims to make Islam, or a certain puritanical reading of
it, into the unique source of political authority. I am not a religious
believer, but even if I were, I could think of few fates more miserable
than living under a theocracy of any kind. After 2001, the old romanticism about terrorists as freedom fighters had lost its last shred of
plausibility.

As far as international politics was concerned, the end of the Cold
War had landed me and my fellow leftists in unfamiliar territory.
Although I had never been a supporter of communist regimes, I had
found it convenient to assume that whenever NATO, the West, or the
United States intervened in some overseas conflict, at least since Viet-
nam, they were committing some kind of political crime, imperiously

asserting their narrow national interests to the great prejudice of everyone else's. It seemed a good rule of thumb that they would always be throwing their weight on the wrong side. But then there was Rwanda: I would have favored a war to prevent the holocaust there, even if it had to be carried out by the usual imperialist suspects and—as would probably have been the case—against the edicts of the United Nations. Shortly afterward, with the help of a new and deservedly popular left-leaning government in Britain, I found myself supporting what was in effect an invasion of Serbia by an alliance of capitalist states. Afghanistan presented another interesting case: Without approving of Soviet imperialism in general, I had always been on the side of the Soviet Union in its attempts to install a progressive, secular regime there, and the project did not lose its appeal when it was taken up belatedly by NATO under the leadership of the United States.

That is why, when it became clear that George W. Bush was intent on intervening in Iraq and toppling Saddam Hussein, I was ready to think it might be a good idea. I cannot imagine agreeing with Bush's judgments on many things, and I was quite unpersuaded by the specific claims he made about Iraq: it always seemed unlikely that Saddam's Baathist regime would have backed Islamicist terrorists or that it could pose any military threat to Europe or the United States. Indeed, it seemed unlikely that Bush's war would be in the immediate interests of the United States or of other Western powers. On the contrary, it was likely to cost them popularity throughout the world. But the important point was not the machinations of the Washington elite or their rich fantasy life (as I said rather sanctimoniously in a discussion at my local Labour Party) but the long-term welfare of the twenty-five million people who live in Iraq and the prospects for the long-oppressed Iraqi left. Up to that point, it had seemed likely that Saddam Hussein and his repressive dynasty would stay securely in power for many decades to come. The measures taken by the United Nations following the invasion of Kuwait were a joke or, rather, an obscenity. They were a standing refutation of the common liberal presumption that the United Nations is always right, as I am still reminded by a slogan stenciled on a wall near where I live: "Sanctions kill 4,000 Iraqi children every month." What the Iraqis needed, I had long thought, was something rather more than gentle reform; they needed a left-wing coup, and suddenly the gate to it had swung open. It was a paradox, to say the least, that the opportunity was being created by the United States under a reactionary president, but that did not make it wrong: it was what leftists used to call dialectics, though *fluke* might be a better word. Iraq's foolhardy defiance of a whole sequence of UN resolutions seemed to provide a good enough pretext for doing what needed to be done. For the most unexpected of reasons, the long-awaited hour of revolution was at hand.

I soon realized that I was almost alone in calling the prospective event a *revolution*. I was not surprised that statespersons such as Bush were inclined to avoid the word; it is, after all, a reminder of the mortality of political institutions, and it sounds rather left-wing. But they spoke freely of *regime change*, which is, after all, *revolution*'s dictionary equivalent, and it would not have been outlandish for the rest of us to scorn the euphemism and use a plain, blunt word instead. Of course, the situation in Iraq did not conform to the nineteenth-century nationalist idea of revolutions, where a people is supposed to rise up spontaneously and overthrow their oppressive rulers without any help from outside. On the other hand, it would be hard to find any actual revolutions that have followed that romantic pattern, and in the existing state of international relations and military power, it would be impossible for there to be any more. There is no point in being a linguistic eccentric, however, so I went along with the consensus and accepted that the events should be called a war, though it struck me that "war in Iraq" (or "invasion of Iraq") would have served better than "war on Iraq." In my own mind, though, I couldn't help making the substitution: "the Iraqi revolution."

The Iraqi revolution, or the war, has not gone anything like as well as I hoped. Things started going wrong before it even began, when it failed to get the backing of Germany, Russia, France, or the United Nations. The doubts that they raised were not unreasonable, especially given the largely irrelevant arguments about self-defense and Islamic terrorism emanating from Washington. But it was clear all along that their opposition was worse than quixotic: the United States would go it alone if it did not go in concert with other countries; and the more alone it was, the bloodier the conflict would be, and the less likely a successful result.

If I have been disappointed with much that has happened in Iraq since the invasion (seventeen months ago as I write, in August 2004), I have been almost as shocked by the poor quality of debates about it in the rest of the world. The immediate blame lies, undoubtedly, with the dark and implausible case for the action that was provided by Bush and his colleagues in Washington and echoed in Europe, particularly in the circles around Tony Blair in the British Labour government. This confusion played straight into the hands of a journalistic class whose attitude to politicians increasingly reminds me of gleeful teenagers intent on barracking their teachers at school and preventing them from doing their job. Journalists as a class like to think of themselves as followers of Socrates—fearless battlers for truth, whatever it may be and wherever it may take them. Unfortunately, they seem to equate telling the truth with revealing an awkward secret rather than devising a persuasive analysis. For them, the amount of annoyance or embarrassment caused by a story becomes a surrogate measure of its accuracy. With a journalist class of that kind, it was inevitable that public discussions of war and revolution in Iraq would focus not on the options and opportunities for the people of Iraq, or the chances of giving them a secular left-wing government, but on the convoluted actions of Bush and Blair, together with their aides and assistants and critics, and on characters like the unfortunate British civil servant David Kelly, who committed suicide after being identified as a source for a BBC story. The fact that Kelly was an expert on Iraqi military affairs who supported the invasion on the grounds that Iraq possessed weapons of mass destruction ready for use within hours was not widely reported; instead, he was allowed to pass as some kind of liberal activist who had laid down his life in the cause of truth, peace, and human rights. But even if Bush, Blair, and Kelly were as black or as white as the media wanted them to be, that had little bearing on the long-term prospects of happiness and prosperity for the Iraqi people, of whom we heard very little at all.

I had to admit that it was ridiculous when the US government likened the situation to World War II, with Saddam as a second Hitler whom the Allies must reluctantly confront. What worried me was that the argument was countered not by attempts to analyze the new configuration of events but by equally evasive attempts to cast Bush as another Hitler or to treat the whole enterprise as a second Vietnam. There was even a comic attempt by some would-be Marxists to retreat into romantic nationalism and equate Iraq with Nazi-dominated France, with the Islamicist insurgents as heroes in a progressive struggle for "national liberation."[6] On every side, people were lunging for historical parallels rather than analyzing what was really going on—a symptom, I suspected, of a disease that was eating away at the sinews of progressive political debate.

It was not just public discussions of Iraq that dismayed me. Much worse was the atmosphere of private conversations among liberals and leftists, conveyed by nods and winks and significant groans over a drink or around a fire. Everyone I met seemed to be passionately "against the war," as they put it, and convinced that all leftists must be of the same opinion. Many of them also laid claim to some specially privileged source of information: the nice Muslim engineer who came to fix their computer or their good Iraqi friends who happened to share their opinion—as if that settled the matter either way, and as if there were not Iraqis and Muslims on every side of the question. It was, of course, clear that my own position, which could be described as wary optimism about the Iraqi revolution, put me in rather embarrassing company: a secular leftist in the same lobby as American neoconservatives and Zionist zealots. But I thought I had my reasons, even though I began to feel like a heretic or a pariah in a conformist culture of liberal dissent. When friends presumed they knew what I thought, I seldom had the courage to correct them.

Throughout its history, progressive politics has depended on taking a somewhat cheerful view of humanity's prospects. The assumption has always been that both scientific knowledge and economic productivity have an inherent tendency to improve over time, that these improvements have generally enhanced humanity's chances of happiness and prosperity, and that they can be expected to continue to do so in the future. Of course, setbacks can occur, but on the whole—if you take a reasonably broad perspective, and if you consider such fundamental indices of happiness as health and longevity, prosperity, education, and tolerance—the optimistic assumption is supported by the historical record. In any case, optimism is a matter of will as much as intellect, and progressive optimism is not just a matter of stumbling on ready-made reasons for hope: it is also a matter of seeking out latent opportunities for improvement and making the most of them, wherever they may be found. One of the most striking things about progressive politics at the end of the twentieth century is that it began to run out of hope. It fell in love with failure and started to wallow in gloom. The idea that no news is good news acquired a somber complexion: every wind was now an ill wind, whichever way it blew. Reports of disaster—especially disasters in Iraq—were greeted with a kind of vindictive glee; bad tidings became an excuse for ecstasies of progressive despondency, creating a new solidarity of despair.

If they knew about it, my friends would have been astonished to learn that I did not support the massive rally that took place on September 28, 2002, in the name of the "Stop the War Coalition." As it happens, I was on the streets of London that day, very close to the route along which hundreds of thousands of people marched. I have always liked demonstrations, and it felt strange not to be taking part in this one; but as I saw the marchers and their banners, I knew it was not the place for me. The members of the Iraqi left who had been living in exile in London for many years were not supporting the march, and I did not want to parade with old British communists loyal to Saddam Hussein or with the men from the Muslim brotherhood whose T-shirts asked me to believe that "Islam is the solution." But what clinched it for me was the would-be leftists with banners bearing the slogan "Not in My Name"—a phrase that amounted to an admission that the purpose of their protest was not to improve the lot of anyone else but to claim a kind of pristine innocence for themselves. The left, I reflected, was no longer a band of committed activists with a debatable analysis and a contentious program; instead, it had dissolved into a broad popular front making common cause with the prophets of doom—a self-regarding conspiracy of moral exhibitionists and beautiful liberal souls. I turned away in dismay.

Since that time, the presumption of opposition to the war or the revolution has become more and more pervasive. It has become like a gloom auction with participants trying to outbid each other for the pessimistic high ground, and the topic is not really the state of the world or the prospects of improvements in Iraq but the apparently pig-headed policies of the US government. One can argue, however, that what is really surprising is that such a bold and progressive venture as the invasion of Iraq should ever have managed to get itself sponsored by any US president, particularly a conservative one. Military adventures overseas are bound to be expensive and to involve losses of life that will be hard to justify to an American electorate, especially if the main beneficiaries are going to be citizens of faraway countries. The real anomaly was that Bush managed to impose the policy—which would have made rather more sense under a left-leaning administration led by a Clinton or a Gore—on the conservatives of the Republican Party.

The liberal position was, by contrast, entirely consistent and predictable. Liberals have always found it hard to support policies that cost lives. They are rightly squeamish about the cynical accountancy that suggests that killing a hundred people may be obligatory if it is going to save the lives of a thousand. They are understandably dismayed if it is pointed out that the loss of lives in Iraq in the year following the invasion was no greater than the annual loss attributed to UN sanctions in the period preceding it. But if their attitudes do credit to their sensibilities, they amount not so much to a political judgment as to a conscientious objection to politics itself.

The representatives of the left, meanwhile—apart from a few unrepentant Saddamites—almost completely failed to mount any distinct arguments for joining the "antiwar coalition." Scarcely anyone recalled the old leftist truism that a purely liberal agenda may mean postponing radical social change to a nonviolent tomorrow that will never come. The left is in danger of a complete loss of nerve when confronted with the appalling costs of action and the sobering thought that the costs of inaction may be even greater. Of course, it is possible that the revolution (or the war) will turn out badly. If it does, this outcome will not prove that it was a bad cause but, rather, that it was a tragedy comparable to that of the Spanish Civil War, where between half a million and a million people were killed in the attempt to defend the republic against religiously inspired insurgents led by Franco. Understandably, it has always been the left's favorite failure: the republic should have been saved, and many other tragedies might have been averted if it had been.

Some twenty years ago, conservatives in the United States started a brilliant campaign against liberals and the left. They commandeered the phrase "political correctness" and used it to insinuate that any attempts to improve the life of the oppressed were motivated by servile conformism, coattailing, and bad faith. And the campaign has been so successful that nowadays no one would be naive enough to lay claim to political correctness without a heavy measure of irony (which perhaps explains the retreat into the self-referential slogan "Not in My Name"). The campaign has been effective because it latches onto an inherent vulnerability of progressive politics, whether leftist or liberal: that its visions of a better world cannot serve as spurs to effective action without also providing excuses for narcissistic saintliness. Unluckily for the old traditions of rational progressivism, the left has chosen not to fight back in the name of politics but to take refuge in soporific self-satisfaction instead. You might say that it has embraced ethical correctness in place of political correctness. Changing the world has become less important than shedding ostentatious tears over its failure to live up to our superior standards. But the ethics is easy, and it's the politics that counts.

# NOTES

1. See "Critique of the Gotha Programme" (1875), in Karl Marx and Friedrich Engels, *Selected Works* (Moscow: Progress, 1970), 3:13–30.

2. From this point of view, Robert Nozick's rigorous deduction of a libertarian society with a "minimal state" as the "only morally justifiable one" (see *Anarchy, State and Utopia* [New York: Basic Books, 1974]) can be read as a demonstration that "moral justification" cannot be the last word in the assessment of a social order.

3. The crux of tragedy was the idea that politics and morality are not only irreconcilable but incommensurable; the philosophers, however, sought to solve the problem (or perhaps to square the circle) by insisting on the supremacy of politics. The theme is implicit throughout Plato's *Republic*; it becomes explicit at the beginning of Book I of Aristotle's *Nichomachean Ethics* (1094a), which argues that politics is the "master art."

4. In the preface to the "Economic and Philosophic Manuscripts of 1844," Marx declared that he would publish "the critique of law, ethics, politics, etc., in a series of distinct, independent pamphlets, and afterwards try in a special work to present them again as a connected whole." See Karl Marx and Friedrich Engels, *Collected Works* (London: Lawrence & Wishart, 1975), 3:231.

5. See especially Michel Houellebecq's fortuitously prophetic *Plateforme* (Paris: Flammarion, 2001), trans. Frank Wynne (New York: Alfred A. Knopf, 2003).

6. "The first, elementary step . . . is solidarity with cause of national liberation in Iraq. The US-led forces have no business there. The Iraqi *maquis* deserves full support in fighting to drive them out." See Susan Watkins, "Vichy on the Tigris," *New Left Review* 28 (July–August 2004): 19.

# 12

# Pages from a Daily Journal of Argument

## NORMAN GERAS

*Editor's Note: The pieces collected here are edited extracts from* norm-blog—*The Weblog of Norman Geras (http://normblog.typepad.com/normblog/). As most readers will know, the Internet served as a major new source of information (and disinformation) on the war in Iraq. Over the last few years, and especially during the war, a new genre called the "blog" has developed and prospered on the Internet. The particular strengths of this genre include its ability to open up the public sphere to voices and critiques that traditionally have been excluded by virtue of the tight control of the means of public discourse. The quality of writing in the "blogosphere" is varied, but it is clear that many notable scholars and public intellectuals have taken on the new genre with verve and sophistication, as is the case with the esteemed political theorist Norman Geras. Geras's thoughts are presented here both for their astute analytical quality as well as for their illustration of this new form of public discourse.*

## 1. IRAQ AND LEFT-LIBERAL OPINION (JULY 2003)

*This is an amended version of part of a talk given to the Workers' Liberty summer school in London on June 21, 2003.*

I want to say something about support for democratic values and basic human rights. We on the left just have it in our bloodstream, do we not, that we are committed to democratic values. And although, for reasons I can't go into here, some on the left are a bit more reserved about using the language of basic human rights, nonetheless, for many of us it was this moral reality, and especially its negation, that played a part in drawing us in: to protest and work against a world in which people could just be used for the purposes of others, be exploited and superexploited, worked maybe to an early death, in any case across a life of hardship; or be brutalized for organizing to fight to change their situation, be "disappeared," or tortured, or massacred, by regimes upholding an order of inequality—sometimes desperate inequality—and privilege. In our bloodstream.

However, there is also a certain historical past of the left referred to loosely under the name "Stalinism" that forms a massive blot on this commitment and these values, on the great tradition we belong to. I am of the generation—roughly 1960s-vintage, post-Stalinist left—educated in the Trotskyist critique of that whole experience, in the new expansion and flourishing of an open, multifaceted and pluralist Marxism; educated in the movement against the war in Vietnam, the protests against Pinochet's murderous coup in Chile and against the role of the United States in both episodes and in more of the same kind. Of a generation that believed that, even though the Western left still bore some signs of continuity with the Stalinist past, this was a dying, an increasingly marginal strand, and that we had put its errors largely behind us. But I fear now it is not so. The same kinds of error—excuses and evasions and out-and-out apologia for political structures, practices, or movements no socialist should have a word to say for—are still with us. They afflict many even without any trace of a Stalinist past or a Stalinist political formation.

I obviously don't have the time or space here to rehearse all of the relevant arguments. I will confine myself to sketching some important features of the broad picture as I see it.

## SEPTEMBER 11

On September 11, 2001, there was, in New York, a massacre of innocents. There's no other acceptable way of putting this: some three thousand people (and, as anyone can figure, it could have been many more) struck down by an act of mass murder without any possible justification, an act of gross moral criminality. What was the left's response? In fact, this goes well beyond the left if what is meant by that term is people and organizations of *socialist* persuasion. It included a wide sector of liberal opinion as well. Still, I shall just speak here, for short, of the left. The response on the part of much of it was excuse and apologia.

At best you might get some lip service paid to the events of September 11 having been, well, you know, unfortunate—the preliminary "yes" before the soon-to-follow "but" (or, as Christopher Hitchens has called it, "throat-clearing"). And then you'd get all the stuff about root causes, deep grievances, the role of US foreign policy in creating these; and a subtext, or indeed text, whose meaning was America's comeuppance. This was not a discourse worthy of a democratically committed or principled left, and the would-be defense of it by its proponents, that they were merely trying to explain and not to excuse what happened, was itself a pathetic excuse. If any of the root-cause and grievance themes truly had been able to account for what happened on September 11, you'd have a hard time understanding why, say, the Chileans after that earlier September 11 (I mean of 1973), or other movements fighting against oppression and injustice, have not resorted to the random mass murder of civilians.

Why this miserable response? In a nutshell, it was a displacement of the left's most fundamental values by a misguided strategic choice—namely, opposition to the United States, come what may. This dictated the apologetic mumbling about the mass murder of US citizens, and it dictated that the United States must be opposed in what it was about to do in hitting back at Al Qaeda and its Taliban hosts in Afghanistan. [A more extended statement of my views on this subject is to be found in "Marxism, the Holocaust and September 11: An Interview with Norman Geras," *Imprints* 6, no. 3 (2002–2003): 194–214.]

## THE LIBERATION OF IRAQ

Something similar has now been repeated over the war in Iraq. I could just about have "got inside" the view—though it wasn't my view—that the war to remove Saddam Hussein's regime should not be supported. Neither Washington nor Baghdad—maybe. But *opposition* to the war—the marching, the petition signing, the oh-so-knowing derision of George W. Bush, and so forth—meant one thing very clearly. Had this campaign succeeded in its goal and actually prevented the war it was opposed to, the life of the Baathist regime would have been prolonged, with all that that entailed: years more (how many years more?) of the rape rooms, the torture chambers, the children's jails, and the mass graves recently uncovered.

This was the result that hundreds of thousands of people marched to secure. Well, speaking for myself, comrades, there I draw the line. Not one step.

Let me now just focus on a couple of dimensions of this issue.

HUMANITARIAN INTERVENTION    First, there is a long tradition in the literature of international law that, although national sovereignty is an important consideration in world affairs, it is not sacrosanct. If a government treats its own people with terrible brutality, massacring them and such, there is a right of humanitarian intervention by outside powers. The introduction of the offense of crimes against humanity at the Nuremberg Trial after World War II implied a similar constraint on the sovereign authority of states. There are limits on them. They cannot just brutalize their own nationals with impunity, violate their fundamental human rights.

Is there then, today, a right of humanitarian intervention under international law? The question is disputed. Some authorities argue that the UN Charter rules it out absolutely. War is only permissible in self-defense. However, others see a contradiction between this reading of the Charter and the Charter's underwriting of binding human rights norms. Partly because the matter is disputed, I will not here base myself on a legal right of humanitarian intervention. I will simply say that, irrespective of the state of international law, in extreme enough circumstances there is a *moral* right of humanitarian intervention. This is why what the Vietnamese did in Cambodia to remove Pol Pot should have been supported at the time, the state of international law notwithstanding, and ditto for the removal of Idi Amin by the Tanzanians. Likewise, with regard to Saddam Hussein's regime in Iraq, it was a case crying out for support for an intervention to bring the regime finally to an end.

Just think for a moment about the argument that this recent war was illegal. That something is illegal does not itself carry moral weight unless legality as such carries moral weight, and legality carries moral weight only conditionally. It depends on the particular law in question, on the system of law of which it is a part, and on the kind of social and ethical order it upholds. An international law—and an international system—according to which a government is free to go on raping, murdering, and torturing its own nationals to the tune of tens upon tens, upon more tens, of thousands of deaths without anything being done to stop it, so much the worse for this as law. It is law that needs to be criticized, opposed, and changed. It needs to be moved forward—which happens in this domain by precedent and custom as well as by transnational treaty and convention.

I am fully aware in saying this that the present US administration has made itself an obstacle in various ways to the development of a more robust and comprehensive framework of international law. But the thing cuts both ways. The war to depose Saddam Hussein and his criminal regime was not of a piece with that. It didn't have to be opposed by all the forces that did in fact oppose it. It could, on the contrary, have been supported—by France and Germany and Russia and the UN, and by a mass democratic movement of global civil society. Just think about that. Just think about the kind of precedent *it* would have set for other genocidal, or even just lavishly murderous, dictatorships—instead of all those processions of shame across the world's cities, whose success would have meant the continued abandonment of the Iraqi people.

It is, in any event, such realities—the brutalizing and murder by the Baathist regime of its own nationals to the tune of tens upon tens, upon more tens, of thousands of deaths—that the recent war has brought to an end. It should have been supported for this reason, irrespective of the reasons (concerning weapons of mass destruction [WMDs]) that George Bush and Tony Blair themselves put up front, though it is disingenuous of the war's critics to speak now as if the humanitarian case for war formed no part of the public rationale of the coalition, since it was clearly articulated by both Bush and Blair more than once.

Here is one approximate measure of the barbarities of the Baathist regime I have just referred to. It comes not from the Pentagon, or anyone in the Bush administration, or Tony Blair or those around him. It comes from Human Rights Watch. According to them, during twenty-three years of Saddam's rule, some 290,000 Iraqis disappeared into the regime's deadly maw, the majority of these reckoned to be now dead. Rounding this number down by as much as 60,000 to compensate for the "thought to be" brings this figure to 230,000. It is 10,000 a year. It is 200 people every week. I'll refrain from embellishing with details, which you should all know, as to exactly how a lot of these people died.

Had the opposition to the war succeeded, this is what it would have postponed—and postponed indefinitely—bringing to an end. This is how almost the whole international left expressed its moral solidarity with the Iraqi people. Worse still, some sections of the left seemed none too bothered about making common cause with, marching alongside, fundamentalist religious bigots and known racists; and there were also those who dismissed Iraqi voices in support of the war as coming from American stooges—a disgraceful lie.

GOOD AND BAD CONSEQUENCES    Second, let's now model this argument abstractly. You have a course of action with mixed consequences, both good consequences and bad consequences. To decide sensibly, you obviously have to weigh the good against the bad. Imagine someone advising, with respect to some decision you have to make, "Let's only think about the good consequences" or "Let's merely concentrate on the bad consequences." You *what*? It's a no-brainer, as the expression now is. But from beginning to end, something pretty much like this has been the approach of the war's opponents. I offer a few examples.

· The crassest are the statements by supposedly mature people—one of these Clare Short, another the novelist Julian Barnes—that this war was not worth the loss of a single life. Not one, eh? So much for the victims of the rape rooms and the industrial shredders, for the children tortured and murdered in front of their parents, and for those parents. So much for those Human Rights Watch estimates and for the future flow of the regime's victims had it been left in place.

· More generally, since the fall of Baghdad, critics of the war have been pointing (many of them with relish) at everything that has gone, or remains, wrong in Iraq: the looting, the lack of civil order, the continuing violence and shootings, the patchy electricity supply, the failure to find weapons of mass destruction. Is this argument fair enough? Yes and no. Yes, because it has to be part of any balanced assessment. But also no if it isn't set against the fact, the massive fact, of the end of a regime of torture, oppression, and murder, of everything that has stopped happening since the regime fell. Typically, however, it isn't set against this massive fact. This fact is passed over or tucked away, because to acknowledge it fully and make a balanced assessment won't come out right for the war's critics. It just won't stack up—this, this, and, yes, also this, but against the end of *all that*—in the way they'd like it to.

- Or else your antiwar interlocutor will freely concede that, of course, we all agree it is a good that that monster and his henchmen no longer govern Iraq; but it is too stupid a point to dwell upon, for it doesn't touch on the issue dividing us, support or not for the war (on grounds of WMD, international law, US foreign policy, the kitchen sink). Er, yes, it does. No one is entitled simply to help themselves to the "of course, we all agree" neutralization of what was and remains an absolutely crucial consideration in favor of the war. They have properly to integrate it into an overall, and conscientiously weighted, balance sheet of both good and bad consequences.

- The same ploy from a different angle: Since the fall of Baghdad, there have been voices—both Iraqi voices and those of Western critics of the war—calling for the immediate departure from Iraq of US and British forces. One can certainly discuss this as a proposition. Would it be better for Iraq and its people or worse, such an immediate or early withdrawal? Personally, I doubt that it would be better. Indeed, it would likely spell disaster of one kind or another. From more than one survey of Iraqi opinion I've seen, it is the view also of many Iraqis that there should be no withdrawal for the time being, until the consolidation of an Iraqi administration. But note, anyway, that the call for a prompt withdrawal is not a call to restore the Baathist regime to power. No, it just starts from where things are now, with the regime gone. That is, it starts from a better starting point than would otherwise have been in place. And this is a good (but not properly acknowledged) achieved by US and British arms.

- If you can't eliminate the inconvenient side of the balance, denature it. The liberation of Iraq from Saddam's tyranny *can't* have been a good, because of those who effected it and of their obviously bad foreign policy record: Vietnam, Chile, Nicaragua, and the rest. It can't therefore have been a liberation. Even allowing the premise to go unchallenged (which in fact I don't, since recent US and British foreign policy also has achievements to its credit: evicting the Iraqis from Kuwait, intervening in Kosovo, intervening in Sierra Leone, getting rid of the Taliban regime in Afghanistan), it is a plain fallacy. A person with a bad record is capable of doing good. There were some anti-Semitic rescuers of Jews during the Holocaust. This argumentative move just fixes the nature of the act via a presumption about those who are responsible for it, sparing one the necessity of examining the act for what it actually brings about and of assessing this in its own right. It's a bit like saying that because the guy who returned me the expensive book he'd borrowed has previously stolen things from others . . . you can fill in the rest yourself, and, yes, it's silly.

- Last and worst here. If the balance doesn't come out how you want it to, you hope for things to change so that the balance will adjust in your favor. In the case under consideration, this is a perilous moral and political impulse. When the war began, a division of opinion was soon evident among its opponents, between those who wanted a speedy outcome—in other words, a victory for the Coalition forces, for that is all a speedy outcome could realistically have meant—and those who did not. These latter preferred that the Coalition forces should suffer reverses, get bogged down, and you know the story: stalemate, quagmire, Stalingrad scenario in Baghdad, and so forth, leading to a US and British withdrawal. But what these critics of the war thereby wished for was a spectacular triumph for the regime in Baghdad, since that is what a withdrawal would have been. So much for solidarity with the victims of oppression, for commitment to democratic values and basic human rights.

Similarly today, with all those who seem to relish every new difficulty, every setback for US forces: what they align themselves with is a future of prolonged hardship and suffering for the Iraqi people—whether via an actual rather than imagined quagmire, a ruinous civil war, or the return of some new and ghastly political tyranny—rather than a rapid stabilization and democratization of the country, promising its inhabitants an early prospect of national normalization. That view is caring more to have been right than for a decent outcome for the people of this long-unfortunate country.

## CONCLUSION

Such impulses have displayed themselves very widely across left and liberal opinion in recent months. Why? For some, because what the US government and its allies do, whatever they do, has to be opposed—and opposed however thuggish and benighted the forces that this stance threatens to put your antiwar critic into close company with. For some, because of an uncontrollable animus toward George Bush and his administration. For some, because of a one-eyed perspective on international legality and its relation to issues of international justice and morality. Whatever the case or the combination, it has produced a calamitous compromise of the core values of socialism, liberalism, or both, on the part of thousands of people who claim attachment to them. You have to go back to the apologias for, and fellow-traveling with, the crimes of Stalinism to find as shameful a moral failure of liberal and left opinion as in the wrong-headed—and, too often, in the circumstances, sickeningly smug—opposition to the freeing of the Iraqi people from one of the foulest regimes on the planet.

## 2. THE THRESHOLD FOR HUMANITARIAN INTERVENTION (MAY 2004)

One of the arguments against the Iraq war that was tirelessly repeated in the run-up to it and hasn't altogether disappeared since is this one (and its variants): If there was a humanitarian case for military intervention against that dictatorship—the regime of Saddam Hussein—why not against other dictatorships as well? I've not hitherto considered it worth taking time to rebut this argument, on account of what I judged to be its morally unperceptive character. If I deal with it now, I do so not because I've changed my mind on that score, but because dealing with it will enable me to delineate the more serious issue behind it, one that any partisan of the regime-change case for the war did—and does—need to address.

Iraq, before the coalition destroyed the Baathist regime, wasn't merely a dictatorship, an authoritarian regime unremarkable among other such regimes. It wasn't, for example, Egypt, Uganda, or Cuba today or Nicaragua under Somoza. According to indices widely known and publicized by human rights NGOs, Iraq under Saddam was a quite exceptionally vicious and murderous regime. On the most basic level, therefore, the argument that, for reasons of consistency, supporting the war to liberate Iraq must entail a commitment to wars to overthrow (all) other dictatorships was beside the point. It was simply misdirected. That Iraq was a dictatorship wasn't the moral threshold being invoked, whether implicitly or explicitly, by the great majority of those who supported the war for regime-change reasons.

I will add that the argument under consideration is a poor one even apart from this point. States going to war put their soldiers in harm's way as well as incur very large costs. This is one of the reasons why wars for exclusively humanitarian reasons virtually never occur. They usually also engage some interest of the states initiating them. Not even as powerful a country as the United States is likely to be in a position to wage simultaneous or quickly successive wars on many x-type regimes (x, here, embodying the relevant moral threshold)—even if it is going to wage war on this particular x-type regime and in part because it is one. Consider the following example: You may send donations to Oxfam and/or the Red Cross and/or the Medical Foundation and/or the RSPCA [Royal Society for the Prevention of Cruelty to Animals] several times a year regardless of the fact that, were you to be fully "consistent" in the matter and donate as much and as often to *all* similar charities, it would prove financially too burdensome for you. You may donate as you do without moral anguish.

The humanitarian argument in support of the Iraq war wasn't, then, that Saddam Hussein's Iraq was a dictatorship but that it lay beyond a much worse moral threshold. I go on now to speak about this threshold. It was well captured in an article in the *New York Review of Books* [May 13, 2004] by Peter W. Galbraith:

> Iraq is free from Saddam Hussein and the Baath Party. Along with Cambodia's Pol Pot, Saddam Hussein's regime was one of the two most cruel and inhumane regimes in the second half of the twentieth century. Using the definition of genocide specified in the 1948 Genocide Convention, Iraq's Baath regime can be charged with planning and executing two genocides—one against the Kurdish population in the late 1980s and another against the Marsh Arabs in the 1990s. In the 1980s, the Iraqi armed forces and security services systematically destroyed more than four thousand Kurdish villages and several small cities, attacked over two hundred Kurdish villages and towns with chemical weapons in 1987 and 1988, and organized the deportation and execution of up to 182,000 Kurdish civilians.
>
> In the 1990s the Saddam Hussein regime drained the marshes of southern Iraq, displacing 500,000 people, half of whom fled to Iran, and killing some 40,000. In addition to destroying the five-thousand-year-old Marsh Arab civilization, draining the marshes did vast ecological damage to one of the most important wetlands systems on the planet. Genocide is only part of Saddam Hussein's murderous legacy. Tens of thousands perished in purges from 1979 on, and as many as 300,000 Shiites were killed in the six months following the collapse of the March 1991 Shiite uprising. One mass grave near Hilla may contain as many as 30,000 bodies.
>
> In a more lawful world, the United Nations, or a coalition of willing states, would have removed this regime from power long before 2003.

Mark the final sentence here. Note particularly "In a more lawful world"; "the United Nations"; "a coalition of willing states."

Even though there may be those who will want to expand Galbraith's pairing of Pol Pot's and Saddam's regimes by the addition of other extremely "cruel and inhumane" candidate regimes, the moral substance of the point Galbraith makes in this passage shouldn't need to be argued among serious-minded people. This was one of the *very worst* of regimes in recent decades.

Consequently, the overriding of the principle of national sovereignty was justified, if it was, not because Saddam Hussein was a dictator but because his regime fell on the wrong side of a moral threshold of extreme inhumanity. That should have delegitimized it as an acceptable member of the community of nations.

There is an established lineage of moral thinking about international affairs, including thinking specifically within the tradition of international law, that believes that respect for national sovereignty, as important as it is, does have its limits. These limits are set high. They do not permit one state to invade another merely because the former disapproves of the latter's internal policies, or because "we" don't share some of "their" values or customs or practices, or because some of those strike us as, or indeed are, bad. However, beyond a certain threshold of what I will call, for short, basic humanity, where a state has begun to violate on a large scale some of the most basic rights and/or needs and/or requirements that go with any kind of tolerable existence, then that state is no longer to be seen as enjoying the protection of the principle of national sovereignty.

I do not try to disguise the ideal-critical character of the norms and threshold that I invoke here—"ideal-critical" in the sense of referring not to any already-established or indisputably authoritative set of criteria but to a set that I would advocate as morally defensible. At the same time, however, I do not just suck them out of my thumb. They make up a well-known strand within the tradition of discussion and of doctrine to which I appeal. In some work I have in progress on the concept of crimes against humanity, I allude to that strand, and the circumstances licensing humanitarian intervention, thus:

> "if a tyrant . . . practises atrocities towards his subjects, which no just man can approve" (Grotius); "if tyranny becomes so unbearable as to cause the Nation to rise" (Vattel); in pursuit of a "higher policy of justice and humanity" (Harcourt); "in behalf of a grievously oppressed people, which has never amalgamated with its oppressors as one nation" (Creasy); "when

a state . . . becomes guilty of a 'gross violation' of the rights of humanity"
(Engelhardt); "where the general interests of humanity are infringed by the
excesses of a barbarous and despotic government" (Wheaton).

> (Source: Jean-Pierre L. Fonteyne, "The Customary Interna-
> tional Law Doctrine of Humanitarian Intervention: Its Cur-
> rent Validity under the U.N. Charter," *California Western
> International Law Journal* 4 [1974]: 214–222)

Now, of course, the key problem is to translate the kind of broad
and sweeping phrases just quoted into a more concrete list of empirically specifiable criteria that would enable us to distinguish situations
that do from situations that don't justify intervening on humanitarian
grounds. This is a demanding task, and I don't pretend to be able to
accomplish it just like that. But I will offer two criteria as arguably justifying humanitarian intervention by external powers in the affairs of a
sovereign nation:

1. Where a state is on the point of committing (or permitting), or
   is actually committing (or permitting), or has recently committed
   (or permitted), massacres and other atrocities against its own
   population of genocidal, or tendentially genocidal, scope

2. Where, even short of this, a state commits, supports, or overlooks murders, tortures, and other extreme brutalities such as to
   result in a regular flow of thousands upon thousands of victims

This proposal, obviously, is provisional. The formulation of (1) and
(2) could doubtless be improved, and the two criteria would certainly
need to be supplemented. Also, they don't justify humanitarian intervention (in every relevant case) regardless of all other considerations.
Those qualifications made, I would say that (1) here—all by itself—certainly provides adequate prima facie grounds for a humanitarian intervention; and I think (2)—all by itself—is also strong enough to do this,
though, because not as strong as (1), it will have to meet a greater volume of counterargument. The regime of Saddam Hussein fell foul of
both (1) and (2).

## 3. NOT BAD ENOUGH (JULY 2004)

One of the more lamentable arguments deployed by those opposed to
the Iraq war has been that, though what went on in Baathist Iraq was
very bad, it wasn't quite bad *enough* to validate a humanitarian or

regime-change justification for the war. As glimpsed in passing, this thought has surfaced here and there throughout the public controversy over the war, and it continues to do so. You could have seen it on an egregious antiwar poster from September 2003; or in John Pilger's description of his feeling of safety when traveling in Saddam's Iraq [*New Statesman*, April 19, 2004]; or, most recently, in scenes from Michael Moore's *Fahrenheit 9/11*, scenes of "children [in prewar Iraq] . . . flying little kites, shoppers . . . smiling in the sunshine . . . the gentle rhythms of life . . . undisturbed" (Christopher Hitchens [in *Slate*, June 21, 2004, http://slate.msn.com/id/2102723]). But the thing has been laid out also as full-blown argument, in order to counter the humanitarian case for the war. Common within formulations of it has been the claim that, for all the horrors perpetrated under Saddam Hussein, the worst of them weren't being perpetrated just then, in the run-up to the war or the period immediately before that. There was no ongoing or imminent *humanitarian crisis*. It is not only antiwar journalists and bloggers who are to be found favoring this argument; it is also, unfortunately, Human Rights Watch, as spelled out in a statement by Kenneth Roth from January 2004.

Critical as I'm bound to be, in the combination of circumstances already set out, of Kenneth Roth's statement on behalf of Human Rights Watch—an organization doing invaluable work—let me begin by registering some of the statement's good points, points in which it is superior to much run-of-the-mill antiwar advocacy.

- Roth's statement registers that in the US-led coalition's justification for the invasion of Iraq, the humanitarian consideration played a part, albeit a minor one. That is the truth, though often denied in antiwar polemics.
- His statement rejects "the argument that humanitarian intervention cannot be justified if other equally or more needy places are ignored."
- And it also rejects "the argument that past U.S. complicity in Iraqi repression should preclude U.S. intervention in Iraq on humanitarian grounds"—an argument people never tire of, no matter how many times it has been seen.

The nub of Roth's and Human Rights Watch's rejection of the humanitarian case for military intervention is this: Although the organization had no illusions about the "vicious inhumanity" of his regime, "by the time of the March 2003 invasion, Saddam Hussein's killing had ebbed." The more extravagant of the blood-letting in Iraq lay in the past—much of it in 1988 and 1991—and "the scope of the Iraqi government's killing in March 2003 was not of the exceptional and dire magnitude that would justify humanitarian intervention."

The brutality of this viewpoint could not be more sharply highlighted than it is being, now, by the steadily unfolding horror of Darfur. Terrible as that horror is in itself, it stands also for one humanitarian crisis after another in which the world community looks on, lazily scratches its backside, talks and talks, talks at the UN, utters its billionth condemnation of Israel, and then reacts finally when it is much too late for thousands, or millions, of dead—if it reacts at all. One might have thought, against this grim reality, that the chance of finally removing a regime that on Human Rights Watch's own estimate was responsible for the slaughter of 290,000 people (290,000, you understand: give one short minute of your time to mourning each of these people, and you'll need to devote 240-odd days to the exercise if you permit yourself four hours sleep on each of the nights of those days), a regime that left, even among those it didn't kill, God knows how many permanently damaged survivors of rape, torture, branding, having their tongues cut out or their ears cut off—that the chance of finally removing this regime should not need to meet the even higher requirement that it wasn't killing enough people when late 2002 was turning into early 2003.

For you have to grasp the full secret of this kind of argument—the argument that military intervention in Iraq might have been justified at some earlier point, but not any longer since the killing had "ebbed"— and this secret is that the great majority of the victims are *already dead.* I can improve on that point, actually. *All* of the victims of murder, whether of mass slaughter or serial individual butchery, are already dead. And some that aren't soon will be already dead. It doesn't take very long to kill a human being, and it doesn't take very long to kill thousands upon thousands of them. In Rwanda, going on a million were done to death in a matter of months. If you discount the already dead from your calculation of the morality of a given regime change, a given humanitarian intervention, you thereby put a value of next to nothing on anyone who is still alive but menaced with the proximate threat of being killed. For there's only a fleeting few moments between being alive and being violently dead, and once people are dead (the way the world works), they're immediately dead already. If their lives, once taken, are worth nothing to the moral case, then the lives of others yet to be taken aren't going to be worth very much.

I don't want to do any distortion to the position as argued by Kenneth Roth for Human Rights Watch. It can be said in his defense that he *doesn't* discount the already dead. For he writes:

> "Better late than never" is not a justification for humanitarian intervention, which should be countenanced only to stop mass murder, not to punish its perpetrators, desirable as punishment is in such circumstances. . . .
> That does not mean that past atrocities should be ignored. Rather, their perpetrators should be prosecuted.

But this is to displace the political question at issue here into a legal one. Of course, bringing the perpetrators of terrible crimes to justice is a necessary and vital pursuit. It does not, however, stand in for the question of whether or not the regime whose thugs the perpetrators were is fit, morally and politically, to survive within the community of nations, fit to have its sovereignty respected, and fit—one cannot avoid saying this bluntly—to enjoy the benefit of marchers, enlightened opinion formers, veteran socialists, spotless liberals, a whole huge planetary wave of protest, mobilizing against the prospect of its being militarily taken down. To discount the already dead in discussing *that* question is falsely to skew the issue in one way.

It's not the only way it gets skewed, however. There's also an implication in some advocacy of this sort that, the killing having "ebbed" in Iraq, the only reasonable counterfactual inference that can be made about future victims of the regime, had the latter not been taken down, is a rate of killing of the "ebbed" kind. This line of thought might be validly applicable to some state or other that has grave crimes (maybe even genocidal ones) in its remote past but that has evolved over decades or more into something more benign. I think I can safely say without additional argument that that wasn't true of the Saddam Hussein regime. Presided over by a political monster, with two sons waiting in the possible succession who had more than shown their own aptitude for cruelties that most of the good peace marchers will find nearly unthinkable without their being overcome by existential revulsion and fear, a regime that was certainly a continuing threat to those living under it and perceived, quite reasonably, as a potential if not immediate threat beyond its borders, Saddam's regime gave no grounds at all for confidence in the hypothesis of an "ebbed" future level of killing.

The criteria for humanitarian intervention deployed by Kenneth Roth (among others) would allow a regime that had just massacred, let us say, two million of its own people, but had finished massacring them, to stand with its sovereignty and its international legitimacy intact. If those are the criteria you uphold, do you not, in effect, say this to every Saddam Hussein, every Robert Mugabe? "It's not the killing of people that will imperil your regime; it's the killing of them too slowly, too continuously, in too ongoing a sort of way."

Not quite a year ago I wrote on this blog of a shameful moral failure of left and liberal opinion. Nothing that has happened in the year since has changed my view about that. One of its most unpleasant symptoms has been the style of argument I've highlighted in this post. That it should have been adopted even by so good an organization as Human Rights Watch is testimony to the sorry state of progressive opinion today across the globe.

# 13

## Liberal Realism or Liberal Idealism
### The Iraq War and the Limits of Tolerance

RICHARD JUST

A few weeks before the Iraq war started, I found myself at a gathering of liberal activists in Washington. The group hadn't convened specifically to talk about the war, and it spent most of the meeting discussing domestic issues—Bush's tax cuts, Social Security, health care, and so on. But war was in the air, so it was unavoidable that the subject would be raised. On the agenda as the last item, someone had written, "What do we do when the bombs start falling?" As the meeting was about to adjourn, a participant pointed out that we hadn't discussed the war. The question was put to the group: What *do* we do when the bombs start falling? There was a moment of awkward silence in the room, at which point someone said, "Duck." It was offered half as a question and almost assuredly was at least half-meant as a joke—gallows humor for what was, in the minds of many of those gathered, a dark moment in American history. But it was pretty much the best anyone in the room had to offer. The meeting was over moments later.

The people in that room were, for the most part, serious, well-intentioned progressives. I imagine many now take some vindication in their prewar views—and it is vindication to which they are at least partially entitled. In advocating for war against Saddam, I and other liberal hawks underestimated how difficult it would be to build a decent society in Iraq and overestimated the extent to which the Bush administration was qualified for that task. Our mission in Iraq has yielded higher costs, in dollars and especially in lives, than many of us expected, and it has yielded fewer immediate benefits than many of us predicted. As a result, it is much more difficult to justify the Iraq war in October 2004 than it was in April 2003.

Difficult—but not impossible. If the war is still justifiable at all—and I now believe that is a big "if"—then it is justifiable only on slightly different grounds than the three traditional, and now suspect, planks on which the case for an invasion originally rested (Saddam's alleged links to Al Qaeda, Iraq's supposed weapons of mass destruction, and the imperative of building a liberal democracy in the heart of the Middle East). What took place in 1991 at the close of the Gulf War was a significant moral failure, one of the great failures of inaction in US history. To leave Saddam in power, knowing full well what he had done to the Kurds in the 1980s, knowing full well what he was doing to the Shia as we watched, and knowing full well what he would continue to do to all Iraqis, was an inexcusable choice. Our decision to leave Saddam entrenched in Baghdad, even after we had evicted him from Kuwait, sent a clear message to the Arab world that American ideals were fungible when Muslim life was at stake. Saddam's continuing presence on the world stage, his continuing oppression of his own people and harassment of his neighbors throughout the 1990s, not to mention his celebration of suicide bombers and vaguely threatening noises toward the United States and its allies, was a reminder of the glaring gap between the Untied States' ideals and its real-world behavior. Removing him was not a sufficient condition for building a better, more liberal Middle East, but it was, I think, a necessary one. He was a stain on our ideals and therefore an impediment to our goals. After 9/11, putting these ideals and goals into practice in the Middle East acquired new urgency. Even in the absence of Al Qaeda links or weapons of mass destruction, even given the extraordinary difficulty of building a democracy in Iraq, it was clearly in our moral interest and self-interest to see Saddam removed from power.

That perspective alone, of course, does not mean the war was the right decision. Indeed, the list of costs and benefits to be weighed in determining whether the war was justified is long and complex. But putting aside other factors, one question worth considering is what price in American and Iraqi lives the liberation of Iraq was worth. That calculation means that the case for war grows weaker by the day. In April 2003, when the war had been won with the deaths of 138 American troops and the deaths of several thousand Iraqi civilians—the Associated Press estimated the number of civilian deaths between March 20 and April 20 to be 3,240 but conceded the real number was almost certainly higher[1]—did the liberation of Iraq and its twenty-five million citizens outweigh the loss of life that had been required to achieve it? I think the answer was yes. (Think about it this way from the perspective of an Iraqi civilian: If you had lived under Saddam Hussein, would you have been willing to accept an approximately one in ten thousand chance that you would die in order to live as a free person? Of course. To be sure, this calculation does not speak to whether the American loss of life was justified.) But is the same true now that the number of American deaths has surpassed one thousand, many thousands more Iraqis (the Associated Press says that estimates range from ten thousand to thirty thousand, including soldiers and civilians)[2] have been killed, and the freedom we promised Iraqis has in fact turned out to be an awful, bloody form of chaos? The answer is far from clear. Would the loss of fifty-eight thousand Americans, the number who died in Vietnam, justify a war in which we brought Saddam to justice and freed his country? Clearly no. There is a real-world price to the fulfillment of liberal goals, and people of principle should not wish away the existence of that price, nor should they shirk the responsibility of attempting reasonable judgments about when a price is worth paying and when it simply costs too much.

The willingness to make such judgments is the cornerstone of idealistic thought in foreign policy. Such judgments are difficult, perhaps borderline impossible—and I concede that putting a price in lives on the liberation of a country grates both the liberal ear and the liberal conscience. But without such calculations, however imperfect, the world is merely a collection of interests, and our action in it remains unguided by moral principle. In retrospect, I am less interested by the fact that most progressives opposed the war than I am by the fact that the language of their opposition has so frequently been the language of realism. The argument that because containment had worked during the Cold War, it would work in Iraq was (never mind the absurdity of the historical comparison) a favorite of many liberals. It was as if they had forgotten that containment, like all actions and inactions, carried some moral cost, a cost that had to be weighed against the cost of other options. The cost of containment during the Cold War (billions living under communist totalitarianism) was acceptable not because it was negligible but because the cost of fighting the Soviet Union (millions dead in a nuclear holocaust) was correctly judged to be far worse. The situation and the costs involved were very different in Iraq.

Liberals, however, seemed less concerned with moral costs and more concerned with what would serve US interests, narrowly conceived. "Containment and deterrence have worked well throughout the last fifty years," said Dennis Kucinich, not normally known as a Cold War realist, in a speech on the day the Iraq war started.[3] Eleven days earlier, Howard Dean had said, "Saddam, in my view, has been successfully contained for twelve years at a relatively low cost. . . . We can stop Saddam Hussein from doing anything for another twelve years if we have to without invading."[4] When Dean said that Saddam had been contained at a "low cost," he could only have been using the term with regard to a very narrow definition of US self-interest. Surely, he did not believe that our decision to leave Saddam in power for twelve years had come at a "low cost" to Iraqis. No, the costs of containment were only low if understood within a realist framework. If understood within a framework that took into account interests *and* moral considerations, containment became a more complex proposition.

And it's not as if Kucinich and Dean were the candidates of the Zbigniew Brzezinski wing of the Democratic Party; they were speaking, in stark realist terms, on behalf of its progressive wing. Then again, where the Iraq war was concerned, those wings were sometimes hard to tell apart. Six months after the war had ended, Brzezinski, whose career as a foreign policy realist stands in opposition to so much of what liberal idealists believe about the world, received a standing ovation at a progressive conference in Washington, where he delivered a keynote speech denouncing Bush for his "quasi-theological formulations."[5]

How was it possible that many liberals embraced realism to explain their opposition to the war? The progressive establishment, I think, has come somewhat unmoored from its proper place in foreign affairs because it has become uncomfortable making the moral judgments that idealism in the world requires. Unwilling to weigh the moral costs of casualties against the moral costs of inaction, many progressives deny the very existence of moral trade-offs in foreign policy and retreat to the safe language of realism. What disturbed me greatly—and disturbs me still—about the liberal response to the Iraq war was not that liberals by and large opposed the war but, rather, that many seemed uninterested in wading into these thorny dilemmas in all their moral complexity. It was not that they were ignoring the question of whether they favored the war; they were ignoring the fundamental obligations of idealism, which have often been, and ought to be, inseparable from the fundamental obligations of liberalism. Too often in the post-9/11 world, when the time has come to translate the moral, and essentially progressive, roots of foreign policy idealism into plans for American action, liberals have said, "Duck."

## II

My colleague Lawrence Kaplan wrote in a *New Republic* cover story in summer 2004 that John Kerry's presidential campaign had adopted a worldview based on realism.[6] Later, during the final weeks of the 2004 campaign, Kerry made some nods in the direction of foreign policy idealism—during the first presidential debate, for instance, he said he would consider deploying US troops to stop the genocide in Darfur.[7]

But the Democratic convention was a far more depressing story. Speeches were almost completely devoid of any mention of human rights, democracy promotion, or universal values. Perhaps in the post-9/11 world these ideas have come to be seen as Republican ideas (which is a shame, because we have seen in the last year that the Republican Party's commitment to these ideas is mostly rhetorical rather than practical). Whatever the reason, the absence of these ideas from the Democratic convention was telling and disturbing. The war on terrorism and the situation in Iraq are clearly our nation's most important foreign policy priorities, as they should be. But for the most part, Democrats who spoke at the convention framed those issues not in a way that connects America's moral mission in the world to its security—as, for instance, Tony Blair did so masterfully in his speech to Congress in July 2003[8]—but in terms of how to restore US international alliances and reduce the US military burden in the Middle East. I do not want to disparage these questions—they are extraordinarily important. But from listening to the Democratic convention, one might have concluded that the United States has no interest—either strategic or moral—in building a more democratic, more free world.

Take Kerry's acceptance speech. The words *human rights* never appeared. Neither did the word *democracy* in relationship to contemporary foreign policy.[9] Instead, Kerry's worldview seemed best expressed in a mantra that he—and other Democrats—have taken to using with frequency: "The United States of America never goes to war because we want to; we only go to war because we have to." One can read this statement in different ways, but the obvious way to read it is as an affirmation of a realist approach to using military force. After all, the United States never *has* to do something for moral reasons; the only rationales on which we *have* to act are self-interested ones—and by self-interest, I refer to the narrow kind, not the broader kind that sees US long-term interests as inextricably bound to democracy promotion. Think about it in practical terms: According to this worldview, the United States was better off not intervening in World War II until 1941 when we were attacked; indeed, had Germany not declared war on us preemptively, we would have been better off fighting only Japan. We did not, after all, *have* to free Europe. We would not have stopped a genocide in Kosovo. Of course, we would not have fought the most recent Iraq war, but we would not have fought the first Iraq war, either. According to this philosophy, we made the right decision in not intervening militarily in Rwanda in 1994. And this worldview would counsel our current inaction in Darfur, Sudan. (If any of the major speakers at the Democratic convention addressed the Darfur genocide, I didn't hear it.) Is this what the majority of liberal activists now believe? Have we all become Scowcroft Democrats? When the party faithful cheered Kerry and the other politicians who invoked that amoral mantra of only going to war because "we have to," they were giving their assent to a hard-bitten worldview based only on interests and not on principles—except for the principle, so popular among progressive activists, that war is almost always wrong, which is not a principle at all but rather a refusal to grapple with competing moral imperatives.

More troubling to me than Kerry's appeal to voters' realist impulses were the speeches of John Edwards and Barack Obama. Both men, who are now widely presumed to represent the future of the Democratic Party, are seeking to do something admirable and important, something that no national Democratic politician has successfully done in more than a decade: reclaim the language of morality for progressives. But they are seeking to do so only on domestic matters. On the one hand, it is refreshing to hear a politician talk, as both men do, about poverty in moral terms. On the other hand, this move to the language of morality on domestic affairs has opened up a gaping disconnect between the way Democrats speak about all things domestic and the rather narrow way they speak about foreign affairs. If moralism can be reclaimed as a liberal strategy—indeed, a liberal value—on domestic matters, why must it be shunned in the realm of foreign policy?

Here is the way that Edwards talked about poverty at the convention:[10]

> We can also do something about thirty-five million Americans who live in poverty every day. Here's the reason we should not just talk about it, but do something about millions of Americans who still live in poverty: because it is wrong. We have a moral responsibility to lift those families up.
>
> I mean, the very idea that in a country of our wealth and our prosperity, we have children going to bed hungry. We have children who don't have the clothes to keep them warm. We have millions of Americans who work full-time every day for minimum wage to support their family and still live in poverty—it's wrong.

Would that a Democratic politician use such idealistic language in talking about foreign affairs. Here is the section of his speech where Edwards came closest:

> And together, we will ensure that the image of America—the image all of us love—America this great shining light, this beacon of freedom, democracy, and human rights that the world looks up to—that that beacon is always lit.

As Democratic rhetoric at the convention went, this was actually a decent nod toward idealism. (And to Edwards's credit, he spoke with passion about Darfur in his debate with Dick Cheney in October.)[11] But while the airy concepts of America as a beacon of freedom in the world are nice enough, they pale in comparison to the stern moral language with which Edwards spoke about poverty. Surely if it's "wrong" that Americans work for minimum wage to support their family and still live in poverty, then it is also wrong that black Africans in Sudan are being systematically exterminated by Arab militias or that Iraqis lived for decades under the oppression of a totalitarian dictator. The idea of framing domestic debates in strident moral terms but framing foreign policy almost solely in realist terms seems like an odd line for liberals to draw. Why should our mode of thinking about one be so different from our mode of thinking about the other?

Every young liberal I know was extremely impressed by Obama's keynote speech. Most Democrats are convinced that Obama will at some point be their party's standard-bearer and perhaps the first black US president. As a state politician, Obama has clearly thought more about domestic policy than about foreign policy; yet, he did talk about both, and, here again, the disconnect in moral tone was plainly evident. The most striking part of Obama's speech was when he called on Americans to view themselves as more than just individuals but as part of a community, one with shared moral responsibilities to its own members:[12]

> If there's a child on the South Side of Chicago who can't read, that matters to me, even if it's not my child. If there's a senior citizen somewhere who can't pay for their prescription and having to choose between medicine and the rent, that makes my life poorer, even if it's not my grandparent. If there's an Arab American family being rounded up without benefit of an attorney or due process, that threatens my civil liberties. It is that fundamental belief—I am my brother's keeper, I am my sister's keeper—that makes this country work.

This was perhaps the most eloquent articulation of the case for collective responsibility that I have ever heard a politician give. But Obama did not apply this same logic to foreign affairs, which he talked about only in terms of its impact on the United States' interests, narrowly defined, not in terms of its broader moral interests. He was eloquent on the subject of the Iraq war's tragic effect on the lives of young soldiers. But he refused to go much further. "We have real enemies in the world," he said. "These enemies must be found. They must be pursued. And they must be defeated." And that was it. No mention of human rights. No mention of universal values. In this respect, Obama was, of course, no different from the majority of Democratic convention speakers. But surely a man who believes that "if there's a child on the South Side of Chicago who can't read, that matters to me, even if it's not my child," also believes that if a child is suffering in Darfur, then it matters to us, even if she is not our child, even if she is not American. And surely one who believes that "if there's a senior citizen somewhere who can't pay for their prescription . . . that makes my life poorer, even if it's not my grandparent," must also believe that a senior citizen evicted from his lifelong home in Bosnia in a burst of ethnic cleansing makes our lives as Americans poorer, even if he is not our grandparent, even if he is not American. And surely one who believes that "if there's an Arab American family being rounded up without benefit of an attorney or due process, that threatens my civil liberties," also must believe that if the entirety of the Arab world continues to live under authoritarian regimes that abuse their people and manipulate their anger into rage toward the Western world, even if those people are not American, then their lack of freedom diminishes us morally and, as we learned on 9/11, threatens *our* freedom as well.

Obama need not have said all this, of course. But it would have been nice to hear some nod in the direction of the importance of pursuing moral ends in foreign affairs from the presumed future leader of the Democratic Party.


## III

While the Democrats' embrace of foreign policy realism is disturbing, perhaps it is only a transient matter of politics; after all, political realities change quickly. In 2000, Republicans were the party of foreign policy realism, and Democrats were proponents of humanitarian intervention. Perhaps by 2008, the parties will have switched again.

So, although I am troubled by the realist rhetoric of Kerry, Edwards, and Obama, I understand that what really matters in the long term is something else: whether the next generation of progressives—my generation of progressives (I am twenty-five)—is predisposed toward an idealist or realist worldview. Obviously, events yet to come will go a long way toward dictating my generation's views on the world by the time it takes power. But even now, it may be possible to hazard some broad guesses about the direction we are headed. I see two major reasons for optimism in this regard and one major reason for pessimism.

The first reason for optimism is that unlike our parents—whose worldview was shaped in large part by Vietnam—our experiences, at least prior to the Iraq war, in witnessing US power in action have been largely positive ones. We have seen, as in the US intervention in the Balkans in 1999, the United States act successfully as a moral force in the world. We have seen, in the aftermath of 9/11 and our invasion of Afghanistan, how closely the United States' moral obligation to promote the spread of liberty is intertwined with our own security. And, prior to Iraq, when we have seen failures of US power, they were not, broadly speaking, failures of *too much* US power but rather *too little*— as in our failure to stop a genocide in Rwanda in 1994, our belated intervention in the Balkans in 1999, and, most important, our failure to take strong military action against Al Qaeda and the Taliban until after 9/11. Even in Iraq, which can of course be seen as a failure of American hubris, an argument can also be made that our biggest mistake was one of omission, not one of commission: a failure to put enough troops on the ground to secure peace in the early days of the occupation.

The second reason for optimism is slightly more nebulous but, I think, important nonetheless. Some have looked at the explosion of young people performing community service and have labeled us a generation of résumé builders (or, in David Brooks's memorable formulation, a generation dominated by "the organization kid").[13] But when you look at my generation's embrace of national service organizations such as AmeriCorps, City Year, and Teach for America, when you look at the proliferation of service groups on college campuses, I think you can see a kind of idealism at work as well: an impatience with the status quo, a preference for direct action to fix problems, and a belief that those with means have an obligation to do what they can to repair the world. I concede that it's a difficult link to draw between a young person's propensity to volunteer in a soup kitchen and his or her propensity to believe in the moral underpinnings of US foreign policy. But there's a fundamental idealism—or, at the very least, a lack of cynicism—that underlies both beliefs, which is one reason I am hopeful about the kind of foreign policy my generation will vote for and, someday, implement.

The reason for pessimism is nebulous as well. It, too, lies in a broad and often-noted characteristic about my generation that may not appear, on the surface, to have much to do with foreign policy: the elevation of "tolerance" as a central guiding value of my generation and, specifically, of liberals of my generation. From an early age, we have been taught that tolerance—of other people, of other value systems, of other opinions—was a key part of living in a democracy. From elementary school through college, tolerance as a generic value was frequently advanced by teachers, parents, and role models as a key component of participating in a healthy educational community and, indeed, of living in a healthy world. Many of us grew up believing that tolerance was an unmitigated good—something that was literally impossible to oppose.

This view has been, by and large, a very good thing. Tolerance *is* a key building block of a healthy democracy, and when you look at some of my generation's political values, it would be hard not to say that a genuine respect for tolerance has served us well. (To take one example: Polls show that our generation is far more supportive of gay rights than previous generations. In the 2002 American Freshman Survey, conducted annually by UCLA, 59 percent of college freshmen favored same-sex marriage,[14] as compared to just 29 percent, according to a recent Pew poll, in the US population as a whole.)[15] When cultural conservatives lament the rise of tolerance as a political value, they are often merely lamenting their losses in the culture wars. After all, debates about tolerance often carry more than a hint of religious-secular disagreement.

But for all the benefits of a reverence for tolerance, I worry that when extended as an all-encompassing value onto the template of world affairs, it translates far too neatly into realism and yields a decidedly nonprogressive result. Over and over again, in conversations with fellow young liberals about the Iraq war, I heard a distinct discomfort with the idea of democracy as a universal value or the ability of the United States to act as an agent of that value. This argument had plenty of different permutations; anyone who has talked politics with young liberals since 9/11 has heard them. One particularly common permutation held that the United States could not be expected to fix the world's problems when it has so many problems of its own at home. You can hear the ethic of tolerance-as-a-good-unto-itself at work in this line of reasoning; after all, if you see human rights problems in the Middle East in the context of mere differences between nations—to paraphrase, crudely: we have our death penalty and homelessness, and they have their genocides and chemical weapons—then it becomes harder to view those abuses with the moral judgment that they require. (Kerry's awful and oft-repeated line, that we shouldn't build firehouses in Baghdad and close them in America, plays to this knee-jerk sense that all countries' problems are morally equivalent and that we ought to take care of our own shortcomings before trying to solve others' difficulties.)[16] The less willing we are to judge other countries—other governments, other world leaders—the less likely we are to contemplate using our power, be it soft power or hard power, toward moral ends.

That is why I worry that a generation raised to be nonjudgmental is more likely to allow moral relativism to creep into its thinking on foreign policy and might therefore be predisposed against foreign policy idealism. Idealism at its very core requires moral judgments—judgments about when a government has behaved so badly as to forfeit its right to sovereignty; judgments about how many American lives it is worth to save the lives of those in other countries; judgments that take into account the fact that inaction can carry moral costs every bit as real as action. Realism and an extreme fetishization of tolerance *could* go hand and hand: the latter invites us to duck the difficult judgments required by the deployment of US power toward humanitarian ends, and the former gives an intellectual framework to the ducking of such judgments.

I am proud to be part of a tolerant generation. But I hope we will recognize that tolerance has its limits—namely, that when we rationalize injustice in other countries, we risk allowing tolerance to spill over into moral relativism. If we are to view the world through the eyes of idealists, we will need to temper our inclination toward tolerance with a reverence for justice. We will need to be unafraid to judge—and not just to judge but to weigh the difficult moral trade-offs that are involved in following these judgments through to their logical policy conclusions. My hope for the next generation of liberals is that we will find a way of thinking about the world that accepts this burden.

Those whom the natural lottery has blessed with both freedom and the means to promote it do not have an obligation to complete the work of righting every wrong in the world, nor do they have an obligation to sacrifice recklessly their own in the pursuit of justice for others. But they do have an obligation to make moral inroads, however small, and to seek moral outcomes, as opposed to merely self-interested ones, when practical. Barack Obama is right: The liberal impulse *is* to be the keepers of our brothers and sisters. This impulse must be tempered by an understanding that the world is not perfectible. But we can be level-headed in our assessment of the way the world works, moderate in the objectives we set, and cautious in the means by which we seek to achieve our ends—and still believe that Obama's impulse is worth following, at home *and* abroad.

This suggestion does not mean an embrace of a militaristic foreign policy. It does not mean that our own national interests should ever be sublimated to our moral ones, only that we should find ways to make the two complement each other whenever reasonably possible. And it does not mean that there is a right answer in a debate over any given war in particular. All it means is that liberals should rediscover our support of ideals. The United Nations, international alliances, European goodwill—these things are not unimportant, but they are, in the final analysis, merely means. It is our ideals that ought to be our ends. And we cannot duck them forever.

# NOTES

1. Niko Price, "AP Tallies 3,240 Civilian Deaths in Iraq," Associated Press, June 10, 2003.
2. Bassem Mroue, "More Than 10,000 Iraqis Die Violently in Baghdad Region Alone," Associated Press, September 8, 2004.

3. Dennis Kucinich, speech to the National Newspaper Association, March 20, 2003, http://www.house.gov/apps/list/speech/ohio_kucinich/030320news papers.html (accessed January 21, 2005).

4. Howard Dean, appearance on *Meet the Press*, March 9, 2003, http://dean2004.blogspot.com/2003_03_09_dean2004_archive.html (accessed January 4, 2005).

5. Zbigniew Brzezinski, "Address to the New American Strategies Conference," October 28, 2003, Washington, D.C., http://www.newamericanstrategies.org/articles/display.asp?fldArticleID=68 (accessed January 21, 2005). I would like to make a full disclosure that one of the cosponsors of the conference was *The American Prospect*, where I was employed as an editor at the time, although I had no role in organizing the conference.

6. Lawrence F. Kaplan, "Springtime for Realism," *New Republic*, June 21, 2004.

7. The first presidential debate of 2004, on September 30, 2004; see the transcript here: http://www.washingtonpost.com/wp-srv/politics/debatereferee/debate_0930.html (accessed January 4, 2005).

8. Tony Blair's speech to the US Congress, July 17, 2003, http://www.cnn.com/2003/US/07/17/blair.transcript/ (accessed January 4, 2005).

9. Made on July 29, 2004; see http://www.johnkerry.com/pressroom/speeches/spc_2004_0729.html (accessed January 4, 2005).

10. Made on July 28, 2004; see http://www.johnkerry.com/pressroom/speeches/spc_2004_0728.html (accessed January 4, 2005).

11. Held October 5, 2004; see http://www.washingtonpost.com/wp-srv/politics/debatereferee/debate_1005.html (accessed January 4, 2005).

12. Made on July 27, 2004; see http://www.dems2004.org/site/apps/nl/content3.asp?c=luI2LaPYG&b=131063&ct=158769 (accessed January 4, 2005).

13. David Brooks, "The Organization Kid," *Atlantic Monthly* (April 2001). I should note that Brooks interviewed me for this article, although I am not specifically quoted in it.

14. See "College Freshmen Spend Less Time Studying and More Time Surfing the Net, UCLA Study Reveals," http://www.gseis.ucla.edu/heri/02_press_release.pdf (accessed January 4, 2005).

15. See for the Pew poll http://www.pollingreport.com/civil.htm (accessed January 4, 2005).

16. See http://www.johnkerry.com/pressroom/speeches/spc_2004_0729.html and http://www.usatoday.com/news/politicselections/nation/president/2004-07-07-kerry-nc-ads_x.htm (accessed January 4, 2005).

# PART FOUR

# EUROPEAN DIMENSIONS

# 14

# Iraq and the European Left

## JOHN LLOYD

Michael Moore's *Fahrenheit 9/11* has begun playing in Europe as this essay is being finished. For many European as well as American reviewers and commentators, the response to it has fallen into a kind of liberal groove: that it's extreme and unfair, but you have to admit it's nice to see Bush and the US administration ridiculed. Thus David Edelstein, a film critic for the Web magazine *Slate*, commented, "I was troubled by the cheapness of Moore's interviewing techniques. But I laughed my ass off anyway."[1]

I didn't, because it seemed to me that the joke was on us: the people of the left, who have split (albeit asymmetrically) over the issue of the invasion of Iraq. And because Iraq has forced new thinking and new alignments, it has come to be a proxy for other, older arguments as on such issues as the abilities (or lack of them) of the European Union and the United Nations, the future of intervention, the promotion of democracy, and the nature and future of American hegemony—or, as some prefer, American imperialism.

Moore's film represents one way out: denunciation. It's one increasingly being taken not just by natural ranters like Moore but by many in the US Democratic fold and by very many of those who pronounce on these issues in Europe, left and far left, but also right and far right. The writer Eric Tarloff, an occasional speechwriter for Democratic presidents and presidential hopefuls, wrote in the *Financial Times Magazine* of the "appalling quiescence and acquiescence on the part of the American political class and media (their British counterparts were not quite so pusillanimous, although the record in both cases is far from stellar)."[2] Both extremists and moderates, then, can agree on the complete moral awfulness of those who supported the Iraq invasion.

Something is at work here, which in more extreme cases—though the extreme becomes more and more the norm—is what Christopher Hitchens called in a *Slate* article on Moore's film "the loaded bias against the work of the mind."[3] It's a habit, which one had thought largely confined to the extremes of left and right, of blotting out both contradictory evidence and facts as well as consideration of the possibility that, in this case, the view that the invasion of Iraq designed to end Saddam's/Baath rule might be a project worth supporting. In Moore's case, the suppression of almost all mention of Saddam's horrors in favor of cartoonlike gags at the expense of Bush and his senior officials renders the film worthless as a piece of argument and totalitarian-like in its method. Hitchens again: "If you leave out absolutely everything that might give your 'narrative' a problem and throw in any old rubbish that might support it, *then you have betrayed your craft*" (his italics).[4]

That's why *Fahrenheit 9/11* can't be dismissed, as moderate leftists tend to do, as "good fun but a bit over the top." It's of a piece with a disturbing movement that is shared by right and left: that toward the "betrayal of the craft" of journalism, and indeed of rational argument, by a mobilization of arguments that are wholly self-serving and by the use of techniques that are designed to ridicule. The examples of shock-jock radio and of the mobilization of the right-wing press against President Bill Clinton have been beguiling ones for the left. Moore and others less successful have learned the wrong lesson—that is, that hyperbolic case making enthuses your base, gets the wry approval of the moderates who incline your way, and reduces those who have a different position on any one of the targets of your wrath to figures of fun.

The success—on both sides of the divide—of ridicule docs could be another nail in the coffin of a search for truth through investigation of the facts; indeed, it could be the death of facts in journalism and debate. So successful has been the line that sees in the Iraq war merely the "ideologically driven" desire to extend US power, coupled with the financially driven mania to control Middle Eastern oil and the faith-driven crusade to batter the crescent with the cross, that it meets almost no argument on the left. The fate of the question "Why was it so wrong to have the removal of Saddam Hussein as a major aim of the US administration, especially since many on the left had called for such an outcome for decades?" has been instructive. It's more or less gone from public discourse, except what are represented as the desperate excuses of the US and UK administrations. Yet it's on the left where, above all, this question has to be posed and reposed—not to get an answer of unequivocal assent but to remind ourselves and others that the goal of tyrant bashing has always been one of our prouder reasons for existence. The fact that one such bashing had been given by a US government of the right is not a reason to wish it, even implicitly, undone.

The United States, more and more, is being seen as The Problem— and Iraq as *its* problem, not ours. Apart from the UK's considerable force based in and around Basra and smaller contingents of Polish, Italian, and other troops, most of the European states have contributed little to the Iraq war. The view that nothing has brought Europe together like the dislike of its greatest ally is at least superficially true. It remains to be seen how deep that dislike goes, though some fear it may have further to go. In *Prospect* magazine in July 2004, Philip Gordon of Brookings, an analyst both knowledgeable about and sympathetic to the EU, wrote that "I am not saying that Europe and America will end up in a military stand-off like that between east and west during the cold war. But if current trends are not reversed, you can be sure you will see growing domestic pressure on both sides for confrontation rather than co-operation."[5]

Europe is a good place to start, for it has become, with the UN, an entity that is appealed to as a peaceful counterweight to a bellicose United States, as a place where power is exercised with subtlety and discretion and a good deal of devolution of power—rather as Britain ran its empire in the periods when there was no native restlessness to deal with. Mark Leonard, the head of the Foreign Policy Centre in London, wrote in 2004 that the EU "is practically invisible. . . . Europe operates through the shell of traditional national structures such as the House of Commons, the British law courts and national civil servants. . . . Europe's invisibility allows it to spread its influence without provocation."[6] Leonard contrasts positively the influence of the EU on its "near abroad—the states which acceded to the EU, and those hoping to do so soon—with the US on its backward, in Latin America." He adds that, "whereas the EU is deeply involved in Serbia's reconstruction and supports its desire to be 'rehabilitated' as a European state, the US offers Colombia no such hope of integration through multilateral institutions or structural funds, only the temporary assistance of American military training missions and aid, and the raw freedom of the American market."[7] Leonard is no America basher; on the contrary, he is an extreme moderate in the European debate. But he is able to make a contrast that redounds to the credit of Europe and the discredit of the United States while not comparing like with like: Europe doesn't have to provoke, because it's not usually a threat—not to nice people, but not to nasty people, either (and which of the United States' neighbors or near-abroaders wants to become part of an ever-closer union with the United States? Canada? Brazil?).

To be sure, both Leonard and the writer Timothy Garton Ash[8] concede that Europe has no coherent line on foreign affairs and security issues, and no forces to put to the service of that line when it comes—though both believe at least the first of these will come about. Both also concede that Europe's military weakness is a problem for it, one that is interpreted in the United States as a lack of will to share an appreciable part of the burden of policing the world's hot spots—indeed, even to protect itself. In a scintillating presentation of his book *Free World* at London's Royal Society for the Arts in July 2004, Ash remarked on "how little even the Madrid attacks galvanized Europe." In a piece in *Prospect* in answer to Philip Gordon's essay, he wrote that the EU must commit itself "to be a serious force outside of its own borders, especially in its own wider neighbourhood, stretching from Casablanca to Vladivostok [and] . . . do this as a strategic partner, and not a rival, of the US."[9]

But the real prospects of such a partnership are still distant. Most of the EU states are giving very little, or nothing, to an effort to bring security in Iraq that is in their interests—even if the invasion was not of their willing, as it is in the United States. Indeed, according to French foreign minister Michel Barnier, France will never deploy any forces in Iraq. European forces *are* engaged in Afghanistan—but not enough. And NATO, which has responsibility for the operations there, finds European member states exceedingly reluctant to increase their commitments. To be sure, the Bush administration did not live up to the promise that Bush had made to Blair to "expend the same amount of energy in the Middle East"[10] as Blair did in keeping a fragile settlement going in Northern Ireland. But we rarely ask, Expend the energy on what? The left, and European comment generally, often gives the impression that US engagement and pressure on Israel would be a more or less instant solution; it ignores the pesky matter of Israeli public opinion and Israeli democratic choice.

Can Europe agree on enough basics of foreign policy and security policy to become what Blair called for three years ago, a "superpower, not a superstate"?[11] Such an accord is not likely soon; and because the long term is made up of a multiple of soons, it's hard to see what could make the difference in the long term. In only the most obvious area of dispute, Britain and France have quite different attitudes toward the United States in the postwar period, since they drew different lessons from the confrontation with the transatlantic ally over the French-British invasion of Suez in 1956. Britain concluded that it was best to remain as far as possible on the US side; France, that it must develop as independent a foreign policy as possible within the general carapace of the Western alliance—outside NATO, with an independent nuclear deterrent and an often sharply differing approach to issues as different as relations with the former Soviet Union and with former colonies in Africa. France was most successful in promoting the Franco-German alliance as the "engine" of the European Union—a machine that still runs, if increasingly wheezily as the French and German economies still languish and as the EU grows beyond a number easily controllable by a political center dominated by two states. Both right- and left-wing governments in France tend to view the promotion of democracy in developing countries more skeptically than the Americans and the British, seeing stability and interstate relations as trumping civil and human rights.

The left in Britain has become increasingly Europhile, though Britain as a whole has not. Much of the left had been against the EU: the Labour Party split on that issue (among others) in the early 1980s, with pro-European leaders such as Roy Jenkins, David Owen, and Shirley Williams creating the Social-Democratic Party, which briefly challenged Labour for the position of the main opposition party until declining, then merging with the Liberal Party in the late eighties. At the same time, the Labour Party shifted, ceasing to regard the EU as a "capitalist club" and seeing it instead as a source of progressive legislation in both labor and civil rights areas. The Conservatives under Margaret Thatcher and since have moved to a "Euroskeptical" position, substantially for the same reason. Though part of the far left remains—quite rationally—attached to the position that this is a grouping with more success in creating a single-market economy than in spreading social democracy Europe-wide, most of the rest have concluded that the cosmopolitanism and idealism of the EU venture—committed, as Mark Leonard has put it, to "peace, multilateralism, compromise"—are more in tune with their beliefs than a nation-state, even one committed to leftist policies, could ever be. Although Tony Blair is generally seen as one who would like some closer integration with the EU—at least so far as adopting the euro to replace sterling—he is also now widely disparaged on the left as one who had not done enough to further the pro-European cause. People on the left were deeply impressed both with the scale of the antiwar protests—the largest, in London in 2002, reached an estimated one million—and with the prevalence of rainbow-colored "Peace" flags flown everywhere on the continent.

This pro-Europeanism, however, has often been a cause of preventing the left from asking hard questions about the EU's efficiency. Philip Gordon has put the situation well. In his *Prospect* article, he calls on Europeans to

> respect America's special role and responsibility for global security and join the US in dealing with the challenges such as terrorism and weapons proliferation. They must acknowledge that European integration and enlargement—while themselves enormous contributions to world peace—are no longer enough, and that Europeans need to do much more to contribute to peace and security beyond their borders. In exchange for a real seat at the table, the EU should agree not to try to constrain American power and instead accept the goal of strategic partnership with the US.[12]

But many Europeans, especially on the left, don't "respect America's special role and responsibility for global security" and don't want to join it. The decision of the new Spanish prime minister, José Luis Rodríguez Zapatero, to pull the Spanish contingent out of Iraq as soon as he came to power in 2004, and the harsh words his administration had for the Anglo-American alliance (he accused Blair and Bush of "waging a war based on lies," while his defense minister, José Bono, called Blair "a complete dickhead"),[13] have played well elsewhere. The Italian left has come to a shaky agreement that it will pull the larger (and effective) Italian contingent out if it wins. The French socialists see Zapatero as a model: In a rally in his honor in Toulouse in June 2004, Zapatero—in the words of the *Financial Times Madrid* correspondent Leslie Crawford—gave a "speech even more anti-American than he would risk back home," ending with the call that "we must not allow one country to decide the future of our planet."[14] Guess which one country?

What faith European leftists have left over from the EU they put in the UN. But the UN is two organizations. One is the world of its agencies, which—at the sharp end—can be heroic and are called on to be so every day. The highest-ranking casualty in Iraq so far has been Sergio Vieira de Mello, the senior UN official charged by Kofi Annan to oversee UN operations in Iraq. Even in UN agencies' everyday work, they constitute a network of regulation, efforts at compromise, and a routinization of agreed international processes that addresses the most outstanding problems and without which it's hard to see the world working as well as it does.

But the other side of the UN is its basis in national sovereignty and realpolitik, which has all but completely stymied large-scale humanitarian intervention and effective policing or enforcement of its own resolutions. It certainly did so in the case of Saddam Hussein—who, in the twelve years after the 1991 Gulf War, breached every one of the provisions of the cease-fire agreements that had ended it. It's usually forgotten, in the race to prove that Iraq instantly and fully disarmed after the Gulf War and was thus no threat to anyone, that the defection of the head of the country's biological weapons program forced a confession that Iraq had continued to produce more than 180 types of biological weapons in violation of the agreement; that Saddam probably had tried, repeatedly, to obtain weapons-grade uranium; and that, as the David Kay report showed, Saddam had been seeking to buy from "dear leader" Kim Jong Il a North Korean missile system. Furthermore, and more immediately murderously, Saddam attacked the unprotected Kurds in instant violation of the agreement. On most days when US and UK aircraft patrolled the no-fly zone in order to stave off further Kurdish massacres, they were fired on. The sanctions put in place, which caused considerable distress in Iraq because Saddam controlled the permitted flow of funds and made sure that the poor suffered, were the object of unremitting criticism from NGOs, activists, and powerful Security Council states, such as France and Russia. If Saddam had rid himself of most of his weapons of mass destruction—probably without his knowledge—his regime remained on the alert to restock the armory once the sanctions/inspection regime dwindled into insignificance, as seemed likely before 9/11.

The UN is, as Philip Bobbitt has put it,[15] "a universal law-creating system actually based on democratic majoritarianism and self determination"—that is, the same sources of power as the parliamentary nation-state. But at the same time as nations solemnly profess allegiance to these sources of authority, they deny them power in practice, once the chips are down. The UN system's worst charge is that it lets tyrants get away with murder—and permits them to remain members—as when Libya was voted chair of the Human Rights Commission and Sudan, the latest largely undisturbed killing field, became and remains a member. Insofar as any effective action is being taken on the Sudan-Darfur humanitarian crisis, it is being taken by states—with the United States in the lead. This is the norm: interventions in Africa are generally done, if at all, by the former colonial powers. These can be relatively effective, as the British in Sierra Leone or the French in Ivory Coast; they can be ineffective, as the United States in Somalia; or they can actually shield the perpetrators of horrors, as the French did in Rwanda in 1994. But it's the nation that does it, for a mixture of raisons d'état and belief, old colonial reflexes, and new NGO-prompted conscience.

The United States has taken the villain's part for the left, worldwide. The consensus on this point has gathered so rapidly and so completely that it leaves little space for anything but invective and skepticism. It has become the agenda for most European commentary, providing the underlying narrative to a range of discrete stories. Is AIDS the story? The United States is not delivering the assistance it promised and is only doing so if the recipients agree to abstinence rather than protected sex. Is the EU the story? The focus is the divisions within it created by the US invasion of Iraq or the gulf that Bush has caused between the United States and Europe. Is Blair the story? He is damaged goods because of his support for the United States.

Not much scope here for what Philip Gordon called for: a view at least sympathetic to the burden of upholding world order or stopping more disorder. In his Royal Society for the Arts talk, Garton Ash spoke a little despairingly of the closing of the British intellectual mind on the United States, producing what amounts to a revulsion against its works that no longer cares to examine its options—or the options for the world if it ceases to act in something like the manner it is now acting. And it is likely to so act, under any conceivable future administration.

In an essay in *Foreign Affairs*, Eliot A. Cohen concludes with this message—one deeply unwelcome to the European left and, indeed, to Europeans as a whole:

> The United States today has less choice about its role in world affairs than its worried leaders and their critics, or its anxious friends and numerous enemies, think. The logic of empire is a logic of extension and the strategic conundrum of empire is that of overcommitment and overstretch. Despite

the wishes of French and Chinese politicians, no countervailing state or federation will restore a balance-of-power system akin to that of Europe in the eighteenth and nineteenth centuries, at least not in the near future. Despite the wishes of idealists, no international institution has proven capable of effective action in the absence of power generated and exercised by states. And a third possibility—anarchy unleashed after a disgusted United States recalls its legions in a spurt of democratic disgust at and indifference to the rest of the planet—is too horrifying to contemplate. The real alternatives, then, are US hegemony exercised prudently or foolishly, safely or dangerously—and for this, US leaders must look back to school themselves in the wisdom that will make such statesmanship possible.[16]

This view is largely right, except that it understates what is possible for Europeans. They have little military capability that the Americans need, though it is up to the Europeans to develop it. They do have, however, roughly the same aims, and they face roughly the same dangers. The forces that wish to do the United States down wish to do Europe down; indeed, those forces are often trying to do so, as the bombs in Madrid showed. Partnership is not just possible but inevitable, if both sides wish to face challenges that include terrorism, nuclear proliferation, the growing power of vast states like China and India, the ongoing stagnation of the Middle Eastern states, and the continuing disasters in Africa. Europe and the United States differ less than the anti-Americans (and, in the United States, the anti-Europeans) would have us think. It was a leftist, postwar government of the UK that did the most to create NATO. It should not be beyond the left to again see clearly enough where our interests, and our common beliefs, lie. It just doesn't seem likely, for now.

## NOTES

1. David Edelstein, "Proper Propaganda," *Slate*, June 24, 2004, http://www.slate.com/id/2102859 (accessed January 21, 2005).

2. Erik Tarloff, "The Charge of the Right Brigade," *Financial Times Magazine*, July 3, 2004.

3. Christopher Hitchens, "Unfairenheit 9/11: The Lies of Michael Moore," *Slate*, June 21, 2004, http://www.slate.com/id/2102723 (accessed January 21, 2005).

4. Ibid.

5. Philip Gordon, "Letter to Europe," *Prospect* (July 2004).

6. Mark Leonard, "Rebranding Europe," unpublished essay prepared for the Foreign Policy Centre. The full text of the essay is available at http://www.fpc.org.uk/fsblob/144.pdf (accessed January 4, 2005).

7. Ibid.

8. Timothy Garton Ash, *Free World: Why a Crisis of the West Reveals the Opportunity of Our Time* (London: Allen Lane, 2004; published in the United States as *Free World: America, Europe, and the Surprising Future of the West* [New York: Random House, 2004]).

9. Timothy Garton Ash, "Letter to America" *Prospect* (July 2004).

10. "President Bush Meets with Prime Minister Blair in Northern Ireland," White House press release, April 8, 2003.

11. Tony Blair quote found in Charles Grant, "EU and US Need to Learn to Play Together," *St. Petersburg Times* (Russia), July 10, 2001.

12. Philip Gordon, "Letter to Europe," *Prospect* (July 2004).

13. José Bono quote taken from Isambard Wilkins, "Spanish Politician Labels Blair an 'Imbecile' on Live Television," *The Telegraph*, January 16, 2004.

14. Leslie Crawford, "Baptism of Ire," *Financial Times Magazine*, July 17, 2004.

15. Philip Bobbitt, *The Shield of Achilles* (New York: Knopf, 2002).

16. Eliot A. Cohen, "History and the Hyperpower," *Foreign Affairs* (July/August 2004).

# 15

## Guilt's End

### How Germany Redefined the Lessons
### of Its Past during the Iraq War

RICHARD HERZINGER

The postwar period is completely over now—that was how German chancellor Gerhard Schröder commented on his invitation to the celebration of the sixtieth anniversary of the Allied landing in Normandy on June 6, 2004. His participation attested to the fact that the liberation of Europe from Hitler had also been a "victory for Germany."

The celebrations confirmed the new historical-political self-awareness of the German government's leader. In the commemorative speeches of the Western statesmen, there were no longer any vanquished, symbolically underscoring that Germany has become accepted without reservation in the circle of Western democracies and that its National Socialist past is no longer being chalked up against it. On the anniversary of D-Day, the Germans were given more than the full rehabilitation by the erstwhile Western coalition of victors. French president Jacques Chirac thanked the United States for its decisive part in the liberation of Europe and termed it an "eternal friend." At the same time, he greeted the chancellor of Germany, the former occupier of France, as his "brother."

With this acknowledgment, Chirac made clear that the historic achievement of the Americans belongs—in his view—to a concluded epoch of tragic wars. Although this achievement must be perceived in the historic consciousness of liberated Europeans, it is no longer instructive as a template of action for the present. George W. Bush's attempt, in the run-up to the anniversary, to transfer the pathos of the war of liberation from Nazi Germany to the common fight of the Western democracies against Islamist terrorism had been brusquely rejected by Chirac and was not repeated by the US president in his D-Day address. Under Chirac's direction, the celebrations foregrounded the imperative to maintain and expand the peace. And the French president left no doubt that this new European consciousness that war had been left behind as an archaic political means was mainly represented by the German-French axis.

With his grand gesture toward the new main ally, Chirac's politics of history consecrated what had already become apparent during the dispute about the Iraq war: the decoupling of the German discourse about the past from the Anglo-American historical narrative about World War II. The latter places the triumph of the liberal civilization of the West over its totalitarian challengers into the center of historical remembrance, which is regularly remobilized during conflicts with dictatorial regimes—and by no means only by conservative US presidents. By contrast, during the transatlantic quarrel prior to the beginning of the Iraq war, Chancellor Schröder and Foreign Minister Joschka Fischer had repeatedly stressed that the Europeans principally resisted war as a method of conflict resolution in the twenty-first century. They had learned in the preceding century that war could bring nothing but horror and destruction. One can only arrive at such an evaluation, however, if one leaves unconsidered that National Socialism could only have been defeated by means of a war and that one could have limited its horrendous scale only if Hitler's regime had been abolished early on—by military means, if necessary.

Thus, during the dispute about the Iraq war, more was at stake than a political difference about the usefulness and legality of a specific warlike intervention. The dispute also expressed more than merely a deep resentment toward the person of the current US president, who some regard as an ideal foil for projections of the "ugly American." Beyond that, the Iraq crisis provided the German public with the exemplary occasion for a fundamental reinterpretation of the historical lessons taught by the experience of totalitarianism and war. Instead of merely stressing the painful experience of war, Schröder and Fischer could also have said that the Europeans, particularly the Germans, must be especially watchful toward dictatorships like Saddam Hussein's—after all, they had experienced the devastating consequences of underestimating the dangers that emanate from totalitarian regimes with their own flesh and blood. Such a line of argument, however, was rejected as ahistorical during the German debate.

Yet the red-green federal government had argued quite differently a few years earlier, on the occasion of the Kosovo war. The Social Democratic minister of defense, Rudolf Scharping, and Foreign Minister Joschka Fischer of the Green Party had at that time justified the military intervention against Milošević with the impending genocide of Kosovo Albanians, drawing parallels to the annihilation policies of the National Socialists. Fischer explained that he had retained two German historical maxims from his leftist socialization: "Never again war!" and "Never again Auschwitz!" In no way did Fischer intend, as was often imputed later, to equate the Serbian massacres in Kosovo with those at Auschwitz. What he meant to say was revulsion against war was not a sufficient lesson to be learned from the German past. One had to recognize equally that targeted, state-sponsored mass murder had to be halted, in the most extreme case even with outside military intervention.

The shock experience that allowed Fischer to come to this insight was the massacre at Srebrenica in Bosnia in the summer of 1995. The UN troops had, without a fight, surrendered the Muslim enclave, which the UN had declared a protective zone, to the Serbian troops of General Ratko Mladić. As chair of the fundamentally pacifist Greens, Fischer had for many years taken a position against any military involvement of the West in the Balkans. Now he changed his position—initially against the majority of his party. However, by the time the Greens entered into the governing coalition with the Social Democrats in 1998, Fischer had pushed through a comprehensive change of course in foreign policy matters, at least in the governing bodies of the party. The Greens, which only a few years earlier had demanded the dissolution of NATO, committed themselves not only to the firm political and cultural integration of Germany into the West but also to military integration into the Western alliance.

The support of the Kosovo war, however, brought the Greens into difficult conflicts with their traditional electorate, who wished to remain true to the radical-pacifist ideals of their founding epoch. But the Green party leadership remained steadfast, and the relative stabilization of peace in the Balkans after NATO's intervention slowly muted the loudest criticism from the left. Remarkably, the harshest attacks against Fischer's foreign policy now emanated from the conservative side. The accusation was that Fischer wanted to compensate for his radical past—in the seventies he had been the leader of a militant extreme left organization in Frankfurt am Main—by behaving particularly submissively now toward the United States, against which he had once fought as the number one imperialist enemy.

Although this accusation did not conform to the facts, it did contain a kernel of truth. Fischer's evolution into an engaged pro-Atlanticist was paradigmatic for a process of learning that the "new left" had undergone since the sixties and seventies. Shock experiences like the disclosure of the crimes of the "anti-imperialist" Pol Pot regime in Cambodia and finally the collapse of the Soviet Union brought their most farsighted thinkers—to whom Joschka Fischer always belonged— to the realization that their former revolutionary utopianism tended to have had totalitarian traits, and that the original impulses of their anti-authoritarian revolt had emerged from the liberal ideals of the West. If they now raised these Western values all the more enthusiastically, they did so not because they embraced mere opportunism but because they were newly convinced that the anchoring in the Western world represents the condition for the realization of "left" enlightenment ideals— and that the United States, in spite of all necessary criticism, is the main guarantor that this Western world exists.

The new loyalty of the left government toward the leading power of the West was strengthened again by September 11. But even though this time only a few defectors among the Greens and Social Democrats resisted Germany's participation in the war in Afghanistan, a subliminal anti-American grumbling was already audible in these parties. For his commitment to "unconditional solidarity" with the United States, which Chancellor Schröder had given immediately after the terrorist attacks in New York and Washington, D.C., he was criticized with increasing vigor. After Fischer, Schröder now also had become suspect of behaving like an overeager vassal of Washington.

The critics missed that Schröder's statement had a specific national political component. With his locution of "unconditional solidarity," Schröder had meant to say not that he was willing to follow the United States uncritically but that Germany's support for the United States would obviously also include an active military contribution. In making this point, he brought to a close a decade-long debate over the legitimacy of military action by Germany's Federal Armed Forces outside the borders of their own country. For a long time, the German Basic Law had interdicted any military engagement that did not directly serve the country's defense. Originally this determination had been intended to make it impossible for Germany, after the catastrophic experience with National Socialism, to ever again conduct a war of aggression.

With its participation in the Kosovo war, but conclusively with the war in Afghanistan, the Federal Republic has stripped itself of this historically rooted restriction on its freedom of military action. Schröder had thus used the crisis after September 11 to finally establish Germany as an equal member of NATO. What looked to many like a devout submission to the United States was in fact another step in creating a new national consciousness, unburdened by the incriminating past.

During the subsequent Iraqi crisis, Schröder skillfully deployed this new consciousness. From the fact that Germany had been unhesitatingly ready to help the United States in the Afghanistan war, he now coined the argument that Germany therefore did not owe the Americans any further proof of solidarity. The duty of solidarity had been paid off by this act of friendship, so to speak. Schröder and Fischer had come under strong public pressure to give evidence of their independence from the American claim of leadership. In the German public, the spontaneous sympathy after September 11 had long since given way to a profound suspicion of the United States' motives for its "war against terror." Conspiracy theory books, according to which the mass-murderous attacks of September 11 could possibly have been organized by the CIA or Mossad in order to give the United States the occasion to realize its plans for world domination, filled the top spots of German best-seller lists. In 2002, 60 percent of Germans told pollsters that they did not believe the US government's official version regarding the background of September 11.

Schröder used this mood for an election campaign with strongly nationalist inflections. He spoke of "a German way" and maintained that German foreign policy was crafted in Berlin, not in Washington. With this point, he implied that it had been merely because of a lack of sovereignty and national strength that Germany so far had never openly resisted US policy. The Iraq war now gave Schröder the occasion to demonstrate to the entire world that this newly won sovereignty would be able to stand up even in an open conflict with the United States.

Schröder thereby gave voice to a new national consciousness that could rhetorically link itself to the traditional "antifascist" core convictions of the left. The United States was now reproached for planning, in contravention of international law, an "aggressive war," which inevitably calls to mind Hitler's wars of aggression. All of a sudden, the moral credo of a Germany purified of its National Socialist past was supposed to be again "Never again war!" The contradiction that the new Germany had only just recently participated in wars in Kosovo and Afghanistan was systematically played down. In any event, Social Democrats and Greens had always preferred to call these events not "wars" but euphemistically "humanitarian interventions" or "crisis deployments." That these warlike actions caused the deaths of numerous enemy soldiers and civilians was never seen as a problem in the German debate. Similarly, the German public never seemed to find it objectionable that Gerhard Schröder, at the high point of the peace campaign, posed with the Russian chief of state Vladimir Putin, urging conformity with international law, while the Russian army in Chechnya continued to be guilty of the most serious crimes against the civilian population there.

It is true that a leftist nationalism, which defines itself as pacifist and "antifascist" in the sense of "antimilitarist" and in sharp distinction from US policy, is nothing new in the German left. It already dominated the attitudes of German Social Democrats during the debates about NATO rearmament during the 1980s. Today, however, this national consciousness on the left can rest on a much greater self-assuredness than in those years. Then, it represented only an oppositional movement—even if broadly based—against official German government policy under the conservative chancellor Helmut Kohl, who strictly supported the US course. During the Iraq conflict, however, the new leftist national pride coagulated into the official government line. It expressed the good conscience with which Germany had thoroughly done its homework in working through its terrible past. In fact, the German democracy had proven to be stable beyond a shadow of a doubt. The Germans had intensively confronted their past and acknowledged their historical responsibility. The commitment to the unconditional working through of the past and the systematic nurturing of the remembrance of the crimes of National Socialism has long since become the credo of the conservative political establishment as well. At the Organization for Security and Co-operation in Europe conference on anti-Semitism in April 2004 in Berlin, the host was applauded even by Jewish international organizations for its engagement against anti-Semitism and racism. Germany's reputation to rank international law and international cooperation above all else in its foreign policy might soon bring it the yearned-for permanent seat on the UN Security Council.

An essential difference to the eighties can also be seen in the fact that deep mistrust of the supposedly belligerent United States is now shared by a large segment of the bourgeois-liberal and conservative public. As long as the Cold War lasted, resentment that had always existed in this milieu against the United States as the military conqueror and "reeducator" of Germany was voiced only sotto voce, because the United States was, after all, indispensable as an anticommunist protective power. With the end of the communist threat, however, this condition has disappeared. In the debate about Iraq, the leadership of the Christian Democratic and Christian Social Parties took positions against the strong wave of anti-Americanism, but such sentiment among their electorate was scarcely less prevalent than among the supporters of left parties. If a conservative politician such as Edmund Stoiber or Angela Merkel had governed the republic at this moment, he or she probably would have tried to escape direct participation in the Iraq war—but without openly taking a position against the United States, thereby remaining in the old transatlantic tradition from Konrad Adenauer to Helmut Kohl. The majority of the members of their party and of its voters, however, felt themselves better represented by Schröder's resounding no, formulated with unmistakable national pathos, than by the conservative party leaders' attitudes, which they felt to be halfhearted and vacillating.

We see, then, that on the Iraq question the overwhelming majority of Germans came together in a national consensus, which rests on a mostly stable national self-image. This stance does not mean an abandonment of the community of shared values with the United States. However, the common values are now prioritized in a different way: peace and stability are ranked first, because they are seen as the condition for the preservation of freedom. A poll taken by the newsmagazine *Der Spiegel* in February 2003 shows how dramatic this break was: 62 percent of the Germans surveyed stated that they no longer felt gratitude to the Americans; 53 percent designated the United States as the greater danger for world peace, whereas only 28 percent mentioned Iraq, and only 9 percent cited North Korea. It is true that Germans, in these views, did not differ significantly from many other Europeans. In Germany, however, the popular conception that the American intention to export democracy with military means was pure irrationalism or a mere pretext for US imperialist expansionism was of special piquancy. After all, the Germans themselves had been put on the way to democracy by war and occupation of their country.

Precisely this fact, however, formed the hidden core problem that the German public worked away at to address on the occasion of the Iraq war. Germany is—justifiably—proud of its transformation into a well-functioning democratic society. Yet the historic blemish remains that the conditions for this change were not created through its own efforts but through those imposed by foreign powers, first among them the United States. This fact continues to hamper the development of a new national consciousness. Consequently, a historical-political discourse has begun that doubts the moral motives of the former victorious and occupying powers and thus seeks to minimize these powers' share in the democratic purification of the Germans after 1945.

Not coincidentally, the Iraq debate was conducted alongside an intensive critical examination of the Allied air war against Germany. The anniversary of the destruction of Hamburg in the "firestorm" of 1943 offered an occasion for this. A best-seller by the historian Jörg Friedrich (*Der Brand*, "The Fire") assigned the quality of a war of annihilation to the Anglo-American air strategy in World War II. Such problematic revisions of the prehistory of the Federal Republic's democracy help it to overcome the feeling of moral inferiority toward the erstwhile democratic reeducators. During the projective interpretation of the Iraq conflict by German opponents of the war, the United States and its president slipped into the role of aggressor and breaker of international law, while the fate of the Iraqi people, who in this conception were the target of the American attack, was identified with the suffering of the German population in the hail of Allied bombs during World War II. The role of Saddam Hussein and the character of his totalitarian dictatorship were largely ignored in this explanatory model. Moreover, the causal connection between National Socialist rule and the destruction of Germany was at times effaced from collective memory.

The moral pathos, however, with which the potential victims of an American "war of aggression"—leading politicians of the ruling coalition prophesied hundreds of thousands of civilian deaths and millions of refugees from the war zone—were pitied ahead of time stood in sharp contrast to the prevailing disinterest among the left for the countless real victims of Saddam's regime. Similarly, the anti-Semitic ideology and thrust of the Baath regime played almost no role in the moral and political classification of US plans for a war in Iraq. The moral arguments of the US president were dismissed as a mere propagandistic pretext for his political and imperialist ambitions. But even if one principally distrusted Bush and his government, one should have recognized the problem that Saddam Hussein's Iraq posed for peace and stability in the entire region and attempted to find a solution for it. Except for a small, isolated group of radical leftists who call themselves "anti-German antifascists," consider Islamism to be a fascist threat, and have written the unconditional defense of Israel on their banners, almost no voices on the left argued in this direction. This was a further indication that the vehement emotional rejection of the United States' war plans was not primarily about the real situation in Iraq but rather about the attempt of an inner purification of feelings of national guilt.

Thus, the condemnation of the Iraq war and the justified outrage about the torture methods of the US Army often resonate with the subliminal satisfaction to be able, finally, to feel superior to the former master teacher in matters of international law, democracy, and human rights. Now that Germany has barely arrived after its "long march to the West" (according to the historian Heinrich August Winkler [see, e.g., Kay Schiller, "Political Militancy and Generation Conflict in West Germany during the Red Decade," *Debatte* 11, no. 1 (May 2003): 19–38]), it can present itself as a competent guardian of Western values: the Germans in a way stylize themselves as better Americans. Such guardianship remains abstract, though, for the time being. By keeping out of a conflict, which is of eminent concern to Germans, Germany has not proven that it would hold on more steadfastly than the United States to basic Western values in an extreme situation—active military engagement for the federal army in Afghanistan, for example, or attacks in Germany similar to those in New York or Madrid. From the vantage point of a higher morality, one can more easily repress such threatening dangers and drown out the lack of concrete strategic perspectives in world politics.

To the extent that the image of an exemplarily changed nation, which has drawn the correct lessons from its terrible history, is solidified, the contours of a new German separate consciousness become delineated. It recalls the former delinquent who believes to have learned his lesson once and for all and believes himself to be better armored against the temptations of evil than his judges, who did not have to undergo such an inner purification. This new national self-assuredness is not rooted, as many on the left had long feared, in denying or minimizing German guilt. Its foundation, rather, is the certainty that it paid off for Germany to have anchored the duty of remembrance of its dark past in its democratic raison d'état.

## NOTE

Translated by Jens Kruse.

# 16

# The Iraq War and the French Left

MICHEL TAUBMANN

Throughout the crisis in Iraq, French socialists melted into the national consensus against the war. This reaction occurred practically without debate—a strange attitude for a party with a habitual taste for internal controversies. Is there a duty to intervene against a dictator? What about the future of the United Nations, NATO, and the European Union? And what about the future of relations between Europe and the United States? Is there any credibility to a "peace camp" that includes Vladimir Putin's Russia? Should one adopt an attitude of critical support or confrontation toward the United States? Should France abstain or use its power of veto in the Security Council? Questions were in fact not lacking. There was plenty to think about in regard to this difficult dilemma between the demands of intentional justice and the liberation of the Iraqi people.

Yet, the socialists, as with a large majority of the French political establishment, reduced an extremely complex situation to a simple choice, more moral than political, between war and peace. Placing George W. Bush on the same footing as Saddam Hussein, they renewed the ancient rhetoric of pacifism. The protests of February and March 2003 in which the socialists found themselves shoulder to shoulder with the communists, the Greens, and "alternative globalists" bathed them in the illusion of a renewal. Having exited 2002 in a groggy state—the year of their presidential election debacle—the socialists had the impression of washing away twenty years of participation in power, seen by many socialists as synonymous with compromise. Their attitude can be explained by examining the roots of French pacifism.

## THE GREAT TRAUMA OF 1914

Flashback: On the eve of World War I, the Section Française de l'Internationale Ouvrière (SFIO), in conformity with Marxist theory, considered that "capitalism brings war just as clouds bring thunder." In the name of internationalism, the majority of European socialist parties called on the proletariat to refuse dying for "salesmen of cannons" in a conflict uniquely motivated, according to their view, by economic rivalries for the conquest of markets. But pacifism collided with an obstacle largely ignored until then by the socialist movement: the irresistible force of national sentiment. Lacking a realistic articulation of the relation between patriotism and internationalism, with the first clarion call, French socialists, like most other European socialist parties, proved incapable of resisting the temptation of the "sacred union."

The war would profoundly divide the left and give birth to communism, leaving socialists full of remorse for abandoning their pacifist ideals. As with the rest of their compatriots, they remained traumatized by the four years of hell that Europe experienced between 1914 and 1918. The call of "Never again!" would henceforth guide the steps of a generation that had just lost one and half million young soldiers in the trenches.

But this refusal of the war prevented the socialists from discerning clearly during the 1930s the nature of the subsequent conflict, because this time, an international civil war between totalitarianism and democracy was at issue. And pacifism, a phenomenon only possible in democracies, could only serve the more aggressive power—in this case, Nazi Germany. If the leadership of the Communist Party between September 1939 and June 1941 refused to endorse the struggle against Hitler due to its solidarity with the Soviet Union, signatory of the German-Soviet Pact, the majority of the SFIO reclaimed for the entire French left the old pacifist line that would lead them to reject in the same breath the "imperialisms" of both England and Germany. With the exception of a courageous minority behind Léon Blum, socialist parliamentarians ended up giving the reigns of powers to Philippe Pétain on July 10, 1940.

This shipwreck should have discredited the ideology of pacifism among socialists, and the trauma of 1940 seemed to have erased the trauma of 1914. In giving privilege to nation, freedom, and democracy, a new generation of French socialists emerged during the Resistance. These men and women, shaped by the struggle against Nazism, would after the war distinguish themselves courageously from the communists and their campaign for "peace," which in reality was destined to serve the expansion of the Soviet dictatorship. This generation of socialists had chosen in 1947 the camp of freedom against Soviet totalitarianism, which, having attained power in Eastern Europe, would imprison those social democrats who refused to bow to the law of its absolute party.

## THE MISSILES ARE IN THE EAST

During the 1950s and the 1960s, the SFIO defined itself resolutely as "pro-Atlantic." Its members believed that the survival of an independent workers' movement in Europe, inseparable from democracy, could not be guaranteed without US protection. This pro-Atlantic orientation would distinguish the socialists for a long time from Gaullism, on the one hand, and communism, on the other. It was put into retirement by the new Socialist Party founded at the Congress of Epinay in 1971, which, henceforth allied with the Communist Party, became converted to an anti-imperialist and third world discourse.

The man who inaugurated this common program, François Mitterrand, never belonged to the SFIO but nevertheless shared the SFIO's profound attachment to the Atlantic alliance. In 1983, having become president of the republic, Mitterrand took the side of the Americans on the issue of the missile crisis, much to the consternation of German pacifists who preferred "better red rather than dead." One had to remind them, however, that whereas the pacifists are in the West, the missiles are in the East. Mitterrand's position did not provoke the slightest murmur among the French left, more preoccupied as they were with "fiscal austerity measures," which substituted their dreams of a "rupture with capitalism," than with questions of foreign policy, which, in any case, belonged to the prerogative of the president of the republic.

## THE AFTERMATH OF ANTICOLONIALISM

Things played themselves out differently in 1991 on the occasion of the Gulf War. This first post–Cold War conflict possessed all the "winning cards" that would be cruelly missing in the second Gulf War of 2003: an immense international coalition, grouping together not only the United States but also the dying USSR, Europe, and a majority of Arab nations; the benediction of the United Nations; and, contrary to 2003, an incontestable violation—the brutal annexation of a small country, Kuwait, by the military and bloody dictatorship of Saddam Hussein.

It was a new type of war, an "international police operation" based on consensus and carried out by nation-states in the absence of any expectations of benefiting directly, the aim of which was deemed as announcing a new world order defined by the absence of conflicts among great powers. François Mitterrand could rightly speak of a "just war." Thus, during the parliamentary vote at the beginning of hostilities, the socialists, with their immense majority, joined the right almost unanimously for the purpose of backing the presidential choice. Only an isolated handful of parliamentarians, among them a few trouble-makers from a new school of socialists—Julien Dray, Jean-Luc Mélenchon, and Marie-Noëlle Lienemann—broke ranks by opposing the war along with the communists and the extreme right.

Yet, twelve days after the commencement of hostilities, Defense Minister Jean-Pierre Chevènement, still at this time a member of the Socialist Party, resigned from his post—an event never seen before in the midst of a conflict. Aside from his exaggerations and cataclysmic prophecies—he had predicted a massacre of French soldiers—he expressed the unease felt by many socialists, including many government ministers. For the generation of Chevènement, Lionel Jospin (at the time, minister of education), Pierre Joxe (interior minister), and Michel Rocard (prime minister), the basic frame of reference was neither Munich nor the Cold War but rather the war in Algeria.

It was a refusal of the SFIO's politics, which seemed incapable of moving beyond a colonial vision of Algeria, that shaped the partisans who came into power in the 1980s. In the final analysis, they could not fail to see the Baathists of Saddam Hussein as a reminder of the National Liberation Front (FLN) and other nationalist movements in the third world, which, even though dictatorial, nevertheless remained "progressive" and anticolonialist. Faced with a choice between the wealthy emir of Kuwait, viewed as a feudal lord sitting on his basket of oil, and the nationalist Iraqi dictator with revolutionary and anti-imperialist tendencies, many socialists were at pains to decide.

But the same people could (and not without reason) deny a posteriori any moral legitimacy to this war when France and the rest of the Coalition, refusing to march on Baghdad, abandoned the Shiite and Kurdish insurgents to a bloody repression by Saddam's troops. Adhering strictly to the mandate of the United Nations, the "just war" simultaneously restored sovereignty to the aggrieved country, Kuwait, and respected the sovereignty of the aggressor, Iraq.

## THE DUTY OF INTERVENTION

In this context, Bernard Kouchner, at the time secretary of state for humanitarian action, gave a sense of "the left," or at least a moral sense, to this first Gulf War. With the support of Danielle Mitterrand, he managed to convince the French president to engage in a rescue operation of the Iraqi Kurdish population. France, Great Britain, and the United States thus created a protected zone, prohibited to Iraqi troops. Thanks to this initiative, four million Kurds would, beginning in 1992, escape from the hands of the Baathist dictator.

Profiting from dividends gained in the "Oil for Food" program under the oversight of the United Nations, the Iraqi Kurds developed a degree of prosperity and liberty—to be sure, relative, but nonetheless without any equivalent in their immediate geographic surroundings. The idea of "humanitarian intervention" advocated for a long time by the founder of Doctors without Borders and by a few antitotalitarian intellectuals deflated the idea of the sanctity of national sovereignty. They would brandish this idea anew in the case of Bosnia when nationalist Serbs massacred two hundred thousand Muslims between 1992 and 1995.

During these years until 1999, the French left, with the exception of a few individuals, observed with "lowered guns" the bloody dismantling of the former Yugoslavia. Television reports on the siege of Sarajevo appeared every day, yet large-scale demonstrations were not organized by the parties of the left, the French labor unions, or the right. Even France's educated youth, ever ready to mobilize itself against the least xenophobic agitation of Jean-Marie Le Pen, remained indifferent toward the massive conflagration of ethnic cleansing happening a few hundred kilometers from their borders.

Having never really learned the lessons of totalitarianism, the entire French left could only perceive in the disintegration of communist Yugoslavia the convulsions of an incomprehensible interethnic conflict. Lacking a more or less "progressive camp" with which to identify as well as a more or less "imperialist" adversary to fight against, the left ensconced itself in a position of nonengagement.

"One should not add war to war," François Mitterrand responded to those who had pressed on him to intervene. Much like the German chancellor, Helmut Kohl, and the majority of European leaders, he had already decried the eventual intervention of European forces as becoming dragged into the Serbian resistance much in the image of Tito's resistance against Hitler's troops.

## THE KOSOVO WAR

It was finally not the left but Jacques Chirac who changed French foreign policy by hardening the tone toward Slobodan Milošević soon after his arrival at the Elysée Palace in 1995. Chirac played an active role in the decision taken by NATO to put an end to the wars in Yugoslavia by means of an intervention to liberate Kosovo in March 1999. This novel "international police action" was far from presenting itself under the same mandate as the 1991 operation against Iraq. It did not receive the endorsement of the United Nations. It was even condemned by China, Russia, and some of the Balkan countries adjoining Yugoslavia, where a reflex action of orthodox solidarity against Albanian Muslims played a significant role. This intervention was carried out by a limited coalition of mainly European troops under US authority and with a NATO mandate.

In France, adversaries against intervention in Kosovo transferred their arguments from those used eight years earlier against the Gulf war: the conflict would be long and deadly; the Serbian people in their patriotic fervor would stand firm behind their leader, Milošević; the orthodox masses of neighboring countries would express their solidarity with an attacked Yugoslavia; and world peace would be threatened by a widening of the conflict, which would require Russia to intervene on behalf of the Serbs. These arguments were pressed into service once again against the war in Afghanistan in 2001 and yet again against the war in Iraq in 2003. Nevertheless, these arguments had few supporters in 1999. These supporters were primarily recruited from the extreme right and "sovereignists," who refused to accept a violation of Serbian sovereignty, a traditional ally of France. One also found them among members of the Communist Party and Trotskyites, for whom the sufferings of the Yugoslavian people began the day a US airplane dared to fly over the territory of a country that had long been considered as a model of "worker-managed" socialism.

The majority of the left, more so than the right, brought its support to the operation in Kosovo. Lionel Jospin, then prime minister, shared the interventionist views of Jacques Chirac, who exercised in this affair his "right of inventory" in honor of François Mitterrand. Within the government of the "plural left," the reservations of Jean-Pierre Chevènement and of the communists were well known, but both parties remained discrete with their reservations. By contrast, the Socialist Party, the Greens, numerous humanitarian associations, artists and intellectuals, and even some people close to the extreme left committed themselves in favor of the Kosovo Albanians. Many were surprised at having supported a military operation executed by the Americans for the first time. And many of them, identifying Milošević with Hitler, placed their action in the tradition of antifascism.

It should be mentioned that the justification for intervention, contrary to the weapons of mass destruction later in the case of the second Iraq war, was spread daily as the lead story of newspapers and television broadcasts around the entire world—namely, the tens of thousands of Kosovar refugees amassing on the frontiers of Albania or neighboring Macedonia. Sweeping away any relative objections to international law, such humanitarian urgency brought the majority of the French left to rally around "the duty of intervention."

## THE KOUCHNER LINE

It was a logical choice that the person who carried forward this concept was given the task of its application. Bernard Kouchner, then minister of health, provisionally quit Jospin's government in order to direct the international protectorate under the mandate of the United Nations, which permitted Kosovo to attain civil peace, democracy, and prosperity—to be sure, precarious, yet previously indispensable. Beyond France, the "duty of intervention" seemed to offer a benchmark for the European left in search of a way of adapting to the challenges of globalization. Accordingly, Tony Blair in the United Kingdom, having become prime minister in 1997, considered the duty of intervention to be the cornerstone of the new internationalism demanded by New Labour.

In Germany, Foreign Minister Joschka Fischer and his old accomplice Daniel Cohn-Bendit imposed a painful cultural revolution on the Green Party, which was coming out of demonstrations during the 1980s and demanding again in its 1998 election platform Germany's departure from NATO. The "Never again!" call by the children of "Germany, Pale Mother," would change its meaning: it no longer signified the refusal of war but rather the refusal of dictatorship. And two years later, on the occasion of the war in Afghanistan, Fischer set into motion a decisive turning point in German history: for the first time since World War II, soldiers of the *Bundeswehr* were deployed in a territorial offensive outside the European continent on the side of the Americans and the English.

## THE WAR IN AFGHANISTAN

Within the French left, the intervention in Afghanistan provoked more reservations than the intervention in Kosovo had. Misery, the complete absence of freedom and social rights, a reign of terror, an obscurantist theocracy, the oppression of women, the dictatorship of the Taliban— all represented a system even more contradictory to the proclaimed values of the left. Nevertheless, it was not the condition of human rights that justified the war but rather the attack against the United States on its own soil on September 11 by a terrorist organization whose headquarters was located in Afghanistan. In a clear case of legitimate self-defense, the actions of the aggrieved party subscribed entirely to the framework of international justice, which "allowed the pursuit of actors, commanders, and accomplices wherever they are to be found," as was proclaimed by the solemn declaration published by the European Union on September 15, 2001.

The military retaliation commenced on October 7, 2001, with the first aerial bombardments of Afghanistan. France associated itself with this retaliation. Prime Minister Jospin agreed with Chirac in sending combat troops on the side of the Americans and the principal European countries. But the commencement of hostilities provoked very violent reactions. The extreme left, as in every conflict, repeated mechanically its Marxist-Leninist analysis. Placing on equal footing George W. Bush and Osama bin Laden, it denounced the imperialist war and the US bombardments, characterizing them as blind strikes against the civilian population. The extreme left in effect expressed the same ignorance of modern warfare and its precision strikes as had been exhibited by Green Party politician Noël Mamère. The presidential candidate of the French Green Party challenged the use of violence and advocated the combat of terrorism through "legal means." The virulence of the French Greens surprised those who remembered their engagement in favor of intervention in Kosovo. This time, the Greens disassociated themselves unambiguously from their German comrades and the French government to which they belonged. For his part, the communist Robert Hue expressed his "feeling of being tested" and "extreme indignation" with regard to the American bombardments, which he could only envision as extremely lethal.

## CULPABLE AMERICA

However, at a party hosted by the newspaper *L'Humanité* two days after the attacks of September 11, Robert Hue expressed clearly "his solidarity" not only with "every American citizen" but also with "the leaders that they chose for themselves." This last phrase provoked heated indignation among those partisans in attendance. For them, it was not a question, once compassion had been expressed for the victims, to say that we are "all Americans," as had invited the title of the editorial of Jean-Marie Colombani, the editor of *Le Monde*, on September 12, 2001. Their reaction was revealing of a fairly widespread mentality—especially among the left, where many easily found themselves playing the role of network pundits on the evening of September 12. While the ruins of the World Trade Center were still smoking, the entertainers of Canal+ could only formulate one reproach against the terrorists: having provided America with the long-desired "pretext" to spread "its" war throughout the world. A terror more disconcerting than that of bin Laden was soon presented in the character of a fairly sympathetic marionette, a sort of Islamic "Robin Hood," fighting with lesser means against a "hyperpower."

"Hyperpower": This expression, made popular by Jospin's foreign minister, Hubert Védrine, quickly imposed itself as self-evident. From a certain point of view, it characterized justly the dominant role of the United States in the world after the Cold War. Yet, didn't the events of September 11 demonstrate the extreme fragility of this "hyperpower" and the whole Western world in the face of suicidal terrorists armed simply with box cutters? This perplexing reality has the implication of considering the United States a victim, a view that could not be accepted by those who had always considered imperialism to be culpable. This idea, widespread in France, undoubtedly explains that country's feeble emotional response after September 11.

In Spain and Germany on September 11, silent demonstrations united tens of thousands of people from different cities. In Berlin on September 14, every political party organized an impressive demonstration united against terrorism. On this day, at precisely noon, the Council of Europe called on the eight hundred million inhabitants of the continent's forty-three countries to observe three minutes of silence in solidarity with the American people. In France, Jacques Chirac and Lionel Jospin, accompanied by numerous dignitaries, participated in a moving ceremony at the American Cathedral in Paris. Instructions had been communicated to the public sector to observe a moment of silence. These instructions were not always followed.

Teachers took the opportunity to speak to their students about September 11 . . . in Chile. Others, by evoking the "more numerous" victims of the Rwandan genocide or the famine in the Sahel, also sought to relativize the tragedy of arguably the richest country on the planet (a designation that presumably made the 9/11 victims slightly culpable).

In certain public sectors, partisans of the line "You reap what you sow" were sharply opposed to the "hand of honor" or the "slap in the face" of exasperated colleagues at the simple mention of the United States: "It serves them well!" "They deserved it!" "It was bound to happen to them one day!"

Interviewed by *Libération* on September 14, 2001, a leader of CGT Renault did not hide the perplexity of his "troops": "of course, the entire world feels solidarity with the victims. But we'll have to wait for the American response. And we'll have to be attentive to the increase in racism. We've seen this on other previous occasions." In an opinion piece published by *Libération* on September 25, 2001, the European Deputy Sami Naïr (close to Jean-Pierre Chevènement), after admitting that the Americans had a right to retaliate, nevertheless called on them essentially to "reflect on what it means to be the object of rejection." In fact, after the wave of sympathy aroused by the tragedy of September 11, the US retaliation in Afghanistan served as a springboard for the amplification of critiques against the United States.

Polling done during the military operations revealed a France divided, with hostility emanating primarily from voters on the left. Within Jospin's government, Minister of Health Bernard Kouchner fiercely defended the duty of intervention not only on humanitarian grounds. His colleagues remained discrete, but no socialist minister openly relayed critiques coming from the rest of the "plural left." And the Socialist Party, conforming to its role, loyally supported the government's policy and most notably the sending of French troops to Afghanistan. Nevertheless, the leaders of the party were to a certain extend relieved by the rapid US victory after five weeks of combat. It was about time—room was needed for campaigning in the upcoming presidential elections.

## THE EMBARRASSMENT OF THE SOCIALISTS

During this election campaign, international questions were strangely absent. And yet, in the streets of Paris and in the French media, everyone seemed to speak only about the conflict in the Near East. Having made Palestine into another Vietnam at the start of the twenty-first century, the extreme left was shaped by a new generation of partisans who hated Israel and the United States. In contrast to "ambient depoliticization," the weeks preceding the election were marked by two impressive street demonstrations: one in support of the Palestinians, bringing together leftists and Islamists; the other in favor of Israel and against anti-Semitism, organized by the Jewish community. In this confrontation over the Middle East, which profoundly tore apart the left, the Socialist Party proved itself to be almost nonexistent.

Minimizing the rise of anti-Semitic acts, which attained a new record in the spring of 2002, and allowing the extreme left to develop with impunity its simplistic vision of the conflict in Iraq, the Socialist Party perhaps lost during these weeks a good part of those votes that would have allowed its candidate, Lionel Jospin, to advance to the second round of elections. Pascal Boniface, one of the principal counselors in the Socialist Party for international affairs, developed an openly hostile stance toward the United States and Israel by underscoring the value of voters of Maghreb origin, who are ten times more numerous than Jewish voters. But this line of argumentation encountered strong internal resistance, and, consequently, the Socialist Party adopted a low profile.

## THE PROGRESSIVE RADICALIZATION OF THE SOCIALIST PARTY

In Jospin's programmatic brochure entitled "I'm Engaging Myself" (*Je m'engage*), the events of September 11 are mentioned only once:

The world is too complex and too diverse such that one power can pretend to resolve its problems only with regard to its national interests. That is why, and even more so after September 11, the collective interest requires that the United States remains open toward others by respecting rules, by sharing in the spirit of dialogue and by concerning itself with the major difficulties of international organizations that deal with the substantial questions facing the world today.

One does not find one word in this brochure about the danger posed by radical Islam to Western democracies. And the lessons of September 11 seem only to concern the United States. The Socialist Party has therefore adopted the prevailing view in France, and especially that of the left, that an American drive to hegemony constitutes the principal problem facing the world today. This view determined the party's approach to the crisis in Iraq.

During most of the summer of 2002, the Socialist Party, not yet reconciled with its debacle in the presidential election, remained entirely self-focused. It does not practically address the Iraq question until the summer university of La Rochelle at the end of August, which marked the Iraq question's reentry into French politics. At the beginning of September 2002, Henri Emmanuelli, one of the leaders of the left wing in the Socialist Party, declared himself "radically opposed to an intervention, regardless of the Security Council's position." But at this time, the majority of the Socialist Party was far from having ideas as clearly formulated as this.

In front of the National Bureau as well as in front of the socialist group in the National Assembly, First Secretary François Hollande declared, "It is up to the Security Council to determine the necessary actions and injunctions." It is also within the United Nations, according to Hubert Védrine, the former foreign minister, that "the Iraqi threat must be assessed." These declarations reveal the ambiguities plaguing the Socialist Party during the fall of 2002, which did not completely exclude eventual support for an intervention under the mandate of the United Nations. The Socialist Party's position was at this moment as hesitant as that of the French executive.

The Socialist Party's position became radicalized under the pressure of public opinion, becoming increasingly more hostile toward a war, and also for tactical reasons. Regarding French diplomacy as continuing to subordinate an eventual military engagement to a UN decision, the socialists increasingly denounced this position's "lack of clarity." The party persuaded itself that Jacques Chirac, regardless of his demonstrations of independence, would finally align himself with the United States, as France had always done in times of great international crisis. It would therefore be unjust to reproach the socialists for any kind of "herd mentality" with respect to Chirac. In actuality, the party saw France apply an intransient attitude vis-à-vis the United States, which they had demanded toward the end of 2002. Calling for the right to exercise a veto in the Security Council, they found themselves in step with the entire left, including the extreme left.

## THE OVERWHELMING VICTORY OF PACIFISM

The Communist Party, the Greens, and the Trotskyites, as well as the National Front, all affirmed unconditionally a hostile attitude toward any kind of intervention against Saddam Hussein's Iraq. On September 10, 2002, the French Communist Party (PCF) organized a colloquium at the National Assembly with its Euro-deputies in order to "prevent war . . . and to bring alternative suggestions with which to develop another conception of the world." For its part, the Ligue Communiste Revolutionnaire (LCR) wanted to create "an international movement" for the purpose of "opposing the worst practices of the American hyper-power and, foremost, its willingness to attack Iraq." The Greens of seven European countries—Austria, Belgium, France, Germany, Italy, Luxemburg, and the Netherlands—published a communal declaration opposed to the "stated intention of the American administration to wage war against or in Iraq." In all of Europe, "the left of the left" decided to bounce a vague alternative globalization off the springboard of an unprecedented international mobilization. This fusion of alternative globalization and pacifism fully surfaced in November 2002 during the European Social Forum (FSE) in Florence. On the basis of the leftist culture of a government that during the 1990s dominated Europe according to the social-liberal fashion of the day, an entire generation discovered the oldest paroles of the socialist movement, such as "Capitalism brings war just as clouds bring thunder."

At the end of the FSE forum on November 12, 2002, almost half a million demonstrators marched down the streets of Florence "against the war in Iraq, for another Europe." Anarchists, communists, members of labor unions, and Catholics found themselves shoulder to shoulder. Some proclaimed, "Make love, not war!" Others proclaimed, "God is with us; pray for peace." Never was it an issue of international justice. And Saddam Hussein was never mentioned at all. The enemy was clearly defined as war and Western liberalism. Orange T-shirts were emblazoned (in English) with "Wanted: Terrorist Number One, Bush!" and "with the complicity of McDonald's, Boeing," as youth shouted themselves out of breath (also in English), "George Bush, Tony Blair, we will fight you!" The tone for the antiwar movement was sounded.

After Florence, the mobilization reached a crescendo in many European countries. The governments of Spain, England, and Italy affirmed themselves in favor of an intervention, but in Germany, Chancellor Schröder undoubtedly secured his reelection by rallying around him completely the pacifists, who were hostile in principle to any intervention independent of the United Nations.

In France, the antiwar fervor did not last long. The movement was controlled by the extreme Trotskyite left that had headed the initiatives behind the first demonstrations. The demonstration of December 12, 2002, could only muster a few thousand demonstrators, but, for the first time since 1968, the extreme left found itself in step with the public opinion of not only the left but also a French majority. "That Saddam Hussein," affirmed the LCR in a communiqué, "is a horrible dictator is clear, but this war, decided by the Bush administration, is essentially about affirming imperial supremacy with the object of securing a monopoly over regional oil reserves."

## BETWEEN CHIRAC'S DEVIL AND THE LEFT'S DEEP BLUE SEA

The Socialist Party extended its support at the December 2002 demonstration, but extremely discreetly. This was also the case in subsequent demonstrations. Why did the Socialist Party identify itself by hoisting up its own placards when, ultimately, nothing separated it from other demonstrators? In fact, the party continued to reaffirm the "horror" inspired in it by Saddam Hussein, yet it was carried away by the tremendous global swell that had already designated George W. Bush as the principal danger for the planet and that had subsumed opposition to the Iraqi war with the combat of all injustices. "No to war against the poor," one could read on the placards brandished in the large demonstration in Paris on February 15, 2003.

On this day, about 150,000 people marched in the streets of the French capital. The turnout was much less than that in other European capitals: London, Madrid, and Rome gathered retinues of about three million people, according to organizers. One must acknowledge that in

Paris, the demonstrations reflected the attitude of the French government. In fact, since the end of January, Dominique de Villepin and Jacques Chirac had raised their tone toward the United States; and France had threatened already to use its veto power in the event of a new Security Council resolution presented by the United States and Britain justifying the use of force.

This position is exactly what the Socialist Party had demanded a few weeks earlier. A number of its leaders did not hide their conviction that Chirac "would not go to the end." They hoped to channel the antiwar movement to their benefit. But the radicalization of French diplomacy deprived the Socialist Party of any autonomous political role.

## KOUCHNER ALONE

Amid the intoxication of this new sacred union "for peace," the socialists this time abandoned one of their acquisitions from their earlier stay in power: the duty of intervention that had allowed saving the Iraqi Kurds in 1991 as well as the Kosovo Albanians in 1999. Bernard Kouchner, who promoted this policy, found himself alone among the socialist leaders in defending the legitimacy of intervention in Iraq under the mandate of the United Nations. In his public appearances, he sketched the contours of a policy that the left could have proposed to France during this crisis. Having broken with the general consensus, he declared at the beginning of March 2003, "Today, Chirac says that we French are not appointed to remove this dictator from the world. That is not my view. We are appointed." Opposed to ambient pacifism, he added, "War is the worst of solutions, but there exists something even worst: allowing Saddam to stay in place." Between Bush and Chirac, he recommended a third way.

"Neither war, nor Saddam": Such is the title of an article that Kouchner authored with Antoine Veil in *Le Monde* in February 2003. He advocated substituting the priority of human rights in Iraq for the struggle against US hegemony that had so far guided the course of French diplomacy. He thereby envisioned, under the UN mandate, France being linked with military pressure on Saddam Hussein, which would permit the removal of the dictator but also avoid war.

> The worst comes from exchanges during the last exchanges among American, German and French leaders. Political reasoning cedes to the virile strategy of an iron hand. To continue in this manner brings war tomorrow. But we have not attempted anything realistic and convincing in order to

avoid war; we have not tried to organize a vigorous diplomacy that could orchestrate the departure of Saddam without recourse to bombardments. We have not wanted to hear the Iraqi people.

In response to Kouchner's suggestions, the leaders of the Socialist Party expressed only silence or jeers. "We prefer a 'French doctor' [in English] rather than Dr. Strangelove," stated Jean-Christophe Cambadélis, Paris deputy and a close associate of Dominique Strauss-Kahn, who is not the most anti-American of the Socialists. Removed from any governmental responsibilities, the socialists seemed to have abandoned any political reflection.

Thus, whereas Tony Blair attempted to save the unity of the Security Council with his resolution of March 2003, which proposed five reasonable and precise demands to the Iraqis along with an ultimatum, scarcely any of the French socialists extended a hand to the leader of the British workers. Rather than working toward a common European position, which would remain equally distant from Schröder's total pacifism and Blair's "pro-Atlantic" view, the French socialists joined the choir of the "sovereigntists" and the extreme left, equally hostile to the "social-liberalism" of New Labour.

In the manner of Jacques Chirac, by pretending to combat simultaneously the Iraqi war and the unilateral temptation of the US administration, the Socialist Party prevented neither the war nor the erosion of international institutions. To be sure, the complexity of what was at stake required a great deal of imagination in order to reconcile the urgency of liberating the Iraqi people with preserving international institutions. There was at least something to debate. Yet the socialists, having forgotten the lessons of their own history, found themselves in the same position as they did in August 1914, this time, however, in a "sacred union" not against a bellicose spirit but for the idolatry of peace, renouncing any autonomous role between the Chirac-Villepin axis and the left. Should they want, however, to play a role again in a credible government, they can ill afford to do without a "theory of war."

## NOTE

This chapter was originally published in *Irak, An 1: Un autre regard sur un monde en guerre*, ed. Pierre Rigoulet and Michel Taubmann (Paris: Le Rocher, 2004), 363–378. Translated by Nicolas de Warren.

# 17

# Tempting Illusions, Scary Realities, or the Emperor's New Clothes II

ANDERS JERICHOW

B oy, they were right: the emperor was quite naked! No weapons of
mass destruction. No Scuds in abundance. No army prepared to
drag invading forces into street warfare. No elite units ready to
sacrifice their lives on behalf of Saddam Hussein, the president, the dictator, the mass murderer.

So governments faced calls for public inquiries, parliamentary commissions, legal scrutiny, and new elections. Why? Two possible reasons
for an inquiry would make sense. First, the well-known reason would
be to force governments to answer the question as to why the Iraq war
was initiated when it was, if Iraq indeed posed no danger to neighbors
or the international community. But a second question for public inquiry
could be, Why was an overthrow of the Iraqi dictator not initiated long
before in realization of the fact that the perpetrator of several wars
and horrible crimes, including the genocide of Kurds during Operation
Anfal in 1987–1989, quite clearly did not enjoy the support of his population, to say nothing of the unwillingness of his own army to come to
his defense?

Needless to say, intelligence about Iraqi war preparations was wrong.
Intelligence on the crimes of Saddam Hussein, however, proved to be
painfully true. Over the course of his rule in Iraq, an estimated three

hundred thousand Iraqis were murdered and thrown into mass graves. The "republic of fear" surely did rest on fear and suppression of the people, whose love and support Saddam Hussein claimed to enjoy. Still, Western and Arab media and political opposition to the US-led war has focused on the critique of war now, leaving aside questions about the failure of the international community to remove Saddam Hussein before 2003. Several democratic governments have come under intense criticism for removing the dictator, yet those democratic governments that allowed him to maintain his barbaric regime have proven immune to criticism.

Tempting illusions and scary realities dominate the whole Iraq affair.

First, for decades European and Arab Middle Eastern countries have nurtured the tempting illusion that no war counts for no bloodshed or even peace. The scary reality is that so-called peace in Iraq and the Middle East frequently has rested on the toleration of brutal dictatorship and bloody suppression in Iraq—and continued occupation and settlements in Palestine—peace, that is, for governments but certainly not for people. Not in Iraq, not in Palestine.

International public perception was generally inclined and even preferred to see the Iraq war as a US, US-British, or Western intervention in Arab affairs. The war, as it was fought, though, included a quite deliberate involvement of one out of three Arab governments. Only Kuwait, still healing its wounds from the Iraqi invasion in 1990, openly allowed US troops to prepare for war on its soil. But six other Arab governments—Saudi Arabia, Jordan, Qatar, Bahrain, the United Arab Emirates, and Oman—permitted American and British presence in local military bases, discreetly contributing to the objective reality of a "Coalition" that was not entirely "Western."

The international public enjoyed seeing French, German, and Russian opposition to the war as proof of the transatlantic rift between Europe and the United States (and its so-called British poodle), although what the war's opponents never acknowledge is the fact that more European members of NATO chose to support the anti-Saddam Coalition rather than French-dominated opposition. Although it is obviously tempting to see the unilateralist Bush government in this light, it may bode ill for some to count small and big, Eastern and Western European, countries equally. Some countries, according to Jacques Chirac, would do best to remain quiet and humble, while the French Big Brother speaks on behalf of Europe.

We, the Europeans, know best, of course. We especially know the Middle East better—after all, weren't European great powers the original colonists of the Arab countries? We, the Europeans, find ourselves truthfully recommending that the United States avoid a clash of civilizations, as if we, the Europeans, have been at the forefront of defending Arab and Muslim pride. Forget about the colonialist past. Who took the leadership role in the liberation of Kuwait? Not Europe. Who turned their backs on Srebrenica and Bosnia more generally, a country facing genocide in the 1990s in the midst of Europe? Europe. Who initiated a humanitarian intervention in Bosnia and later in Kosovo? The United States. It is tempting, especially in Europe, to see an absence of armed action as upholding peace, as if armed action by itself negates peace. The scary reality—in Kuwait, in Bosnia, in Kosova, and later in Afghanistan—is that the opposite of peace is not armed action to prevent aggression but aggression itself. And armed intervention, unfortunately, may be necessary to preserve peace and limit aggression.

Would Saddam Hussein have left Kuwait unharmed if the international Coalition had not initiated a war against the Iraqi dictator and his act of agression? Would Serb killers have left the men and boys of Srebrenica unharmed if Europe had turned its back on Bosnian Muslims? Well, Europe did turn its back to Srebrenica, which merely emboldened further Serbian agreesion. Now, Bosnia in fact is the case in which a European government did indeed shoulder its responsibility for atrocities by holding back. The Dutch government accepted the responsibility for holding Dutch UN soldiers back when the killings in Srebrenica began in earnest. The Dutch government, realizing its moral and military failure, honorably took responsibility for its failure. Unfortunately, the UN leadership did not accept its own responsibility in the same way for neglecting warnings of a genocide in Rwanda. UN peacekeeping forces in the neighborhood witnessed the atrocities being planned, yet they were kept back and received no enforcement, and the absence of international action paved the way for the reality of eight hundred thousand people's unnecessary deaths.

No outside powers have accepted any responsibility for the continued regime of Saddam Hussein for twenty-three gruesome years. It is tempting to foist all responsibility on the dictator himself. In reality, however, supporters as well as opponents of the war in March 2003 share a terrible moral responsibility for tolerating and even aiding Saddam for decades. During the first decade of his reign, Saddam received massive support from abroad. Arab Gulf countries ensured supplies of money that enabled this warmonger to continue his aggression against Iran. Western countries—among them the United States and Britain—shared intelligence with the Iraqi secret services. Western as well as Eastern European partners, including France and Russia, supplied Saddam with vast amounts of military matériel. Germany assisted in selling Saddam ingredients for chemical weapons, used at first to kill Iranian child soldiers, later to eradicate Kurdish communities from the soil of northern Iraq.

Yes, the United States did share a responsibility in the making of Saddam Hussein. So did France. So did Russia. So did Arab governments. They did so fully aware of the fact that the Iraqi people, including the Kurds, paid a heavy price. Later, many of those who aided and abetted Saddam would question whether the international community could send in the marines to remove the dictator. But Saddam Hussein, even by Middle Eastern standards, was not just another dictator. He deliberately inflicted wars on neighbors and willingly accepted the price of hundreds of thousands of lives lost in such wars. He made the decision to commit genocide in Kurdistan. He cold-bloodedly suppressed and killed dissidents and relatives of dissidents at large—and for no other reason than to uphold his own power. No other dictator, no government, no terror organization, no state in the Middle East can match the atrocities of this extraordinarily cruel ruler. Yet for most of his rule, he was assisted from abroad, not challenged. And although for ten years he was subjected to sanctions, both neighbors and the international community knew that the sanctions harmed the Iraqi population more than the dictator himself.

In 2002–2003, the UN Security Council was deeply split on the interpretation of intelligence collected in Iraq. Yet, on the table the council considered only the potential risk to the international community posed by Iraq and never the danger to the Iraqi people posed by respecting and privileging the sovereignty of Iraq and Saddam Hussein and his right to rule, not the danger to the Iraqi people by respecting such so-called sovereignty—in this case, the right of the ruler to rule. Supporters and opponents of an armed intervention against Iraq were both right and wrong. Supporters happened to be wrong in their assessment of Iraqi weapons of mass destruction, but they were right in their assesment of the destabilizing effect of Saddam Hussein on the Middle East. Opponents happened to be right that Saddam Hussein had disposed of his weapons of mass destruction, but they were awkwardly wrong in their perception of a willingness of Saddam Hussein to cooperate. The point is that none of them knew for sure. Even Hans Blix, the Swedish head of the UN arms inspectors and an opponent of the war, admits that he personally expected weapons of mass destruction to be hidden somewhere in Iraq. As a civil bureaucrat, Blix had the job solely to look for documentation, while governments had to make decisions and act accordingly.

In his recent book, Blix, a former head of International Atomic Energy Agency (IAEA), the UN nuclear agency, found comfort in the fact that IAEA had been correct in the assesment that Iraq no longer had a nuclear program. As things turned out, he and the IAEA fortunately were right. It is useful to consider, however, that over the course of ten years, the IAEA had not exposed Pakistani export of components for nuclear weapon production to North Korea, Iran, or Libya. Imagine that events had turned out the other way around, with prior disclosure of the Pakistani export to North Korea but not to Iraq. Hardly comforting. Not only the war but the whole Middle East could have changed drastically during the 2003 war in Iraq.

A tempting illusion of those who opposed the Iraq war is that if no government had intervened in Iraq, the Middle East would have had peace. But as the UN inspectors as well as the US weapons inspector David Kay agree, Saddam Hussein apparently accepted the destruction of his most lethal weapons, but he never canceled his dream of producing weapons of mass destruction again. And the troubling reality is that supporters as well as opponents of the war were wrong in their estimation of the power of Saddam Hussein. He proved to be less dangerous to the outside world than the supporters of the war had assumed. But he was more dangerous to his own people than the opponents were prone to admit.

As the story went before the war, a father and his son step on a bus in Baghdad. The boy points at the ever-present poster of Saddam Hussein and says, "That's the evil man, Dad, that you and Mum curse every night." The man grabs the boy, holds him toward people in the bus, and asks, "Who is the father of this boy, talking like that about our beloved leader?" Supporters and opponents of the war unwillingly became subjects of a remake of the story of the emperor's new clothes After all, it was hardly a coincidence or even a mistake that Saddam Hussein never published any documentation of the whereabouts of his previous weapons of mass destruction. Certainly he was not aware that his own forces were not willing to fight for his survival. The dictator could do without weapons of mass destruction, as long as the perception of his power could survive. But his power could not survive an absence of the cornerstone of his power—fear.

The UN Security Council in November 2002 called in the cards. Saddam Hussein gambled and, as usual, made his people pay the price. He could have produced the necessary documentation of his previous weapons of mass destruction. He could finally have accepted the offer of asylum in the United Arab Emirates. But, as before, Saddam Hussein initiated and lost a war that he could have avoided. In short-term tactics he was second to none, always willing to accept losses on behalf of his enemies, his dissidents, and even his own clan and family. In the long term, he was a disaster, taking charge of one of the potentially most prosperous Arab countries, only to leave it in ruins—initiating wars, only to lose them.

Only rarely have human rights–focused liberals or the European left called for the overthrow of Saddam Hussein. Publicly, political parties from the center to the left criticized American intimations of war. And distrust of the motives of the United States and Britain overshadowed interest in understanding the plight of Iraqis. Admittedly, the Bush government had given them reasons for skepticism by staying out of the Kyoto protocol, refusing to join the International Criminal Court for war crimes, and allowing the war on terror to infringe on civil liberties in the United States and abroad. Before the Iraq war, still fewer political parties accepted the UN sanctions on Iraq because of the burden that sanctions put on the Iraqi people, not on Saddam Hussein. The European debate slowly, but unmistakingly, moved toward calling for the abolishment of sanctions altogether, leaving Saddam Hussein in power, while the US government tried promising new "smart sanctions" that targeted Saddam and his regime, not his people. Then war came and resulted in the removal of Saddam Hussein, his army, intelligence agencies, the army, and the police.

The Iraqi people have paid a heavy price, not only for twenty-three years of brutal dictatorship but also for shifting and capricious international policies. The effects of the internal dictatorship is well documented. The impact of international policies is still a subject for more academic research and political discussion. It is beyond doubt, however, that Saddam Hussein was armed by the West as well as by the East, financed to a large extent by Arab government loans and grants, and accepted by all as a sovereign and autonomous member of the UN, even as torture prevailed in his prisons, Kurds were subjected to ethnic cleansing, Shia marsh territory was destroyed, and young men were called to fight and die in wars inflicted on their country by the dictator, always ruling by fear. The Iraqi people paid for his tyranny in blood, the absence of welfare, and lack of security. They paid for shifting policies, from the time of the first Iraq war to the second, in more blood, more fear, and a greater absence of security. And after the last war, relieving them of Saddam Hussein, they have been victims of a new reality of insecurity, this time due to the vacuum left over from the abolishment of all police and army apparatus.

Though not internationally acknowleged, most European members of NATO did contribute to the Coalition forces and the process of social reconstruction. In most of these countries, these efforts were not supported by popular majorities, although in Denmark they generally were. In the media and politics, attention focused on the opposition of the French and German governments and on the impact of the Iraq war on the dwindling popularity of Prime Minister Tony Blair in Britain. To Iraqis, this reaction should not have come as a big surprise. Waiting for the solidarity of the outside world has turned out to be a central feature of the Iraqis' fate. Waiting for independence from colonial European powers. Waiting for military coups and countercoups and internationally supported military bureaucrats to pack their bags. Waiting for big powers to stop arming and financing their suppressors. Waiting for international recognition of popular needs contrary to the rights of regimes. And, having finally gotten rid of their dictator, waiting for support of the international community to reconstruct Iraq.

Since the latest war, Iraqis have been waiting for international assistance to ensure security. The majority of European governments, contrary to the wishes of the United States, wanted the UN to take leadership. When in June 2004 the United States finally accepted the UN in a leading role, paving the way for a reunited UN Security Council, France, Germany, and Russia still had no intention of sending soldiers or to provide extensive debt relief as requested by the new, UN-recognized interim government in Baghdad (the latter policy changed, however, as of July 2004). And the Spanish government, elected on a promise to call back its troops, certainly had no plans to reintroduce Spanish soldiers in Iraq if asked by the UN or an internationally recognized sovereign Iraqi government.

Not only France, Germany, Russia, and Spain but Arab governments as well preferred to keep the Iraqis waiting, subject to new terror. Large parts of Arab as well as European media and politics have seen the continued violence as a kind of liberation struggle against the US presence in Iraq, although most of the violence has targeted and killed Iraqi civilians, not Americans in uniform. It is hardly surprising that the United States has primarily counted and stressed its own fatalities in the war. But neither have Arab nor European media or governments focused on Iraqi victims of mass violence (terror, suicide bombings, etc.), which is aimed at destroying the first chance of an Arab people to create their own society, a new constitution, a balance of their own choice between state and religion—in short, to build a democratic society. While all major Iraqi political parties and religious factions have proven sensitive to the risks of failure in potential ethnic and religious division, and have accepted new federal structures and respect for human rights, European and Arab media have focused primarily on the failures of the American occupation.

American preparations for state building did leave much to be desired; abolishing the old police without offering a new security system, for example, and disassembling the old civil administration without a new administration at hand were predictably bad policies. The Abu Ghraib torture scandal only served to confirm Arab and European expectations of American hypocrisy—that is, Americans talking about the value of human rights while at the same time allowing soldiers to dehumanize Iraqi prisoners, even taking pictures of naked prisoners for family albums back in the States.

Still, what did the European and Arab governments want for Iraqis? Sovereignty? Promised by the United States and the Coalition in June 2004. Human rights? Recognized by all major Iraqi parties and important religious leaders. Federalism? Recognized by major Iraqi political parties and the UN, including all permanent members of the Security Council. The biggest problem is that, while the interim Iraqi government (appointed by Lakhdar Brahimi and the UN, and recognized by the the UN Security Council) has asked for international assistance, both European and Arab governments have to some extent turned their backs on Iraq.

Clearly, Iraqis have become hostages to the transatlantic rift as well as to the ongoing Western-Arab clash of interests. If acknowledged rhetorically by all, international human rights still are the privilege of few. The Iraqis have become victims of a perceived conflict of aims between the United States and Europe. The conflict may be real, although in reality Iraq serves as merely a symbol in the transatlantic rift about American unilateralism; the future role of NATO; the need for binding multilateralism, including the International Criminal Court and the Kyoto protocol; and so forth. In Iraq, Western aims and hopes for the Iraq's future must be basically the same. Nonetheless, it would be naive to neglect the limited interest on the part of autocratic Arab governments to invest seriously in the establishment of a federal, democratic Iraq, based on freedom of religion and universal human rights, at a time when reforms in their own countries are still a delicate, sensitive, and highly controlled issue, left for the future.

But Iraqis may not have time to wait for the resolution of other transatlantic rifts—or for Arab reforms elsewhere—to see an international, responsible involvement in the reconstruction of their country. The Iraqis may unwillingly serve as symbols, again, in the forthcoming dispute on reforms in the Arab world. Other Arab populations have not been asked. Supreme Arab state leaders generally do not stand for election or on trial, for that matter. Free political parties, such as those the Iraqis have called for, are not allowed in other Arab countries. Freedom of speech, as Iraqis clearly desire, is not allowed in most Arab countries. Torture, as Iraqis did not appreciate—before, during, and after Abu Ghraib—still prevails in most of the Arab world, as remedies and mechanisms of social control of their ruling regimes.

Nevertheless, economic, political, and legal reforms of the countries of the Arab world have come to dominate the international agenda. It would not be presumptuous to expect Arab populations to be in favor of reforms and the expansion of their freedom. But it is obvious that governments or regimes of the Arab world are no more eager to follow the wishes of their subordinates than to submit to pressure by the United States or Europe. Engulfed by international opposition to its shortcomings and failures in Iraq, to put it mildly, the Bush government quickly decided to adjust its calls for Arab reforms. Originally a grand plan for political and legal reform across Arabia, the proposal was finally presented at the G8 summit in June 2004, as a humble recommendation of financial investment and government cooperation, leading Europeans to praise a diplomatic victory. In the eyes of Europe—center-left as well as liberal and conservative—dialogue rather than confrontation leads to stability.

An approach of this kind was tried prior to the fall of the Soviet empire and the wall separating East and West in Europe—cooperation and ideological challenge or even confrontation at the same time. European governments may find it tempting to duplicate the old Helsinki process now in the Arab-European theater. But the somewhat problematic—even scary—reality is that, contrary to the situation in central

Europe before the end of the Cold War, the Western liberal, democratic, free governments for decades have been openly sponsoring and even arming the dictators whom they now want to relieve of their duties. During the same decades, European as well as US policies have been based on the assumption that, as long nobody would rock the boat in the Middle East and North Africa, stability would survive, whereas any challenge to the present rulers might lead to turbulence, religious totalitarianism, conflict, and armadas of refugee boats crossing the Mediterrenean toward Europe. Today European as well as American assessments have become inverted, now openly expecting turbulence, social unrest, terror, and conflict if reforms are not introduced.

But with whom do you cooperate, if the autocrat is not particularly interested in paving the way for his exit? As in a tango, it takes two for a dialogue to unfold. In most Arab countries, the present governments postpone the moment when they will have to accept liberalization of NGO cooperation across borders and even international contributions to the development of Arab civil society. Only in one Arab country, Iraq, is totalitarianism left behind, one hopes, enabling an Arab population for the first time to determine its own future, looking already for international assistance and cooperation in a historic reconstruction. Had the outside world paid the same respect to international human rights and expressed solidarity with the people of Iraq, Saddam Hussein could have been removed long before 2003, to everyone's advantage. The emperor eventually was much weaker than perceived but dressed in impressive clothes of aggression, locally and internationally. Only in the end, he was naked.

# PART FIVE

# SOLIDARITY

# 18

## Antitotalitarianism as a Vocation
An Interview with Adam Michnik

THOMAS CUSHMAN AND ADAM MICHNIK

*Adam Michnik, a leading force in the Solidarity trade union movement and the founder and editor of the largest Polish daily newspaper, Gazeta Wyborcza, was an outspoken supporter of the war in Iraq. In this interview, which occurred in Warsaw on January 15, 2004, Michnik clarifies his position on the war and discusses the responses of other European intellectuals.*

THOMAS CUSHMAN: I'd like to focus on the response of Polish intellectuals and former anticommunists and activists to the war in Iraq, Polish relations with the United States more generally, and how the latter have affected relations between Poland and other European countries, especially those that were against the war. I am an American liberal who supported the war in Iraq on humanitarian grounds. It's somewhat difficult to find such people in the United States, so I've had to come all the way to Poland to find liberals who support the war. In your essay "A View from the Left: We, the Traitors" [*Gazeta Wyborcza*, May 29, 2003, and in English in *World Press Review* (June 2003)], you took a very strong position of support for the war in Iraq and noted that you share that position with other former dissidents. Could you explain this in more detail?

ADAM MICHNIK: I look at the war in Iraq from three points of view. Saddam Hussein's Iraq was a totalitarian state. It was a country where people were murdered and tortured. So I'm looking at this through the eyes of the political prisoner in Baghdad, and from this point of view I'm very grateful to those who opened the gates of the prison and who stopped the killing and the torture. Second, Iraq was a country that supported terrorist attacks in the Middle East and all over the world. I consider that 9/11 was the day when war was started against my own work and against myself. Even though we are not sure of the links, Iraq was one of the countries that did not lower its flags in mourning on 9/11. There are those who think this war could have been avoided by democratic and peaceful means. But I think that no negotiations with Saddam Hussein made sense, just as I believe that negotiations with Hitler did not make sense. And there is a third reason. Poland is an ally of the United States of America. It was our duty to show that we are a reliable, loyal, and predictable ally. America needed our help, and we had to give it. This was not only my position. It was also the position of Havel, Konrád, and others.

TC: Yes, you specifically mention that this is a view you share with Václav Havel and György Konrád.

AM: We take this position because we know what dictatorship is. And in the conflict between totalitarian regimes and democracy, you must not hesitate to declare which side you are on. Even if a dictatorship is not an ideal typical one, and even if the democratic countries are ruled by people whom you do not like. I think you can be an enemy of Saddam Hussein even if Donald Rumsfeld is also an enemy of Saddam Hussein.

TC: This is a difficult position to find on the left in the United States. It seems as if many people would not support the fight against totalitarianism because it was being waged by a government that they did not like.

AM: Susan Sontag's speech from the Frankfurt Book Fair will be published in *Gazeta Wyborcza*.[1] I think that if she heard what I'm saying here, she'd no longer extend her hand to me.

TC: But unlike Sontag, who never had any direct experience of totalitarianism, your position seems to be directly related to your experience as a revolutionary, as an antifascist and an anticommunist. Is your view on the war a natural progression from this experience?

**AM:** It's simply that life has taught me that if someone is being whipped and someone is whipping this person, I am always on the side of those who are being whipped. I've always criticized US foreign policy for forgetting that the United States should defend those who need to be defended. I would object to US policy if it supported Saddam Hussein, and I have always criticized the United States for supporting military regimes in Latin America.

**TC:** In your writing, you often criticize utopian politics. It seems that George W. Bush's vision (or that of his neoconservative advisers) is a utopian vision: destroying totalitarianism and instituting democracy. A large part of the reaction against Bush seems to be focused on his revival of some kind of American messianism. How do you reconcile your criticism of utopian thinking with support of this seeming American utopianism?

**AM:** Bush has a utopian ideology . . . maybe not Bush, but maybe his circle. Perhaps I'm being naive, but I don't think it is utopian to want to install democratic rule in Iraq. If it won't be an ideal democracy, let it be a crippled democracy, but let it not be a totalitarian dictatorship. I don't like many things in today's Russia, but we have to say that there is a difference between Putin and Stalin. In my opinion, the religious visions of Bush's circle are anachronistic. I can't believe that John Ashcroft has personal conversations with God every day, who tells him what to do. But if God told him that he should destroy Saddam, then this was the right advice, because a world without Saddam Hussein is better than a world with Saddam Hussein.

**TC:** This is a fundamental political ideological position.

**AM:** Yes, but I can imagine that even a bad government guided by a bad ideology can enter into a just war.

**TC:** In "We, the Traitors," you mention that you communicated with Havel and other European intellectuals about the war in Iraq and that there seems to be some solidarity between Eastern European intellectuals and the United States vis-à-vis the war in Iraq. On the other hand, many, if not most, Western European intellectuals, particularly in France, and also left intellectuals in the United States, took a diametrically different position. Given your long-standing positive relations with American and European intellectuals, have you experienced any backlash against your position?

**AM**: Yes.

**TC**: And what do they say? I find that when I try to debate the issue with many left intellectuals, they just shut down, refuse to hear the arguments. Many of them simply express a visceral hatred of George Bush, and this seems to block any meaningful discussion of the antitotalitarian justification of the war. They simply cannot understand, nor do they seem to want to understand, how a liberal intellectual could support the war in Iraq.

**AM**: Well, who was worse, Ronald Reagan or Leonid Brezhnev? If I were American, I would never have voted for Reagan, but as a Pole, I liked the tough position of Reagan toward Brezhnev. Perhaps Reagan did not quite understand what he was doing, and maybe Bush doesn't understand, either. But the facts are that, suddenly, Libya has begun to speak a different language. Syria has begun to speak a different language. Even North Korea has started to speak a different language. This is not to say that Bush is always right. Of course not. But you must see the hierarchy of threats, of dangers. I asked my French and German friends, "Are you afraid that tomorrow Bush will bomb Paris? And can you really be sure that terrorists and fundamentalists will not attack the Louvre? So which side are you on?"

**TC**: So it's either-or—you're either with us or against us.

**AM**: Unfortunately, yes.

**TC**: But this is the attitude of fundamentalists.

**AM**: No, it's not fundamentalist because I don't believe that there are nations that are, let's say, cursed. I remember that the United States of America, after the bloody war with Germany and Japan and Italy, helped these countries become democracies. When I visit my friends in Spain, who always criticize the United States, I ask them, "In 1945, were you mad at Americans for not overthrowing Franco, or did you expect them to do this?" And they say that it was awful that the United States did not go into Spain and overthrow Franco. In some ways Franco was worse than Saddam Hussein.

**TC**: But the average left intellectual in the United States won't listen to this argument. If one supports the war on liberal grounds, then antiwar liberals disagree with the prowar position—and, of course, those on the right who support the war don't agree with the liberal justification.

**AM:** Well, we had a similar situation under communism because even though we hated the communists, they fought about the border with Germany, and we anticommunists had exactly the same position as they did.[2]

**TC:** How do your friends in Europe reply to this argument?

**AM:** Well, they say that Americans want to have power over the whole world. They criticize unilateralism. They say that they do not agree that the United States of America should dictate to the whole world. They also say that international law is being abused, that the United Nations did not consent to this. So I simply say that it's not that I want the United States to have all the power in the world but that I prefer this to Saddam Hussein.

**TC:** So would it be right to say that you believe that there is a moral imperative that is greater than international law?

**AM:** Of course.

**TC:** But this is the paradox, the problem that we face. The moral argument confronts the body of international law and falls flat.

**AM:** What is international law when you have the human rights commission in Geneva headed by Libya?

**TC:** In one of your earlier articles in *Kritika*, called "Three Kinds of Fundamentalism,"[3] you stress the dangers of fundamentalism: it expresses "the conviction that one possesses a prescription for the organization of the world, a world free of conflicts other than the conflict between good and evil, free of conflicts between interests and different points of view." This is exactly what many American and European intellectuals say about George Bush.

**AM:** They're right. They are absolutely right. The only thing they are wrong about is the war in Iraq.

**TC:** So the war is acceptable in spite of the fact that George W. Bush, with his rhetoric of evil, might be something of a fundamentalist and is engaging in dangerous politics?

**AM:** I don't think his international policies are dangerous. I think it is the way he justifies these policies.

**TC:** What about his justifications?

**AM:** I think it's always dangerous to make political arguments in a religiously ideological way. And it's very dangerous to treat as traitors to the American nation those who think differently. I think it's very dangerous to use foreign policy to achieve goals in internal policy. But, still, I think that the decision to overthrow Hussein was right and just. Of course, you can win the war and you can lose the peace, and this is what I'm afraid of now. I'm afraid today that the spirit of triumphalism is ascendant in US policy. So if President Bush asked me, I would advise him to involve the United Nations in Iraq. I would seek reconciliation with the countries in Western Europe that criticized the war in Iraq. I think that it was a mistake not to use NATO structures in this war. It is impossible for the United States to deal with the whole world on its own. The United States must look for allies . . . should reunite its country with Europe. You must not be offended with Europe because the United States has much in common with, say, France. This conflict is a gift for terrorists and fundamentalists.

**TC:** Throughout your revolutionary period, when you were fighting against communism, you always took a position of nonviolence. Now, in supporting the war you are advocating violence. Can you explain this? I ask this because many people in the United States admired you for your nonviolent stance against communism. But now they say, "Michnik advocates nonviolence, but he's supporting this war." Isn't it paradoxical to advocate the promotion of human rights through violent means? I realize that this is a difficult question

**AM:** No, it's a very easy one. I can't remember any text of mine where I said that one should fight Hitler without violence; I'm not an idiot. Against [Polish premier Wojciech] Jaruzelski you could fight without violence, even against Brezhnev. This is clear if you look at [Soviet dissidents] Andrei Sakharov and Aleksandr Solzhenitsyn. But never against Saddam Hussein. In the state of Saddam, the opposition could find a place only in cemeteries.

**TC:** So some situations call for violence in order to overthrow totalitarianism, fascism?

**AM:** Of course. I've never been a pacifist.

**TC:** No, I know that. But I repeat: In the United States, people say that Michnik was for nonviolence, and now he's for violence. This is what people tell me.

**AM:** There are dictatorships against which you can fight without violence—for example, the British Empire in India. But in the Third Reich of Hitler, there was no possibility of this.

**TC:** Let me ask you about the role of Israel. Given your Jewish background, are you ever subjected to accusations of serving Israeli interests?

**AM:** Not even in Poland have I ever been accused of this! We have the whole universe of anti-Semitic dispositions in Poland, but I've never been accused of serving Israeli interests. I'm not even accused of being pro-American, because most Poles are pro-American. You can say that I look at Israel and the Middle East from the point of view of a Polish intellectual who likes the country but does not like Ariel Sharon. Israel is the only country in the Middle East where Arabs can be elected to the parliament in a democratic election.

We invited several Iraqi journalists to our newspaper, to *Gazeta Wyborcza*, for a roundtable. What they said about Saddam Hussein's regime, well, you can't imagine. I would advise my critical friends in the United States to talk to the Iraqi people. Let them talk to Iraqi journalists who suffered in silence for so many years. In relation to Iraq, critics of the war only hear the voices of the neoconservatives.

**TC:** Why are Western European intellectuals deaf to this moral argument?

**AM:** Well, Hans Magnus Enzensberger, Bernard Kouchner, and others aren't deaf. It's related to why so many Western European intellectuals did not want to hear about Stalin's crimes for so many years.

**TC:** It's an interesting problem for the sociology of intellectuals and ideology. There is some continuity in the deafness to moral argument, some relation between past and present.

**AM:** It's a sociological and historical problem. Look at France. France can never accept that it is no longer a dominating power in the world of culture. This is true both of the French right and the French left. They keep thinking that Americans are primitive cowboys or farmers who do not understand anything. If Americans do not understand the difference between Sunnis and Shiites, what do they know about the world? But this doesn't change the method. Americans could never understand the difference between the right and the left in Germany, but they knew that Hitler should be defeated!

**TC:** Now we have a situation in which Polish troops are involved actively in Iraq. How do you feel about the fact that there are Polish troops supporting what many see as an American imperial venture? For many years the Poles were put down by empires, by Russia, by Austria-Hungary, by Germany, and all of a sudden the Poles are the allies of the new American empire.

**AM:** No, we are not in Iraq as part of the empire; we are there for freedom. If America were to occupy a foreign country only because it's not friendly toward the United States, we would be against it.

**TC:** This does not represent some kind of will to power on the part of Poland?

**AM:** Oh, sure, the Polish people dream about Baghdad being our colony!

**TC:** But still, in all seriousness, here are the Poles, the Americans, the Australians, the British, and they're occupying this country, and so the rest of the world looks at Poland, and the perception is that it's part of the imperial project of America.

**AM:** Did they criticize the fact that four countries—the United States, Britain, France, and the Soviet Union—occupied Germany after World War II?

**TC:** In my discussions with some other Polish intellectuals, who are critical of the war, they claim that Iraq is not the same kind of situation.

**AM:** It's never the same.

**TC:** They say that the intellectuals who support the war in Iraq don't understand that Saddam Hussein is not Adolf Hitler, and so on. I interviewed Jacek Kuron the other day, and, as you know, he was against the war. He was critical of the idea that the fight against Saddam Hussein is the same thing as the fight against Hitler.

**AM:** Well, it's obvious that Saddam is not Hitler. Pol Pot was not Hitler, either. My fundamental question is, What would Saddam Hussein have to do for my dear friend Jacek to agree that he's as bad as Hitler? What more would he have had to do? Invade Poland and build gas chambers in Auschwitz one more time?

**TC:** Have you changed your position at all on the war in Iraq now that it's over?

**AM:** No. But I wonder whether the United States is not making mistakes after the victory. Regarding the decision to overthrow Saddam Hussein, I have no doubts. Still, I don't know if the policy of stabilization is optimal. Here, I'm afraid of American arrogance, the lack of sensitivity to the culture in Iraq, to the Iraqi people. The State Department should get Americans of Iraqi background more involved in Iraq, and, so far as I know, they are not doing this.

**TC:** So are you more negative about the postwar situation than you were about the war itself?

**AM:** The war was just and fair. But what's happening now requires different methods. It's not enough that we have technology; we must help the people there. And I'm afraid of the ignorance and arrogance of the Americans.

**TC:** What do you mean by American arrogance? How do you define it?

**AM:** They do not understand the sense of Iraqi dignity, the dignity of Saddam's enemies. If you're powerful, you are much more likely to be blind and deaf to signals from outside.

## NOTES

This interview was originally published in *Dissent* (Spring 2003): 28–30. © Thomas Cushman. The interviewer would like to thank the US ambassador to Poland, Christopher Hill, and Patricia Hill for arranging this interview. Helena Luczywo served as the translator for the interview.

1. In this speech, published as "The Fragile Alliance" in the *Guardian*, October 18, 2003, Sontag focuses on the rift between American and European civilization. She offers distinct criticism of the polarizing rhetoric that has been at the base of much of the Bush administration's war against terrorism and of American unilateralism as principal causes of the current US-European tensions. Her position stands in contrast to Michnik's focus on antitotalitariansim and the perils of Saddam Hussein and terrorism. She makes virtually no mention of internal European politics as a source of tension between the United States and Europe.

2. The issue of the Polish-German border was a matter of dispute throughout the twentieth century. In 1950, the Oder-Neisse line was established at the border, but it was not initially accepted by West Germany, because many Germans were displaced from Polish lands without being granted the right of return and because of concerns over the rights of the German minority in Poland. Eventually, the Federal Republic of Germany accepted the border

as a condition of reunification, but throughout the process, it was a contentious issue around which dissidents and communists in Poland tended to unite.

3. This essay appears in *Letters from Freedom: Post–Cold War Realities and Perspectives* (Berkeley and Los Angeles: University of California Press, 1998), 253–259.

# 19

# Sometimes, a War Saves People

## JOSE RAMOS-HORTA

The new Socialist government in Spain has caved in to the terrorist threats and withdrawn its troops from Iraq. So have Honduras and the Dominican Republic. They are unlikely to be the last. With the security situation expected to worsen before it improves, we have to accept that a few more countries—which do not appreciate how much the world has at stake in building a free Iraq—will also cut and run.

No matter how the retreating governments try to spin it, every time a country pulls out of Iraq, it is Al Qaeda and other extremists who win. They draw the conclusion that the Coalition of the Willing is weak and that the more terrorist outrages occur, the more countries will withdraw.

As a Nobel Peace laureate, I, like most people, agonize over the use of force. But when it comes to rescuing an innocent people from tyranny or genocide, I've never questioned the justification for resorting to force. That's why I supported Vietnam's 1978 invasion of Cambodia, to end Pol Pot's regime, and Tanzania's invasion of Uganda in 1979, to oust Idi Amin. In both cases, those countries acted without UN or international approval—and in both cases they were right to do so.

Perhaps the French have forgotten how they, too, toppled one of the worst human rights violators without UN approval. I applauded in the early 1980s when French paratroopers landed in the dilapidated capital of the then–Central African Empire and deposed "Emperor" Jean Bedel Bokassa, renowned for cannibalism. Almost two decades later, I applauded again as NATO intervened—without a UN mandate—to end ethnic cleansing in Kosovo and liberate an oppressed European Muslim community from Serbian tyranny. And I rejoiced once more in 2001 after the US-led overthrow of the Taliban liberated Afghanistan from one of the world's most barbaric regimes.

So why do some think Iraq should be any different? Only a year after Saddam Hussein's overthrow, they seem to have forgotten how hundreds of thousands perished during his tyranny, under a regime whose hallmark was terror, summary execution, torture, and rape. Forgotten, too, is how the Kurds and Iraq's neighbors lived each day in fear, so long as Saddam remained in power.

Those who oppose the use of force at any cost may question why overthrowing Saddam was such a priority. Why not instead tackle Robert Mugabe, the junta in Myanmar, or Syria? But while Mugabe is a ruthless despot, he is hardly in the same league as Saddam—a tyrant who used chemical weapons on his own people, unleashed two catastrophic wars against his Muslim neighbors, and defied the UN.

Saddam's overthrow offers a chance to build a new Iraq that is peaceful, tolerant, and prosperous. That's why the stakes are so high and why extremists from across the Muslim world are fighting to prevent it. They know that a free Iraq would fatally undermine their goal of purging all Western influence from the Muslim world, overthrowing the secular regimes in the region, and imposing Stone Age rule. They know that forcing Western countries to withdraw from Iraq would be a major step toward that goal, imperiling the existence of moderate regimes—from the Middle East to the Maghreb and Southeast Asia.

If those regimes were to fall, hundreds of thousands of Muslims who today denounce the "evils" of Western imperialism would flock to Europe, the United States, Canada, and Australia, seeking refuge. As in Iran, Muslims might have to experience the reality of rule by ayatollahs before they realize how foolish they were not to oppose these religious zealots more vigorously.

Fortunately, that remains a remote scenario. If we look beyond the TV coverage, there is hope that Washington's vision of transforming Iraq might still be realized. Credible opinion polls show that a large majority of Iraqis feel better off than a year ago. There is real freedom of the press with newspapers and radio stations mushrooming in the new Iraq. There is unhindered Internet access. Nongovernmental organizations covering everything from human rights to women's advocacy have emerged. In short, Iraq is experiencing real freedom for the first time in its history. And that is exactly what the religious fanatics fear.

Iraq's Shiite majority has acted with restraint in the face of provocation by extremist elements in the Sunni minority, Saddam loyalists, and Al Qaeda and other foreign mercenaries. The Coalition authorities would be wise to cultivate responsible Shiite clerics more closely and ensure that their legitimate concerns are met. While a Shiite-dominated regime might not meet America's goal of a Western-style democracy, it is still far preferable to risking the return of Saddam's thugs. The United States must reiterate that building democracy will not marginalize Islam. Democracy and Islam coexist in Indonesia, Malaysia, and Bangladesh, while Israel offers an example of a state built on a single religion. That could be the case in Iraq, too, as long as it is led by wise clerics who are able to deliver freedom and good governance. The most probable contender to fill this role is Grand Ayatollah Ali al-Sistani, who has emerged as the national leader the country needs to keep it together. He may not be a democrat in the Western mold, but the United States needs to cultivate him and provide whatever support is required to ensure that he emerges as ruler of the new Iraq.

The United States also needs to repair the damage done by the mistreatment of Iraqi prisoners. While it's important to remember that those involved only represent a tiny fraction of US servicemen in Iraq, the fact remains that the abuse was allowed to continue for many months after organizations such as the normally secretive Red Cross sounded alarm bells. Only thorough investigation, including action against those responsible, can restore US standing in Iraq.

Now is the time for Washington to show leadership by ensuring that the UN plays the central role in building a new Iraq. As an East Timorese, I am well aware of the international body's limits, having seen firsthand its impotence in the face of Indonesia's invasion of my country in 1975. The UN is the sum of our qualities and weaknesses, our selfish national interests and personal vanities. For all its shortcomings, it is the only international organization we all feel part of; it should be cherished rather than further weakened. While the United States will continue to play a critical role in ensuring security in Iraq, a UN-led peace-keeping force would enable many Arab and Muslim nations to join in and help isolate the extremists.

In almost thirty years of political life, I have supported the use of force on several occasions and sometimes wonder whether I am a worthy recipient of the Nobel Peace prize. Certainly I am not in the same category as Mother Teresa, the Dalai Lama, Desmond Tutu, or Nelson Mandela. But Mr. Mandela, too, recognized the need to resort to violence in the struggle against white oppression. The consequences of doing nothing in the face of evil were demonstrated when the world did not stop the Rwandan genocide that killed almost a million people in 1994. Where were the peace protesters then? They were just as silent as they are today in the face of the barbaric behavior of religious fanatics.

Some may accuse me of being more of a warmonger than a Nobel laureate, but I stand ready to face my critics. It is always easier to say no to war, even at the price of appeasement. But being politically correct means leaving the innocent to suffer the world over, from Phnom Penh to Baghdad. And that is what those who would cut and run from Iraq risk doing.

## NOTE

"Sometimes, a War Saves People" is reprinted from the *Wall Street Journal*, May 13, 2004.

# 20

# Gulf War Syndrome Mark II

## The Case for Siding with the Iraqi People

JOHANN HARI

G ulf War Syndrome Mark II has not been officially diagnosed, but the political classes of Britain and the United States are now lurching into the advanced stages of the disease. Its symptoms are simple and—for Iraqis—deadly. The carrier automatically assumes that a majority of Iraqi people agree with his position on the invasion of Iraq. He does not seek any evidence for this belief; indeed, all evidence derived from the real world (as opposed to common sense) is denounced as "unreliable" or "contradictory." Because the sufferer knows through some unexplained telepathic link what Iraqis think, he feels free to speak on their behalf, while—with no irony—he mocks others who might have taken greater care to discover Iraqi opinion as "imperialists." That is the illness's sole and overriding symptom, and it has crippled the response of progressive forces to the second Iraq war.

When it became obvious in late 2001 that the Bush administration was considering overthrowing Saddam Hussein's regime, progressive forces across the world began to succumb to the disease. They assumed automatically that the Iraqi people did not want the war to proceed and began to speak on their behalf. Gary Younge, a *Guardian* columnist whom I like and respect, argued, for example, that "we should side with the Iraqi people."[1] It did not seem to occur to him that this required him to actually find out what Iraqis said; he automatically claimed them for the antiwar movement. George Bush and Tony Blair—in a mirror-image offensive—assumed the Iraqi people were on *their* side, longing for liberation and the sight of a Stars and Stripes or Union Jack. I was genuinely unsure about the position of the Iraqi people; these parallel appropriations of the voices of an oppressed and tyrannized people seemed to me both distasteful and conjectural.

I could see how both sides plausibly claimed to have most Iraqis with them. On the one hand, the antiwar lobby argued that Iraqis did not want their country to be assaulted with cluster bombs and depleted uranium by a country that only two decades ago had helped to arm and fund Saddam. Yet, on the other hand, prowar liberals could also say that, after three decades of being held hostage by Baathism, Iraqis wanted somebody—anybody—to intervene in the slow drip-drip of blood stretching out beyond Saddam, beyond Uday and Qusay, like a long Mesopotamian morgue. And out there, in the heart of the Middle East, were the cowed, anxious people of Iraq with the answers to these questions, if only we could discover them.

It became clear to me that the only way to take a principled left-wing stance toward this war was to discover what most Iraqis wanted and to back their wishes consistently. It is not my job—as a progressive Westerner in the privileged position of writing for a British newspaper—to speak on behalf of the oppressed. It is my job to find out what the oppressed say, hope, and dream and to amplify their suppressed voices to a wider public. I have tried to do this, in my short career, with the British poor, the Palestinians resisting Israeli occupation, the people across the developing world resisting the International Monetary Fund (IMF) and World Bank, and elsewhere.

I tried to apply this approach to the new crisis in the Middle East. Iraqis were capable of weighing the dangers of a US invasion against the dangers of eternal Baathism. A progressive position should, it seemed to me, be determined by Iraqis, not by our own gut prejudices. If Iraqis wanted the war, then we on the left would have to grit our teeth and support US tanks and bombs, while lobbying hard for a democratic transition to follow.

But how could we discover what Iraqis want? As I made arrangements that foggy autumn to visit Iraq, I met with as many Iraqi exile groups based in my hometown, London, as I could. Over 20 percent of the Iraqi population was tyrannized into exile by Saddam's regime, and London has the largest Iraqi population in the world outside the Middle East, so there were plenty of community centers and pressure groups to visit. Clear majorities explained that their families "back home" were reluctantly hoping the war would proceed. "They cannot say it clearly—all calls are intercepted—but we can talk on the telephone in a way that makes our meaning clear," they explained time and again. These prowar Iraqi majorities rose to near unanimity when it came to the Kurds. Through these visits, I met and became close friends with a group of Iraqis my age—in their midtwenties—who had formed the Iraqi Prospect Organisation (IPO) to campaign for the overthrow of Saddam and a democratic Iraq.

But I was aware that exiles obviously have a particular and unusual interest in regime change. I forced myself to remain skeptical about their reporting of Iraqi opinion as I endured their memories of Baathist rape and acid baths. It was in Saddam's Iraq itself that I knew the answers lay; therefore, I touched down in Damascus and headed for the border in September. From the moment I entered the country, it was hard to escape the minders helpfully loaned to any Western visitor by the regime; harder still to escape the constant feeling that, even if you shook off these particular thugs, you were being watched. I was in Baghdad for Saddam's referendum on his glorious rule. My hotel held a celebration party for the "Yes, All Hail Saddam" campaign. It happened the night before Iraqis went to the polls.

The country was taut and hypertense, waiting for a loud bang from any direction. Baghdad that autumn was a city that smoked. The kids smoked. The adults smoked. The elderly smoked. And they didn't go in for any low-tar rubbish, either. If New York is the city that doesn't sleep, Baghdad was the city that dare not sleep. Even late into the night, people scurried around, smoking, always smoking. But how to broach the subject obviously obsessing everyone?

The first hint of real Iraqi opinion came on my third day in the country, in a *souq* (market) in Mosul. A tiny, dignified old man was delighted to hear I was British. "I visited Britain many times in the 1970s and 1980s, before . . . before . . . ," he explained, smiling. He asked after his favorite restaurants and offered sweet tea. "We Iraqis love British democracy," he said softly. "You understand? We love British democracy." A taxi driver taking me to Saddam City explained that the area used to have a different name. "Who knows—perhaps we will change the name once more?" he asked, with a smile held just a fraction too long.

But these sparks of candor were rare. In Sumawi in southern Iraq, I was driven through the concrete slums into which the Marsh Arabs have been "relocated." A couple and their four children invited us into their home for tea. Once inheritors of a five-thousand-year-old life on the marshes, they now—thanks to Saddam—lived in a corrugated tin shack in the desert, and their marshes were poisoned and drained. Their traditional skills were now worthless, they had barely any money, yet they insistently refused to accept any cash compensation for the tea. As we left reluctantly, I noticed that they had been forced to hang a picture of Saddam—the man who had destroyed their people—on their Spartan wall. I asked about the dictator and the approaching bombs. "We love Saddam," she said very slowly and very carefully, before she turned away. She looked back at me, as if she wanted to continue. She glanced again at Saddam and wished me good-bye.

The extent to which speech is constrained in a totalitarian state only struck me properly in a Baghdad museum called—in a David Irving–like parody of history—the Museum for the Martyrs of Persian Aggression. As we wandered around, looking at the grim exhibits, one of the soldiers on duty guarding the museum told me that three of his brothers had died in that war. Everybody in the country had lost somebody, yet it is almost impossible to get anybody to talk about it. They speak in a small number of bloodless stock phrases. "It was a heroic war, led by our great leader Saddam Hussein," they would bark in a Pavlovian fashion. After more than a dozen of these encounters, it suddenly hit me that the people of Iraq were not even allowed to grieve their huge numbers of dead in their own way. They were permitted only a regulation measure of state-approved grief, which had to be expressed in Saddam's language: that of martyrdom and heroism, rather than wailing agony about the futility of a war that slaughtered more than a million people yet left the borders unchanged and achieved nothing. If they could not be candid about such private matters, how much courage did it take for the small minority who dared to talk to me about the forthcoming war?

Tantalizing encounters happened everywhere. I left concluding that very few Iraqis saw the war as uncomplicatedly bad, and many wanted it to proceed. If I am honest, I did not want to draw these conclusions. I returned to find almost all of my friends and political allies energized by the growing antiwar movement. Almost everybody I admired politically—with the exceptions of Tony Blair and Christopher Hitchens—was delivering rousing speeches and writing dazzling columns opposing the invasion. The politicians I most despised in the developed world—George Bush, Dick Cheney, Silvo Berlusconi, the British Tory Party—

were lining up as the war's greatest cheerleaders. I did not want, on a visceral level, to support Republican bombs, but how could I ignore my discoveries about Iraqi opinion? How could I oppose the tyrannized Iraqi people just to massage my own political comfort? Ah, but these discoveries were anecdotal, impressionistic, I kept reminding myself; I was still wavering.

I was tipped over into full support for the war by a survey conducted by the International Crisis Group (ICG), an independent and widely respected Brussels-based think tank. They had sent monitors into Iraq to conduct more methodically and systematically the same secret experiment that I had attempted. After speaking to dozens of Iraqis across the country, they reported that "a significant number of those Iraqis interviewed, with surprising candor, expressed their view that, if (regime change) required an American-led attack, they would support it. The notion of leaving the country's destiny in the hands of an omnipotent foreign party has more appeal than might be expected—and the desire for a long-term US involvement is higher than expected."[2]

It seemed clear that most Iraqis wanted the war to proceed. This was a good case for invasion, not the preposterous nonsense about weapons of mass destruction that was being spouted by the US and—to my great regret—British governments. I believed desperately that it was the job of the left to back the Iraqi people, and I could not understand why so many of my political friends and allies derided this as a "pro-Bush" or "neoconservative" position. When I saw significant parts of the left cheering George Galloway—a repellent antiwar Stalinist who had saluted Saddam's "courage, strength, and indefatigability" in Baghdad in the early 1990s—I felt disorientated. What was happening here?[3] I knew Iraqi opinion was an inconvenient factor in an otherwise glossy antiwar script that could use some great tunes about international law, peace not war, and so on. But didn't it matter just a bit? Indeed, shouldn't it be at the core of a progressive stance toward the war?

I accompanied my friends from the Iraqi Prospect Organisation to several antiwar rallies, where they tried to explain the wishes of their Iraqi relatives still trapped under Saddam's rule. At best, they were ignored or offered lame arguments. Sama Hadad, for example, whose father was murdered by the regime, was told by one peace protester that this could be solved by sending in human rights inspectors as well as weapons inspectors. "And tell me," Sama asked, "when these inspectors find massive evidence of human rights violations on every street corner, what then?" The "peace" protester looked blank. "We'll tell

Saddam to stop," she said after a long pause. "And if he won't? The only alternative is to invade, isn't it?" "Oh, no, I don't believe in violence," the protester replied. At least this protestor bothered to engage, however loosely; I saw my friends from the IPO hissed and even spat at by supposed advocates of "peace."

(No, these people were not typical of the antiwar movement, which was overwhelmingly stocked with decent people. But these incidents nonetheless reveal how marginal actual Iraqi people seemed to many people participating in the antiwar protests. Indeed, a significant pròportion seemed to be motivated almost entirely by intense hatred of George Bush. I share this feeling, but it hardly seems enough to overrule solidarity with the Iraqis.)

It was only months later, once the war was over, that I discovered just how right the small weather vanes of Iraqi opinion like the ICG report and the patient explanations of the IPO had been. Full opinion polls began to be conducted for the first time ever on Iraqi soil. They used exactly the same techniques as those of the polls that successfully predict general election results across the world. The result? As I write—in the summer of 2004—almost every single one of the dozens of opinion polls have found that a clear majority of Iraqis wanted the war to proceed. Not some war, some day—this specific invasion. (Even Hayder Sabbar Abd, the torture victim who was famously led on a leash by Lyndie England, carefully explained that he had wanted the US invasion to proceed.)[4]

So it is now beyond dispute that, on the day of the huge antiwar rallies across the world in February 2003, a majority of Iraqis would have been marching in precisely the opposite direction if they had been free to do so. The opponents of the war who claimed to be speaking on behalf of the Iraqi people were proved conclusively wrong. It is testimony to how deeply ingrained Gulf War Syndrome Mark II has become that this fact sounds alien to so many, despite the evidence for it having been in the public domain for more than a year. Before the war, there was some plausible doubt about what Iraqis thought about the war; since the war, there is none.

So did the progressive opponents of the war apologize for claiming incorrectly to speak for most Iraqis? Did they adjust their moral compass to account for this new awareness and stop abusing anybody who supported the majority of Iraqis as Bush-loving maniacs? We all know the answer. I would have respected anybody who admitted that, yes, the Iraqis wanted one thing, but we Western progressives believe we know better than them what is in their best interests. True, that would have been an imperialist argument, but it would have had the bonus of being honest.

Those few progressives who do not deny the evidence of the opinion polls instead question the wisdom of Iraqis and more generally of majorities. One colleague of mine—a distinguished antiwar commentator— said to me recently, "We support minorities all the time. So only a minority of Iraqis was smart enough to see through the US invasion. So what? Only a minority of Americans is smart enough to see that the death penalty is wrong."

I give him extra credit for conceding that the antiwar movement had few Iraqis on its side. His argument sounds persuasive at first; he seems to have pointed out a major hole in my approach. There are many instances in which I (and all progressives) support a minority against a majority. I do not believe in abandoning the tiny number of gay activists in the Arab world, for example, because there is a thumping homophobic majority. I do not believe the death penalty is legitimate even in countries where it is supported by most citizens.

But there is a crucial proviso. On the fundamental question of how a state should be constructed—where the locus of sovereignty itself should reside—majorities of citizens are never wrong. The British people, for example, have decided collectively to be a political unit, to be self-determining, and to be broadly democratic. However you might quibble about what it is legitimate for them to do collectively within that democratic national unit, these basic questions about where to invest their sovereignty cannot be judged wrong unless the very concept of democracy is renounced.

In the same way, majorities of Iraqis can be wrong on individual issues, but on the very question of whether their state should exist as their collective property (as opposed to Saddam Hussein's), no democrat can legitimately question their judgment. The decision by a majority of Iraqis to support the invasion was one of these foundational questions. It was a decision to constitute their collective identity above and beyond Saddam Hussein and the state that served him.

Sadly, these difficult questions were ignored by progressives. Instead, the process of trashing the Iraqi polls began, a process of denial that at times seemed reminiscent of the darkest moments of the history of the left. The *Guardian*'s comment editor, Seumas Milne, for example, sniffed that "the dwindling band of cheerleaders for war have seized on contradictory and questionable Baghdad opinion surveys conducted by

Western pollsters to back [their case]."[5] He implied that Iraqis were not being honest with Western pollsters, perhaps because they were afraid.

This possibility should be seriously considered. If Iraqis are not talking freely even now, then much of the evidence I am drawing on is questionable. Yet in one BBC poll (hardly a prowar source) that found majority support for the invasion, less than 10 percent of Iraqis said that they had confidence in the occupying forces, and 41 percent admitted that they found the invasion "humiliating." Why would Iraqis be candid on so many negative points and only hold back on the question of whether they wanted the invasion itself to proceed? Because they felt free to be extremely critical on every other issue, it seems fair to assume Iraqis are telling the truth about the most basic issue of all. If opponents of the war wish to maintain their belief that most Iraqis did not want the war to proceed, they must now argue that opinion-polling techniques that work all over the world have somehow, inexplicably, broken down more than fifty times in Iraq.

Other critics of the polls have claimed that Iraqis would—if given the option—have preferred simply the lifting of UN sanctions against the country, without any invasion: Saddam without sanctions. Noam Chomsky has been at the forefront of arguing that Iraqis could have overthrown Saddam themselves in these circumstances.[6] Again, this argument deserves serious attention. It is true that no opinion poll has offered the straightforward lifting of sanctions in early 2003 as an option to Iraqis, but, equally, Iraqis are not stupid. Asked the question "Did you think the invasion of Iraq was right?" it is not beyond the wit of the most educated population in the region to say, "No, I would have preferred an end to sanctions." Many of the minority of Iraqis who did answer no might well have done so for this reason.

It seems, incidentally, naive at best to presume that Iraqis could have liberated themselves if only the shackle of sanctions had been lifted. (I speak as somebody who always opposed sanctions; invasion invariably seemed a better option than a medieval embargo.) Iraqis had no sanctions throughout the 1980s and could not overthrow Saddam then; when they tried to do so in 1991, when sanctions had barely begun to kick in, more than one hundred thousand were slaughtered by Saddam's armies. Does Chomsky believe that Saddam (or Uday and Qusay) would at any point have reacted with less than full and vicious force to an uprising? Would Iraqis have ever been strong enough, even postsanctions, to destroy Saddam's totalitarian machine alone? Would even an uprising that somehow succeeded really have claimed fewer lives than the war? It is a legitimate intellectual and moral position to claim that the continuation of Baathism was less bad than a US invasion and a resulting leap into the unknown. To pretend, however, that these were not the two options—that somehow, magically, Iraqis without sanctions could bloodlessly rise—is not.

But siding with the Iraqi people in favor of a US-led invasion is plainly not enough for progressives who seek a clean conscience. The charge against prowar liberals and leftists—led by Chomsky and his followers—is that we are shallow cheerleaders for US power, contriving to find softheaded excuses for hard bullets, convinced that "our boys" are deep down better than those of any other tribe. If we are to prove this claim wrong, two obligations fall upon us.

The first obligation is that we should never delude ourselves or others about the intentions of US state power. We can (and must) formulate a progressive agenda based on siding with Iraqis—but we must not kid ourselves that George Bush and Dick Cheney are sitting in the Oval Office doing the same. It is not yet clear why the United States decided to embark on this war. It now seems fairly obvious that weapons of mass destruction were, at best, a legalistic pretext in a much wider process of justifying invasion. Other motives may include the long-term stability of oil supplies, the removal of a key strategic opponent of Israel, and perhaps a desire to reverse the long process of American-led crushing of democracy in the region. But we are not here to sugarcoat US state power. We are not here to pretend that a government that would offer positions to John Negroponte (with his record of vicious antidemocratic thuggery in Central America) and laud Henry Kissinger (a genocidal war criminal) can be taken at face value when it professes support for Iraqi democracy and human rights.

We should therefore work on the assumption that there has been a passing coincidence between the wishes of a majority of Iraqis and the interests of US state power. Nothing more. It was right to exploit that coincidence to get rid of Saddam and wrong to deny that it existed. But to imply that the United States did this primarily for humanitarian reasons—that Donald Rumsfeld leads the Praetorian Guard for Amnesty International—is absurd. I came dangerously close to making this mistake myself at times. I teetered in my columns near to implying that humanitarian intent was a significant motive on the part of the Bush administration. The evidence does not support this claim—particularly if one looks at the tyrant-supporting behavior of the Bush administration in other parts of the world or its contempt for human rights both at home and in detention facilities in Iraq, Afghanistan, and Guantánamo Bay. So for any progressive who wishes to support Iraqis, backing the invasion can only have been the first page of a long book.

The second obligation that falls upon prowar liberals who want to show they are not dupes for the Bush administration follows neatly from this point. We must keep backing the Iraqi people *even—especially— when their interests diverge from the interests of US state power.* If we "liberal hawks" backed the war because most Iraqis did, too, then we must back the Iraqis on other foundational political questions for years to come. We must show that our allegiance is not to the states we happen to live in but to a tyrannized people who wish to rebuild their lives.

This is no longer a hypothetical situation. It is already essential. The polls showed that almost no Iraqis at all supported the US Army's murderous excursion into Fallujah, where at least eight hundred Iraqi civilians were pointlessly killed. There was no need to assault the nationalist insurgency in this way, especially since they were going to be offered an amnesty just a few months later anyway. Radicals need to be locked into Iraq's emerging democracy, not blasted out of it. Following Fallujah and the revelations of torture in Abu Ghraib—sanctioned by the US government, according to Seymour Hersh[7]—the polls found that most Iraqis wanted an immediate handover of power to an Iraqi government and very rapid elections leading to the withdrawal of occupying forces, unless a democratic Iraqi government explicitly asked them to stay.

If we do not support Iraqi opponents of the leveling of Fallujah, if we do not support Iraqi demands for much faster elections, then we have failed in the role of good progressives, just as surely as the opponents of the war failed when they did not support the prowar majority of Iraqis. And this is even more true when it comes to opposing the imposition of a failed strategy of market fundamentalism on Iraq through the IMF and World Bank. For Iraqi democracy to be meaningful, an elected Iraqi government must be able to determine the structure of the Iraqi economy. This matter sounds laughably basic, but it is not by any means guaranteed. The Iraqi government must be free to set its own tax rates and decide over the nature of contracts and provision of services within Iraq. Without these minimal prerequisites, democracy is reduced to a technocratic sham.

Yet this scenario is precisely what the next Iraqi government is supposed to accept. Contracts signed by Paul Bremmer in his time as unelected proconsul to Iraq (often handing over great slabs of the Iraqi economy to Bush administration crony corporations) are fixed and unchangeable. Here is evidence that the right, too, has succumbed to Gulf War Syndrome Mark II: they are simply assuming that Iraqis agree with them about massive economic reforms that would only be accompanied in a democratic country by decades of debate. This is not democracy; it is market fundamentalism that argues for a US invasion of Capitol Hill to impose similarly "business-friendly" conditions on the Senate.

It is important to understand: the economic model imposed on Iraq by the IMF is *not* US-style capitalism (never mind European social democracy). It is a strain of capitalism far more extreme than anything ever attempted in a democratic country, with full-scale privatization of extremely basic services and almost no recourse for the government and public opinion against corporations. The United States, for example, is involved in a protracted public debate about whether to privatize Social Security, but the IMF coerces poor countries (including Iraq) to privatize Social Security as a matter of course, even if a democratic majority opposes the idea.

Nor is the IMF agenda a guarantee of economic success, a temporary measure necessary to secure a flourishing Iraq. As Nobel Prize–winning economist and former chief economist at the World Bank Joseph Stiglitz has explained, these IMF-led "development programs" are almost invariably disastrous for everybody except international capital—particularly ordinary citizens and the poor. After the Russian economy was virtually subcontracted to the IMF, life expectancy in post-Soviet Russia, incredibly, actually fell below the dismal levels of Soviet communism. Stiglitz told me recently that the IMF approach to Iraq is "almost an exact repeat of Russia. It's as if they thought Russia was a major success, and the only problem is that they didn't go far enough." If the IMF and its supporters in the West really believe that their reforms will deliver for the Iraqi people (as opposed to Western multinationals), why not subject them to the democratic process?

The battle in Iraq is, therefore, part of a much wider battle to reform the IMF so that independent and democratic development in poor countries becomes possible. No opinion polling in Iraq has been conducted about this restructuring agenda, but democratic Iraqi trade unions—free at last to organize—are protesting across the country. (You can give cash online at www.iraqitradeunions.com—here's a way to give real support to a force for secular, democratic reform in Iraq.) If we do not support Iraqis in resisting this program, then we have lost our ability to claim the second half of the "prowar left" tag. We can support bombs to destroy Baathism and proudly remain on the left; we cannot support the undemocratic imposition of an über-Thatcherite program and do so.

It is not too late for liberals and leftists in the United States and across the developed world to support their allies—or, if you prefer, comrades—in Iraq. Gulf War Syndrome Mark II is easily treated. Turn off the Rumsfeld press conference, take a pill for your Bush-induced nausea, and listen. Listen to the Iraqi people. They have been trying to talk to us for a very long time.

## NOTES

1. Gary Younge, "Twin Vision of Empire," *The Guardian*, February 10, 2003.

2. International Crisis Group, "Voices from the Iraqi Street," Middle East Briefing No. 3, December 4, 2002, http://www.crisisweb.org/home/index .cfm?id=1825&l=1 (accessed January 22, 2005).

3. George Galloway, "Empire Builders and Homicidal War: George Galloway's Historic Speech," Al Jazeera, October 30, 2003, http://www .globalresearch.ca/articles/GAL311A.html (accessed January 22, 2005).

4. Ian Fisher, "Iraqi Recalls Beatings, Piles of Naked, Hooded Prisoners," *New York Times*, May 5, 2004.

5. Seumas Milne, "Iraq Has Now Become the Crucible of Global Politics," *Guardian Unlimited*, September 25, 2003, http://www.guardian.co.uk/comment/ story/o,,1049198,00.html (accessed January 22, 2005).

6. Noah Chomsky, "The Invasion of Iraq," posted by the author on his own personal weblog, March 27, 2004. The full article is found at http://blog .zmag.org/ttt/archives/000032.html (accessed January 22, 2005).

7. Seymour M. Hersh, "Torture at Abu Ghraib," *New Yorker*, May 10, 2004, http://www.newyorker.com/fact/content/?040510fa_fact (accessed January 22, 2005).

# 21

# "They Don't Know One Little Thing"

PAMELA BONE

The quote that serves as the title for this essay is by an Iraqi woman in Jordan, being interviewed by the BBC at the time of the toppling of the statue of Saddam Hussein. She provided his response when she was asked about antiwar protesters, together with other women who were gathered together to recount the horrors of the regime of Saddam Hussein.

I wondered at first whether the women were exaggerating. They told me that in Iraq, the country they had fled, women were beheaded with swords and their heads nailed to the front doors of their houses, as a lesson to other women. The executed women had been dishonoring their country with their sexual crimes, and this behavior could not be tolerated, the then–Iraqi leader, Saddam Hussein, had said on national television. More than two hundred women had been executed in this manner in the previous three weeks, the women of the Committee in Defense of Iraqi Women's Rights told me. This was in Melbourne, Australia, in November 2000. The women talking to me that day were just a few of the four million Iraqi exiles around the world who had fled Saddam's regime.

Because the claims seemed so extreme, I checked Amnesty International's country report, which said that numerous reports had been filed from Iraq about executions, without charge or conviction, of prostitutes or women alleged to be prostitutes. Some of the women's "sexual crimes" were having been raped by one of Saddam's sons. One of the women executed was a doctor who had complained of corruption in the government health department. Surma Hamid, one of the protesters in Melbourne that day, said the international sanctions against the Iraqi regime should be lifted, because by generating resentment against the West, they were helping Saddam to stay in power. "By committing these crimes, the regime is providing more excuses for the United States and the UK to maintain the sanctions, and these sanctions have proved very beneficial for this regime," she said.

I thought of these women often in the weeks before the US-led invasion of Iraq. I had always, without thinking about it too deeply, assumed I was a pacifist. It seemed part of being a left-leaning, feminist, agnostic, environmentalist internationalist. I'd been to peace conferences where I'd been buoyed by the possibilities of a world united. In my newspaper columns, I'd scorned military affairs and deplored the amount that my country and other developed countries spent on defense instead of on foreign aid. Yet, in February 2003, when asked to speak at a rally for peace, I politely declined. But I added, less politely, that if there were to be a rally condemning the brutality Saddam Hussein was inflicting on his people or protesting at the treatment of women in the Middle East in general, I would be glad to speak at it.

For as long as public opinion polls have been taken, they have shown women to be less eager for war than men. Indeed, the early feminists believed that it was important to emphasize women's abhorrence of killing. If women ruled, there would be no wars, this argument went (and still goes). The Bloomsbury feminist Virginia Woolf asserted at the time of World War I that "scarcely a human being in the course of history has fallen to a woman's rifle."[1] (Opposing this view was a long line of women posing as men in order to go into battle or handing out white feathers to men not in uniform.)

Today nearly every feminist Web site has a strong antiwar statement on it. As with other wars, fewer women than men supported the war in Iraq. In Australia, according to Newspoll, just before it began 56 percent of men but only 46 percent of women were for the war.[2] Yet bigger differences exist within groups of men and women than between them. In Australia, political allegiance was more important than gender in the support for war or lack of it. Three-quarters of supporters of the conservative Liberal-National Coalition were prowar, whereas only 37 percent of Labor voters were. In the United States, the racial gap was far bigger than the gender gap, with 68 percent of black Americans opposing the war. Where did that leave me, a Labor-voting feminist, in supporting the invasion? Like many others, at the beginning I had hoped against hope that Saddam Hussein might somehow be deposed without war. In the end I believed that he had to go, even if it meant war.

Almost everything I write and think on this issue has been colored by having been in Rwanda in the aftermath of the 1994 genocide, seeing children with machete scars on their hands where they had put them up to shield their heads, hearing the people's stories of whole families massacred, watching bodies being exhumed from mass graves. In the space of one hundred days, an estimated one million people were killed. What happened in Rwanda happened because the world allowed it to: because when the killings started, the United Nations pulled out all but a handful of its troops, while the Security Council debated whether to call what was happening a genocide, which would have obliged it to act. It is colored by having been through the regions of southern Africa in 2003 where a silent holocaust of famine and AIDS was wiping out populations. No protest rallies for starving African children. It is colored by having listened, years before September 11, before most people had even heard of the Taliban, to exiled Afghan women asking in anguish, "Why does the West not help us?" And it is colored by having talked to the Iraqi women refugees, who asked the same question: "Why does the West not help us?"

The essays in this book are written by liberals who supported the war. We, the prowar liberals, are a minority. Yet from the beginning it has seemed to me odd that most opposition to the war has come from women and the left. Surely, showing solidarity with oppressed people is a tradition of the left? Surely, feminists could see that a large part of the reason the Islamist terrorists who had attacked the West hated us was the freedom of women in Western societies? Using the definitions of the 1948 Genocide Convention, the Baath regime headed by Saddam Hussein can be charged with carrying out two genocides: one against the Kurdish population in the late 1980s and another against the Marsh Arabs in the 1990s. In addition, as many as three hundred thousand Shiites were killed in the six months following the collapse of the March 1991 uprising against his government. "A person stands a better chance of being tried and judged for killing one human being than for killing one hundred thousand," the former UN human rights commissioner Jose Ayala Lasso observed some years ago.[3] The slow growth of international humanitarian law, built up over the past century—the Nuremberg Trial, the international criminal tribunals for Rwanda and the former Yugoslavia, and, more recently, the International Criminal Court—was to change this situation: to put an end to impunity for rulers who murdered, tortured, or otherwise carried out large-scale abuses of the human rights of their citizens. International public opinion, especially on the left, was generally supportive of this idea. The notion of national sovereignty as a protection for mass murderers was to be no more valid than the old, discredited idea that a man's home is his castle and that he has the right to bash his wife and children within its walls if he wants to.

I was in Vienna in 1993, at the time of the big UN International Human Rights Conference. What brave hopes then for international solidarity and for women's rights! Thousands of women were there, demonstrating, holding up posters that said, "Women's Rights Are Human Rights." It was asserted in the declaration of that conference that human rights are universal, not culturally or economically determined. (Consider for a moment what this statement means. If human rights are not culturally determined, it means that such things as honor killings, female genital mutilation, and stonings for adultery cannot be justified in the name of tradition or culture; if human rights are not economically determined, it implies an obligation on the part of rich countries to provide economic aid to those countries that are unable to provide basic goods to their citizens.) At that conference, then–UN secretary-general Boutros Boutros-Ghali warned that the international community would take over states if they failed to fulfill their human rights obligations.[4] Australia's then–foreign minister Gareth Evans told the conference that despite different cultural and religious traditions, throughout history all philosophies had recognized that within human relations, some things were always right and some always wrong.

Where had all those fine words gone in March 2003? In a UN Security Council whose members were so filled with self-interests that they could not agree to enforce their own resolutions or to show solidarity against a dictator who had murdered hundreds of thousands of his own citizens, invaded two neighboring countries, and forced millions into exile; in Western public opinion gripped in a determined anti-imperialism and a cultural relativism so broad that it saw the United States, rather than despotic rogue states, as the greatest danger to world peace; in the anger of peace marchers, expressed not at the tyrant Saddam Hussein but at George W. Bush and Tony Blair.

The emerging global consensus that human rights override national sovereignty broke down over Iraq. Why? Because international public opinion is opposed to war (and it is good, a sign of great hope, that it is). And to many, this was a war being waged by the world's only super-power against one of the world's poorest nations. Many did not know or chose not to reflect much on the fact that Iraqi children had been dying from malnutrition while their leader continued to build palaces and monuments to himself. So the millions marched, and Saddam saw that the Western world had no stomach for war and was encouraged. It was not their intention, but the antiwar demonstrators gave courage to one of the most monstrous regimes of recent history. That they did is undeniable; the former Iraqi foreign minister, Tariq Aziz, said so at the time.

"Have people gone completely and utterly mad?" wrote the British author William Shawcross at the time. "How come they don't realize they are undermining the United Nations, and making war more likely?"[5] The war could have been justified on the basis of human rights alone. Yet humanitarian considerations were not the principal reason the leaders of the "Coalition of the Willing" put forward for invading Iraq. Although Bush and Blair spoke of the need for regime change, Australia's prime minister, John Howard, said he could not "justify on its own the military invasion of Iraq to change the regime . . . much and all as I despise the regime."[6] The leaders believed (correctly, as it turned out) that removing the possibility that weapons of mass destruction could be used by rogue states or terrorists was the cause people would be more likely to support. With respect to all those who opposed the war who were well informed, many protesters did not really know what kind of regime existed in Iraq. "Well, I've never heard anything about that, Pam," said my sister when I told her. "We wanted the UN to do it," said a friend. Of course we did. And that is another positive thing: that public opinion was wise enough to know that if the regime of a sovereign nation is to be toppled, such action should be taken with the authority of the UN (opinion polls showed majority support for an invasion if it had UN backing).[7]

But what if—after the millions had marched, after the years of failed sanctions and broken UN resolutions, after the Security Council had spent months squabbling and then failed to agree on action, after so many threats and ultimatums—the United States and its handful of the willing had simply backed down and gone home? How would Saddam and every other murdering dictator in the world have been emboldened?

How would every jihadist across the Middle East have been strengthened in his belief that the West was weak and that a worldwide Islamic state was achievable?

Iraq brought together the war against terrorism, Islam versus democracy, national sovereignty versus human rights, secularism versus religious fundamentalism. This war, which continues, is a war of ideas as much as a war of armies. It is part of a struggle far more complex than the Cold War, because it engages more than ideology: it engages a religious faith, which means it can claim the authority of God for whatever it wishes to impose.

I agree with the Samuel P. Huntington thesis that there is a clash of civilizations.[8] Moreover, I believe that a large part of the clash is about the freedoms of women. Truly, the war in Iraq was not fought for the emancipation of women. No war ever has been. Whereas South Africa was subjected to years of sanctions over the oppression of blacks, no sanctions are applied to countries because they condone or promote the oppression of the female half of their population. Under the Taliban, women were banned from public life, whipped for showing an inch of flesh, and buried up to their necks and stoned to death if suspected of adultery. Nothing was done by Western governments to help them—until Osama bin Laden became a threat, when, suddenly and miraculously, there was Cherie Blair, wife of Tony, and Laura Bush, wife of George W., making speeches about the rights of Afghan women. It is also true that by the standards of the region, women were not particularly oppressed under the Saddam regime—notwithstanding the executions of women for "sexual crimes"; the gang rape of the wives, daughters, and mothers of dissidents in front of their families; or, in an attempt to win favor with his fundamentalist neighbors, a decree issued by Saddam allowing men to kill their female relatives to preserve family "honor."[9]

However, a large part of what is at stake in the new Iraq, echoed across the Middle East, is the right of men to control women. In the name of religion, still today, in the twenty-first century, thousands of women are legally murdered every year over family honor, little girls are forced into marriages with old men, women are stoned and beaten for having sex outside marriage, and women are covered and segregated and denied such basic freedoms as the right to go in public without a male relation or to drive a car. In Jordan, the penalty for honor killing is set at six months in jail. In rural Pakistan, a young girl belonging to the family of a murderer is offered as compensation to the family of the murder victim. In Iran until recently, the legal age of marriage for a girl was nine years. We tip-toe around these dreadful practices and say cultural change must come from within. Strange that no one ever said of the treatment of blacks under the apartheid system in South Africa, or of nineteenth-century slave owners, that cultural change needed to come from within.

Fear of women's sexuality is a driver of religious fundamentalism, whether Christian, Jewish, Hindu, or Muslim. The freedoms of Western women, their open sexuality, are a large part of the hatred Islamist men feel for the West. They would, if they could, spread their joyless, sex-denying, life-denying version of religion over the world. They've said, many times, that this is what they want. They would, if they could, have all our daughters in burkas.

The hatreds of bin Laden and his kind will not be assuaged, but, in general, fundamentalism wanes as prosperity increases. According to the 2003 Arab Human Development Report (written for the UN by Arab academics), a significant part of the reason so many countries in the Middle East are overpopulated, economic basket cases is the repression of women.[10] Countries across the world demonstrate a clear correlation between equality between men and women and the prosperity, democratic freedoms, and quality of life of the society as a whole. If the new Iraq is to become the hoped-for example of peace and democracy to other Arab states, one of the most effective measures that those charged with its rebuilding can take is to encourage the participation of women at every level of society. This idea is recognized by global organizations such as the United Nations and the World Bank. The United States also appears to recognize it. "Women's rights and opportunities figure prominently in US support for Iraq's transition to democracy," said a media release of the US State Department on International Women's Day, 2004.[11]

"The women's movement here is strong," said Mishkat al-Mumin, of Baghdad University's law school. Mishkat, who spoke to me from her home in Baghdad in June 2004, had watched the statue of Saddam Hussein come toppling down, with a mixture of awe and elation. "But I didn't feel freedom then. Not until they captured him. Now I do feel freedom," she said. Under Saddam, Mishkat said, women suffered two kinds of damage: "They suffered the damage of losing their husbands and fathers and sons in the wars he started. And they also suffered the damage of discrimination. When women tried to get a job, they were told there was a government instruction to prefer men." Yes, since the war, women have suffered from the lack of security, she said. "There are many obstacles to us still, the lack of training, the violence against women. But most women are glad Saddam has gone. Before there were no women in decision making. Now we have women in decision-making roles. We have so far managed to operate in difficult circumstances. I think we will overcome these obstacles," she added. "Now Iraqi women have a future. That is the most important thing."

Since the initial invasion, suicide bombings and other terrorist attacks have killed hundreds of Iraqi civilians. Support for the occupying forces, initially high, plummeted. The torture of Iraqi prisoners by US soldiers at Abu Ghraib prison did immeasurable harm, not only to the victims but to the cause of instituting change across the Middle East, because it allowed Islamists to claim that Westerners are no better than they are.

But some things are better: sanctions have been lifted; money on a scale not seen since the Marshall Plan is being spent on water, sanitation, hospitals, and health centers; local people have been trained; millions of children have been vaccinated. In town council elections, ordinary Iraqis demonstrated a great enthusiasm for democracy, and most of those elected have been educated moderates. More than eighty new women's groups have been formed. Pressure from Iraqi women succeeded in overturning the draft Resolution 137, put up by the former governing council, that would have put family law into Islamic courts, with laws being administered by clerics.[12] The constitution gives women, who make up about 60 percent of the population in Iraq, more rights than they have in any neighboring states. The interim government, formally recognized by the UN, is the most broadly representative government in the Middle East and includes six women.

The good news in Iraq is seldom told. As a journalist, I have found it disillusioning to see the one-sided reporting of the war—including from Australia's national broadcaster, the ABC—by left-liberal journalists who opposed the war in the first place and do not want to acknowledge that any good could come of it. It has also been hard to take the daily deluge of hostile and abusive e-mails from people who had assumed that as a liberal commentator, I would have automatically been opposed to the war.

I believe that the leaders of the United States, Britain, and Australia acted honorably, if not always competently, in liberating Iraq. I supported the invasion because I believed that in the twenty-first century, genocidal dictators should not be left to torture and murder their citizens with impunity. And because I believed the example of a decent democratic state in Iraq might begin a process of democratization and liberalization across the region. And also because this process might result in a better future for women in those countries.

Much is written about the rage of Arab men against the West. But across the Arab world, and in Iran and Afghanistan, this phenomenon is also happening: Muslim women are forging a new feminism, sometimes at great risk even to their lives. Hundreds of Web sites have been set up by women fighting against fundamentalism. Just as Christian women (with varying success) have, Muslim women are demanding that their religion accommodate women's equality. Some are challenging the way men have hijacked a religion that they say does grant them rights, some say that parts of the Koran need to be reinterpreted, and some believe that women's liberation can only come through a complete separation of church and state. Yes, these brave women are still a small minority, but their numbers are growing. Just as Western women have, feminist women in Islamic countries have to fight other women. Unfortunately, they also get little support from many Western feminists who, in the name of tolerance, buy the line of those educated, middle-class Muslim women, living in Western countries under the protection of Western laws, who insist that in Islam women have "a different kind of freedom." The reason is that the new left, along with much of modern-day feminism, have abandoned the principle of justice as their primary virtue and have replaced it with tolerance, apparently not seeing that tolerance can imply being tolerant of the intolerant and the intolerable.

As British prime minister Tony Blair said in April 2004 of the rebuilding of Iraq: "Against us in this task are ranged every variety of reactionary forces: sympathizers of Saddam Hussein, outside terrorists, religious fanatics."[13] The important word here is *reactionary*. Paradoxically, much of the new left aligns itself with those reactionary forces, who hold values diametrically opposed to liberalism: religious fundamentalist, racist, misogynist, homophobic tendencies—everything liberalism is opposed to. In so doing, they let down the progressive movements from within those societies that are fighting to change the cultures that the new left "tolerates."

There were valid reasons to be against the war, some of which have been borne out. But being a woman is not large among them: to cling to the notion of women as the world's peacemakers implies that women are not capable of seeing when a war might be just. Neither is being a liberal: the conventional wisdom is that the war was not justified because there was no immediate threat from weapons of mass destruction and no (strongly proven) link with Al Qaeda. In brief, it was not justified because we were not threatened. This is not a liberal-left position. Conservatives worried that attacking Iraq would stir up a hornet's nest in the region. Conservative principles teach that countries should only go to war in defense of their national interest and security. This is not what liberal principles teach. Liberal principles teach international solidarity. Critics of the humanitarian justification for the war frequently point out that other regimes in the world, such as Burma and North Korea, starve and oppress their peoples, and these are not attacked. This is tantamount to saying that because we cannot save every starving child, we need not try to save any. Just because we can't immediately remove every evil dictator in the world, it doesn't mean we shouldn't remove those we can. Critics also point out the American hypocrisy in having supported Saddam Hussein in the past. Should the people of Iraq not be freed because those who would free them are hypocrites?

What of all the innocent people who were killed? This is the hardest question. In the long term, the invasion and occupation probably saved more people than it killed. But this perspective would be no consolation to those who have lost husbands, parents, children. How can you trade lives off against each other, saying that these lives must be sacrificed to save other lives? Yet this is what war is. Humanity has not yet found an alternative to physical force as the ultimate sanction against a genocidal regime. And if it were only right to attack another country in self-defense, it would not have been right for the Allied forces to attack Hitler in order to rescue the Jews, as long as Hitler had been no threat to outside countries.

Many times, listening to the BBC news in the early sleepless hours of the morning, I have asked myself, How could you have supported this? But if the war had not occurred, Saddam Hussein would still be there, keeping his citizens in misery. And then I talk to a doctor who works with the Survivors of Torture Foundation in Melbourne. He tells me of an eight-year-old Iraqi boy he is treating for trauma, who was made to watch his father being tortured by Saddam's thugs and whose father was also made to watch while his son's arms were broken, slowly.

If the UN had kept a united front against Saddam, his bluff just possibly might have been called and war averted. But the UN is only as good as its member states, and in democracies, at least, those member states are only as good as their citizens force them to be. Ordinary citizens allow governments to get away with not signing international treaties, to give meager amounts of overseas aid, to exploit poor countries through unfair trade rules, and to require those poor countries to pay back impossible debts.

What can be done now? Iraq badly needs the world to believe it can become a normal country. Whatever their views about the war, all people of goodwill should hope that Iraq can be rebuilt as a decent democratic state, where people have the same right to pursue prosperity and happiness as we in the West do. And that the United Nations—which the former Irish ambassador to the UN, Conor Cruise O'Brien, once described as "humanity's prayer to itself to be saved from itself"—can also be rebuilt.[14] We need it more than ever.

There is no choice but to continue to hope that somehow, all of us can be better than any of us. That superpower, international public opinion, should now use its power to push for a war to end the inequality, poverty, and injustice in the world—if it's peace it wants.

## NOTES

1. Virginia Woolf, *Three Guineas* (New York: Harcourt, Brace, 1938), 8.

2. Newspoll Market Research, "Australian Opinion on War," April 1, 2003, http://www.newspoll.com.au/cgi-bin/display_poll_data.pl (accessed January 11, 2005).

3. Quoted by Kofi Annan to the Mexican Congress at The International Conference on Financing for Development, March 19, 2002. The full speech is available at www.un.org/ffd/pressrel/19b.htm (accessed January 22, 2005).

4. See http://www.unhchr.ch/html/menu5/d/statemnt/secgen.htm (accessed January 11, 2005).

5. William Shawcross, "Support for Bush and Blair Is Good for the U.N., Bad for Saddam," *The Age*, February 16, 2003, http://theage.com.au/articles/2003/02/15/1044927847862.html (accessed January 5, 2005).

6. John Howard quote in Albert Langer, "Albert Langer: Latham v. Reality: The Looming Crisis," www.lastsuperpower.net, June 14, 2004. The full article is available at http://www.theage.com.au/articles/2004/06/13/1087065029879.html (accessed January 5, 2005).

7. See the poll of March 4, 2003, posted at http://www.newspoll.com/au/cgi-bin/display_poll_data.pl (accessed (January 11, 2005).

8. Samuel P. Huntington, "The Clash of Civilizations," *Foreign Affairs* 72, no. 3 (Summer 1993): 22.

9. Cited in "Iraq Human Rights Report," March 16, 2001, http://www.arabicnews.com/ansub/Daily/Day/010316/2001031630.html (accessed January 5, 2005).

10. The full report is available at www.religiousconsultation.org/Special_Features/Arab_Human_Development_Report_2003.htm (accessed January 5, 2005).

11. Tami Longaberger, "Improving the Human Rights of Women and the Gender Perspective: U.S. Statement," April 5, 2004, http://www.humanrights-usa.net/statements/0405LongabergerItem12.htm (accessed January 5, 2005).

12. Darlisa Y. Crawford and Kathryn McConnell, "Constitution Marks New Start for Iraqi Women, Minister Says: International Women's Day Conference in Washington," http://usinfo.state.gov/dhr/Archive/2004/Mar/10-394031.html (accessed January 22, 2005).

13. Tony Blair quoted in "Bush, Blair Discuss Sharon Plan; Future of Iraq in Press Conference," statement made at the White House, April 16, 2004, http://www.whitehouse.gov/news/releases/2004/04/20040416-4.html (accessed January 22, 2005).

14. The O'Brien quote was cited in a speech to the UN General Assembly by Australian foreign minister Alexander Downing on September 24, 2003. The full speech is available at http://www.foreignminister.gov.au/speeches/2003/030924_general_assembly_ny.html (accessed January 22, 2005).

# 22

# "Why Did It Take You So Long to Get Here?"

ANN CLWYD

It was an early evening in Baghdad when I arrived at the office of the Institute of War and Peace Reporting, but still many young students were there working on leads and storylines. The institute works in many of the world's hot spots. It seeks to aid the process of rebuilding postconflict nations by teaching journalism.

The students were an illustration of the rapid change that had taken place in Iraq. Twelve months earlier such a gathering would have been impossible. For decades, journalism in Iraq consisted of reporting the words of Saddam Hussein for publications owned by other members of his family. Integrity and independent analysis were not encouraged. The arbiters of our information-driven age, the satellite dish and Internet, were largely absent.

Now journalism offered possibilities of a stimulating career as all forms of media blossomed in post-Saddam Iraq. New newspapers appeared on a daily basis, and satellite dishes cluttered the Baghdad rooftops. Internet cafés linked Iraqis to the outside world. Radio stations gave voice to those who had long been unheard. Everywhere there was a thirst for information and the signs of Baghdad returning to its role as an intellectual hub of the Middle East.

I had been invited to talk to the students in my role as Special Envoy to the Prime Minister on Human Rights in Iraq. But I reminded them that I had been a journalist before I became a member of Parliament. It was as a journalist that I had first been introduced to Iraq.

In 1977, a group of Iraqi students studying at Cardiff University told me about their lives and the oppression that both they and their families faced in Iraq. Even when studying overseas, Iraqis were not free of the long arm of Iraqi state control; their international student organization was little more than a branch of the secret police. Those who spoke out against the regime while abroad soon found their families being threatened at home. The students themselves were often attacked on university campuses in the UK by pro-Saddam students.

It was testimony to the courage of those students and their families that they refused to remain silent. The Committee against Repression and for Democratic Rights in Iraq (CARDRI) was established by brave Iraqis studying in Britain and concerned Britons. I became the chair of that organization in 1984. In those years of repression and exile, CARDRI was a lifeline for the many persecuted within Iraq. It reported the crimes of the regime of Saddam Hussein and protested against the tacit support that he received throughout the eighties from Western governments.

For the students who sat before me now in Baghdad, I could have been describing another world rather than the history of their parents' generation. The generous funding of education was long past, a victim of Saddam's wars. Overseas education was rare. I told the students that the role of a journalist was to ask the difficult questions of those in power. A hand shot up. The question was to the point. Raising the issue of regime change, the student asked, "Why did it take you so long to get here?"

## SADDAM'S IRAQ

This question goes to the heart of the debate that surrounded the conflict in Iraq. What was the rationale for intervention? If this rationale had been based on the need for humanitarian action, why then had it taken so long to act?

The evidence of atrocities had been growing since the early years of the Saddam regime. The testimonies passed on by Iraqi students in Britain painted a picture of a brutal police state that sometimes verged on the incredible. Names of those executed were publicized. Little was done.

These crimes took place in the latter years of the Cold War. The development of universal human rights, although enshrined long ago in the United Nations Declaration on Human Rights and a multitude of treaties and pronouncements, was still seen as secondary to the real-politik of the Cold War. Human rights abuses were viewed as an internal matter, beyond the sanction of the international community.

The Iran-Iraq war provided a cover and excuse for the regime's atrocities. The prevailing logic from the United States was that the Iranian revolution was the principal threat to the region; as a result, any criticism of Saddam was muted. This silence even extended to the use of chemical weapons by the Iraqi forces, despite the use of chemical and biological weapons being strictly prohibited by the Geneva Protocol of 1925. Condemnation, when it came, was measured and evenhanded, laying blame at the doors of both Iranians and Iraqis.

Throughout this period, reports had also been made of brutal action taken against the Kurdish population in northern Iraq. Since the creation of modern Iraq, there has been a tension between the center and the Kurdish region. Political solutions had failed. Now the government in Baghdad tried to undercut support for the Kurdish cause in rural areas. A policy of Arabization was adopted, as Kurdish communities were forcibly moved and their villages destroyed.

In the late 1970s, 1,189 villages were annihilated and their inhabitants dispersed.[1] In hindsight, this policy would be seen as a prelude to the more serious crimes against the Kurds that became known as the Anfal.

The Anfal campaign continued the policy of destroying villages. But now the population was also a legitimate target for attack by the Iraqi military. Kanan Makiya emphasized this change in policy. "The real hallmark of the operation was the bureaucratically organized, routinely administered mass killings of village inhabitants for no other reason than that they happened to live in an area that was now designated as "prohibited for security reasons."[2] The Anfal saw the repeated use of chemical weapons against a civilian population. In the run-up to the war in Iraq in 2003, the Kurdish town of Halabja became more widely known as an example of Saddam's brutality. The bombing of Halabja owed its notoriety to the numbers killed and the presence of television cameras to record the aftermath. But away from the cameras, from February through September 1988, there were many more Halabjas as the Anfal campaign raged across Iraqi Kurdistan. The Kurds claimed that 182,000 had been killed during this period. When Ali Hasan al-Majeed, widely known in Iraqi Kurdistan as "Chemical Ali," the military commander with sole responsibility for the area, was confronted with this figure, he scoffed. "What is this exaggerated figure of 182,000? It couldn't have been more than 100,000."[3] The huge military defeat suffered by Saddam in Kuwait ultimately resulted in greater freedom for Iraqi Kurds but also heralded the beginning of another bloody episode in Iraqi history. This time the victims were the Shia of southern Iraq.

After 1991, the story of the Anfal could be told because it was possible to physically get to Iraqi Kurdistan. The rubble of thousands of destroyed villages was easy to see. As the Baathist security services fled Sulaymaniyah and Arbil, they left behind tons of documents that provided meticulous detail of the brutality meted out to opponents of the regime. No such evidence was available outside the Iraqi Kurdish safe haven. It was only after April 2003, when Saddam's regime had been toppled, that the evidence also began to be uncovered of the terrible abuse in the south of the country.

In June 2003, I watched as the bodies were dug out at the mass grave at Al Hillah, sometimes with bare hands in chaotic scenes, as relatives scrabbled through the dirt to find any remains of their lost loved ones. It appeared that everyone had known of the existence of the sites of these mass graves, but it was only now that they could go to them. The graves were filled with those slaughtered by the Baathists in the aftermath of the failed uprising at the end of the war in Kuwait. Thousands of bodies had been buried there. No one has yet been able to put an exact figure on the numbers killed. Sadly, however, the exhumations have presently been halted because of security problems.

The majority of those found in the graves around Al Hillah would have been members of the Iraqi Shia community. They had already suffered at the hands of Saddam in the previous decade. The main Shia political party, the Dawa, had been outlawed in March 1980, and membership of it was punishable by death.[4] The following month the spiritual leader of the Dawa, Muhammad Baqir al-Sadr, was executed. It was the first time in the history of the modern Middle East that a grand ayatollah had been executed.[5] Many more Shia were executed, while others fled into exile.

The Shia uprising at the end of the war with Kuwait was put down with great brutality. One haven of safety had been the vast expanse of the marshlands that straddle the border with Iran in the south of the country. These became Saddam's next target. New dams and canals were constructed that effectively drained the marshes. This construction was coupled with military action against the Marsh Arab population.

Iraqi security forces used napalm and other chemical weapons, shelled and burned villages, assassinated local leaders and other prominent community members, and abducted heads of families. Other tactics employed by Iraqi authorities included the deliberate contamination of water supplies, the poisoning of the fishing grounds, commercial blockades, the denial of aid and the refusal of access to aid agencies.[6]

It was a widespread misconception that abuses under Saddam's regime were largely historical by the time regime change had become a policy option. Sanctions and international pressure in the 1990s had not in fact ended the atrocities. The oppression of the marshland communities continued throughout the final years of the regime and only came to an end with its demise.

The same was true of the Arabization programs around Kirkuk. Kirkuk has always been a disputed city. Home to a large Kurdish community, it is surrounded by large oil reserves. Ever since the discovery of oil, the issue of who should run the city and own its mineral resources has been contested. The last years of Saddam's regime saw a concerted effort to alter the ethnic makeup of the city decisively. A UN High Commissioner for Refugees (UNHCR) report estimated that one hundred thousand had been displaced as a result of this policy. The report explained the rationale for their expulsion: "They were sent to Northern Iraq for several reasons, yet the majority of them were accused of having affiliations with the opposition parties in the north or abroad. Being a Kurd or Turkmen also sufficed as a reason."[7] This was a clear policy of ethnic cleansing, which was carried out until the regime was deposed in 2003.

## INTERNATIONAL RESPONSES TO HUMAN RIGHTS ABUSES AND GENOCIDE

One of the achievements of the late twentieth century was the development of an international community that is committed to the protection and development of human rights. A network of nongovernmental bodies has emerged that reports on abuses wherever they occur in the world. A body of law has been developed to protect those who face persecution. However, the laws are only effective if there is the necessary will to implement them.

In 1948, the Universal Declaration of Human Rights stated in clear language the rights of every person. The Universal Declaration is seen, rightly, as the cornerstone of human rights. Less widely celebrated is the resolution that the United Nations General Assembly had adopted the day before, the UN Convention on the Prevention and Punishment of the Crime of Genocide.

The UN Convention on Genocide built on the principles established by the Nuremberg Trial, which defined what constituted war crimes and crimes against humanity. Both crimes would be punishable under international law. In addition to these crimes, genocide was added per a UN General Assembly Resolution of 1946. The UN Convention on Genocide established a definition of what constituted genocide:

ARTICLE II

In the present Convention, genocide means any of the following acts committed with intent to destroy, in whole or in part, a national, ethnical, racial or religious group as such:

· Killing members of the group;
· Causing serious bodily or mental harm to members of the group;
· Deliberately inflicting on the group conditions of life calculated to bring about its physical destruction in whole or in part;
· Imposing measures intended to prevent births within the group;
· Forcibly transferring children of the group to another group.[8]

All states that signed up to the convention undertook to act against genocide, as defined in the agreement. The convention was signed but then largely ignored; it could not bypass the paralysis of the Cold War era. Acts of genocide occurred in Cambodia and Uganda, but they were ended by local action rather than international intervention from the UN.

The 1990s marked a shift in the debate both on human rights and on the responsibility of states to protect those whose rights were threatened, whether at home or abroad. The end of the Cold War offered the prospect of the UN Security Council acting in a way envisaged by its initial founding charter.[9] The number of peacekeeping missions approved by the UN Security Council increased significantly.

However, this greater commitment to intervention was not what would be remembered when the major disputes of the decade were reviewed. When the UN was called on to act over gross human rights abuses in Bosnia, Rwanda, and Kosovo, it was found wanting. The Convention on Genocide appeared to work against its stated ambition, as it became more important to avoid triggering any legal duty to act by using the word *genocide* than to act against the abuses. This tendency reached its nadir as the genocide in Rwanda unfolded, with Amnesty International reporting that the White House forbade the use of the word by its officials. "The rationale behind this policy was to first and foremost avoid negative public reactions triggered by the intervention in Somalia; but the second reason was to avoid the legal obligation to prevent genocide and to punish those responsible, as outlined in the Convention on Genocide."[10]

If the rapid slaughter in Rwanda did not warrant the description "genocide," there seemed little prospect of the atrocities in Iraq being labeled as such. Human Rights Watch tried, when it stated publicly in July 1993 that it considered the Anfal campaign to be an act of genocide.[11] The persecution of the communities of the Arab marshlands was condemned, but it was not labeled "genocide." This view emerged despite growing evidence of action by the Iraqi government that would fall under the convention definition of "deliberately inflicting on the group conditions of life calculated to bring about its physical destruction in whole or in part."

### INDICTING SADDAM

In an attempt to try to begin the process of bringing the perpetrators of human rights abuses in Iraq to justice, I helped to establish the organization INDICT. INDICT was set up to campaign for the prosecution of the leading members of Saddam's regime and to collect the evidence that would be used in such trials. As I said at the launch event of INDICT in the House of Commons, "Saddam Hussein should not continue to escape prosecution for his war crimes and crimes of genocide. It is essential that he should not cheat justice."[12]

The task of INDICT was helped by the creation of the safe haven for Iraqi Kurds, again after my report of having witnessed the Kurds fleeing from the helicopter gunships of Saddam Hussein on the mountains of Iran and Iraq in 1991. Now a part of Iraq offered evidence that could be collected and witnesses who could be interviewed. Investigations were not only restricted to those still inside Iraq, however; wherever witnesses were available, statements would be collected. At the end of the process, evidence had been collected in fifteen countries. The interviews were always conducted on the basis that the evidence given could eventually be used in a criminal court. INDICT always insisted on the highest standard for the evidence it gathered. It was told by an eminent international lawyer that, short of getting Saddam to sign a confession in his own blood, the organization had all the material needed to support his indictment.

INDICT illustrated how the politics of solidarity and human rights had developed by the mid-1990s. A body of law now existed that could be used to bring human rights abusers to court. INDICT aimed to do so. Slowly national courts were taking on international cases. We pursued cases in Norway, Switzerland, Belgium, and the UK.

However, the development of international law was slow. Even if the law existed, its application was dependent on institutions that had their own political agendas. In Britain, the then–attorney general referred the case against Tariq Aziz to Scotland Yard. This action effectively meant the case had been shelved. Requests to indict heads of state were not allowed under a new ruling of the International Court of Justice. Even though Slobodan Milošević was indicted for crimes against humanity while still head of state, the UN failed to do the same in the case of Iraq. I was told that moves by the United States and Britain were blocked at the UN Security Council by China, Russia, and France.

Now the argument has been overtaken by events. But I believe that the indictment of Saddam and leading members of his regime was a missed opportunity to bring pressure on Saddam and leaders of his regime to account for their human rights record. Indictments would have sent a clear message to the leadership of the regime that they stood accused of the most serious crimes by the international community. It would have been part of a process that would have stripped the regime in Iraq of the international credibility that it still craved right up to its demise. The evidence of the crimes that it committed against its own citizens would have been there for all to see. Indictments would have signaled that if Iraq wanted to be part of the international community again, these individuals would have to stand trial. Other leaders might also understand that they could not act with impunity, thereby preventing abuses elsewhere.

## NO OTHER WAY

INDICT ran out of time. The argument for prosecuting the regime was lost by default as the possibility of regime change moved ever closer. I had not wanted to see another war in Iraq. The Iraqi people had already suffered from nearly continuous conflict since Saddam had assumed his rule. The war with Iran, which cost a million lives, was followed by the Anfal campaign in Iraqi Kurdistan, and then the invasion of Kuwait was followed by the bloody repression of uprisings in the

south and north of the country. The 1990s continued with savage punishment meted out to anyone who threatened the regime.

When I visited Iraqi Kurdistan in the weeks before the conflict, I was
told of the credible intelligence received there of plans to attack the
population with chemical weapons. In the local markets, disposable
diapers were being sold as makeshift gas masks. People were already
leaving the towns for the safety of the countryside. The Iraqis I spoke to
told me that there could be no peace while Saddam was still in power
and that they could see no other way of being rid of him than through
foreign intervention.

It was impossible to argue against the logic of this opinion. If the
only way the Iraqis could be free of this vile dictatorship was through
external intervention, then I had to support it. It was the only option
left that offered the chance of a better future for the people I had
worked with for so long. When I returned to Britain and the debate in
the run-up to war, I repeated what the Iraqis had told me and voted for
the military action.

## AFTER SADDAM

I have considered the lead-up to war in some detail because I believe
that this history offers a revealing insight into the work of individuals
and groups that want to effect change for the better. It illustrates the
development of human rights law in the last quarter-century, the opportunities that this development provides, and its limitations. In contrast,
the aftermath of regime change in Iraq shows how much work needs to
be done in planning for the rebuilding of countries that have been
scarred by conflict.

## SOLIDARITY AND HUMAN RIGHTS

The original work of organizations such as CARDRI was based on the
distribution of information through whatever channels were available.
The work was supported by contributions from the labor movement,
the academic community, British and exiled Iraqi students, and the
wider Iraqi diaspora. Conferences were held, books and pamphlets
published. On a limited budget, a great deal could be achieved. The
strength of the organization was its ability to act as a focal point of solidarity for all Iraqis who had suffered at the hands of the regime.

However, the openings for solidarity organizations were limited. A group could lobby to change government policy or work to influence the policies of opposition parties. But it was dependent on others to act. The opportunity for a group itself to initiate change was limited.

The end of the Cold War did not bring about a new world order but resulted in new possibilities for the development of human rights. It became easier to refer to a universal set of human rights and have some prospect of these being protected by international legal institutions. By the end of the 1990s, international law had developed to such an extent that a head of state could finally be held to account for the crimes committed by his or her government, as the proceedings against Milošević and Augusto Pinochet illustrated. However, these actions also showed the difficulties of using the courts. INDICT was an organization that reflected this new era, with its emerging possibilities and very real limitations.

What was needed was the ability to somehow channel the collective resources of those involved with the solidarity movement with those campaigning to bring leading members of Saddam's regime to justice. Although many Iraqis and some others did support both organizations, I believe that those who hope to bring an end to atrocities and widespread abuse of human rights must give further consideration about how that can be done. Backing the indictment of Saddam and leading members of his regime could have been a way forward and may have even prevented the need for military force to be used to oust the regime. I will return to discuss these issues in further detail later.

## INSTITUTIONS AND HUMAN RIGHTS

In the span of a decade, Saddam Hussein launched two campaigns of genocide in Iraq. The international community did not act. Although we now live in a world where in theory it is not possible for a major human rights abuse to take place "in a faraway country of which we know little,"[13] a huge gulf between knowledge and action still exists. The Convention on Genocide has existed for more than half a century, yet it remains unused.

However, signs in recent years have indicated an acceptance of the need to rethink ideas of intervention in response to major human rights abuses. As Kofi Annan noted in early 2000, "If humanitarian intervention is, indeed, an unacceptable assault on sovereignty, how should we respond to a Rwanda, to a Srebrenica—to gross and systematic violations of human rights that offend every precept of our common humanity?"[14] What is required is the political will both to take action on genocide and to make the resources available to act quickly when genocide is reported. The case must be stated that the failure to act may be expedient in the short term but will have long-term consequences.

The failure to act against the Anfal campaign led directly to the humanitarian disaster of 1991, when thousands of Kurds perished on the mountains of Kurdistan, fleeing Saddam's helicopter gunships, which I witnessed myself.

The slow-motion destruction of the Arab marshlands, in the south of Iraq, resulted in large outflows of refugees to neighboring countries and a regional environmental disaster. The long-term costs of trying to right this destruction will be vast. Though I have myself witnessed the positive effects of the current reflooding of the area, it will be impossible to re-create that ecosystem completely and to expect all refugees to return. The effects of genocide and massive human rights abuses can no longer be contained within the borders of a single nation.

We need only look to Afghanistan to see that the failure of the poorest states can provide the ideal environment for future terrorists. Genocide destroys state structures; it creates regional crisis and instability. In a modern interdependent world, the ripples of instability spread further. Genocide is the responsibility of the entire world, and it is vital, therefore, that we create international institutions that can respond to prevent genocide.

Resources need to be provided so that forces are available to act on short notice. These forces should be credible, which will require the richer nations of the world to foot the bill. Although all nations must bear responsibility, the argument will be most relevant to the United States, as it is the United States, as the world's only superpower, that can currently provide the military capability to prevent genocide. The use of military force in humanitarian interventions, however, should always be a final step, when all other avenues of actions have been exhausted. Once military forces have been deployed, it is vital that they act in accordance with the existing Geneva Conventions on warfare and postconflict occupation.

## LEARNING THE LESSONS OF INTERVENTION

If a nation pursues military action in the name of humanitarianism, it must ensure that the actions of its forces conform to humanitarian and human rights law. This must be emphasized throughout military training. Sadly, this has not always happened in postconflict Iraq. Individuals within a force that brought liberation from a vile dictatorship have been found guilty of the abuse and torture of prisoners.

For those of us who argued for the intervention in Iraq on humanitarian grounds, the abuse of Iraqi prisoners by their Coalition captors has been a sickening revelation. In my role as Special Envoy to the Prime Minister on Human Rights in Iraq, I had been investigating a single case of abuse from the summer of 2003. I hoped that it was an isolated incident, but in time it became apparent that it was illustrative of a wider systemic failure in the treatment of those detained by the Coalition forces. The abuse scandal was just the worst manifestation of the disregard for detainees' rights.

The disregard for the rights of detainees not only offended human rights sensibilities but also represented a strategic failing. Images of abuse spread quickly. Immediately the job of policing Iraq became more difficult for Coalition forces. Those who were seeking recruits to fight the Coalition now had the propaganda they needed.

It could be argued that the care of prisoners is not as important as achieving other, more tangible military objectives. This argument not only is morally defective but also overlooks the changes that occurred in the last decades of the twentieth century. A war is fought and won as much in the media as on the battlefield. Technology has advanced quickly: cheap digital cameras are widely available, and images can be sent around the world in seconds. Whereas in the past it may have been possible to hide abuse, such secrecy today is no longer an option.

Protection for those deprived of their liberty in the aftermath of a conflict is enshrined in the 1949 Geneva Conventions. The importance of applying these rules cannot be overstated. If our ambition is to replace dictatorship with democracy and respect for human rights, we have to be seen to uphold the high standards of the Geneva Conventions.

## THE RULE OF LAW

If we seek to rule through law, it is imperative that planning to have those systems in place after intervention should be a priority. This scenario initially was not the case in Iraq, and the collapse of the old judicial system only added to the problems that the Coalition faced in administering justice.

Central to rebuilding the Iraqi judiciary will be the handling of the trial of the members of the former regime. These trials are an opportunity to demonstrate how society has changed. There is, however, a tension inherent in setting up the legal process: Iraqis want to prove to the world that they are capable of staging a trial of this magnitude, whereas the international community is concerned that a trial in Iraq might not be regarded as fair.

There is an urgent need to find a way through this tension. Saddam Hussein's trial will have an enormous impact both inside and outside Iraq. It will be an opportunity for the record of Saddam's reign to be laid bare before the world, particularly to the Middle East. The pivotal nature of the trial highlights the importance of having the truth told, even when reconciliation may be some way off. Providing the necessary resources for the process should therefore be a seen as a priority.

## RETHINKING THE DEBATE ON IRAQ

The Iraq debate still dominates British politics. It will have a significant impact on the future policy of British governments. It has also influenced Britain's relationships with European neighbors and will impact the development of international institutions.

The most striking thing about the debate in Britain, past and present, is how little of it has to do with conditions within Iraq or the views of Iraqis. The debate in Britain has become a vehicle for other concerns, most of them inward looking. The debate prior to war, which contained many divergent views on the reasons for intervention in Iraq, has in time been narrowed down to a single argument about weapons of mass destruction, centered on how government worked and how it chose to disseminate information. Subsequently, the message in much of the media has been reduced to a convenient shorthand: the government lied.

As this debate has evolved, what is noticeable is the absence of Iraqi voices. Those whom I heard in Iraqi Kurdistan before the war believed that attacks with chemical weapons were imminent. If Saddam deceived us, it appears that he had also deceived those closer to him. This suggests that the issue of whether or not Saddam was in possession of weapons of mass destruction was less clear-cut than hindsight may have us believe.

The debate was also characterized in some quarters by a knee-jerk rejection of any policy coming from the United States. Central to this argument was the assertion that the Bush administration was the most right-wing in recent history, controlled by a sinister grouping of neo-cons. Any engagement with the substance of the Bush administration's policies toward Iraq was not necessary after such pronouncements: it was guilt by association.

A year later, a deep ambivalence persists toward the development of democracy in Iraq. Iraqi politicians are dismissed either as puppets or exiles without any real connection to the Iraqi people.

Having known and worked with the opposition to Saddam for more than two decades, I find the description of brave individuals as "puppets" deeply offensive. Interim prime minister Iyad Allawi was nearly killed in 1978 in the UK when he was attacked by a Baathist assassin with an axe. The deputy prime minister, Barham Salih, was imprisoned at the age of sixteen for his political activities. The deputy foreign minister, Hamid al-Bayati, was imprisoned in Abu Ghraib and had five members of his family killed by Saddam's regime. Eight thousand members of Foreign Minister Hoshyar Zebari's family clan disappeared in 1983 and have never been seen since.

The difficulty facing the Iraqi interim government (IIG) as Iraq moves toward elections in 2005 will be dealing with the continuing security challenge without reverting to a repressive form of government. I met with ministers a month or so after the handover in July 2004. They were aware of the balancing act that will be required but made it clear that in the short term, the restoration of security had to be the over-whelming priority. In political terms, there is no doubt the IIG will be under considerable pressure to take whatever measures are deemed nec-essary to end the violence.

Given, however, that a human rights ethos and the rule of law have not yet taken root in Iraq and that the security situation is unlikely to improve for some time, the IIG must continue to explain the safeguards being put in place to protect fundamental rights and the need for any particular derogations. In addition, those Iraqis working to uphold and promote basic human rights require ongoing assistance.

Routine calls are made to "end the occupation" without any clear statement of what would follow. The internationalism that informed earlier struggles and was strengthened by fraternal links through the labor and trade union movement is now replaced by simplistic slogans. We need to re-create the bonds of internationalism if we are to move toward a more informed domestic debate.

This renewed internationalism will also be required to push through the reform of international institutions if they are to deliver justice in the future. An energetic debate needs to take place at national and international levels to make this happen.

At a national level, there needs to be agreement that it is a desirable objective to work toward a reformed UN and also to provide the funding to make it possible to establish standing forces that can be called on for speedy interventions when required. This approach must be combined with building political support for intervention. The events of 9/11 made the case for the failed state being a threat to global security, but I would also argue that we have a basic moral responsibility, as citizens of the world, to protect those at risk.

At an international level, there needs to be a commitment to reconsider how the UN works. This view is apparent on both sides of the debate. The UN is often criticized for its failure to act, while simultaneously being denied the resources to allow it to work effectively. However, the model of state sovereignty enshrined in the UN Charter is, at times, an obstacle to effective action against human rights abuses. The work of the International Commission on Intervention and State Sovereignty[15] is a welcome sign of a new debate emerging on how ideas of state sovereignty can be recast in our interdependent world. In this new doctrine, state sovereignty also carries responsibilities, as this summary of the commission's work illustrates:

> That the General Assembly adopt a draft declaratory resolution embodying the basic principles of the responsibility to protect, and containing four basic elements:
>
> · an affirmation of the idea of sovereignty as responsibility;
> · an assertion of the threefold responsibility of the international community of state—to prevent, to react and rebuild—when faced with human protection claims in states that are either unable or unwilling to discharge their responsibility to protect;
> · a definition of the threshold (large scale loss of life or ethnic cleansing, actual or apprehended) which human protection claims must meet if they are to justify military intervention; and
> · an articulation of the precautionary principles (right intention, last resort, proportional means and reasonable prospects) that must be observed when military force is used for human protection purposes.[16]

These reforms will not be limited to the UN alone; other international institutions, governmental and nongovernmental, have a part to play in responding to major human rights abuses. Of course, I applaud the efforts of those who helped in getting the International Criminal Court set up; I myself campaigned for it. Its success, however, will depend, as ever, on political will and adequate resourcing. The United States' acceptance of the International Criminal Court would also be a major step forward in developing international law in the human rights area.

## CONCLUSION

Returning to the topic of Iraq, we should reflect on where we are now, more than two years after the fall of a brutal dictatorship. It is a period that has seen progress in rebuilding the shattered infrastructure of a country, both its physical network and its civil society. At the end of a difficult period, a political process is still moving forward, toward a new constitution that will be forged democratically. This process edges forward despite the many dire predictions of civil war, the numerous bloody terrorist attacks that have attempted to trigger it, and the mistakes of the Coalition. That the process is ongoing is testimony to the determination and optimism of the vast majority of Iraqis.

Iraqis now have freedom of speech and association. A new civil society is emerging in the shape of political parties, human rights organizations, and pressure groups of all descriptions. The media are flourishing as never before.

Awaiting trial are leading members of the Baathist regime. In the months to come, they will have to face justice, a privilege that was denied to their victims. The trials will allow the true story of those years to be told, to both the Iraqi people and the rest of the world. I have also been told that the evidence that INDICT has collected from hundreds of those who suffered at the hands of Saddam's regime will be used in these trials.

I began this chapter recalling a student asking me why it had taken the international community so long to act against Saddam. My answer touches on the history of the solidarity movement that I was part of. We should reconsider that solidarity again. The international community, at different times and through different agencies, failed the Iraqi people during the years of dictatorship. We should have dealt effectively with Saddam sooner. But now that he has been removed, we need to commit ourselves to working with the Iraqi people, to build a new society, based on the ideals of democracy and human rights. And we need to stay the course to enable them to succeed.

# NOTES

I would like to thank Robert Smith for his valuable help in preparing this chapter.

1. Kanan Makiya, *Cruelty and Silence* (London: Penguin, 1994), 167.
2. Ibid.
3. Ibid., 168.
4. F. A. Jabar, *The Shi'ite Movement in Iraq* (London: Saqi Books, 2003), 233.
5. Ibid., 234.
6. J. Fawcett and V. Tanner, *The Internally Displaced People of Iraq*, The Brookings Institution–SAIS Project on Internal Displacement (Washington, D.C.: Brookings Institution, October 2002), 31, quoting numerous reports from the Special Rapporteur of the Commission on Human Rights from 1992 to 2001 and Christopher Mitchell, "Assault on the Marshlands," in *Iraqi Marshlands Prospects* (London: International Charitable Foundation, May 21, 2001).
7. UNHCR/African Centre for the Constructive Resolution of Disputes (ACCORD) Report, November 14, 2000.
8. UN Convention on the Prevention and Punishment of the Crime of Genocide, December 9, 1948.
9. International Commission on Intervention and State Sovereignty (ICISS), *The Responsibility to Protect* (Ottawa: International Development Research Centre, 2001), 7.
10. K. J. Campbell, *Genocide and the Global Village* (New York: Palgrave, 2001), 78, quoting Amnesty International, USA, "The World Fails to Respond," in *Forsaken Cries: The Story of Rwanda*, videotape (New York: Author, 1997).
11. Human Rights Watch, "Genocide in Iraq: The Anfal Campaign against the Kurds," July 1993, http://www.hrw.org/reports/1993/iraqanfal/ (accessed January 22, 2005).
12. INDICT press release, January 15, 1997.
13. Neville Chamberlain speaking about Czechoslovakia in 1938.
14. ICISS, *The Responsibility to Protect*, 2, quoting Kofi Annan in his 2000 Millennium Report to the General Assembly.
15. ICISS, *The Responsibility to Protect*.
16. Ibid., 74.

# PART SIX

# LIBERAL STATESMANSHIP

# 23

# Full Statement to the House of Commons, 18 March 2003

TONY BLAIR

beg to move the motion standing on the order paper in my name and those of my Right Honorable friends.

At the outset I say: it is right that this House debate this issue and pass judgment. That is the democracy that is our right but that others struggle for in vain. And again I say: I do not disrespect the views of those in opposition to mine.

This is a tough choice. But it is also a stark one: to stand British troops down and turn back; or to hold firm to the course we have set. I believe we must hold firm. The question most often posed is not why does it matter? But: why does it matter so much? Here we are: the Government with its most serious test, its majority at risk, the first Cabinet resignation over an issue of policy. The main parties divided.

People who agree on everything else, disagree on this and likewise, those who never agree on anything, finding common cause. The country and Parliament reflect each other: a debate that, as time has gone on has become less bitter but not less grave.

So: why does it matter so much? Because the outcome of this issue will now determine more than the fate of the Iraqi regime and more than the future of the Iraqi people, for so long brutalized by Saddam. It will determine the way Britain and the world confront the central security threat of the 21st century; the development of the UN; the relationship between Europe and the US; the relations within the EU and the way the US engages with the rest of the world. It will determine the pattern of international politics for the next generation.

But first, Iraq and its WMD [weapons of mass destruction].

In April 1991, after the Gulf War Iraq was given 15 days to provide a full and final declaration of all its WMD. Saddam had used the weapons against Iran, against his own people, causing thousands of deaths. He had had plans to use them against allied forces. It became clear after the Gulf War that the WMD ambitions of Iraq were far more extensive than hitherto thought. This issue was identified by the UN as one for urgent remedy. UNSCOM, the weapons inspection team, was set up. They were expected to complete their task following the declaration at the end of April 1991.

The declaration when it came was false—a blanket denial of the program, other than in a very tentative form. So the 12 year game began. The inspectors probed. Finally in March 1992, Iraq admitted it had previously undeclared WMD but said it had destroyed them.

It gave another full and final declaration. Again the inspectors probed but found little. In October 1994, Iraq stopped co-operating with UNSCOM altogether. Military action was threatened. Inspections resumed.

In March 1995, in an effort to rid Iraq of the inspectors, a further full and final declaration of WMD was made. By July 1995, Iraq was forced to admit that too was false.

In August they provided yet another full and final declaration.

Then, a week later, Saddam's son-in-law, Hussein Kamal, defected to Jordan. He disclosed a far more extensive BW program and for the first time said Iraq had weaponized the program; something Saddam had always strenuously denied. All this had been happening whilst the inspectors were in Iraq. Kamal also revealed Iraq's crash program to produce a nuclear weapon in 1990. Iraq was forced then to release documents which showed just how extensive those programs were.

In November 1995, Jordan intercepted prohibited components for missiles that could be used for WMD. In June 1996, a further full and final declaration was made. That too turned out to be false. In June 1997, inspectors were barred from specific sites. In September 1997, another full and final declaration was made. Also false. Meanwhile the inspectors discovered VX nerve agent production equipment, something always denied by the Iraqis.

In October 1997, the US and the UK threatened military action if Iraq refused to comply with the inspectors. But obstruction continued. Finally, under threat of action, in February 1998, Kofi Annan went to Baghdad and negotiated a memorandum with Saddam to allow inspections to continue. They did. For a few months. In August, co-operation was suspended. In December the inspectors left. Their final report is a withering indictment of Saddam's lies, deception and obstruction, with large quantities of WMD remained unaccounted for. The US and the UK then, in December 1998, undertook Desert Fox, a targeted bombing campaign to degrade as much of the Iraqi WMD facilities as we could.

In 1999, a new inspections team, UNMOVIC, was set up. But Saddam refused to allow them to enter Iraq. So there they stayed, in limbo, until after Resolution 1441 when last November they were allowed to return. What is the claim of Saddam today? Why, exactly the same claim as before: that he has no WMD. Indeed we are asked to believe that after seven years of obstruction and non-compliance finally resulting in the inspectors leaving in 1998, seven years in which he hid his program, built it up even whilst inspection teams were in Iraq, that after they left he then voluntarily decided to do what he had consistently refused to do under coercion.

When the inspectors left in 1998, they left unaccounted for: 10 thousand litres of anthrax, a far-reaching VX nerve agent program, up to 6,500 chemical munitions, at least 80 tonnes of mustard gas, possibly more than ten times that amount unquantifiable amounts of sarin, botulinum toxin and a host of other biological poisons, an entire Scud missile program.

We are now seriously asked to accept that in the last few years, contrary to all history, contrary to all intelligence, he decided unilaterally to destroy the weapons. Such a claim is palpably absurd.

1441 is a very clear Resolution. It lays down a final opportunity for Saddam to disarm. It rehearses the fact that he has been, for years in material breach of 17 separate UN Resolutions. It says that this time compliance must be full, unconditional and immediate. The first step is a full and final declaration of all WMD to be given on 8 December. I won't to go through all the events since then—the House is familiar with them—but this much is accepted by all members of the UNSC.

The 8 December declaration is false. That in itself is a material breach. Iraq has made some concessions to co-operation but no-one disputes it is not fully co-operating. Iraq continues to deny it has any WMD, though no serious intelligence service anywhere in the world believes them.

On 7 March, the inspectors published a remarkable document. It is 173 pages long, detailing all the unanswered questions about Iraq's WMD. It lists 29 different areas where they have been unable to obtain information. For example, on VX it says: "Documentation available to UNMOVIC suggests that Iraq at least had had far reaching plans to weaponize VX. . . . Mustard constituted an important part (about 70%) of Iraq's CW arsenal . . . 550 mustard filled shells and up to 450 mustard filled aerial bombs unaccounted for . . . additional uncertainty with respect of 6526 aerial bombs, corresponding to approximately 1000 tonnes of agent, predominantly mustard.

"Based on unaccounted for growth media, Iraq's potential production of anthrax could have been in the range of about 15,000 to 25,000 litres. . . . Based on all the available evidence, the strong presumption is that about 10,000 litres of anthrax was not destroyed and may still exist." On this basis, had we meant what we said in Resolution 1441, the Security Council should have convened and condemned Iraq as in material breach. What is perfectly clear is that Saddam is playing the same old games in the same old way. Yes, there are concessions. But no fundamental change of heart or mind.

But the inspectors indicated there was at least some co-operation; and the world rightly hesitated over war. We therefore approached a second Resolution in this way. We laid down an ultimatum calling upon Saddam to come into line with Resolution 1441 or be in material breach. Not an unreasonable proposition, given the history. But still countries hesitated: how do we know how to judge full co-operation? We then worked on a further compromise. We consulted the inspectors and drew up five tests based on the document they published on 7 March. Tests like interviews with 30 scientists outside of Iraq; production of the anthrax or documentation showing its destruction. The inspectors added another test: that Saddam should publicly call on Iraqis to co-operate with them.

So we constructed this framework: that Saddam should be given a specified time to fulfil all six tests to show full co-operation; that if he did so the inspectors could then set out a forward work program and that if he failed to do so, action would follow. So clear benchmarks;

plus a clear ultimatum. I defy anyone to describe that as an unreasonable position. Last Monday, we were getting somewhere with it. We very nearly had majority agreement and I thank the Chilean President particularly for the constructive way he approached the issue. There were debates about the length of the ultimatum. But the basic construct was gathering support.

Then, on Monday night, France said it would veto a second Resolution whatever the circumstances. Then France denounced the six tests. Later that day, Iraq rejected them. Still, we continued to negotiate. Last Friday, France said they could not accept any ultimatum. On Monday, we made final efforts to secure agreement. But they remain utterly opposed to anything which lays down an ultimatum authorizing action in the event of non-compliance by Saddam.

Just consider the position we are asked to adopt. Those on the Security Council opposed to us say they want Saddam to disarm but will not countenance any new Resolution that authorizes force in the event of non-compliance. That is their position. No to any ultimatum; no to any Resolution that stipulates that failure to comply will lead to military action. So we must demand he disarm but relinquish any concept of a threat if he doesn't. From December 1998 to December 2002, no UN inspector was allowed to inspect anything in Iraq. For four years, not a thing. What changed his mind? The threat of force. From December to January and then from January through to February, concessions were made. What changed his mind?

The threat of force.

And what makes him now issue invitations to the inspectors, discover documents he said he never had, produce evidence of weapons supposed to be non-existent, destroy missiles he said he would keep? The imminence of force. The only persuasive power to which he responds is 250,000 allied troops on his doorstep. And yet when that fact is so obvious that it is staring us in the face, we are told that any Resolution that authorizes force will be vetoed.

Not just opposed. Vetoed. Blocked. The way ahead was so clear. It was for the UN to pass a second Resolution setting out benchmarks for compliance; with an ultimatum that if they were ignored, action would follow. The tragedy is that had such a Resolution issued, he might just have complied. Because the only route to peace with someone like Saddam Hussein is diplomacy backed by force.

Yet the moment we proposed the benchmarks, canvassed support for an ultimatum, there was an immediate recourse to the language of the veto. And now the world has to learn the lesson all over again that weakness in the face of a threat from a tyrant, is the surest way not to peace but to war.

Looking back over 12 years, we have been victims of our own desire to placate the implacable, to persuade towards reason the utterly unreasonable, to hope that there was some genuine intent to do good in a regime whose mind is in fact evil. Now the very length of time counts against us. You've waited 12 years. Why not wait a little longer?

And indeed we have. 1441 gave a final opportunity. The first test was the 8th of December. He failed it. But still we waited. Until the 27th of January, the first inspection report that showed the absence of full co-operation. Another breach. And still we waited.

Until the 14th of February and then the 28th of February with concessions, according to the old familiar routine, tossed to us to whet our appetite for hope and further waiting. But still no-one, not the inspectors nor any member of the Security Council, not any half-way rational observer, believes Saddam is co-operating fully or unconditionally or immediately.

Our fault has not been impatience. The truth is our patience should have been exhausted weeks and months and years ago. Even now, when if the world united and gave him an ultimatum: comply or face forcible disarmament, he might just do it, the world hesitates and in that hesitation he senses the weakness and therefore continues to defy.

What would any tyrannical regime possessing WMD think viewing the history of the world's diplomatic dance with Saddam? That our capacity to pass firm resolutions is only matched by our feebleness in implementing them. That is why this indulgence has to stop. Because it is dangerous. It is dangerous if such regimes disbelieve us. Dangerous if they think they can use our weakness, our hesitation, even the natural urges of our democracy towards peace, against us. Dangerous because one day they will mistake our innate revulsion against war for permanent incapacity; when in fact, pushed to the limit, we will act. But then when we act, after years of pretence, the action will have to be harder, bigger, more total in its impact. Iraq is not the only regime with WMD. But back away now from this confrontation and future conflicts will be infinitely worse and more devastating.

But, of course, in a sense, any fair observer does not really dispute that Iraq is in breach and that 1441 implies action in such circumstances. The real problem is that, underneath, people dispute that Iraq is a threat; dispute the link between terrorism and WMD; dispute the whole basis of our assertion that the two together constitute a fundamental assault on our way of life.

There are glib and sometimes foolish comparisons with the 1930s. No-one here is an appeaser. But the only relevant point of analogy is that with history, we know what happened. We can look back and say: there's the time; that was the moment; for example, when Czechoslovakia was swallowed up by the Nazis—that's when we should have acted. But it wasn't clear at the time. In fact at the time, many people thought such a fear fanciful. Worse, put forward in bad faith by warmongers.

Listen to this editorial—from a paper I'm pleased to say with a different position today—but written in late 1938 after Munich when by now, you would have thought the world was tumultuous in its desire to act.

"Be glad in your hearts. Give thanks to your God. People of Britain, your children are safe. Your husbands and your sons will not march to war. Peace is a victory for all mankind. And now let us go back to our own affairs. We have had enough of those menaces, conjured up from the Continent to confuse us." Naturally should Hitler appear again in the same form, we would know what to do. But the point is that history doesn't declare the future to us so plainly. Each time is different and the present must be judged without the benefit of hindsight.

So let me explain the nature of this threat as I see it. The threat today is not that of the 1930s. It's not big powers going to war with each other. The ravages which fundamentalist political ideology inflicted on the 20th century are memories. The Cold War is over. Europe is at peace, if not always diplomatically. But the world is ever more interdependent. Stock markets and economies rise and fall together. Confidence is the key to prosperity. Insecurity spreads like contagion. So people crave stability and order. The threat is chaos. And there are two begetters of chaos. Tyrannical regimes with WMD and extreme terrorist groups who profess a perverted and false view of Islam.

Let me tell the House what I know. I know that there are some countries or groups within countries that are proliferating and trading in WMD, especially nuclear weapons technology. I know there are companies, individuals, some former scientists on nuclear weapons programs, selling their equipment or expertise. I know there are several countries—mostly dictatorships with highly repressive regimes—desperately trying to acquire chemical weapons, biological weapons or, in particular, nuclear weapons capability. Some of these countries are now a short time away from having a serviceable nuclear weapon. This activity is not diminishing. It is increasing.

We all know that there are terrorist cells now operating in most major countries. Just as in the last two years, around 20 different nations have suffered serious terrorist outrages. Thousands have died in them. The purpose of terrorism lies not just in the violent act itself. It is in producing terror. It sets out to inflame, to divide, to produce consequences which they then use to justify further terror. Round the world it now poisons the chances of political progress: in the Middle East; in Kashmir; in Chechnya; in Africa. The removal of the Taliban in Afghanistan dealt it a blow. But it has not gone away. And these two threats have different motives and different origins but they share one basic common view: they detest the freedom, democracy and tolerance that are the hallmarks of our way of life. At the moment, I accept that association between them is loose. But it is hardening. And the possibility of the two coming together—of terrorist groups in possession of WMD, even of a so-called dirty radiological bomb is now, in my judgment, a real and present danger. And let us recall: what was shocking about 11 September was not just the slaughter of the innocent; but the knowledge that had the terrorists been able to, there would have been not 3,000 innocent dead, but 30,000 or 300,000 and the more the suffering, the greater the terrorists' rejoicing.

Three kilograms of VX from a rocket launcher would contaminate a quarter of a square kilometre of a city. Millions of lethal doses are contained in one litre of anthrax. 10,000 litres are unaccounted for. 11 September has changed the psychology of America. It should have changed the psychology of the world.

Of course Iraq is not the only part of this threat. But it is the test of whether we treat the threat seriously. Faced with it, the world should unite. The UN should be the focus, both of diplomacy and of action. That is what 1441 said. That was the deal. And I say to you to break it now, to will the ends but not the means that would do more damage in the long term to the UN than any other course. To fall back into the lassitude of the last 12 years, to talk, to discuss, to debate but never act; to declare our will but not enforce it; to combine strong language with weak intentions, a worse outcome than never speaking at all. And then, when the threat returns from Iraq or elsewhere, who will believe us? What price our credibility with the next tyrant? No wonder Japan and South Korea, next to North Korea, has issued such strong statements of support.

I have come to the conclusion after much reluctance that the greater danger to the UN is inaction: that to pass Resolution 1441 and then refuse to enforce it would do the most deadly damage to the UN's future strength, confirming it as an instrument of diplomacy but not of action, forcing nations down the very unilateralist path we wish to avoid. But there will be, in any event, no sound future for the UN, no guarantee against the repetition of these events, unless we recognize the urgent need for a political agenda we can unite upon.

What we have witnessed is indeed the consequence of Europe and the United States dividing from each other. Not all of Europe—Spain, Italy, Holland, Denmark, Portugal—have all strongly supported us. And not a majority of Europe if we include, as we should, Europe's new members who will accede next year, all 10 of whom have been in our support. But the paralysis of the UN has been born out of the division there is. And at the heart of it has been the concept of a world in which there are rival poles of power. The US and its allies in one corner. France, Germany, Russia and its allies in the other. I do not believe that all of these nations intend such an outcome. But that is what now faces us.

I believe such a vision to be misguided and profoundly dangerous. I know why it arises. There is resentment of US predominance. There is fear of US unilateralism. People ask: do the US listen to us and our preoccupations? And there is perhaps a lack of full understanding of US preoccupations after 11th September. I know all of this. But the way to deal with it is not rivalry but partnership. Partners are not servants but neither are they rivals. I tell you what Europe should have said last September to the US. With one voice it should have said: we understand your strategic anxiety over terrorism and WMD and we will help you meet it. We will mean what we say in any UN Resolution we pass and will back it with action if Saddam fails to disarm voluntarily; but in return we ask two things of you: that the US should choose the UN path and you should recognize the fundamental overriding importance of re-starting the MEPP [Middle East peace process], which we will hold you to.

I do not believe there is any other issue with the same power to re-unite the world community than progress on the issues of Israel and Palestine. Of course there is cynicism about recent announcements. But the US is now committed, and, I believe genuinely, to the Roadmap for Peace, designed in consultation with the UN. It will now be presented to the parties as Abu Mazen is confirmed in office, hopefully today. All of us are now signed up to its vision: a state of Israel, recognized and accepted by all the world, and a viable Palestinian state. And that should be part of a larger global agenda. On poverty and sustainable development. On democracy and human rights. On the good governance of nations.

That is why what happens after any conflict in Iraq is of such critical significance. Here again there is a chance to unify around the UN. Let me make it clear. There should be a new UN Resolution following any conflict providing not just for humanitarian help but also for the administration and governance of Iraq. That must now be done under proper UN authorization. It should protect totally the territorial integrity of Iraq. And let the oil revenues—which people falsely claim we want to seize—be put in a trust fund for the Iraqi people administered through the UN.

And let the future government of Iraq be given the chance to begin the process of uniting the nation's disparate groups, on a democratic basis, respecting human rights, as indeed the fledgling democracy in Northern Iraq—protected from Saddam for 12 years by British and American pilots in the No Fly Zone—has done so remarkably. And the moment that a new government is in place—willing to disarm Iraq of WMD—for which its people have no need or purpose—then let sanctions be lifted in their entirety. I have never put our justification for action as regime change. We have to act within the terms set out in Resolution 1441.

That is our legal base. But it is the reason, I say frankly, why if we do act we should do so with a clear conscience and strong heart. I accept fully that those opposed to this course of action share my detestation of Saddam. Who could not? Iraq is a wealthy country that in 1978, the year before Saddam seized power, was richer than Portugal or Malaysia. Today it is impoverished, 60% of its population dependent on Food Aid. Thousands of children die needlessly every year from lack of food and medicine. Four million people out of a population of just over 20 million are in exile. The brutality of the repression—the death and torture camps, the barbaric prisons for political opponents, the routine beatings for anyone or their families suspected of disloyalty—are well documented. Just last week, someone slandering Saddam was tied to a lamp post in a street in Baghdad, his tongue cut out, mutilated and left to bleed to death, as a warning to others.

I recall a few weeks ago talking to an Iraqi exile and saying to her that I understood how grim it must be under the lash of Saddam. "But you don't," she replied. "You cannot. You do not know what it is like to live in perpetual fear." And she is right. We take our freedom for granted. But imagine not to be able to speak or discuss or debate or even question the society you live in. To see friends and family taken away and never daring to complain. To suffer the humility of failing courage in face of pitiless terror. That is how the Iraqi people live. Leave Saddam in place and that is how they will continue to live.

We must face the consequences of the actions we advocate. For me, that means all the dangers of war. But for others, opposed to this course, it means—let us be clear—that the Iraqi people, whose only true hope of liberation lies in the removal of Saddam, for them, the darkness will close back over them again; and he will be free to take his revenge upon those he must know wish him gone. And if this House now demands that at this moment, faced with this threat from this regime, that British troops are pulled back, that we turn away at the point of reckoning, and that is what it means—what then? What will Saddam feel? Strengthened beyond measure. What will the other states who tyrannize their people, the terrorists who threaten our existence, what will they take from that? That the will confronting them is decaying and feeble. Who will celebrate and who will weep? And if our plea is for America to work with others, to be good as well as powerful allies, will our retreat make them multilateralist? Or will it not rather be the biggest impulse to unilateralism there could ever be. And what of the UN and the future of Iraq and the MEPP, devoid of our influence, stripped of our insistence?

This House wanted this decision. Well, it has it. Those are the choices. And in this dilemma, no choice is perfect, no cause ideal. But on this decision hangs the fate of many things. Of whether we summon the strength to recognize this global challenge of the 21st century and meet it. Of the Iraqi people, groaning under years of dictatorship. Of our armed forces—brave men and women of whom we can feel proud, whose morale is high and whose purpose is clear. Of the institutions and alliances that will shape our world for years to come.

## NOTE

# 24

## The Threat of Global Terrorism

TONY BLAIR

N o decision I have ever made in politics has been as divisive as the
decision to go to war to in Iraq. It remains deeply divisive today.
I know a large part of the public want to move on. Rightly they
say the government should concentrate on the issues that elected us in
1997: the economy, jobs, living standards, health, education, crime. I
share that view, and we are.

But I know too that the nature of this issue over Iraq, stirring such
bitter emotions as it does, can't just be swept away as ill-fitting the preoccupations of the man and woman on the street. This is not simply
because of the gravity of war; or the continued engagement of British
troops and civilians in Iraq; or even because of reflections made on the
integrity of the Prime Minister. It is because it was in March 2003 and
remains my fervent view that the nature of the global threat we face in
Britain and round the world is real and existential, and it is the task of
leadership to expose it and fight it, whatever the political cost; and that
the true danger is not to any single politician's reputation, but to our
country if we now ignore this threat or erase it from the agenda in
embarrassment at the difficulties it causes.

In truth, the fundamental source of division over Iraq is not over
issues of trust or integrity, though some insist on trying to translate it

into that. Each week brings a fresh attempt to get a new angle that can prove it was all a gigantic conspiracy. We have had three inquiries, including the one by Lord Hutton conducted over six months, with more openness by government than any such inquiry in history, that have affirmed there was no attempt to falsify intelligence in the dossier of September 2002, but rather that it was indeed an accurate summary of that intelligence.

We have seen one element—intelligence about some WMD [weapons of mass destruction] being ready for use in 45 minutes—elevated into virtually the one fact that persuaded the nation into war. This intelligence was mentioned by me once in my statement to the House of Commons on 24 September and not mentioned by me again in any debate. It was mentioned by no one in the crucial debate on 18 March 2003. In the period from 24 September to 29 May, the date of the BBC broadcast on it, it was raised twice in almost 40,000 written parliamentary questions in the House of Commons; and not once in almost 5,000 oral questions. Neither was it remotely the basis for the claim that Saddam had strategic as well as battlefield WMD. That was dealt with in a different part of the dossier; and though the Iraq Survey Group have indeed not found stockpiles of weapons, they have uncovered much evidence about Saddam's program to develop long-range strategic missiles in breach of U.N. rules.

It is said we claimed Iraq was an imminent threat to Britain and was preparing to attack us. In fact this is what I said prior to the war on 24 September 2002: "Why now? People ask. I agree I cannot say that this month or next, even this year or next he will use his weapons."

Then, for example, in January 2003 in my press conference I said: "And I tell you honestly what my fear is, my fear is that we wake up one day and we find either that one of these dictatorial states has used weapons of mass destruction—and Iraq has done so in the past—and we get sucked into a conflict, with all the devastation that would cause; or alternatively these weapons, which are being traded right round the world at the moment, fall into the hands of these terrorist groups, these fanatics who will stop at absolutely nothing to cause death and destruction on a mass scale. Now that is what I have to worry about. And I understand of course why people think it is a very remote threat and it is far away and why does it bother us. Now I simply say to you, it is a matter of time unless we act and take a stand before terrorism and weapons of mass destruction come together, and I regard them as two sides of the same coin."

The truth is, as was abundantly plain in the motion before the House of Commons on 18 March, we went to war to enforce compliance with U.N. resolutions. Had we believed Iraq was an imminent direct threat to Britain, we would have taken action in September 2002; we would not have gone to the U.N. Instead, we spent October and November in the U.N. negotiating U.N. Resolution 1441. We then spent almost four months trying to implement it.

Actually, it is now apparent from the Survey Group that Iraq was indeed in breach of U.N. Resolution 1441. It did not disclose laboratories and facilities it should have; nor the teams of scientists kept together to retain their WMD, including nuclear expertise; nor its continuing research relevant to CW and BW [chemical and biological weapons]. As Dr. Kay, the former head of the ISG [International Survey Group] who is now quoted as a critic of the war, has said: "Iraq was in clear violation of the terms of Resolution 1441." And "I actually think this [Iraq] may be one of those cases where it was even more dangerous than we thought."

Then, most recently is the attempt to cast doubt on the attorney general's legal opinion. He said the war was lawful. He published a statement on the legal advice. It is said this opinion is disputed. Of course it is. It was disputed in March 2003. It is today. The lawyers continue to divide over it—with their legal opinions bearing a remarkable similarity to their political view of the war.

But let's be clear. Once this row dies down, another will take its place and then another and then another.

All of it in the end is an elaborate smokescreen to prevent us seeing the real issue: which is not a matter of trust but of judgment.

The real point is that those who disagree with the war, disagree fundamentally with the judgment that led to war. What is more, their alternative judgment is both entirely rational and arguable. Kosovo, with ethnic cleansing of ethnic Albanians, was not a hard decision for most people; nor was Afghanistan after the shock of September 11; nor was Sierra Leone.

Iraq in March 2003 was an immensely difficult judgment. It was divisive because it was difficult. I have never disrespected those who disagreed with the decision. Sure, some were anti-American; some against all wars. But there was a core of sensible people who faced with this decision would have gone the other way, for sensible reasons. Their argument is one I understand totally. It is that Iraq posed no direct, immediate threat to Britain; and that Iraq's WMD, even on our own case, was not serious enough to warrant war, certainly without a specific U.N. resolution mandating military action. And they argue: Saddam could, in any event, be contained.

In other words, they disagreed then and disagree now fundamentally with the characterization of the threat. We were saying this is urgent; we have to act; the opponents of war thought it wasn't. And I accept, incidentally, that however abhorrent and foul the regime and however relevant that was for the reasons I set out before the war, for example in Glasgow in February 2003, regime change alone could not be and was not our justification for war. Our primary purpose was to enforce U.N. resolutions over Iraq and WMD.

Of course the opponents are boosted by the fact that though we know Saddam had WMD, we haven't found the physical evidence of them in the 11 months since the war. But in fact, everyone thought he had them. That was the basis of U.N. Resolution 1441.

It's just worth pointing out that the search is being conducted in a country twice the land mass of the U.K., which David Kay's interim report in October 2003 noted, contains 130 ammunition storage areas, some covering an area of 50 square miles, including some 600,000 tons of artillery shells, rockets and other ordnance, of which only a small proportion have as yet been searched in the difficult security environment that exists.

But the key point is that it is the threat that is the issue.

The characterization of the threat is where the difference lies. Here is where I feel so passionately that we are in mortal danger of mistaking the nature of the new world in which we live. Everything about our world is changing: its economy, its technology, its culture, its way of living. If the 20th century scripted our conventional way of thinking, the 21st century is unconventional in almost every respect.

This is true also of our security.

The threat we face is not conventional. It is a challenge of a different nature from anything the world has faced before. It is to the world's security, what globalization is to the world's economy.

It was defined not by Iraq but by September 11th. September 11th did not create the threat Saddam posed. But it altered crucially the balance of risk as to whether to deal with it or simply carry on, however imperfectly, trying to contain it.

Let me attempt an explanation of how my own thinking, as a political leader, has evolved during these past few years. Already, before September 11th the world's view of the justification of military action had been changing. The only clear case in international relations for armed intervention had been self-defense, response to aggression. But the notion of intervening on humanitarian grounds had been gaining currency. I set this out, following the Kosovo war, in a speech in Chicago in 1999, where I called for a doctrine of international community, where in certain clear circumstances we do intervene, even though we are not directly threatened. I said this was not just to correct injustice, but also because in an increasingly interdependent world, our self-interest was allied to the interests of others; and seldom did conflict in one region of the world not contaminate another. We acted in Sierra Leone for similar reasons, though frankly even if that country had become run by gangsters and murderers and its democracy crushed, it would have been a long time before it impacted on us. But we were able to act to help them and we did.

So, for me, before September 11th, I was already reaching for a different philosophy in international relations from a traditional one that has held sway since the treaty of Westphalia in 1648; namely that a country's internal affairs are for it and you don't interfere unless it threatens you, or breaches a treaty, or triggers an obligation of alliance. I did not consider Iraq fitted into this philosophy, though I could see the horrible injustice done to its people by Saddam.

However, I had started to become concerned about two other phenomena.

The first was the increasing amount of information about Islamic extremism and terrorism that was crossing my desk. Chechnya was blighted by it. So was Kashmir. Afghanistan was its training ground. Some 300 people had been killed in the attacks on the U.S.S. *Cole* and U.S. embassies in East Africa. The extremism seemed remarkably well financed. It was very active. And it was driven not by a set of negotiable political demands, but by religious fanaticism.

The second was the attempts by states—some of them highly unstable and repressive—to develop nuclear weapons programs, CW and BW materiel and long-range missiles. What is more, it was obvious that there was a considerable network of individuals and companies with expertise in this area, prepared to sell it.

All this was before September 11th. I discussed the issue of WMD with President Bush at our first meeting in Camp David in February 2001. But it's in the nature of things that other issues intervene—I was about to fight for re-election—and though it was raised, it was a troubling specter in the background, not something to arrest our whole attention.

President Bush told me that on September 9th, 2001, he had a meeting about Iraq in the White House when he discussed "smart" sanctions, changes to the sanctions regime. There was no talk of military action.

September 11th was for me a revelation. What had seemed inchoate came together. The point about September 11th was not its detailed planning; not its devilish execution; not even, simply, that it happened in America, on the streets of New York. All of this made it an astonishing, terrible and wicked tragedy, a barbaric murder of innocent people. But what galvanized me was that it was a declaration of war by religious fanatics who were prepared to wage that war without limit. They killed 3,000. But if they could have killed 30,000 or 300,000, they would have rejoiced in it. The purpose was to cause such hatred between Muslims and the West that a religious jihad became reality; and the world engulfed by it.

When I spoke to the House of Commons on 14 September 2001 I said: "We know, that they [the terrorists] would, if they could, go further and use chemical, biological, or even nuclear weapons of mass destruction. We know, also, that there are groups of people, occasionally states, who will trade the technology and capability of such weapons. It is time that this trade was exposed, disrupted, and stamped out. We have been warned by the events of 11 September, and we should act on the warning."

From September 11th on, I could see the threat plainly. Here were terrorists prepared to bring about Armageddon. Here were states whose leadership cared for no one but themselves; were often cruel and tyrannical towards their own people; and who saw WMD as a means of defending themselves against any attempt external or internal to remove them and who, in their chaotic and corrupt state, were in any event porous and irresponsible with neither the will nor capability to prevent terrorists who also hated the West, from exploiting their chaos and corruption.

I became aware of the activities of A. Q. Khan, former Pakistani nuclear scientist, and of an organization developing nuclear weapons technology to sell secretly to states wanting to acquire it. I started to hear of plants to manufacture nuclear weapons equipment in Malaysia, in the Near East and Africa, companies in the Gulf and Europe to finance it; training and know-how provided—all without any or much international action to stop it. It was a murky, dangerous trade, done with much sophistication and it was rapidly shortening the timeframe of countries like North Korea and Iran in acquiring serviceable nuclear weapons capability.

I asked for more intelligence on the issue not just of terrorism but also of WMD. The scale of it became clear. It didn't matter that the Islamic extremists often hated some of these regimes. Their mutual enmity toward the West would in the end triumph over any scruples of that nature, as we see graphically in Iraq today.

We knew that al Qaeda sought the capability to use WMD in their attacks. Bin Laden has called it a "duty" to obtain nuclear weapons. His networks have experimented with chemicals and toxins for use in attacks. He received advice from at least two Pakistani scientists on the design of nuclear weapons. In Afghanistan al Qaeda trained its recruits in the use of poisons and chemicals. An al Qaeda terrorist ran a training camp developing these techniques. Terrorist training manuals giving step-by-step instructions for the manufacture of deadly substances such as botulinum and ricin were widely distributed in Afghanistan and elsewhere and via the Internet. Terrorists in Russia have actually deployed radiological material. The sarin attack on the Tokyo Metro showed how serious an impact even a relatively small attack can have.

The global threat to our security was clear. So was our duty: to act to eliminate it.

First we dealt with al Qaeda in Afghanistan, removing the Taliban that succored them.

But then we had to confront the states with WMD. We had to take a stand. We had to force conformity with international obligations that for years had been breached with the world turning a blind eye. For 12 years Saddam had defied calls to disarm. In 1998, he had effectively driven out the U.N. inspectors and we had bombed his military infrastructure; but we had only weakened him, not removed the threat. Saddam alone had used CW against Iran and against his own people.

We had had an international coalition blessed by the U.N. in Afghanistan. I wanted the same now. President Bush agreed to go the U.N. route. We secured U.N. Resolution 1441. Saddam had one final chance to comply fully. Compliance had to start with a full and honest declaration of WMD programs and activities.

The truth is disarming a country, other than with its consent, is a perilous exercise. On 8 December 2002, Saddam sent his declaration. It was obviously false. The U.N. inspectors were in Iraq, but progress was slow and the vital cooperation of Iraqi scientists withheld. In March we went back to the U.N. to make a final ultimatum. We strove hard for agreement. We very nearly achieved it.

So we came to the point of decision. Prime ministers don't have the luxury of maintaining both sides of the argument. They can see both sides. But ultimately, leadership is about deciding. My view was and is that if the U.N. had come together and delivered a tough ultimatum to Saddam, listing clearly what he had to do, benchmarking it, he may have folded and events set in train that might just and eventually have led to his departure from power.

But the Security Council didn't agree.

Suppose at that point we had backed away. Inspectors would have stayed but only the utterly naive would believe that following such a public climb-down by the U.S. and its partners, Saddam would have cooperated more. He would have strung the inspectors out and returned emboldened to his plans. The will to act on the issue of rogue states and WMD would have been shown to be hollow. The terrorists, watching and analyzing every move in our psychology as they do, would have taken heart. All this without counting the fact that the appalling brutalization of the Iraqi people would have continued unabated and reinforced.

Here is the crux. It is possible that even with all of this, nothing would have happened. Possible that Saddam would change his ambitions; possible he would develop the WMD but never use it; possible that the terrorists would never get their hands on WMD, whether from Iraq or elsewhere. We cannot be certain. Perhaps we would have found different ways of reducing it. Perhaps this Islamic terrorism would ebb of its own accord.

But do we want to take the risk? That is the judgment. And my judgment then and now is that the risk of this new global terrorism and its interaction with states or organizations or individuals proliferating WMD, is one I simply am not prepared to run.

This is not a time to err on the side of caution; not a time to weigh the risks to an infinite balance; not a time for the cynicism of the worldly wise who favor playing it long. Their worldly wise cynicism is actually at best naiveté and at worst dereliction. When they talk, as they do now, of diplomacy coming back into fashion in respect of Iran or North Korea or Libya, do they seriously think that diplomacy alone has brought about this change? Since the war in Iraq, Libya has taken the courageous step of owning up not just to a nuclear weapons program but to having chemical weapons, which are now being destroyed. Iran is back in the reach of the IAEA. North Korea in talks with China over its WMD. The A. Q. Khan network is being shut down, its trade slowly but surely being eliminated.

Yet it is monstrously premature to think the threat has passed. The risk remains in the balance here and abroad.

These days decisions about it come thick and fast, and while they are not always of the same magnitude they are hardly trivial. Let me give you an example. A short while ago, during the war, we received specific intelligence warning of a major attack on Heathrow. To this day, we don't know if it was correct and we foiled it or if it was wrong. But we received the intelligence. We immediately heightened the police presence. At the time it was much criticized as political hype or an attempt to frighten the public. Actually at each stage we followed rigidly the advice of the police and Security Service.

But sit in my seat. Here is the intelligence. Here is the advice. Do you ignore it? But, of course intelligence is precisely that: intelligence. It is not hard fact. It has its limitations. On each occasion the most careful judgment has to be made taking account of everything we know and the best assessment and advice available. But in making that judgment, would you prefer us to act, even if it turns out to be wrong? Or not to act and hope it's OK? And suppose we don't act and the intelligence turns out to be right, how forgiving will people be?

And to those who think that these things are all disconnected, random acts, disparate threats with no common thread to bind them, look at what is happening in Iraq today. The terrorists pouring into Iraq, know full well the importance of destroying not just the nascent progress of Iraq toward stability, prosperity and democracy, but of destroying *our* confidence, of defeating *our* will to persevere.

I have no doubt Iraq is better without Saddam; but no doubt either, that as a result of his removal, the dangers of the threat we face will be diminished. That is not to say the terrorists won't redouble their efforts. They will. This war is not ended. It may only be at the end of its first phase. They are in Iraq, murdering innocent Iraqis who want to worship or join a police force that upholds the law not a brutal dictatorship; they carry on killing in Afghanistan. They do it for a reason. The terrorists know that if Iraq and Afghanistan survive their assault, come through their travails, seize the opportunity the future offers, then those countries will stand not just as nations liberated from oppression, but as a lesson to humankind everywhere and a profound antidote to the poison of religious extremism. That is precisely why the terrorists are trying to foment hatred and division in Iraq. They know full well, a stable democratic Iraq, under the sovereign rule of the Iraqi people, is a mortal blow to their fanaticism.

That is why our duty is to rebuild Iraq and Afghanistan as stable and democratic nations.

Here is the irony. For all the fighting, this threat cannot be defeated by security means alone. Taking strong action is a necessary but insufficient condition for defeating. Its final defeat is only assured by the triumph of the values of the human spirit.

Which brings me to the final point. It may well be that under international law as presently constituted, a regime can systematically brutalize and oppress its people and there is nothing anyone can do, when dialogue, diplomacy and even sanctions fail, unless it comes within the definition of a humanitarian catastrophe (though the 300,000 remains in mass graves already found in Iraq might be thought by some to be something of a catastrophe). This may be the law, but should it be?

We know now, if we didn't before, that our own self-interest is ultimately bound up with the fate of other nations. The doctrine of international community is no longer a vision of idealism. It is a practical recognition that just as within a country, citizens who are free, well educated and prosperous tend to be responsible, to feel solidarity with a society in which they have a stake; so do nations that are free, democratic and benefiting from economic progress, tend to be stable and solid partners in the advance of humankind. The best defense of our security lies in the spread of our values.

But we cannot advance these values except within a framework that recognizes their universality. If it is a global threat, it needs a global response, based on global rules.

The essence of a community is common rights and responsibilities. We have obligations in relation to each other. If we are threatened, we have a right to act. And we do not accept in a community that others have a right to oppress and brutalize their people. We value the freedom and dignity of the human race and each individual in it.

Containment will not work in the face of the global threat that confronts us. The terrorists have no intention of being contained. The states that proliferate or acquire WMD illegally are doing so precisely to avoid containment. Emphatically I am not saying that every situation leads to military action. But we surely have a duty and a right to prevent the threat materializing; and we surely have a responsibility to act when a nation's people are subjected to a regime such as Saddam's. Otherwise, we are powerless to fight the aggression and injustice which over time puts at risk our security and way of life.

Which brings us to how you make the rules and how you decide what is right or wrong in enforcing them. The U.N. Universal Declaration on Human Rights is a fine document. But it is strange the United Nations is so reluctant to enforce them.

I understand the worry the international community has over Iraq. It worries that the U.S. and its allies will by sheer force of their military might, do whatever they want, unilaterally and without recourse to any rule-based code or doctrine. But our worry is that if the U.N.—because of a political disagreement in its Councils—is paralyzed, then a threat we believe is real will go unchallenged.

This dilemma is at the heart of many people's anguished indecision over the wisdom of our action in Iraq. It explains the confusion of normal politics that has part of the right liberating a people from oppression and a part of the left disdaining the action that led to it. It is partly why the conspiracy theories or claims of deceit have such purchase. How much simpler to debate those than to analyze and resolve the conundrum of our world's present state.

Britain's role is try to find a way through this: to construct a consensus behind a broad agenda of justice and security and means of enforcing it.

This agenda must be robust in tackling the security threat that this Islamic extremism poses; and fair to all peoples by promoting their human rights, wherever they are. It means tackling poverty in Africa and justice in Palestine as well as being utterly resolute in opposition to terrorism as a way of achieving political goals. It means an entirely different, more just and more modern view of self-interest.

It means reforming the United Nations so its Security Council represents 21st century reality; and giving the U.N. the capability to act effectively as well as debate. It means getting the U.N. to understand that faced with the threats we have, we should do all we can to spread the values of freedom, democracy, the rule of law, religious tolerance and justice for the oppressed, however painful for some nations that may be; but that at the same time, we wage war relentlessly on those who would exploit racial and religious division to bring catastrophe to the world.

But in the meantime, the threat is there and demands our attention. That is the struggle which engages us. It is a new type of war. It will rest on intelligence to a greater degree than ever before. It demands a difference attitude to our own interests. It forces us to act even when so many comforts seem unaffected, and the threat so far off, if not illusory. In the end, believe your political leaders or not, as you will. But do so, at least having understood their minds.

## NOTE

Parliamentary copyright material is reproduced from the House of Commons Official Report (*Hansard*) with the permission of the Controller of Her Majesty's Stationery Office on behalf of Parliament. This speech, dated March 5, 2004, may be found at http://www.number-10.gov.uk/output/Page5461.asp (accessed January 22, 2005).

# Contributors

**PAUL BERMAN** is a cultural and political critic whose essays and reviews appear in the *New Republic*, the *New York Times Magazine*, the *New York Times Book Review*, *Dissent*, and other journals. He is the author of *A Tale of Two Utopias: The Political Journey of the Generation of 1968* (W. W. Norton, 1997) and *Terror and Liberalism* (W. W. Norton, 2003) and the editor of two readers: *Debating P.C.: The Controversy over Political Correctness on College Campuses* (Dell, 1992) and *Blacks and Jews: Alliances and Arguments* (Dell, 1992). Over the years, he has been on the staff of the *Village Voice*, *Slate*, and the *New Yorker*.

**TONY BLAIR** is the prime minister of Great Britain.

**PAMELA BONE** is a columnist and associate editor of the *Age*, one of Australia's most respected newspapers. She began work as a journalist at the *Shepparton News* (in Victoria) in 1980 and joined the *Age* in 1982. She has received many awards for her journalism, including a United Nations Media Peace prize, an award from the Human Rights and Equal Opportunity Commission, an award from Results Australia for writing on issues of poverty and hunger, and an award from the New South Wales Office of the Status of Women for writing on women's affairs, and she has twice received the Melbourne Press Club's Quill Award for best newspaper columnist. She has traveled widely in developing countries. In September 2002, she went to southern Africa to research an article on famine and AIDS, and she coordinated an appeal by the *Age* that raised more than $1 million.

**IAN BURUMA** lived and worked in Japan and Hong Kong for many years. He is the author of *Bad Elements: Chinese Rebels from Los Angeles to Beijing* (Vintage, 2003); *The Missionary and the Libertine: Love and War in East and West* (Vintage, 2003); *Anglomania: A European Love Affair* (Orion, 2001); *A Japanese Mirror* (New American Library, 1985); *God's Dust: A Modern Asian Journey* (Noonday, 1990); *The Wages of Guilt: Memories of War in Germany and Japan* (Phoenix, 2002); and *Playing the Game* (Farrar, Straus & Giroux, 1991). He is currently the Luce Professor at Bard College.

**ANN CLWYD** has been the Labour MP for the Cynon Valley since 1984; she was previously a Member of the European Parliament for Mid and West Wales (1979–1984). She is the vice chair of the Parliamentary Labour Party, chair of the All Party Parliamentary Human Rights Group, and chair of INDICT, the campaign to bring Iraqi war criminals to justice. She was appointed in May 2003 to be the Special Envoy to the Prime Minister on Human Rights in Iraq, and she has since then visited Iraq four times for the prime minister. As a longtime campaigner on human rights in Iraq, in 1991, she was an eyewitness when thousands of Kurds fled on foot on the mountains of Iran and Iraq from the attacks by Saddam Hussein. Clwyd was influential in setting up the "safe havens" for the Kurds. She has returned to Iraqi Kurdistan several times since and on one occasion brokered a peace settlement between the two warring sides, which resulted in forty-four Kurds being released from prison. She visited northern Iraq in February 2003 before the outbreak of war.

**MITCHELL COHEN** is the coeditor of *Dissent* magazine and a professor of political science at Bernard Baruch College and the Graduate School of the City University of New York. His books include *The Wager of Lucien Goldmann* (Princeton University Press, 1994); *Zion and State* (Columbia University Press, 1992); and, as coeditor, *Princeton Readings in Political Thought* (Princeton University Press, 1996).

**THOMAS CUSHMAN** is a professor of sociology at Wellesley College and the founder and editor in chief of the *Journal of Human Rights*. He is the author of numerous books and articles on cultural dissidence in Russia, the war in Bosnia and Hercegovina, genocide, and the sociology of intellectuals and war. His books include *This Time We Knew: Western Responses to Genocide in Bosnia* (New York University Press, 1996); *George Orwell: into the Twentieth Century* (Paradigm, 2004); and *The Human Rights Case for War: Ethics, International Law, and the Conflict in Iraq* (Cambridge University Press, Forthcoming). He is the editor of two book series, Post Communist Cultural Studies and Essays in Human Rights, both published by Penn State University Press. He was a Mellon Foundation New Directions Fellow for 2002, a fellow of the Salzburg Seminar academic core session on International Law and Human Rights chaired by Lloyd Cutler and Richard Goldstone, and a former visiting scholar at the Carr Center for Human Rights Policy at Harvard University; he is currently a faculty associate at the Center for Cultural Sociology, Yale University.

MIENT JAN FABER was born in the Netherlands under German occupation. He is from a Calvinist background. He was an assistant professor in the Department of Mathematics at the Free University in Amsterdam from 1968 to 1974. From 1974 to 2003, he was secretary-general of the Interchurch Peace Council (IKV) in the Netherlands. When the churches launched a public campaign against his views on Iraq and military intervention, he was dismissed from his post and left the institute. He is currently a professor on the faculty of political and social science at the Free University in Amsterdam.

NORMAN GERAS is professor emeritus in the Department of Government at the University of Manchester. His books include *The Legacy of Rosa Luxemburg* (New Left Books, 1976); *Marx and Human Nature: Refutation of a Legend* (Verso, 1983); *Solidarity in the Conversation of Humankind: The Ungroundable Liberalism of Richard Rorty* (W. W. Norton, 1995); and *The Contract of Mutual Indifference: Political Philosophy after the Holocaust* (Verso, 1998).

JOHANN HARI is an award-winning journalist and playwright. He is a columnist for the *Independent*, one of Britain's leading broadsheet newspapers, and writes regularly for the *Times Literary Supplement*, *Attitude* (Britain's main gay magazine), and the *New Statesman*. His work has also appeared in *Le Monde*, *El Mundo*, *The Guardian*, *Ha'aretz*, the *Melbourne Age*, the *Sydney Morning Herald*, the *Irish Times*, and a wide range of other international newspapers and magazines. In 2003, he was named Young Journalist of the Year by the Press Gazette Awards in the UK. His first book, *God Save the Queen?* was published in 2002 by Totem Books.

**JEFFREY HERF** is a professor of modern European and German history at the University of Maryland in College Park. His publications include numerous articles in scholarly journals. He is the author of *Divided Memory: The Nazi Past in the Two Germanys* (Harvard University Press, 1997). He won the American Historical Association's George Louis Beer Prize in 1998; in September 1996, he was awarded the Fraenkel Prize in Contemporary History by the Institute of Contemporary History and the Wiener Library in London. Herf is also the author of *War by Other Means: Soviet Power, West German Resistance, and the Battle of the Euromissiles* (Free Press, 1991) and *Reactionary Modernism: Technology, Culture, and Politics in Weimar and the Third Reich* (Cambridge University Press, 1984). He is now completing *The Jewish War: Nazi Propaganda in World War Two* (Harvard University Press, 2005). He has also published political essays in *Partisan Review* and reviews in the *New Republic*, as well as in *Die Zeit*, the *Frankfurter Allgemeine Zeitung*, *Die Welt*, and he has lectured widely in the United States, Europe, and Israel. He was a contributing editor to *Partisan Review* and is a member of the editorial board of *Central European History*.

**RICHARD HERZINGER** is the editor in politics of the German weekly *Die Zeit*. He has written and lectured extensively on topics such as anti-Semitism, Islamism, terrorism, and individualism and social responsibility. He is a prominent voice in the European dialogue on Middle East relations and the roles of the European Union. He is the author of *Masken der Lebensrevolution: Vitalistische Zivilisations- und Humanismuskritik in Texten Heiner Müllers* (Fink, 1992) and *Endzeit-Propheten, oder, Die Offensive der Antiwestler: Fundamentalismus, Antiamerikanismus und neue Rechte* (Rowohlt, 1995).

**CHRISTOPHER HITCHENS** is the author of more than ten books, including, most recently, *A Long Short War: The Postponed Liberation of Iraq* (Plum, 2003); *Why Orwell Matters* (Basic Books, 2002), *The Trial of Henry Kissinger* (Verso, 2001); and *Letters to a Young Contrarian* (Basic Books, 2001). He is a contributing editor to *Vanity Fair* and has written prolifically for American and English periodicals, including the *Nation*, the *London Review of Books*, *Granta*, *Harper's*, the *Los Angeles Times Book Review*, *New Left Review*, *Slate*, the *New York Review of Books*, *Newsweek International*, the *Times Literary Supplement*, and the *Washington Post*. He is also a regular television and radio commentator.

**ANDERS JERICHOW** is a columnist at the Danish daily *Politiken* and a frequent radio and TV commentator on Middle East and European international relations. He was the editor for foreign affairs at *Weekendavisen* from 1985 to 1993, foreign editor at *Politiken* from 1993 to 1998, and editor in chief and managing director of *Aktuelt* from 1998 to 2001. He has published a number of books on questions of human rights, development, and democratization issues in the Middle East, including *The Saudi File—People, Power, Politics* (St. Martin's, 1998) and *Saudi Arabia, Outside Global Law and Order* (Curzon, 1997). He coedited *The Wrath of the Damned: An Encounter between Arabia and the West* (Danish PEN, 2004).

**RICHARD JUST** has been editor of the *New Republic Online* since January 2004. He was previously the editor of the *American Prospect Online* and a writing fellow at the *American Prospect*. He graduated cum laude from Princeton University in 2001, with a degree from the Woodrow Wilson School of Public and International Affairs. At Princeton, he was the editor in chief of the *Daily Princetonian*.

**DANIEL KOFMAN** has been a lecturer in philosophy at Pembroke College, Oxford, for the past four years. He has also held lectureships at Lincoln, Balliol, Wadham, and Christ Church Colleges, Oxford University. He has published articles and book chapters on self-determination, sovereignty, theory of rights, nationalism, and moral issues in various national conflicts from the Balkans to the Middle East. He is currently completing a book on self-determination and secession and editing a volume called *The Idea of a Jewish State: Liberal, Communitarian, or Racist?*

**JOHN LLOYD** is the editor of the *Financial Times Magazine*. Born in Scotland, he was educated at Edinburgh and London Universities. He has worked for newspapers, radio, and TV; for much of his career he has been a correspondent for the *Financial Times* in the UK, Central Europe, and Russia. His books include *Loss without Limit* (Sutton, 1986) on the British miners' strike of 1984–1985 and *Rebirth of a Nation* (Michael Joseph, 1998) on the emergence of Russia. Lloyd is also the author more recently of *What the Media Are Doing to Our Politics* (Constable & Robinson, 2004).

**ADAM MICHNIK**, a leading force in the Solidarity trade union movement against communist totalitarianism, is the founder and editor in chief of the largest Polish daily newspaper, *Gazeta Wyborcza*.

**MEHDI MOZAFFARI** is a professor of political science at Aarhus University, Denmark. He is a graduate of the Sorbonne. His latest book is *Globalization and Civilizations* (Routledge, 2002), and his most recent published research is on how to combat Islamist terrorism without combating Islam and on Islamism and international relations.

**JAN NARVESON** is a professor of philosophy at the University of Waterloo in Ontario, Canada. He is the author of a couple hundred papers in philosophical periodicals and anthologies, mainly on moral and political theory and practice, and of several books, including *Morality and Utility* (Johns Hopkins University Press, 1967); *The Libertarian Idea* (Temple University Press, 1989; 2nd ed., 2002); *Moral Matters* (Broadview, 1993; 2nd ed., 1999); and *Respecting Persons in Theory and Practice* (Rowman & Littlefield, 2002). He is on the editorial boards of many philosophic journals, is a frequent contributor to conferences in many countries, was elected a Fellow of the Royal Society of Canada in 1989, and was made an Officer of the Order of Canada in 2003.

**JOSE RAMOS-HORTA** has been an activist for independence and democracy in East Timor since 1969. He served as the East Timorese representative to the United Nations and later as the foreign minister of East Timor. He is founder of the Diplomacy Training Program in the United Nations Human Rights System for indigenous peoples, minorities, and human rights activists in the Asia Pacific region. In 1996, he received the Nobel Peace Prize for his work toward peace and justice in East Timor. He recently cofounded the Indonesian and East Timorese Commission on Truth and Friendship. He is author of *Funu: The Unfinished Saga of East Timor* (Red Sea, 1987). He currently continues his advocacy work for peace and justice encouraging democracy in Iraq and in Burma.

**JONATHAN RÉE** is a freelance philosopher who used to teach at Middlesex University in London and was for many years was associated with the magazine *Radical Philosophy*. His work has appeared in the *Times Literary Supplement*, the *London Review of Books*, and elsewhere. His books include *Proletarian Philosophers* (Clarendon, 1984); *Philosophical Tales: An Essay on Philosophy and Literature* (Routledge, 1987); and *I See a Voice: Deafness, Language, and the Senses—A Philosophical History* (Metropolitan, 1999).

**ROGER SCRUTON** is a self-employed writer and philosopher who lives in rural Wiltshire and is the author of more than thirty books, including

*The West and the Rest* (ISI Books, 2003); *Death-Devoted Heart* (Oxford University Press, 2004); and *News from Somewhere* (Continuum, 2004). He was a professor of philosophy at Boston University from 1992 to 1995 and subsequently a professor at Birkbeck College, London.

MICHEL TAUBMANN is a journalist and the chief redactor of the French news office of ARTE, the European cultural television station. With the historian Pierre Rigoulot, he is the coeditor of *Irak An 1: un autre regard sur un monde en guerre* (Le Rocher, 2004), which includes twenty-four other authors, among them André Glucksmann, Pascal Bruckner and Pierre-André Taguieff, and Stephane Courtois, and which criticizes aspects of US foreign policy but also the anti-Americanism and anti-Zionism of French politics.

# Index

Abdullah II, King of Jordan, 109
Abu Ghraib prison scandal, 82
  damage to US, 18, 266, 283, 304,
    320
  Iraqi opinion of, 20
  sanctioned by US government, 44, 294
  victim led on leash in, 290
Adenauer, Konrad, 239
Afghanistan, 32
  environment for future terrorists, 319
  French policies for, 250–251
  interventions in, 33
  motivations for war in, 118–119
  Oriental despotism in, 117
  refugees returning to, 37
  Taliban evicted from, 33–34, 250,
    282, 346
Africa, casualties in, 111
Agent-relative duties, moral aspects of,
    140–142
Albania in support of Iraq war, 14
Albanians, Kosovar. See Kosovo, inter-
  ventions in
Algeria
  Oriental despotism in, 117
  in rentier economy, 114
Ali, Tariq, 153, 154, 155
Allawi, Iyad, 322
Al Qaeda, 32
  emergence of, 46
  eviction from Afghanistan, 33–34
  suspected connection with Saddam
    Hussein, 43, 45
  threat posed by, 103

  use of asylum laws, 100
  weapons used by, 346
Amnesty International, 297, 314–315,
    325n
Anderson, Perry, 116, 123n
Anfal campaign against Kurdish popula-
    tion, 311–312, 315, 319
Anglophobia, European, 155–156
Annan, Kofi, 79, 318, 331
Anscombe, Elizabeth, 140, 144n
Anti-Americanism
  in Germany, 239
  global revival of, 12
  history of, 155, 156–157
Anti-imperialism, 157
Anti-Semitism
  in France, 253
  in Poland, 277
  spread of, 148
Anti-Western radicalism in Arab and
    Islamic world, 45–46
Antitotalitarianism as vocation, 271–280
Antiwar position. See Opposition to Iraq
    war
Aquinas, Thomas, 164
Arab governments
  attitude toward postwar Iraq,
    265–268
  support for Saddam Hussein, 262
Arab Human Development Report of
    2003, 303, 308n
Arab League, 110
Aristotle, and just war tradition, 161,
    164

Ash, Timothy Garton, 226, 230, 232n
Ashcroft, John, 273
Asian states in support of Iraq war, 14
Asiatic mode of production
  and Oriental despotism, 116
  and rentier economy in Middle East,
    113–115
al-Assad, Bashar, 109
al-Assad, Hafiz, 84, 121
Asylum laws, consequences of, 100–101
Augustine, St., and just war tradition,
  161, 164
Aurelius, Marcus, 101
Australian views on Iraq war, 298–299,
  307n
Austrian opposition to Iraq war, 255
Ayala Lasso, Jose, 299, 307n
Azerbaijan support of Iraq war, 14
Aziz, Tariq, 118, 170, 301, 316

Baath Party
  founding of, 148, 153
  against new Iraqi government, 54
  virtual collusion with, 2, 30
Baathist regime
  barbarities of, 195
  ideology of, 41–42
  members awaiting trial, 324
Bahrain
  contribution to Iraq war, 260
  in rentier economy, 114
  with seat at UN, 37
Barnes, Julian, 196
Barnier, Michel, 226
al-Bayati, Hamid, 322
Beblawi, Hazem, 114, 123n
Belgium in opposition to Iraq war, 255
Benn, Tony, 129, 130, 155
Berlusconi, Silvo, 288
Berman, Paul, 3, 22, 147–151
bin Laden, Osama, 33, 346
  in Afghanistan, 118–119
  compared to Saddam Hussein, 83
  George W. Bush compared to, 250
Blair, Cherie, 302
Blair, Tony
  arguments for war in Iraq, 7, 42–43,
    52, 186
  assumptions about Iraqi people, 286
  attitudes toward European Union, 228
  full statement to House of Commons
    in 2003, 329–339
  on future of Iraq, 305, 308n
  internationalism of, 249
  meeting with President Bush, 226
  resolution of March 2003, 258
  search for weapons of mass destruc-
    tion, 83–84
  speech of 1999, 32–33, 38n
  speech to US Congress in 2003, 211,
    219n
  on threat of global terrorism in 2004,
    340–351
Blix, Hans, 81, 85, 86, 91n, 263
Blum, Léon, 244

Bobbitt, Philip, 229, 232n
Bodin, Jean, 127, 143n
Bokassa, Jean Bedel, 282
Bone, Pamela, 297–308
Boniface, Pascal, 253
Bono, José, 228, 232n
Bosnia
  genocide in, 4, 13, 235, 247, 261
  interventions in, 10
Boutros-Ghali, Boutros, 300
Brahimi, Lakhdar, 266
Bremmer, Paul, 284
Brezhnev, Leonid, 274
Brooks, David, 216, 219n
Brzezinski, Zbigniew, 210, 219n
Buchanan, Patrick J., 80, 83
Bulgarian support of Iraq war, 14
Buruma, Ian, 152–159
Burundi, massacre in, 111
Bush, George H. W.
  decision for Desert Storm in Kuwait, 78
  Gulf War destroying civilian infra-
    structure, 168–169
  pro-Arab policy of, 111
Bush, George W.
  assumptions about Iraqi people, 286
  case for Iraq war, 4, 7, 42–43, 52,
    101, 122, 124n
    false assertions in, 54
  Christian response to military postur-
    ing of, 173
  compared to Osama bin Laden, 250
  foreign policies of, 275–276
  French view of, 243
  German view of, 234
  humanitarian arguments of, 4, 7, 9, 10
  interventions in Afghanistan, 33
  loss of credibility, 54, 55, 88
  meeting with Tony Blair, 226
  motives of, 293
  occupation of Iraq as disaster, 53
  plans for intervening in Iraq, 184–185,
    188
  policy for Middle East, 110
  prosecution of Iraq war, 87–89, 90
  reelection of, 70
  search for weapons of mass destruc-
    tion, 83–84
  seen as principal danger, 256
  utopian ideology of, 273
  vilification of, 10, 11, 148, 151
Bush, Laura, 302

Cambadélis, Jean-Christophe, 258
Canadian Council of Churches, 170
Capitalism, criticisms of, 155–156
Carlyle Group, 32
Carter, Jimmy, 111
Castro, Fidel, 12
Casualties
  for invaded states, 66–67, 75n
  for invading states, 67–68
  and US military personnel as volun-
    teers, 68
  for victims of tyranny, 67

Chamberlain, Houston Stewart, 156
Cheney, Dick, 79, 288
  mistaken outlook for postwar Iraq,
    52–53
  motives of, 293
  optimistic views of Iraq war, 43
  speech of 2002, 47
Chevènement, Jean-Pierre, 246, 249, 252
China in opposition to Iraq war, 7
Chirac, Jacques
  alliance with Saddam's Iraq, 21
  as conservative, 147
  criticism of Letter of the Eight, 13–14
  on disarmament of Iraq, 85–86
  foreign policy of, 81, 87, 248, 258
  friendship with Germany, 233–234
  response to September 11 attack in
    US, 252
  as spokesman for Europe, 260
Chomsky, Noam, 130, 143n, 155, 158,
    292, 293, 296n
Chrétien, Jean, 170
Church positions
  in contacts with dissident groups,
    174–175
  on Iraq war, 160–161
  and American debate, 166–171
  and European debate, 171–174
  just war tradition in, 161–162
  on Kosovo war, 162
  pacifism in, 160, 162, 170
Churchill, Winston, 50, 52, 55
  allied with Roosevelt and Stalin, 79,
    83
Citizenship detached from national idea,
    100, 105n
Clarke, Richard, 33
Clausewitz, Carl von, 161
Clinton, William J., 10, 30, 31, 38n, 118
  reaction to Al Qaeda, 103
Clwyd, Ann, 309–325
Coalition of the Willing in 2003, 13, 265
  critics of, 14
  troops withdrawn from Iraq, 281
Cohen, Eliot A., 230–231, 232n
Cohen, Mitchell, 76–92
Cohn-Bendit, Daniel, 250
Colombani, Jean-Marie, 251
Committee against Repression and
    for Democratic Rights in Iraq
    (CARDRI), 310, 317
Conflict resolution, and international
    law, 97–102
Congo
  civil war in, 31
  UN indifference to, 13
Consequences
  intended and unintended, distinctions
    between, 141–142
  of war, ethical issues in, 9
Consequentialism, issues in, 131,
    137–142
Containment as ineffective for global
    threats, 349–350
Cosmopolitan universalism, 18

Cosmopolitanism, 101–102, 105n
Costs of war
  to invaded state, 65–67
  to invading state, 67–70
  economic costs, 69–70
  military casualties, 68–69
Council of Churches
  Canadian, 170
  Dutch, 174, 178n
  Middle East, 170, 172
  National, 162, 170, 176n
  World, 162–163, 172–173
Crawford, Leslie, 228, 232n
Critiques of the left
  by Berman, 147–151
  by Buruma, 152–159
  by Faber, 160–178
  by Geras, 191–206
  by Just, 207–219
  by Rée, 179–190
Croatian support of Iraq war, 14
Cushman, Thomas, 1–24
  interview of Adam Michnik, 271–280
Czech Republic support of Iraq war, 13

Darfur, genocide in, 204, 211, 212
Dean, Howard, 210, 219n
Defense of Iraq war. *See* Support of Iraq
    war
Democracy as possible problem in Iraq,
    64
Democratic regimes, taxation systems in,
    115
Democratic stability, order in, 110
Democratization
  of Middle East
    as American project, 122
    as justification for Iraq war, 120,
      121
    types of, 121
Denmark in support of Iraq war, 13, 337
Deontology, ethical doctrine of, 138
Desert Fox campaign, 331
Despotic states, decisions for war against,
    104, 106–124
Despotism
  Oriental, 115–117
  taxation affecting, 115
Dictatorial stability, 109
  in Middle East, 110
Dictatorships, rise of, 156
Doyle, Michael, 141, 144n
Dray, Julien, 246
Duelfer, Charles, report on weapons of
    mass destruction, 26n, 54
Dutch Council of Churches, 174, 178n
Dworkin, Ronald, 138, 144n

Eastern European countries, threat from
    USSR, 110
Economies
  Asiatic mode of production in, and
    rentier economy, 113–115
  of Middle East, 112
Edelstein, David, 223, 231n

Edgar, Bob, 170
Edwards, John, 212–213, 219n
Egypt
    Oriental despotism in, 117
    in rentier economy, 114
    as static region, 109
    as tentatively democratic state, 121
Emigration from Islamic countries, 100,
    111–112, 131
Emmanuelli, Henri, 254
England. See United Kingdom
Enzenberger, Hans Magnus, 277
Estonian support of Iraq war, 14
Ethical issues. See Moral and ethical
    issues
Etzioni, Amitai, 122, 124n
Europe
    attitudes toward Middle East, 260–261
    church positions on Iraq war, 169,
    171–174
    opposition to Iraq war, 21
    policies in postwar Iraq, 265–268
    support of Iraq war, 7, 13–14
    taxation systems in, 115
European Social Forum (FSE) in 2002,
    255
European studies
    by Herzinger, 233–242
    by Jerichow, 259–268
    by Lloyd, 223–232
    by Taubmann, 243–258
European Union
    British attitudes toward, 227–228
    foreign policy of, 225–227
    founding of, 96
    response to September 11 attack on
    US, 250
Evans, Gareth, 300
Exxon, 117–118

Faber, Mient Jan, 4, 11, 160–178
Failed states, danger of, 30, 31–32, 36
Faisal, King of Iraq, 121
Fallujah assault in Iraq, 294
Fascism
    and Baathist regime, 41, 148, 153
    capitalism linked to, 156
    and Islamism, 241
    meaning of, 151
    movements influenced by, 148,
    149–150
Fiorenza, Joseph, 169
Fischer, Joschka, 234, 235, 236, 250
Foreign policy of European Union,
    225–227
Fox News, Vidal's outlook on, 152–153
France, 243–258
    alliance with Germany, 227
    against Anglo-American alliance, 228
    anti-Semitism in, 253
    antiwar demonstrations in, 256–257
    in Atlantic alliance, 245
    attitudes toward US, 227, 277
    belief in Iraqi weapons of mass
    destruction, 86

    Communist Party activities in, 255
    opposition to Iraq war, 7, 21, 47,
    85–86, 226, 255, 260, 265, 337
    policies for Afghanistan, 250–251
    refusal to aid postwar Iraq, 265
    response to September 11 attack in
    US, 251–252, 253–254
    Socialist Party positions in, 253–255
    support for Palestinians, 253
    support for Saddam Hussein, 262
    vetoes of UN Resolutions, 333
    in World Wars I and II, 244–245
France, Anatole, 79
Friedrich, Jörg, 240
Fundamentalism
    dangers of, 275
    Islamic, coexistence with secular total-
    itarianism, 46, 55n
    religious, oppression of women in,
    303, 305

G8 Conference in 2004, 122, 267
Gaddis, John Lewis, 49, 56n
Galbraith, Peter W., 200–201
Galloway, George, 289, 296n
Geneva Conventions, 99–100, 120, 311,
    320
    ignored for Iraqi prisoners, 44
Genocide
    in Bosnia, 4, 13, 247, 261
    in Darfur, 204, 211, 212
    of Kurds, 175–176, 200, 229, 259,
    299
    of Marsh Arabs, 175, 200, 299
    prevention of, 4, 9
    as responsibility of entire world, 319
    in Rwanda, 4, 13, 31, 111, 204, 215,
    261, 284, 299, 314–315
    UN convention on, 31, 299, 314,
    325n
    use of word forbidden by White
    House, 314–315
Geras, Norman, 191–206
Germany
    in Afghanistan war, 237
    alliance with France, 227
    belief in Iraqi weapons of mass
    destruction, 86
    border dispute with Poland, 275,
    279n–280n
    church leaders against Iraq war, 172
    conditions after World War II, 52
    friendship with France, 233–234
    Iraq debate in, 239, 240–241
    nationalism of, 237–238
    occupied after World War II, 278
    opposition to Iraq war, 7, 21, 47–48,
    255, 256, 265, 337
    refusal to aid postwar Iraq, 265
    response to September 11 attack in
    US, 252
    support for Kosovo war, 235, 237
    support for Saddam Hussein, 262
    suspicion of US motives, 237, 239
Globalization, criticisms of, 156–157

Gordon, Philip., 225, 226, 228, 231*n*, 232*n*
Gore, Al, 10
Greeley, Andrew, 166–167, 169, 177*n*
Gregory, Wilton D., 169, 177*n*
Grotius, Hugo, 122
Gulf Cooperation Council, 110
Gulf War in 1991
    actions of Saddam Hussein after, 229
    civilian infrastructure destroyed in, 168–169
    French politics in, 246–247
Gulf War Syndrome Mark II, 285–296

Hadad, Sama, 289
Haidar, Jorg, 80
Halliburton company, 32
Hamid, Surma, 298
Hari, Johann, 12, 285–296
Harries, Richard, 163, 177*n*
Hart, H. L. A., 130, 143*n*
Hassan, Prince of Jordan, 109
Havel, Václav, 14, 147, 158, 272
Heidegger, Martin, 155, 156–157
Herf, Jeffrey, 7, 39–56
Hersh, Seymour, 294, 296*n*
Herzinger, Richard, 21, 233–242
Historical aspects of Iraq war, 39–56
Hitchens, Christopher, 29–38
    approval of Bush's war, 158, 288
    on Bush administration, 4
    on Michael Moore, 224, 231*n*
    on President Clinton and Al Gore, 10
    on Saddam Husein, 7
    on September 11 terrorism in US, 193
    vilification of, 11
Hitler, Adolf, 9
Hobbes, Thomas, 62
Holland in support of Iraq war, 337
Hollande, François, 254
Houellebecq, Michel, 183, 190*n*
Howard, John, 301, 307*n*
Howard, Michael, 54–55, 56*n*
Hue, Robert, 251
Human rights
    and democratic values, 192
    humanitarian interventions for, 175–176
    ideology of, 180–181
    and solidarity organizations, 317–318
Human Rights Watch
    on Anfal campaign against Kurds, 315, 325*n*
    on Baathist regime, 195, 196
    on motives for Iraq war, 2, 9, 203, 204
Human security principle in humanitarian interventions, 166
Humanitarian interventions
    applied to Iraq war, 9–10, 135–137, 160
    criteria for, 199–202
    ethical and moral issues in, 7–9
    good and bad consequences in Iraq, 196–199

    in human rights interventions, 175–176
    human security principle in, 166
    and international law, 300
    in Kosovo, 165, 344
    military force in, 2
    as moral right, 194–196
    original advocates of, 247
    as pretext for aggression, 9
    resistance to arguments for, 11–12
    responsibilities in, 319–320
    as wars of conscience, 163
Hungary in support of Iraq war, 13
Huntington, Samuel P., 302, 307*n*
Hussein, King of Jordan, 109
Hussein, Qusay, 31
Hussein, Saddam, 2, 5, 7, 10
    actions after 1991 Gulf War, 229
    agreements violated by, 84
    compared to Osama bin Laden, 83
    crimes of, 258–260, 282, 310–313
    failed indictment of, 315–316, 318
    genocides planned by, 175–176, 299
    invasion of Kuwait, 77–78, 208
    Iraqi resistance to, 12
    manipulation of UN procedures, 19, 22
    oppressive regime of, 174, 208, 338–339
    political victims of, 66, 77, 90*n*, 136, 154
    rallies against, in Western countries, 173
    sanctions affecting, 98, 228
    supported by Western nations, 172, 261–262
    as threat to world security after 9/11, 119
    totalitarian regime of, 41–42
    trial of, concerns for, 321
    weapons deployed by, 84–85
Hussein, Uday, 31

Idealism
    in domestic affairs, 212–214
    and moral judgments, 217
INDICT organization for justice, 315–316, 324, 325*n*
Indonesia, Suharto regime in, 158
Institute of War and Peace Reporting, 309
Intelligence organizations
    assessments before preemptive war, 51, 52
    failures concerning weapons of mass destruction, 47, 86–87, 92*n*
Interchurch Peace Council (IKV), 160–161, 175
Interfaith Peace Council in Netherlands, 11
International Atomic Energy Agency, 85, 263
International Commission on Intervention and State Sovereignty (ICISS), 323

International Criminal Court, 324
International Crisis Group (ICG), 289, 296*n*
International Declaration of Human Rights, 2
International law
 change needed in, 349
 confronted by moral imperatives, 275
 defined by Kant, 97
 difficulties with, 316, 318
 humanitarian issues in, 300
 and military campaigns, 164
 moral and ethical issues in, 7–9, 140–142, 194–195
 restricting war engagement, 162
 supported by Germany, 238
 violation by Iraq, 43
 on war crimes and crimes against humanity, 314
International Monetary Fund (IMF), 295
International relations
 national view of, 95–96, 102–104
 transnational views of, 96–102
Internationalism
 liberal, Third Force of, 3
 renewal of, 322–323
Iran
 illegal weapons sought by, 33
 Iraqi war against, 77, 311
 Islamic revolution in 1979, 121
 nuclear plants in, 34
 oil production in, 117–118
 opportunism of, 31
 oppression of women in, 302–303
 Oriental despotism in, 117
 response of global left to, 26*n*
 as static region, 109
 as tentatively democratic state in 1950s, 121
Iraq
 American debate on, 166–171
 costs of war in, 118, 208–210
 economic plans in, 294–295
 European debate on, 171–174, 264
 and failure of left-liberal opinion, 191–199
 Fallujah assault in, 294
 French view of, 243–258
 German views on, 239, 240–241
 as global challenge, 338–339, 340
 good and bad consequences of war in, 196–199
 human rights abuses in, 160–161
 interim government in, 322
 invasion of Kuwait, 77–78
 journalism in, 309
 judicial system in, 320–321
 and trials for Baathist regime members, 324
 Oil for Food program in, 30, 98, 247
 oil production in, 117–118
 postwar period in. *See* Postwar Iraq
 regime change as revolution in, 184–185
 rights of women in, 302, 304
 as rogue state or failed state, 30, 31
 sanctions against, 2, 98, 229, 264, 292, 298
 as sponsor of Islamic violence, 29–30
 support for US invasion in, 291–294
 three areas of, 64
 Vidal's outlook on, 152
 voices of Iraqi people, 286–296
 war against Iran, 77, 311
Iraq Liberation Act of 1998, 29, 38*n*
Iraq Memory Foundation, 54
Iraq Survey Group, 86
Iraqi Prospect Organisation (IPO), 287, 289
Islamic triad, 111–112
Islamism
 as fascist threat, 241
 forces in Middle East, and interventions needed, 34–37
 and fundamentalism coexistence with secular totalitarianism, 46, 55*n*
 insurgents seen as heroes, 186, 190*n*
 roots of, 119
Islamists
 as emigrants and terrorists, 111–112
 as immigrants in European states, 100
Islamocracy, 112
Islamofascism war against democracy, 3, 5, 22
Israel
 and anti-Zionists, 157
 as democracy, 108–109, 277
 in rentier economy, 114
 sins of, 148
 as static region, 109
Israeli-Palestinian relations
 breakdown in 2004, 35–36
 Iraq as distraction from, 81, 91*n*
 Roadmap for Peace, 337
Italy, changing attitudes toward Iraq war, 13, 228, 255, 256, 337

Japan
 decisions linked to war in Europe, 50–51
 support of Iraq war, 14
Jaruzelski, Wojciech, 276
Jenkins, Roy, 227
Jerichow, Anders, 259–268
Jihad forces
 organization of, 35
 state support of, 35
Jordan
 contribution to Iraq war, 260
 oppression of women in, 302
 Oriental despotism in, 117
 in rentier economy, 114
 as static region, 109
Jospin, Lionel, 246, 249, 250, 251, 252
 brochure after September 11 attack, 253–254
Journalism in Iraq, 309
Journalist reactions to war in Iraq, 186
Joxe, Pierre, 246
Just, Richard, 6, 207–219

Just war tradition, 160, 161–162, 176*n*
 checklists used in, 167
 four principles in, 164–165
 misuse of, 167
Justification of military interventions
 costs to invaded state in, 65–67
 costs to invading state in, 67
 in Iraq, by Bush and Blair governments, 42–43
 objectives for invading state in, 70–72
 national interests in, 71–72
 regime change in, 58–59
  desired properties of new regime in,
   63–65
  necessary conditions for, 63–74
  problems with, 59–63
  prospect of success for new regime,
   72–74

Kamal, Hussein, 330
Kant, Immanuel, 18–19, 62, 70, 96–97,
 99, 102, 106, 108
Kaplan, Lawrence, 211, 219*n*
Kay, David, 34, 86, 92*n*, 229, 263, 343
Kazakhstan support of Iraq war, 14
Kelly, David, 85, 91*n*, 186
Kerry, John, 211–212, 217, 219*n*
Khaldun, Ibn, 113, 123*n*
Khan, A. Q., 33, 35, 345, 348
Khatami, Mohammed, 109
Kim family in North Korea, 98
 Kim Jong II, 229
 contact with Iraq, 34
Kirkuk community in Iraq, 313
Kissinger, Henry, 159, 293
Koestler, Arthur, 154
Kofman, Daniel, 4, 125–144
Kohl, Helmut, 238, 239, 248
Konrád, György, 272
Korea. *See* North Korea; South Korea
Kosovo, interventions in, 10, 13, 155,
 282
 church positions on, 162–166
 French policies in, 248–249
 German support of, 235–236
 and UN Security Council, 168
Kouchner, Bernard, 247, 248–249,
 252–253, 277
 policies promoted by, 257–258
Kucinich, Dennis, 210, 219*n*
Kurdish area of Iraq, 64
Kurds
 campaigns against, 77, 311–312, 319
 genocide by Saddam Hussein,
  175–176, 200, 229, 259, 299
 in Kirkuk community, 313
 protected zone created for, 247, 315
 rebellion against Saddam Hussein,
  77–79
 US commitment to, 36–37
Kuron, Jacek, 278
Kuwait. *See also* Gulf War in 1991
 contribution to Iraq war, 260
 invasion by Saddam Hussein, 77–78,
  91*n*, 99, 184, 208

Oriental despotism in, 117
 in rentier economy, 114

Latvian support of Iraq war, 14
Law, international. *See* International law
League of Nations, 96, 99
Lebanon
 as democracy, 109
 in rentier economy, 114
Left-wing groups
 in Britain, attitudes toward European
  Union, 227
 response to anti-Americanism, 12
 selective solidarity with victims of
  repression, 12
Legitimacy of war, moral issues in, 10
Leonard, Mark, 225–226, 228, 231*n*
Lepard, Brian, 8
Le Pen, Jean-Marie, 80, 247
Letter of the Eight in support of Iraq war,
 13
Levitt, Jean-David, 85–86, 91*n*
Liberal internationalism
 antitotalitarianism in, 6
 basic values of, 3–4
 Third Force of, 3
Liberal societies
 external and internal nonviolence in,
  64–65
 freedoms guaranteed in, 64
 wars against nonliberal regimes, 106
Liberalism
 classic principle of, 62
 cosmopolitan, 102
 language of realism in opposition to
  Iraq war, 209–211
Libya
 illegal weapons sought by, 33
 Oriental despotism in, 117
 in rentier economy, 114
 weapons surrendered by, 34, 87, 144,
  347–348
Lienemann, Marie-Noëlle, 246
Lithuania in support of Iraq war, 14
Lloyd, John, 223–232
Locke, John, 62, 75*n*, 127
Lopez, George, 167–169, 177*n*
Luciani, Giacomo, 114, 123*n*
Luxemburg opposition to Iraq war, 255

Macedonia in support of Iraq war, 14
Machiavelli, Niccolò, 101, 115, 123*n*
al-Majeed, Ali Hasan, 311
Makiya, Kanan, 2, 54, 311, 325*n*
Mamère, Noël, 251
Mandela, Nelson, 284
Margalit, Avishai, 157
Marsh Arabs
 campaigns against, 77, 287–288,
  312–313, 315, 319, 325*n*
 genocide by Saddam Hussein, 175,
  200, 299
Marx, Karl, 113, 116, 122, 123n, 181,
 182, 190*n*
Mazen, Abu, 337

Mélenchon, Jean-Luc, 246
Merkel, Angela, 239
Michnik, Adam, 6, 14, 82, 147, 158
    interviewed by Cushman, 271–280
Middle East
    Asiatic mode of production and rentier
        economy in, 113–115
    backwardness of, 112
    complexity of, 112
    democratization of
        as American project, 122
        as justification for Iraq war, 120, 121
    dictatorial stability in, 110
    economies of, 112
    events affecting world peace and secu-
        rity, 111–112
    as fragmented region, 110–111
    oil production in, 111, 118
    oppression of women in, 302–303
    Oriental despotism in, 115–117
    as outlaw region, 108–113
    roots of terrorism and Islamism in, 119
    as threat to world stability, 107
Middle East Council of Churches, 170,
    172
Middle East peace process (MEPP),
    future of, 337, 339
Mill, John Stuart, 62
Milne, Seumas, 196n, 291–292
Milošević, Slobodan
    compared to Saddam Hussein, 10
    ethnic cleansing by, 154, 165
    eviction from international scene, 32,
        129, 130
    French policies toward, 248
    legal proceedings against, 316, 318
    NATO bombing of, 162, 164
Mitterand, Danielle, 247
Mitterand, François, 245, 246, 248,
    249
Mladić, Ratko, 235
Modernism, reactionary, 45, 55n
Mongolia in support of Iraq war, 14
Montesquieu, Charles de, 116, 123n
Moore, Michael, 11, 82, 83, 203,
    223–224
Moral and ethical issues
    in arguments for war, 125–144
    in choices of churches, 160–176
    in consequences of war, 9
    in idealism, 217
    in international law, 7–9, 275
    in just war tradition, 161–162
Moral racism, 157
Morocco
    Oriental despotism in, 117
    in rentier economy, 114
Mosaddeq, Mohammad, 121
al-Mumin, Mishkat, 303
Mozaffari, Mehdi, 15, 106–124
Mugabe, Robert, 282
Murray, Williamson, 50, 56n
Museum for the Martyrs of Persian
    Aggression, 288
Muslims. *See* Islamists

Naïr, Sami, 252
Narveson, Jan, 57–75
National Council of Churches, 162, 170,
    176n
National interests in justifications of war,
    71–72
National view of international relations,
    95–96, 102–104
    deterrence and preemptive force in, 96
    and going to war against despotism,
        104
    self-correcting aspects of, 103
NATO campaign in Yugoslavia,
    162–165, 235, 248
Negroponte, John, 293
Netherlands
    Interfaith Peace Council, 11
    opposition to Iraq war, 255
    support of Iraq war, 13
Nonviolence, and support of war, 276
North Korea
    illegal weapons sought by, 33
    missile system in, 34, 229
    sanctions affecting, 98
    Vidal's outlook on, 152
Nozick, Robert, 138, 144n
Nuclear Non-proliferation Treaty, 85
Nuclear weapons
    black market in, 87
    desired by terrorists, 344
    missile system in North Korea, 34, 229
    program in Iraq, 85, 330
        and reactor bombed by Israel, 84,
            91n
    targeting innocent civilians, 140
    trade in, 345–346

Obama, Barack, 213–215, 218, 219n
O'Brien, Conor Cruise, 307, 308n
Oil
    and authoritarian rule, 114, 115
    production in Middle East, 111
    revenues benefiting Saddam Hussein,
        42, 46, 53
    as US motivation for war, 117–118
Oil for Food program in Iraq, 30, 98,
    247
Oman
    contribution to Iraq war, 260
    in rentier economy, 114
Opposition to Iraq war
    censure forviolating orthodoxies of, 11
    concerns in, 2–3
    criticisms of, 10–13, 125
    and dogma of imperialist intrusions in
        Iraq, 88
    by France, Germany, and Russia, 7,
        21, 47, 337. *See also specific
        countries*
    strange political bedfellows in, 80
    two-sided critique in, 4–5
Organization of Petroleum Exporting
    Countries (OPEC), 118
Oriental despotism, 115–117
Orwell, George, 22

Outlaw states
  decisions for wars against, 104,
    106–124
  types of, 121
Owen, David, 227
Oxford Research International, 16–18, 20

Pacifism
  as Christian doctrine, 160, 162, 170
  and European opposition to Iraq war,
    255
  problems with, 59–61, 166–167
  roots in France, 244–256
Pakistan
  oppression of women in, 302–303
  Oriental despotism in, 117
Palestine
  Israeli-Palestinian relations, 35–36, 81,
    91n
  Roadmap for Peace, 337
  as static region, 109
Palestinians, French support for, 253
Pax Christi, 171–172, 178n
Peace of Augsburg in 1555, 127
Peoples, categories of, 106
Pétain, Philippe, 245
Philippines in support of Iraq war, 14
Philosophical arguments
  by Kofman, 125–144
  by Mozaffari, 106–124
  by Scruton, 95–105
Physicians for Human Rights, 15
Pilger, John, 203
Pinochet, Augusto, 318
Pinter, Harold, 155
Poland
  border dispute with Germany, 275,
    279n–280n
  support of Iraq war, 13, 271–272, 278
Political correctness, campaign for, 189
Politicians, goals of, 22–23
Politics
  distinct from ethics or morality,
    181–182, 190n
  progressive
    despair in, 187
    vulnerability of, 189
  strange bedfellows in, 79–80
Pollack, Kenneth, 40, 55n
Portugal in support of Iraq war, 337
Postel, Danny, 26n
Postwar Iraq
  attacks by Baath Party in, 54
  lawlessness in, 44, 47
  Muslim extremists in, 282, 283
  negative aspects of, 20
  occupation as disaster, 53
  optimistic view of, 43
  problems in, 265–268
  UN role in, 283
  US policies in, 279, 283
Powell, Colin, 79
Preemptive war
  debates over, 49–52
  political judgments in, 51–52

Prisoners of war, torture of, 120
Progressive politics
  despair in, 187
  vulnerability of, 189
Public opinion surveys in Iraq, 15–18
Putin, Vladimir, 47, 238, 243

Qatar
  contribution to Iraq war, 260
  in rentier economy, 114

Rabin, Yitzhak, 84, 91n
Racism, moral, 157
Raiser, Konrad, 162–163, 165–166,
    173–174
Ramos-Horta, Jose, 14, 158–159,
    281–284
Rawls, John, 18–20
  on individual rights, 138
  *The Law of Peoples*, 2, 20, 106–108,
    123n, 124n
  principles for liberal societies,
    119–121
  on stability, 109
Raz, Joseph, 139, 144n
Reactionary modernism, 45, 55n
Reactions to Iraq war, polarized dis-
    course in, 6
Reagan, Ronald, 111, 274
Realism
  in foreign policy, 211–212, 213, 215
  in opposition to Iraq war, 209–211
  and tolerance, 217–218
Rée, Jonathan, 179–190
Regime change
  arguments for, 2, 4–5, 9–10, 29
    by Cohen, 76–92
    by Herf, 39–56
    by Hitchens, 29–38
    by Narveson, 57–75
  Iraqi support of, 289
  as justification of military interven-
    tions, 58–59. *See also* Justifica-
    tion of military interventions
  as revolution, 185
Religion, and oppression of women,
    303, 305
Rentier effect
  modernization effect in, 114
  repression effect in, 114
Republican government defined by Kant,
    97, 104n
Resistance to Iraq war. *See* Opposition to
    Iraq war
Revolutions, justification of, 62
Rice, Condoleeza, mistaken outlook for
    postwar Iraq, 52–53
Ridicule, problems with, 224
Ritter, Scott, 85, 91n
Rocard, Michel, 246
Rodríguez Zapatero, José Luis, 228
Rogue states
  danger of, 30, 32, 36
  and international law, 97
Romania in support of Iraq war, 14

Roosevelt, Franklin D., 52, 55
  allied with Churchill and Stalin, 79, 83
  declaration of war, 103
Ross, Michael L., 114, 115, 123n
Roth, Kenneth, 203–204, 205, 206
Roy, Arundathi, 153, 154
Rumsfeld, Donald, 44, 79, 293
  mistaken outlook for postwar Iraq,
    52–53
Russia
  opposition to Iraq war, 7, 21, 47, 337
  propaganda from, 156
  refusal to aid postwar Iraq, 265
  support for Saddam Hussein, 262
  as threat to Eastern European coun-
    tries, 110
Russian Revolution, results of, 179–180
Rwanda, genocide in, 4, 13, 31, 111,
    204, 215, 261, 284, 299, 314–315

Sabri, Naji, 92n
al-Sadr, Muhammad Baqir, 312
Said, Edward, 129, 130
Said, Nuri, 163
Sakharov, Andrei, 276
Salih, Barham, 322
Sanctions against Iraq, 2, 98, 229, 264,
    292, 298
Sanctity of states, 61–62. *See also*
  Sovereignty
Saudi Arabia
  contribution to Iraq war, 260
  opportunism of, 31
  Oriental despotism in, 117
  in rentier economy, 114
  as static region, 109
Scharping, Rudolf, 235
Schiller, Kay, 241
Schröder, Gerhard, 21, 80–81, 233
  on international law, 238
  opposition to Iraq war, 47–48
  support of United States, 236–237
Scruton, Roger, 95–105
Section Française de l'Internationale
  Ouvrière (SFIO), 244, 245
September 11, 2001, in US, 343, 345
  affecting US foreign policy, 49
  response to, 192–193, 250, 251–252,
    272, 336
  suspected connection with Saddam
    Hussein, 45
Sharon, Ariel, 277
Shawcross, William, 301, 301n
Shea, Jamie, 163–165, 167, 177n
Shia area of Iraq, 64
Shiite rebellion against Saddam Hussein,
    77–79, 312
Shinseki, Eric, 44
Short, Clare, 196
Singapore in support of Iraq war, 14
al-Sistani, Ali, 283
Slovakia in support of Iraq war, 14
Slovenia in support of Iraq war, 14
Solidarity with the weak
  by Bone, 297–308

  by Clwyd, 309–325
  by Cushman and Michnik, 271–280
  by Hari, 285–296
  and human rights, 317–318
  by Ramos-Horta, 281–284
  for victims of repression, selectivity of,
    12, 26n
Solzhenitsyn, Aleksandr, 276
Sontag, Susan, 272, 278n
South Korea in support of Iraq war, 14
Sovereignty
  of individuals, 62, 127
  of Iraq, 29, 77, 126, 262
  and rule of law, 95–97
  of states, 61–63, 166
    and human rights, 301
    limits to respect for, 201
Soviet bloc countries in support of Iraq
    war, 14
Spain
  anti-American views of, 228, 274
  response to September 11 attack in
    US, 252
  support of Iraq war, 13, 14, 256, 337
  withdrawal of, 265, 281
Spanish Civil War, 6
Srebrenica massacre in Bosnia, 235,
    261
Stability
  democratic, 110
  dictatorial, 109
  in Middle East, 110
Stalin, Joseph, allied with Roosevelt and
    Churchill, 79, 83
Starvation resulting from sanctions, 98
States
  immune to outside interference, 58
  sanctity of, 61–63. *See also* Sovereignty,
    of states
  types of, 120–121
Stiglitz, Joseph, 295
Stoiber, Edmund, 239
Stone, I. F., 142
Strauss-Kahn, Dominique, 258
Sudan, UN indifference to, 13
Sunni area of Iraq, 64
Support of Iraq war
  antitotalitarianism in, 5–6
  forty-eight countries in, 13–14
  values of liberal internationalism in,
    3–4
Syria
  alliances of, 83
  Baath coup in, 84, 109, 121
  Oriental despotism in, 117
  in rentier economy, 114
  as static region, 109

Taliban regime, 119
  eviction from Afghanistan, 33–34,
    250, 282, 346
  oppression of women by, 302
Tarloff, Eric, 224, 231n
Taubmann, Michel, 243–258
Taxation, and fall of despotism, 115

Terrorism
  increase of, 344
  by Muslims, 111–112
  romanticism about, 183
  roots of, 119
  spread of, 335–336
  targets for, 110
  and weapons of mass destruction,
    341, 344
Terrorists moving into Iraq, 348
Thatcher, Margaret, 227
Third world, liberation movements in,
  156
Thomson, Judith Jarvis, 139, 144*n*
Timmerman, Kenneth, 21
Tolerance
  for alternative views, need for, 12–13
  as political value, 216–218
  and realism, 217–218
Torture of prisoners of war, 120
Totalitarianism
  and antitotalitarianism as vocation,
    271–280
  in Germany and Russia, 98
  and Middle Eastern realities, 88–89
  secular, coexistence with Islamic fun-
    damentalism, 46, 55*n*
Transnational view of international rela-
    tions, 96–102
  corruption of bureaucracies in, 98
  effects of sanctions in, 98
  goal of peace in, 98
  and impact of asylum laws, 100–101
  laws imposed in, 98
Tunisia
  Oriental despotism in, 117
  in rentier economy, 114
Turkey, opportunism of, 31
Tyranny, dangers posed by, 14

United Arab Emirates
  contribution to Iraq war, 260
  in rentier economy, 114
United Kingdom
  Anglophobia in Europe, 155–156
  antiwar protests in, 188, 228
  attitudes toward EU, 227–228
  attitudes toward US, 227
  church leaders against Iraq war,
    171–172
  Stop the War Coalition in, 188,
    189
  support for Saddam Hussein, 262
  war with Iraq
    as difficult judgment, 342–343
    justification of, 343–350
    legal opinions of, 342
    support for, 13, 256
United Nations
  Commission on Human Rights, 19
  Convention on Genocide, 314, 325*n*
  Development Programme reports,
    112, 123*n*
  endorsement of international coalition
    in Kuwait, 77–78

General Assembly Resolution of 1946,
    314
  High Commissioner for Refugees, 313
  and international law, 150
  manipulation of procedures in, 18
    by Saddam Hussein, 19, 22
  Oil for Food program, 30, 98, 247
  realpolitik practices of, 6, 229
  reforms needed, 323, 350–351
  resolutions on weapons of mass
    destruction, 29, 34
  role in postwar Iraq, 283
  sanctions against Iraq, 2, 98, 229,
    264, 292, 298
  Security Council, 2, 7, 8, 162, 164
    and Kosovo intervention, 168
    lack of mandate in, 168
    policies for postwar Iraq, 266
    relations with Iraq, 262–263
    Resolution 688, 176
    Resolution 1441, 5, 92*n*, 331, 332,
      334, 336, 338, 342, 343, 346
    splits in, 46
  Special Commission in Iraq, 85
  toleration of tyrants, 13
  as two organizations, 229–230
  Universal Declaration on Human
    Rights, 311, 350
United States
  Anti-Americanism in Europe, 155,
    156–157
  church positions on Iraq war, 166–171
  Conference of Catholic Bishops,
    169–170, 177*n*
  divided politics in, 55
  French attitudes toward, 227, 277
  German attitude toward, 237, 239,
    240–241
  invective against, 230
  motivations for war
    in Afghanistan, 118–119
    in Iraq, 117–122
  policies in postwar Iraq, 279
  resentment of, 337
  support for military regimes, 273
  support for Saddam Hussein, 262, 306
Universal Declaration of Human Rights,
    2, 4, 313
Universalism, cosmopolitan, 18
Unjust peace, consequences of, 77
Unocal pipeline in Afghanistan, 32
Uzbekistan support of Iraq war, 14

Védrine, Hubert, 251, 254
Veil, Antoine, 257
Vidal, Gore, 152–153, 154, 155, 158
Vieira de Mello, Sergio, 229
Villepin, Dominique de, 257
Vilnius 10 in support of Iraq war, 14

War
  conduct of
    *jus in bello* principle in, 162, 163,
      168
    principles in, 119–120

War *(continued)*
  consequential issues in, 137–142
  decisions for, *jus ad bellum* principle
    in, 162, 164, 167–168
  as extension of politics, 161
  feasibility of, 119
    support affecting, 134
  moral arguments for, 125–144
  opposition to, 131–135
    and agent-relative duties, 140–142
    intentional fallacies in arguments
      for, 135–136, 137
  against outlaw regions, 108–113
  against outlaw states, 107
  position of feasibility skepticism, 131,
    132
    diffident, 132–135, 142
    total, 132
  position of principled oppositions,
    131–132, 133
  preemptive
    debates about, 49–52
    political judgments in, 51–52
  tradition of just wars, 160, 161–162,
    176n
    checklists used in, 167
    four principles in, 164–165
    misuse of, 167
Warduni, Shlemon, 170
Water as factor in rise of Oriental despotism, 116
Waugh, Evelyn, 155
Weapons, illegal, sought by nations,
  33
Weapons of mass destruction (WMDs)
  belief in, 144n
  deployed by Saddam Hussein, 84–85,
    119, 262–263

  Duelfer Report on, 26n, 54
  intelligence failures, 47, 86–87, 92n
  prolonged search for, 83–87, 91n,
    330–334, 346–347
  UN resolutions on, 29, 34
  US concerns with, 40, 57–58
  use by terrorists, 341
Weber, Max, 22, 80
Weigel, George, 161, 167
Westphalia Treaties of 1648, 122, 127,
  344
Williams, Shirley, 227
Winkler, Heinrich August, 241
Wittfogel, Karl, 116, 123n
Wolfowitz, Paul, 79
  mistaken outlook for postwar Iraq,
    52–53
Women
  human rights for, 300, 302–305
  in Iraq, treatment of, 297–298
  opposition to Iraq war, 299
Woolf, Virginia, 298, 307n
World Council of Churches, 162–163
  antiwar campaign of, 172–173
World War II, transnational view of con-
  flict in, 96

Yasin, Abdul Rahman, 30
Yemen
  fall of Imams in, 121
  Oriental despotism in, 117
  in rentier economy, 114
Younge, Gary, 285, 296n
Yugoslavia, NATO campaign in,
  162–165. *See also* Bosnia

al-Zarqawi, Musad Abu, 33, 35
Zebari, Hoshyar, 322

Compositor: Michael Bass Associates
Indexer: Herr's Indexing Service
Illustrator: Michael Bass Associates
Text: 10/13 Sabon
Display: Akzidenz Grotesk
Printer and binder: Maple-Vail Manufacturing Group